Commercial Driver's License Exam

AUG - - 2009

The Complete Preparation Guide

1st Edition

LEARNINGEXPRESS®

NEW YORK

Library of Congress Control Number: 2008909893

A copy of this title is on file with the Library of Congress.

Printed in the United States of America

9 8 7 6 5 4 3 2 1

First Edition

ISBN: 978-1-57685-659-8

Regarding the Information in This Book

We attempt to verify the information presented in our books prior to publication. It is always a good idea, however, to double-check such important information as minimum requirements, application and testing procedures, and deadlines with your local Department of Motor Vehicles, as such information can change from time to time.

For more information or to place an order, contact LearningExpress at:

   2 Rector Street

   26th Floor

   New York, NY 10006

Or visit us at:

   www.learnatest.com

List of Contributors

C. Rudy Fox is the director of truck driver training at Caldwell Community College in Hudson, North Carolina, as well as a part-time truck driver with Cargo Transporters. He has more than 40 years of experience in the trucking industry as a mechanic, driver, manager, and educator. In his current position, he supervises the instruction of about 200 students each year in commercial truck driving and safety courses. He previously worked for Ryder Truck Rental, Southwest Freight Carriers, and Newton Transportation. He currently resides in Granite Falls, North Carolina.

Tina Frindt is the director of driver training for Northhampton Community College in Bethlehem, Pennsylvania. She began her career in the trucking industry 10 years ago as a driver for Exclusive Transportation for Industry in Allentown, Pennsylvania. She then worked as the site manager for Truck Driving Academy, Inc., assisting new students enrolling in the truck driver training program. In her current position, she assigns instructors, evaluates performance, and works closely with her staff to ensure the quality of training. She lives in Nazareth, Pennsylvania.

Northeast Editing, Inc., a full-service development house in Jenkins Township, Pennsylvania, has been creating educational content for publishers since 1992. The company's experienced authors, instructors, editors, and designers produce print and online test-preparation products for students of all ages. Northeast Editing, Inc. is a member of the American Book Producers' Association (ABPA) and the Association of Educational Publishers (AEP).

Contents ▶

CONTENTS

How to Use This Book ▶

Congratulations on deciding to become a commercial driver! You'll find a career in the trucking industry to be both rewarding and financially beneficial. As a commercial driver, you'll work in one of the most important industries in the United States. Have you ever heard the saying, "If you've got it, a trucker brought it"? It's true! Each day, thousands of truckers transport goods from manufacturing centers to distribution centers to retail outlets. Truckers transport clothing, automobiles, furniture, food, liquids, animals, construction equipment—even people. While many goods travel by ship, train, or plane for part of their journey, almost everything travels at least part of the way by truck.

Truck drivers are a constant presence on America's highways, and the job outlook is good for those wanting to become commercial drivers. In fact, the U.S. Department of Labor expects the number of trucking jobs to increase in the coming years.

You need a commercial driver's license (CDL) to operate a commercial motor vehicle (CMV). To get a CDL, you have to pass tests, most of which are given at your local Department of Motor Vehicles (DMV). While some of these tests measure your knowledge of CMVs, others test your skills in driving them. The following chapters will teach you what you need to know to pass the tests required for a CDL.

▶ Chapter 1—Introduction to the Commercial Driver's License (CDL)

In this chapter, you'll learn about the trucking industry and the qualifications you must meet to become a commercial driver. You'll learn about the tests you must take to get a CDL as well as about other tests you may have to take, depending on the type of commercial vehicle you wish to drive.

▶ Chapter 2—Driving Safely, Part 1

Since commercial vehicles are large and heavy, you must learn how to drive them safely to protect your own life and the lives of others on highways and interstates. This chapter offers advice for staying alert and provides instruction on how to shift gears, back up, communicate with other drivers, and manage speed and space.

▶ Chapter 3—Driving Safely, Part 2

In this chapter, you'll learn how to drive commercial vehicles in difficult weather. You'll learn how to drive at night, in the winter, in hot weather, in rain, in fog, in the mountains. You'll also learn how to safely cross railroad tracks and how to recover from skids.

▶ Chapter 4—Vehicle Inspection

When you become a commercial driver, you need to inspect your vehicle often to avoid facing problems on the road. You'll learn how to inspect your vehicle in this chapter and what you should look for during an inspection.

▶ Chapter 5—Transporting Cargo

Commercial drivers transport many different types of cargo. Cargo must be loaded correctly or it can fall off your vehicle or cause your vehicle to roll over. This chapter teaches you how to inspect, load, and secure cargo.

▶ Chapter 6—Air Brakes

Most newer CMVs have air brakes, which work using compressed air. They are a safe and an effective way to stop large, heavy vehicles. If you want to drive a commercial vehicle with air brakes, you need to take and pass both a knowledge test and a skills test about air brakes. This chapter teaches you what you need to know to pass these tests.

▶ Chapter 7—Combination Vehicles

Many commercial vehicles are combination vehicles, meaning they are actually two or more vehicles coupled, or attached. If you want to drive a combination vehicle, you need to take a knowledge test about combination vehicles. In this chapter, you'll learn the different types of combination vehicles and how to drive them. You'll also learn how to couple and uncouple combination vehicles and how to inspect them.

▶ Chapter 8—Skills Test

All drivers applying for a CDL must take and pass a skills test. In this chapter, you'll learn what's on each of the three parts of the Skills Test: The Pre-Inspection Test, the Basic Vehicle Control Operations Test, and the Road Test.

▶ Chapter 9—Doubles and Triples

If you plan to drive doubles and triples, which are very long combination vehicles, you need to take the Doubles and Triples Test. In this chapter, you'll learn what you need to know to pass this test, including how to pull double and triple trailers, how to inspect them, and how to couple and uncouple them.

▶ Chapter 10—Tank Vehicles

Tank vehicles, or tankers, are used to transport liquids. You need to take and pass the Tank Vehicle Endorsement Test to receive a license to drive them because driving these vehicles requires special knowledge and skills. In this chapter, you'll learn what you need to know to pass this test, including the different types of tanks and how to drive them.

▶ Chapter 11—Hazardous Materials

Hazardous materials are those that pose a risk to people, property, and the environment. You need to take the Hazardous Materials Endorsement Test before you can transport hazardous materials. In this chapter, you'll learn what you need to know to pass this test, including regulations about hazardous waste and how to handle and transport this type of cargo.

▶ Chapter 12—Passenger Transport

Bus drivers are commercial drivers. In this chapter, you'll learn what you need to know to pass the Passenger Transport Endorsement Test and become a bus driver. You'll learn the rules and regulations regarding the transportation of passengers as well as safety precautions.

If you plan to ...	Study these chapters ...
Drive a combination vehicle	Chapters 1, 2, 3, 4, 5, 6, 7
Drive a CMV with air brakes	Chapters 1, 2, 3, 4, 5, 6, 7
Drive a tank vehicle	Chapters 1, 2, 3, 4, 5, 6, 10
Transport hazardous waste	Chapters 1, 2, 3, 4, 5, 6, 0, 11
Drive a double or a triple	Chapters 1, 2, 3, 4, 5, 6, 7, 9
Drive a school bus	Chapters 1, 2, 3, 4, 5, 6, 8, 12

Introduction to the Commercial Driver's License (CDL)

CHAPTER SUMMARY

If you work in the transportation industry as a commercial driver, you'll travel to new places and earn a good living. To become a commercial driver, you need a commercial driver's license (CDL). All CDL applicants must pass a General Knowledge Test and a Skills Test to show that they have knowledge about commercial vehicles and know how to drive them.

Jobs are hard to come by in today's economy, but this isn't the case in the transportation industry. Trucking is one of the most important industries in the United States because everything—food, clothes, supplies, medicine, farm animals, and even people—has to be transported from place to place. Nearly 500,000 trucking companies have 4.5 million trailers and over 1.7 million tractors on the road that travel over 118 billion miles each year.

Trucking companies come in all shapes and sizes. Some are large, publicly traded companies that operate throughout America. Others are medium-sized with about a half-dozen tractor-trailers. Many are small partnerships with one or two tractor-trailers. Smaller companies might operate within a specific region or state. Specialized trucking companies might have vehicles designed to transport liquids or hazardous waste.

So many trucking companies means it's more likely that you'll find a trucking job that suits you. Some truckers drive only within a 200-mile radius, so they can spend nights at home with their spouses and children. Others are grateful for the chance to travel across America and see small towns, large cities, and national landmarks that most people never have the chance to see. Some truckers work for companies that encourage them to bring their spouses along for the ride. During summer and holiday breaks, these truckers can also take along their children. And many truckers travel with their loyal canines by their sides.

As a truck driver, you'll earn a good living. Even entry-level trucking jobs pay well—usually around $35,000 per year plus benefits. Experienced truckers and those who stay on the road for longer stretches of time can expect to earn between $40,000 and $60,000 per year. Trucking industries frequently offer high salaries, great benefits, new trucks, and even bonuses to attract and keep good drivers.

▶ The Commercial Driver's License (CDL)

Years ago, becoming a truck driver required little or no knowledge about the vehicle you wanted to drive. In some states, you needed only a driver's license to drive a tractor-trailer or a bus. In other states, you had to pass a test showing that you had some knowledge about commercial motor vehicles (CMVs), but you didn't have to show that you knew how to operate them. In yet other states, you weren't required to pass a knowledge test, but you did need to complete a road test in a CMV. Granting licenses so easily put everyone driving on a highway at risk.

Since the federal government didn't keep track of licenses issued to CMV drivers, and it was very easy to get a license in some states, some CMV drivers had licenses in more than one state. This was a very dangerous practice. Suppose a CMV driver was caught driving under the influence of alcohol in Pennsylvania and had his license revoked in this state. The driver could still drive, because he also had licenses in New Jersey and New York—he just couldn't drive in Pennsylvania. Allowing truck and bus drivers to have more than one license put many people in harm's way. Today, to keep people safe, all commercial drivers must obtain a Commercial Driver's License (CDL). And drivers are

allowed only one CDL issued in the state in which they live. All states are connected to one computerized system to share information about CDL drivers, so they can check drivers' records to make certain they have only one CDL.

▶ The Commercial Vehicle Safety Act of 1986

The CDL began with the Commercial Vehicle Safety Act of 1986, which was signed into law on October 27, 1986. The goal of this act was to improve the quality of those licensed to drive CMVs by making sure they have knowledge about the vehicles and know how to drive them. While this act still gave the states the right to issue licenses to truck and bus drivers, states had to follow minimum national standards, which meant they had to be sure truck and bus drivers knew what they were doing. By 1992, all CMV drivers were required to have a CDL, and to get this license, they had to pass both knowledge and skills tests—they had to show that they knew about trucks and buses and that they were able to drive them properly. These knowledge and skills tests still vary from state to state, but they're based on a national model. To find out exactly the kinds of questions on your state's test, contact your local Department of Motor Vehicles (DMV) or search for this information online if you have access to a computer.

You need a CDL to drive

- a single vehicle with a gross vehicle weight rating (GVWR) of 26,001 or more pounds
- a combination of vehicles with a gross combination weight rating (GCWR) of 26,001 pounds or more towing a trailer weighing less than 10,000 pounds

- a combination of vehicles with a GCWR of 26,001 pounds or more if the trailer being towed weighs more than 10,000 pounds
- a bus designed to transport a certain number of people—usually around 15, not including the driver
- a school bus designed to carry 11 or more passengers, including the driver
- any vehicle that transports hazardous materials requiring placards

You do *not* need a CDL to drive

- military equipment used for a military purpose while on active duty
- some fire and emergency equipment owned by a fire company
- recreational vehicles and personal vehicles, including rental vehicles of up to 26,000 pounds
- some motorized construction equipment
- farm equipment meeting exemption requirements

▶ Federal Motor Carrier Safety Regulations (FMCSR)

Most of the rules and terminology related to CDLs come from the Federal Motor Carrier Safety Regulations (FMCSR), a large body of regulations created by the U.S. Department of Transportation Federal Motor Carrier Safety Administration (FMCSA). CDL regulations are described in Part 383 of this document. The following are some of the rules discussed in FMCSR Part 383:

- the purpose of the CDL program
- definitions related to the program

- the number of licenses a commercial driver may hold
- who should be notified if a commercial driver is convicted for driving violations
- the employer's responsibilities regarding CDLs
- the reasons a commercial driver may be disqualified from holding a CDL
- how a driver may apply for a CDL
- why a driver must consent to drug and alcohol testing
- the classification of CMVs
- the required knowledge and skills a commercial driver must have
- the tests a commercial driver must take to get a CDL and the minimum passing scores

▶ Classes of Vehicles

The kind of CDL you apply for depends on the type of CMV you plan to drive. CMVs are divided into the following classes.

Commercial Class A: Combination Vehicles

If you're issued a Class A license, you can drive any combination of vehicles with a GCWR of 26,001 or more pounds if the GVWR of the vehicle being towed is more than 10,000 pounds. You can also operate vehi-

Figure 1.1. Examples of Class A vehicles: truck-trailers and tractor-trailers

Your CDL will contain the following information:

- the words "Commercial Driver's License" or "CDL"
- your full name, signature, and address
- your date of birth, sex, and height
- a color photograph or digitized image of you
- your state license number
- the name of the state issuing you the license
- the date your license was issued and the date it expires
- the class(es) of vehicle(s) you're authorized to drive
- notation of the "air brake" restriction, if you didn't take or pass the Air Brakes Test
- the endorsement(s) for which you have qualified

cles for which a Class B or Class C license is issued if you have a Class A license.

Commercial Class B: Heavy Single Vehicles

If you hold a Class B license, you can drive any single vehicle with a GCWR of 26,001 or more pounds or a combination vehicle where the power unit is over 26,001 pounds. You're also qualified to drive vehicles for which a Class C license is issued if you have a Class B license.

Commercial Class C: Small Vehicles

If you have a Class C license, you can drive any one vehicle or combination of vehicles that isn't Class A or Class B and that has a GCWR of or less than 26,000 pounds.

Figure 1.2. Examples of Class B vehicles: straight trucks

Figure 1.3. Examples of Class C vehicles: small trucks, vans, and buses

▶ CDL Tests

You read in the beginning of this chapter that you need a CDL to drive a truck or a bus—and that you have to pass tests to get your CDL. Try not to get anxious about these tests, even if you have had negative experiences with tests in the past. You have a lot of time to study for them. And the material in this book and in your state's Commercial Driver's Manual will give you all the information you need to learn to pass.

You can take the tests you need to get your CDL at your local DMV. You need to take these tests in this order:

1. Knowledge tests
2. Skills test

A **knowledge test** tests what you *know*. It's a written test that requires you to answer multiple-choice questions. It's similar to tests you may have taken in school. A **skills test**, on the other hand, is a performance test. To pass a skills test, you need to show what you can *do*. When you take a skills test, you drive with an examiner on an approved course in the type of vehicle for which you're applying for a license. Why do you need to pass two different kinds of tests to get a CDL? Think about it this way: Answering questions about how to parallel park a CMV is different from actually parallel parking one. You must be able to demonstrate your ability to operate a CMV correctly and safely.

Knowledge Tests

You just learned that a knowledge test tests what you know. There are seven knowledge tests: a General Knowledge Test, an Air Brakes Test, a Combination Vehicle Test, and four endorsement tests. (Some states combine the General Knowledge and the Combination Vehicle Tests for Class A applicants.) Don't let the number of tests scare you—most drivers take only three or four of the knowledge tests. The number of tests you take depends on your state's requirements and the kind of vehicle you want to drive. This book covers the information on all the knowledge tests. You should also study the Commercial Driver's Manual for your state, so you know exactly what information your particular state will include on the test. You have to pass the knowledge tests to take the skills test, and you have to pass the skills test to get your CDL. It might help to know, however, that the knowledge tests aren't timed. When you get to the DMV, you can take a deep breath, relax, and take your time. And you can take the knowledge tests and the skills test over and over again until you pass. Only one attempt at each knowledge

test is allowed per day in some states and per week in others, however, and you may have to pay another application fee after three attempts. You can retake a skills test, but you must wait a certain period of time before you can retest. Some states allow you to retest in 24 hours, while others require 2 weeks before retesting. Generally, each component must be passed to move on to the next component. (You'll learn about the three components of a skills test later in this chapter.)

All the knowledge tests are multiple-choice. You need to choose the answer choice that correctly

- completes the sentence
- answers the question
- fills in the blank

In most states, multiple-choice questions consist of four answer options. You choose the answer option that correctly completes the sentence or answers the question. Fill-in-the-blank questions are rare on knowledge tests for the CDL.

Knowledge tests may be paper-based, which means you write your answer on a score sheet or fill in the correct circle with a pencil, or computer-based, which means you push button A, B, C, or D or touch the screen to indicate the correct answer. Don't be intimidated if you're asked to take a knowledge test on a computer. Computer-based tests are set up to be user friendly even for people with no computer experience, and you can always ask for help using the computer if you need it.

The General Knowledge Test

All drivers applying for a CDL have to take the General Knowledge Test. The questions on this test are multiple-choice. In most states, you must choose one correct answer from four answer choices (A, B, C, D), but in some states, you're given only three answer choices (A, B, C). Of the 50 questions on the General

- Read each question carefully. The CDL tests usually aren't timed, so relax and take your time.

- Answer the easy questions first. Then go back and spend time on the harder questions. You may not be able to do this with computer-based testing. Some computer-based testing allows you to skip a question, but the skipped question may be inserted later in the test.

- If you're not sure of an answer, narrow down your choices by eliminating answer choices that you know are incorrect.

- Look out for answer options that have the words "all," "every," "always," or "never" in them. These choices usually aren't correct. It's difficult for something to always or never be true!

- Don't change your answer. Your first instinct is usually best.

- Double-check to make sure you're marking the right question with the right answer.

- Don't leave any questions blank—they'll be marked wrong on the knowledge tests for the CDL. If you can't figure out an answer to a question, take a guess.

Knowledge Test, you need to correctly answer 40, or 80 percent, to pass. The following is a list of topics that you may be asked questions about on the General Knowledge Test. You'll learn about each of these topics in detail later in this book:

- inspection
- basic vehicle control (accelerating, steering, stopping, backing safely, etc.)
- shifting gears
- seeing ahead and to the sides and rear
- communicating using signals
- controlling using signals
- managing space
- seeing hazards
- avoiding distractions
- using in-vehicle equipment correctly
- driving at night, in winter, in fog, in hot weather, and in the mountains
- crossing railroad tracks
- braking
- handling emergencies

- skid control and recovery
- accident procedures

The Air Brakes Test

Air brakes work using compressed air. If air brakes are well-maintained and properly used, they're a safe, effective way to stop large vehicles. Because of this, air brakes are commonly used on large CMVs, including buses and most trailers. If you plan to drive any of these vehicles, you need to take a knowledge test on air brakes. On the Air Brakes Test, you'll be asked questions about

- the parts of an air brake system
- dual air brake systems
- inspecting air brake systems
- using air brakes

There are 25 multiple-choice questions on the Air Brakes Test, and you need to correctly answer 20, or 80 percent, to pass. After you take and pass the knowledge test on air brakes, you have to take and pass a skills test.

Figure 1.4. All Class A vehicles have air brakes.

To receive a Class A CDL, you must take and pass the General Knowledge Test and the Skills Test along with the Combination Vehicle Test. Since all Class A vehicles have air brakes, you must also pass a knowledge test and a skills test about air brakes.

Combination Vehicle Test

If you plan to drive a combination vehicle (a Class A vehicle), you need to take the Combination Vehicle Test. A combination vehicle is a tractor-trailer, a double, a triple, or a straight truck with a trailer over 10,000 pounds. A combination vehicle is longer and heavier than a straight vehicle, so you need additional knowledge and skills to safely operate it.

Like the other knowledge tests, the Combination Vehicle Test is multiple-choice, and you'll select the correct answer from three or four answer choices, depending on your state. On the Combination Vehicle Test, you'll be asked questions about

- driving combination vehicles safely
- combination vehicle air brakes
- antilock braking systems
- coupling and uncoupling
- inspecting a combination vehicle

Of the 20 questions on the Combination Vehicle Test, you need to correctly answer 16, or 80 percent, to pass.

▶ Endorsements

You learned earlier that there are different classes of CDLs for different types of vehicles. To operate some of the vehicles in these classes, you need an endorsement on your CDL. An **endorsement** is an additional permission not granted with a regular CDL. To obtain some endorsements, you need to pass only a knowledge test. For others, you need to pass both a knowledge test and a skills test. The following are endorsements and the tests you need to take and pass to receive them:

Endorsement	Test(s)
Double/triple trailers	Knowledge test
Passenger vehicles	Knowledge test and skills test
Tank vehicles	Knowledge test
Hazardous materials	Knowledge test and a security threat assessment

Once you pass a test required for an endorsement, a letter code is added to your CDL. Many states use the following letter codes:

- **T** Double/triple trailer
- **P** Passenger vehicle
- **N** Tank vehicle
- **H** Hazardous materials
- **X** Combination of tank vehicle and hazardous materials

▶ Restrictions

You just learned that an endorsement is an addition. A **restriction**, on the other hand, is a limitation—it limits what you're allowed to do. For example, if you want to drive a commercial vehicle with air brakes, you have to take and pass a knowledge test and a skills test on air brakes. If you don't take these tests, or if you fail them, you'll have a restriction on your CDL.

Like endorsements, restrictions are indicated with a letter or number code. These are some common restrictions:

L   Restricts the driver to vehicles not equipped with air brakes
B   Passenger endorsement restriction—can't drive Class A buses
C   Passenger endorsement restriction—can't drive Class A or B buses
8   Restricts Class A drivers to no tractor-trailer (truck-trailer only)
(Note that your state may use other letter or number codes for these restrictions.)

▶ Endorsement Tests

As you just learned, you have to take an endorsement test, a separate knowledge test, to operate these vehicles or transport this type of cargo:

- doubles and triples
- tankers
- hazardous materials
- passengers

Doubles and Triples

If you plan to drive doubles and triples, you need to take both the Combination Vehicle Test and the endorsement test for doubles and triples. Why the extra endorsement test? Pulling two or three trailers is difficult—doubles and triples are less stable than other CMVs and are more likely to roll over or jackknife. Driving these vehicles safely requires a great deal of knowledge and skill. On the Doubles and Triples Test, you'll be asked questions about:

- pulling double and triple trailers
- coupling and uncoupling
- inspecting doubles and triples
- doubles and triples air brake check

The Doubles and Triples Test contains 20 multiple-choice questions, and you must correctly answer 16, or 80 percent, to pass.

Tank Vehicles

You must take and pass the Tank Vehicles Test if you plan to haul liquid or liquid gas in a permanently mounted cargo tank or a portable tank that holds 1,000 or more gallons. Driving a tanker requires special knowledge and skill because of the tanker's high center of gravity and because the liquid in the tank moves as you drive.

On the Tank Vehicles Test, you'll be asked questions about

- inspecting tank vehicles
- driving tank vehicles
- safe driving rules

Of the 20 multiple-choice questions, you need to answer 16, or 80 percent, correctly to pass.

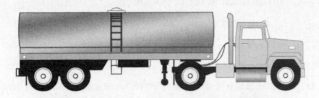

Figure 1.5. A tanker has a high center of gravity, which means it's more likely to roll over.

Hazardous Materials

Hazardous materials, often abbreviated as HAZMAT, include explosives, certain gases, certain solids, and flammable and combustible liquids. Hazardous materials pose a risk to people, property, and the environment. For this reason, some vehicles transporting hazardous materials must be **placarded**, which means signs are placed on the outside warning others of the danger. Placards are placed on the outside of the front and rear of the vehicle and on both sides.

Not all hazardous materials must be placarded, however. It depends on the class. (You'll learn more about this later in this book.) If a CMV is loaded with hazardous materials and the vehicle doesn't have to have placards, you don't need a hazardous materials endorsement on your CDL to drive it. If placards are required, however, you need this endorsement.

The Hazardous Materials Test will test your knowledge of the following:

- the intent of the regulations
- who does what during hazardous materials transportation
- communication rules
- loading and unloading
- bulk packaging marking, loading, and unloading
- driving and parking rules when transporting hazardous materials
- emergencies

Of the 30 questions on this test, you must correctly answer 24, or 80 percent, to pass.

The USA PATRIOT Act requires that all first-time applicants for a hazardous materials endorsement have a background record check (including fingerprints) and a threat assessment status.

Figure 1.6. Hazardous Materials Placards

Passenger Transport

You must have a CDL with the passenger "P" endorsement if you plan to drive a vehicle designed to transport 15 or more adult passengers (not counting the driver). You aren't considered a bus driver, however, if you drive only family members for personal reasons. You need to take and pass both a knowledge test and a skills test to get a P endorsement on your CDL.

On the Passenger Transport Test, you'll be asked questions about

- vehicle inspection
- loading and trip start
- driving a bus on the road
- after-trip vehicle inspection
- prohibited practices
- the use of brake-door interlocks

The Passenger Transport Test has 20 questions, and you need to correctly answer 16, or 80 percent, to pass.

If you plan to drive a school bus, you may also need a school bus "S" endorsement on your CDL.

Some states have a separate knowledge test for school bus drivers.

The Skills Test

Once you pass the General Knowledge Test and take any other required knowledge and endorsement tests, you are eligible to take the Skills Test. To take this test, you need to make an appointment with the DMV. You have to take the test with an examiner in the type of vehicle that matches the class and type listed on your learning permit. On the Skills Test, you need to demonstrate that you can inspect and drive the vehicle properly and safely with less than the predetermined maximum number of points (mistakes) allowed.

The Skills Test consists of three components:

1. Pre-Trip Inspection Test
2. Basic Vehicle Control Skills Test
3. Road Test

A state may "grandfather" a driver with a good driving record and significant driving experience from taking the skills test. The vast majority of CDL applicants have to take the skills test, however.

Pre-Trip Inspection Test

During the pre-trip inspection, you must show your examiner that the vehicle is safe to drive, usually by pointing to or touching each part and explaining what you need to look for to make sure that it's working properly and safe to drive. You may have to inspect items under the hood or crawl under the vehicle. During your inspection, you'll likely look for the following:

- an engine start
- an in-cab inspection
- inspection of the entire vehicle or part of the vehicle

(You'll learn more about each of these in Chapter 8 of this book.)

What happens if you do a good job on the pre-trip inspection but your *vehicle* doesn't pass? Your examiner will mark your test as being incomplete, and you'll have to reschedule, so you can take the test in a safe vehicle.

Basic Vehicle Control Skills Test

During the Basic Vehicle Control Skills portion of the Skills Test, you'll have to move the vehicle forward and backward. You'll move the vehicle forward to set up for backing and in some states perform a measured right turn. For backing maneuvers, you'll be asked to perform skills such as straight line backing, alley dock, and parallel parking. The Basic Vehicle Control Skills Test is usually given in an area marked with lines and traffic cones.

The Road Test

During the Road Test, you'll drive your vehicle on a route specified by the examiner. Some of the skills you'll have to demonstrate during the road test include making turns, choosing the correct gear to match your speed, merging into traffic, and coming to a smooth stop. You may also be asked to perform an emergency stop during the Road Test.

Deductions on the Skills Test

As you learned, to pass the three components of the Skills Test, you must have a minimal number of points deducted for errors. Your examiner will deduct points for each of these errors:

- **Pre-Trip Inspection Test**—Missing or incorrectly identified items
- **Basic Vehicle Control Skills Test**—A pull-up (stopping and reversing the direction of

Regulatory Signs

Turn and Lane Use

Movement Regulation

One Way/Divided
Highway Crossing

Weight Limit

Weigh Station

Truck Route

Seat Belt

Warning Signs

Turn and
Curve

Intersection

Advance Traffic
Control

Merge and Lane
Transition

Width
Restriction

Divided
Highway

Hill/Downgrade

Pavement
Condition

Lane
Transition

Low Clearance

Playground

Speed Hump

Work Zones

Road Work

Double Reverse
Curve

Figure 1.7. Commercial drivers must know the meaning of road signs.

your vehicle to better position it); an encroachment (touching a cone or a line)

- **Road Test**—Touching a curb during a turn; failure to reduce speed properly for an intersection; failure to use turn signals properly

▶ Driver Requirements

According to the Commercial Motor Vehicle Safety Act of 1986 and the Motor Carrier Safety Improvement Act (MCSIA) of 1999, you must meet the following requirements to get a CDL:

- **Residency requirement**: You must live in the state where you're applying for a CDL.
- **Age requirement**: You must be at least 21 years old to get a Class A CDL. In most states, you can get a Class A, Class B, or Class C CDL at 18 years of age. If you're under 21,

however, you can only drive **intrastate**, which means within the state. You can't cross state lines, transport passengers in a bus, or transport hazardous materials.

- **Language requirement**: You must be able to speak English well enough to have conversations with others including officials, to make entries in records and reports, and to understand road signs that are in English.
- **Medical requirement**: The federal government requires that you undergo a physical and mental examination before you apply for a commercial driver learner's permit to make sure that you don't have any physical or mental conditions that might interfere with your ability to operate a CMV. Once you pass your medical exam, you'll be issued a medical examiner's certificate, which you'll take with you to the DMV.

▶ Your Commercial Driver Learner's Permit

Once you have your medical examiner's certificate and have studied for the General Knowledge Test, other required knowledge tests, and any necessary endorsement tests, you're ready to apply for your commercial driver learner's permit. While you don't need an appointment at the DMV, processing—taking the tests, filling out paper work, and getting photographed—takes about 3 hours. At some DMVs, you may have to wait to start the process, so allow yourself plenty of time to get everything done. Remember not to arrive at the DMV near closing time or you may not have enough time to complete the process. In some instances, the DMV will not allow you to start the process because it's too close to the end of the day. You need to bring the following items with you:

- your driver's license
- your Social Security card
- your medical examiner's certificate
  (Note that your state may require additional documentation for proof of identity and residency.)

Once you receive your commercial driver learner's permit, you can drive a vehicle of the class and type that matches your permit. According to law, however, you must be accompanied by a driver holding a CDL of the same or higher class with the proper endorsements. This driver must be with you at all times. You're also not authorized to transport material requiring hazardous materials placards. When you're ready, you can make an appointment with the DMV to take the Skills Test.

▶ Disqualifications

If you're disqualified to operate a CMV, you can't operate a CMV either for a period of time or for life. In most states, you'll lose your CDL for at least 1 year for a criminal offense, such as driving a CMV with a blood alcohol concentration (BAC) of 0.04 percent or more. (In some states, the BAC is lower than this.) If you refuse to take a test for alcohol, you'll be treated as though you were driving under the influence and be disqualified. Be aware that alcohol affects a driver's judgment, vision, coordination, and reaction time. If you drink while driving, you might be unable to respond to hazards in time to prevent accidents.

Driving under the influence of a controlled substance is also a disqualifying criminal offense. Controlled substances are often called Schedule I drugs, and you can obtain a list of these drugs by contacting the Office of Motor Carrier Standards. (The address is listed in the Appendix of this book.) You should know that some medications prescribed by your doctor are Schedule I drugs. Check with your doctor to find out if your medication is safe to take while driving. Even cold medicine can make you drowsy and affect your ability to drive safely.

You can lose your CDL for a year if you're tested for alcohol and your blood alcohol concentration (BAC) is 0.04 percent or more. If you weigh between 180 and 200 pounds and have two drinks in an hour, your BAC will be around this percentage. Three drinks will put you over the limit. Don't risk it!

Possession, transportation, or unlawful use of Schedule I drugs while on duty and leaving the scene of an accident while driving a CMV are both considered a felony. You'll be disqualified for committing these crimes. If you're driving a vehicle that's placarded for hazardous materials, you'll be disqualified for a

	Effects of Alcohol on Your Body and Ability to Drive	
BAC	**Effects on Body**	**Effects on Driving**
.02	Body feels slightly warm; person feels mellow.	Driver is less inhibited.
.05	Person is noticeably relaxed.	Driver is less alert and focused; driver's coordination and judgment are impaired.
.08	Person's judgment and coordination are significantly impaired.	Driver's impaired coordination and judgment are apparent in driving.
.10	Person is noisy and has mood swings.	Driver's reaction time is reduced.
.15	Person's balance is impaired, and person is clearly drunk.	Driver is unable to drive.

longer time. Subsequent offenses usually carry a longer disqualification period and stiffer penalties.

In most states, if you commit two or three serious traffic violations within a specified time, you'll lose your CDL for 2 or 3 years. Serious traffic violations include speeding 15 miles per hour (mph) over the speed limit, reckless driving, following a vehicle too closely, improper or erratic lane changes, operating a CMV without a CDL, operating a CMV without a CDL in your possession, and operating a CMV without the proper class of CDL or endorsement.

If a federal or state inspector finds your vehicle to be unsafe during an inspection, he or she will order your vehicle "out of service." This means you can't operate the CMV until it's fixed. If you do, it's a violation of an out-of-service order. You'll lose your license for a period of time—usually 90 days—if you operate it out of service. For each additional time you operate your CMV out of service, the length of time increases.

CMV drivers must follow federal, state, and local regulations at railroad tracks. Failure to do so will result in a disqualification. Depending on the laws, you may be required to slow down and check that the railroad tracks are clear before crossing, or you may be required to come to a complete stop when hauling hazardous materials. A first violation usually results in a disqualification of 60 days and a second usually results in a disqualification of 90 days.

Because hazardous materials are dangerous, you may be disqualified from your hazardous materials endorsement for the following reasons: if you renounce your U.S. citizenship, you're wanted or under indictment for certain felonies, you have a conviction for certain felonies, you've been committed to a mental institution, or the Transportation Security Administration considers you a safety threat.

According to the MCSIA of 1999, CDL holders can be disqualified for certain offenses committed in their personal vehicles. These are serious offenses,

CDL License Rules

The following are some rules that affect drivers of CMVs:

- You can't have more than one license. If you do, a court may fine you up to $5,000 or put you in jail.
- If you're convicted of a traffic violation other than parking, you must notify your employer within 30 days.
- If you're convicted in another state of a traffic violation other than parking, notify your state's motor vehicle licensing agency within 30 days.
- If your CDL license is suspended, revoked, canceled, or disqualified, you must notify your employer within one working day.

however, such as leaving the scene of an accident, being under the influence of alcohol or drugs, or committing a felony involving a motor vehicle. For a complete list of disqualifications according to the FMCSR, see the Appendix of this book.

Chapter 1 Review Quiz

1–10: Circle the correct answer.

1. What letter code would most likely be added to your CDL if you receive an endorsement to drive a tanker?
   a. P
   b. N
   c. T
   d. H

2. You need a CDL if you drive a single vehicle with a gross vehicle weight rating (GVWR) of ____ or more pounds.
   a. 10,000
   b. 12,000
   c. 15,001
   d. 26,001

3. You do NOT need a CDL to drive a
   a. school bus.
   b. recreational vehicle.
   c. combination vehicle.
   d. straight truck.

4. An additional permission not granted with a regular CDL is called
   a. an endorsement.
   b. a restriction.
   c. an exception.
   d. a placard.

5. Which of the following is an example of a Class C vehicle?
   a. a medium-sized flatbed
   b. a small truck
   c. a garbage truck
   d. a tractor-trailer

6. To take a(n) ____ test, you drive with an examiner on an approved course in the type of vehicle for which you're applying for a license.
   a. skills
   b. restriction
   c. knowledge
   d. endorsement

7. All truck and bus drivers were required to get a CDL beginning in
   a. 1986.
   b. 1988.
   c. 1990.
   d. 1992.

8. Which of these is an endorsement test?
   a. Air Brakes Test
   b. Combination Vehicle Test
   c. Hazardous Materials Test
   d. General Knowledge Test

9. Which endorsement test would you take if you wanted to drive a vehicle that pulls two trailers?
   a. Tankers
   b. Doubles and Triples
   c. Passengers
   d. Hazardous Materials

10. Which of these is NOT a combination vehicle?
    a. a straight truck with a trailer
    b. a tractor-trailer
    c. a truck-trailer
    d. a garbage truck

11–15: Indicate whether each statement is true or false.

_____ **11.** You can take the General Knowledge Test only once.

_____ **12.** You don't need a hazardous materials endorsement to drive a vehicle that doesn't require placards.

_____ **13.** There are 20 questions on the Tank Vehicles Test.

_____ **14.** When you stop and reverse the direction of your vehicle to better position it, it's called an encroachment.

_____ **15.** You must get a medical examiner's certificate to apply for a CDL.

Check your answers on page 293.

CHAPTER

2 ▶ Driving Safely, Part 1

CHAPTER SUMMARY

Driving safely is the most important aspect of any commercial driver's job. This chapter and the following chapter explain the essential skills you need to safely operate your CMV and protect yourself and others from harm.

It's important to know how to drive a CMV safely—and not just to pass the knowledge and skills tests for a CDL! As a responsible driver of a large vehicle, you need to be concerned with the safety of everyone on the road, including yourself. While you can't control the way others drive, you can anticipate problems and adjust your own driving before a problem occurs or in time to avoid a problem altogether. You must also learn how to maintain total control of your CMV at all times and in all conditions. Many questions on the General Knowledge Test are about safe driving, so read this section carefully and study the material until you're sure you know it.

▶ Stay Visually Alert

A **hazard** is any condition or person on or near a road (driver, pedestrian, cyclist, etc.) that poses a risk to you and to other drivers. You need to stay visually alert to be aware of hazards, so you can avoid causing or being involved in an accident. Consider this scenario: Car 1 is traveling at a high rate of speed on an interstate highway. When the driver approaches an off-ramp, he hits his brakes hard. Car 1 is a hazard. The driver of Car 2—the car directly in front of you—doesn't notice Car 1's brake lights. An accident—an emergency—is about to happen right in front of you. What do you do? If you're visually alert, you'll put on your four-way flashers and tap your brakes as an additional warning, so the drivers behind you also slow down and avoid hitting you. After you slow down, if possible, you should put on your turn signal and change lanes. If you weren't visually alert, you might have been involved in an accident and caused the drivers behind you to become involved as well.

Look Ahead

If you look ahead of your vehicle, you're more likely to be ready to stop quickly, change lanes, and perform other maneuvers to avoid getting into an accident. Good drivers typically look at least 12 to 15 seconds ahead of their vehicles. How do they do this? It's not as hard as it sounds. If you're driving slowly, 12 to 15 seconds is about one-eighth of a mile—the length of one city block—so you keep an eye out for hazards this far ahead. If you're driving faster, such as when you're on a highway, 12 to 15 seconds is about one-quarter of a mile. By looking ahead, you give your mind time to understand what is happening in front of your vehicle. You should also have time to adjust your driving to compensate for and avoid a problem before it requires quick, evasive action.

What should you look for when you look 12 to 15 seconds ahead? Look for hazards. Try to spot accidents *before* they occur. When you're driving a CMV, pay attention to what other drivers are doing and take note of road conditions. Look for vehicles turning, changing lanes, slowing down, and merging onto and off the highway. Watch for signs that these actions are about to occur, such as brake lights and turn signals. Traffic signs become even more important when you drive a

large vehicle. They allow you to think ahead and be prepared for a change in traffic patterns, different terrain, bridge weights, underpass heights, and other important information. Look for traffic signs warning of upcoming hills and curves. You may have to change lanes or adjust your driving based on road conditions because of rain and snow. Pay close attention to traffic signals. When you see a **stale green light**—a light that's already green when you see it and has probably been green for a while—assume that it's about to change and slow down, so you're prepared to stop. Good drivers not only anticipate problems before they occur, but also adjust their driving to ensure, as much as possible, that problems don't occur at all.

Use Your Mirrors

The mirrors on your CMV are an important tool to help you see the vehicles alongside and behind you. Check your mirrors often to keep track of nearby vehicles. Is a vehicle about to overtake yours? Is someone riding in one of your blind spots? Could you make a quick lane change if you had to? Regularly checking your mirrors will help you answer these questions. Just as looking ahead helps you prepare for potential problems, mirrors help you spot and compensate for problems created by other drivers. When mirrors are adjusted properly, they allow a driver to make better decisions. Check and adjust your mirrors before every trip—when your trailer is straight—to make sure that you're getting the most accurate view of what's happening around you. Don't forget to clean your mirrors when they are dirty, so your view of the space around you isn't diminished.

Watch Out for Blind Spots

Unfortunately, you can't see everything that's going on around you by looking in your mirrors. The places that you can't see in your mirrors are called **blind spots**. Blind spots are a common problem for drivers because

they can make lane changes challenging. They're another reason why you need to stay visually alert. Another driver might not notice that he is driving in your blind spot. Even though you can't see the driver's car, it's your responsibility to know it's there. How do you do this? Use your mirrors to see the car before it reaches your blind spot, and use your eyes to see the car after it has passed your vehicle. All vehicles have blind spots, but CMVs have large blind spots that correspond with the size of the vehicle. It is a professional driver's responsibility to know where they are and how to compensate for them. By keeping your eyes moving and scanning your mirrors every 5 to 8 seconds, you become aware of vehicles before they enter your blind spots. By knowing what—if anything—is in your blind spots, you can make better decisions for lane changes or evasive maneuvers.

your mirrors to the road—to see nearby vehicles and know what they're doing.

You should understand the type of mirrors that are on your vehicle. Large vehicles have flat mirrors that allow you to see objects in the distance—approximately three-quarters of the way back on your trailer and beyond. Most large vehicles are also equipped with curved mirrors, sometimes called **convex**, **fisheye**, **bug-eye**, or **spot mirrors**, that allow you to see beside and back to the rear of your trailer. Be aware, though, that the images in these mirrors appear smaller and farther away than they actually are. Where your convex mirror leaves off, your flat mirror should pick up. The two mirrors complement each other and should overlap to complete your visual picture. Many trucks are equipped with spot mirrors on the front fenders that help eliminate blind spots. Fender mirrors are an additional tool drivers can use to stay visually alert to their

Figure 2.1. A Truck's Blind Spot

Know How to Use Your Mirrors

There's a right way and a wrong way to use your mirrors. Some drivers focus too long on their mirrors or glance at their mirrors so quickly that they don't see what's happening. Using your mirrors incorrectly isn't only wrong—it's also dangerous! Look at your mirrors quickly, but look long enough—back and forth from

surroundings. It's important to look at all of your mirrors *and* the road to get a full picture of what's going on all around your vehicle.

Check Your CMV

You can use the mirrors on your CMV to watch for any problems that may be occurring on your vehicle. Look

Always use your mirrors in these situations:

- **Lane changes.** Your mirrors will help you figure out if you have enough room to make a safe lane change without causing other drivers to slow down. Check your mirrors before you change lanes, after you've signaled that you're about to change lanes, immediately after you've started to change lanes, and after you've completed the lane change.
- **Merges.** Because your vehicle is large, merging is sometimes tricky. Use your mirrors to determine whether you'll have enough space to safely merge your vehicle with the others on the road.
- **Turns.** Use your mirrors when you turn to make sure that your vehicle won't make contact with another vehicle or an object. Be especially careful during right turns when vehicles can attempt to squeeze between your trailer and the curb.
- **Tight spaces and congested roads.** When in congested traffic areas or tight spaces, check your mirrors to make sure that you have enough room to operate your vehicle without hitting anything.

Staying visually alert is one of the most important factors in ensuring not only your safety, but also the safety of everyone on the road. A trip without incident is a successful one.

into your mirrors every so often to check your vehicle for mechanical problems. Smoke could indicate overheated brakes, tire failure, or even a cargo fire. Underinflated tires can substantially increase the risk of tire fire. An untreated tire fire can put everyone on the road in danger. If you're carrying open cargo, use your mirrors to look out for loose straps or chains, as well as for ballooning tarps, all of which are hazards. If your cargo isn't properly tethered, stop and adjust it immediately, or as soon as it's safe and legal to do so, for the safety of all drivers on the road.

▶ Shifting Gears

Shifting gears correctly is important to maintain control of your vehicle. Improper shifting or incorrect gear choice can lessen your control and create a hazard.

Shifting Up with a Manual Transmission

How do you know when to shift up? When you become an experienced driver, you may be able to figure this out simply by listening to the sounds of your engine. In the meantime, however, you can take other cues from your vehicle.

One way you can tell when to shift up, or upshift, is to watch your revolutions per minute (RPM) on your tachometer. Different vehicles have different operating RPM ranges. Read the owner's manual for your vehicle to find out its operating RPM range. Then watch your tachometer as you drive and upshift when your vehicle reaches the top number of the range. In some vehicles, you may use a method called "progressive" shifting, in which the RPM at which you shift becomes higher as you move into higher gears.

Another way to gauge when to shift is to watch your speedometer. Before you can do this, however, you need to know which speeds are best for each gear. Each gear has a road-speed range that corresponds to that particular gear based on the type of vehicle you're driving. When your vehicle reaches the maximum speed for a gear, you must upshift. When it reaches the minimum speed for that gear, you need to downshift. Then use your MPH on your speedometer as an indicator of when to shift.

How do you execute an upshift? The basic procedure for shifting up is a five-step process:

1. Release the accelerator, push in the clutch, and shift to neutral at the same time.
2. Release the clutch.
3. Allow the engine and gears to slow down to the RPM required for the next gear.
4. Push in the clutch and shift to the higher gear at the same time.
5. Release the clutch and press the accelerator at the same time.

To properly use the clutch in a CMV, you must depress the clutch pedal approximately 1 to 2 inches beyond the free play area. Never push the clutch all the way to the floor when shifting gears up or down. Engaging the clutch brake at the bottom of the clutch stroke will make it nearly impossible to get to the next higher or lower gear.

Shifting using double clutching can be difficult. The only way to master double clutching is to practice. Remember that staying in neutral for too long can make it difficult for you to shift to a higher gear when necessary, but you should never force the shift. Instead, while in neutral, increase the engine speed so that it matches the road speed and then try again.

Shifting Down with a Manual Transmission

How do you know when to shift down? Again, watch your tachometer and speedometer. You should also downshift before heading down a hill. Shift down to a gear lower than the one required to climb the hill. This allows you to reduce your speed and go easy on your brakes so that they don't overheat and malfunction. It's also best to downshift before entering a curve. This allows you to maintain power through the curve and speed up once you're out of the curve. It also keeps your vehicle stable throughout the curve.

Executing a downshift is also a five-step process:

1. Release the accelerator, push in the clutch, and shift to neutral at the same time.
2. Release the clutch.
3. Press the accelerator, and increase the engine and gear speed to the RPM required in the lower gear.
4. Push in the clutch and shift to the lower gear at the same time.
5. Release the clutch, and press the accelerator at the same time.

Remember, only depress the clutch beyond the free play area and not all the way to the floor.

Multi-Speed Rear Axles and Auxiliary Transmissions

Many CMVs today are equipped with multi-speed rear axles and auxiliary transmissions, which give the driver extra gears. The gearshift lever of the main transmission usually has a selector knob and switch. Note that different shift patterns exist for different CMVs, so you'll have to learn the pattern for the specific CMV you're driving.

Automatic Transmissions

Some vehicles have automatic transmissions. **Automatic transmissions** change gear ratios automatically as you're driving. This means, for the most part, the vehicle controls the gears. When going down grades, however, select a low range to improve engine braking (also known as compression braking). Using a lower range prevents the transmission from shifting up beyond the selected gear (unless the governor RPM is exceeded). This braking effect is very important when you're going down grades.

Automated Transmissions

Some CMVs now come with automated transmissions. An **automated transmission** has a clutch and a gear selector, but you use the clutch only to start and stop the vehicle. When the CMV is in motion, sensors monitor the speed and RPM, and shifting is automatic. Note that some states restrict the use of vehicles outfitted with automated transmissions on driving tests. Also be aware that some states add a restriction to your license if you take the driving test in a vehicle with an automatic transmission. This restriction prevents a driver from legally driving a CMV with a manual transmission.

Retarders

Some vehicles contain **retarders**, which help slow down a vehicle without causing major brake wear. The four main types of retarders are (1) exhaust, (2) engine, (3) hydraulic, and (4) electric. Retarders can be turned on or off, and some can be adjusted to distribute varying amounts of power. When a retarder is turned on and a driver lets up on the accelerator pedal all the way, the retarder applies braking power to the drive wheels only. This is a handy feature that can extend the life of your brakes, but you should *always* turn off the retarder when driving on wet, snowy, or icy roads. When the drive wheels don't have good traction, using

the retarder can cause your vehicle to skid. Also note that some areas, such as heavily populated cities, prohibit the use of retarders, so be sure to know when you can or can't use them. Restrictions on the use of retarders came about because some drivers modify the exhaust systems on their CMVs, causing the retarders to be very loud. The noise level of a CMV with retarders with no modification is slightly louder than an accelerating truck.

▶ Backing Safely

Backing is one of the most difficult maneuvers to execute. Because your view of your surroundings is very limited, *backing is always dangerous*, and you should avoid it altogether if possible. It's much safer to park where you'll be able to pull forward when you leave. Once in a while, however, you may find yourself in a situation where backing is unavoidable. You'll also be required to demonstrate your backing ability on the Skills Test.

Knowing these simple rules will help you back in the safest way possible:

- **Look at your path.** Before you begin to back, look at your path. Then get out of your vehicle and walk around it. Check the clearance above and around your vehicle along the path that you intend to take.
- **Back slowly.** Use the lowest reverse gear and back very slowly, in case you need to adjust your steering or stop suddenly. Eliminate distractions and make sure that your full focus is on the task at hand.
- **Back and turn toward the driver's side.** Backing to the right (blindside) is very dangerous because your view is limited. Back toward the driver's side whenever possible,

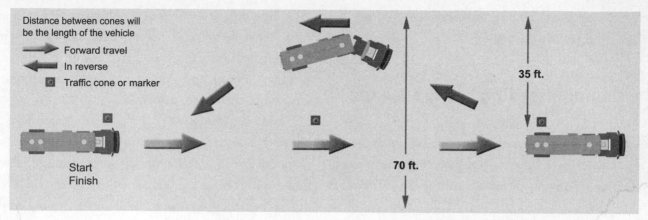

Distance between cones will be the length of the vehicle

→ Forward travel

← In reverse

◻ Traffic cone or marker

35 ft.

Start
Finish

70 ft.

Figure 2.2. The Correct Way to Back With a Trailer

using your mirrors to help you see the rear of your vehicle. Never park your vehicle in a way that prevents you from backing to the driver's side. Also, never lean out of the driver's side window or door when backing. This prevents you from using both of your side mirrors. If you feel that your view of your surroundings is too limited to back safely, you may have to stop your vehicle, get out, and walk your path once again.

- **Use a helper whenever possible.** A helper is an important asset when backing because a helper can see what you can't see in your blind spots. First, agree upon the hand signals your helper will use, and make sure you come up with a clear sign for "stop." Have your helper stand near the back of the vehicle in a spot where you can see your helper and his or her hand signals. If at any time you lose sight of your helper, stop immediately. Don't resume backing until you have your helper in your line of sight.

Backing with a Trailer

Backing with a trailer is even more difficult than backing with a straight truck, a bus, or a car. When backing these types of vehicles, turn your steering wheel toward your intended direction. When backing a trailer, however, turn your steering wheel in the *opposite* direction of intended travel. When the trailer begins to turn, turn your steering wheel the other way so that your vehicle follows the trailer.

Follow these tips to help you back safely:

- The best path to take when backing with a trailer is a straight line. If your path isn't straight, be sure to back to the driver's side for safety reasons.
- Back slowly and use your mirrors to monitor the trailer for drifting.
- If your trailer does begin to drift, make sure you correct the drift immediately by turning the steering wheel in the direction of the drift.
- Pull forward to reposition your vehicle as necessary. This is called making a pull-up. (You learned about pull-ups in Chapter 1. When you make a pull-up on your Skills Test, your examiner will score it as an error.)
- Always use a helper when one is available. Again, have your helper stand at the rear of the vehicle, and make sure that you can see your helper before you begin to back. It's very important to make sure that your

helper uses the agreed-upon hand signals, especially the one for "stop."

▶ Communicating on the Road

Communication is essential to staying safe on the road. You need to signal other drivers to let them know what you plan to do and to make sure they're aware that you're there.

Signaling to Other Drivers

It's very important that you let other drivers know what moves you intend to make. You might also want to signal other drivers to make them aware of information they might not know, such as an accident ahead or an upcoming hazard that will require everyone to reduce speed and stay alert. Never assume that other drivers know what you're going to do or that they have access to information. Use your signals to communicate these things to them.

Signaling a turn. Drivers follow three general rules when signaling a turn:

1. **Signal early.** Signal several seconds before you turn, so that other drivers won't try to pass you as you're executing the turn.
2. **Signal continuously.** To execute a safe turn, you must have both hands on the wheel throughout the turn. Don't remove your hands from the wheel to cancel the signal until you have completed the turn.
3. **Cancel your signal.** If your vehicle doesn't have a self-canceling signal, remember to turn off your signal once you've completed a turn. Leaving your signal on will confuse other drivers and can be a hazard.

Signaling a lane change. Always put on your turn signal before you make a lane change. Then change lanes slowly to give a driver in your blind spot a chance to honk and alert you or move out of your way if you failed to see him or her.

Slowing down. Always let drivers behind you know that you're slowing down, so they'll have a chance to do the same. Lightly tap the brake pedal a few times so your brake lights flash. Other drivers will take this as a warning to slow down. If you're driving very slowly or you're stopped, turn on your four-way emergency flashers if permitted by state law.

Many situations require you to slow down, including these:

- **Trouble ahead.** Your CMV is much larger than most vehicles on the road. This can make it difficult for those behind you to be aware of hazards ahead. If you spot a hazard, flash your brake lights to warn other drivers to slow down.
- **Tight turns.** Slow down when making a tight turn in your CMV to avoid tipping your vehicle. Car drivers don't have to slow down as much during a tight turn, so they might not understand how much you actually have to slow down. When you make a tight turn, brake early and slowly to allow drivers behind time to adjust their own driving.
- **Stopping on the road.** CMV drivers often stop to unload cargo or passengers. Depending on the state, you might also be required by law to stop at railroad tracks. Because a sudden stop can be very dangerous for all drivers, warn drivers behind you by flashing your brake lights. It's also a good idea to put on your four-way emergency flashers before you start to slow down.

(Some states require that you use your four-way emergency flashers for stops at railroad tracks. CMVs carrying passengers or hauling a placarded load must stop at all railroad crossings and proceed only when it is clear and safe to do so.)

- **Other slow-driving situations.** No matter what the situation, use your four-way emergency flashers when you must drive under the speed limit. (Some states require the use of four-way emergency flashers in slow-driving situations, while others forbid it. Be aware of the laws in the state or states that you're driving in.) This lets a driver who is far away and might not be able to gauge your speed know that you're driving slowly.

As a general rule, *never use your signals to direct traffic.* Some drivers think that they're helping others on the road by signaling when it's safe to pass. This is unsafe and could cause an accident, for which you'll be liable. Let other drivers gauge when it's safe to pass.

All of the signals reviewed up to this point—turn signals, brake lights, and emergency flashers—are mechanical signals. Keep in mind, though, that drivers also send signals with their body movements. A good driver picks up on these body signals to determine what another driver intends to do. For example, if you're driving your CMV on the interstate and a car is merging onto the highway, you should notice whether or not the other driver has looked into his mirror or glanced over his shoulder before entering the highway. If he hasn't done a visual scan, you'll know that he has no idea you're in the lane he is merging into. A light tap of your horn will warn the driver that you're there and will prevent you from having to quickly get out of his way. By combining both mechanical signals and body movements, you can increase your awareness of your surroundings and keep both you and your vehicle safe.

Communicating Your Presence

Sometimes other drivers aren't visually alert and might not see your CMV even though it's large and in plain sight. In the following situations, it's crucial that you alert other drivers of your presence to avoid an accident:

Passing. The general rule when passing is to always assume that those around you—vehicles, motorcyclists, bicyclists, or pedestrians—haven't seen you and might suddenly move in front of you. As long as it's legal, lightly tap the horn to let them know you're there. At night, you might also flash your lights from low to high beams and back again as a warning that you're there. It's your responsibility to drive slowly and cautiously so that you're able to prevent an accident if others don't see or hear your warning signals.

Impaired visibility conditions. Sometimes drivers have a difficult time seeing at dawn and dusk. Driver visibility is also impaired in inclement weather such as rain, snow, or fog. If it's hard for you to see other vehicles, assume that they're having difficulty spotting you as well. Under these conditions, turn on your headlights, which should be bright enough to alert other drivers of your presence (don't use just your identification or clearance lights) but not so bright that

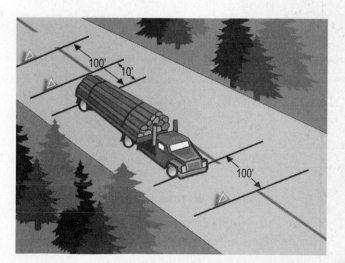

Figure 2.3. The Proper Placement of Reflective Triangles

they cause problems for other drivers (don't use high beams even during the day).

Some companies have a policy that requires drivers to have headlights and clearance lights on at all times. Even if your company does not require lights on, it's a good safety habit to follow.

Parking at the side of the road. If you must stop on the side of the road, turn on your four-way emergency flashers, especially at night. This way, drivers who see your taillights won't assume your vehicle is moving and crash into the rear of your vehicle.

If you must stop on the side or shoulder of the road, put out emergency warning devices such as reflective triangles within 10 minutes of stopping. The sooner you do this, the better. Place reflective triangles at the following sites, holding the triangles out between yourself and other drivers so that they can see you:

- On a two-lane road with traffic in both directions, place triangles within 10 feet of the front or rear corners of the vehicle, on the traffic side, to mark the location of the vehicle. Also place triangles approximately 100 feet behind and ahead of the vehicle, on the shoulder or lane in which you're stopped.
- On a one-way or divided highway, place triangles at 10-foot, 100-foot, and 200-foot points toward the approaching traffic.
- On a hill, curve, or other area with an obstruction that prevents drivers from seeing you, place the last triangle up to 500 feet behind your vehicle.

Your horn can serve as a warning to others, but use it only when absolutely necessary because the sound of your horn can startle drivers. Use your horn as a last resort to get a driver's attention.

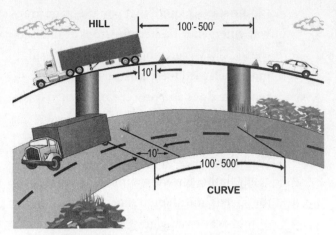

Figure 2.4. If you're stopped on a hill or a curve, place the last reflective triangle 500 feet from your vehicle.

▶ Managing Speed

Many fatal crashes occur because one or more drivers were driving too fast. You need to know how to manage your speed to stay safe. Although it's important to follow posted signs when assessing an appropriate speed, you should also factor in driving conditions such as traction, curves, visibility, traffic, and hills.

Speed and Stopping Distance

You probably know that you can't instantly come to a complete stop. You have to allow your CMV some distance to stop completely. Three factors dictate stopping distance:

Your **perception distance** is the distance your vehicle moves from the time that your eyes spot a hazard until your brain recognizes it. An alert driver will process this information in three-quarters of a second. If you're traveling 55 mph, your perception distance will be 60 feet.

Your **reaction distance** is the distance your vehicle moves from the time your brain recognizes the hazard until your foot moves off the accelerator and pushes the brake pedal. An alert driver will react in an additional three-quarters of a second. At 55 mph, your vehicle will travel an additional 60 feet before your foot hits the brakes.

Your **braking distance** is the distance it takes for your vehicle to stop once your foot has pushed the brake. A truck traveling 55 mph on a dry road with good brakes won't be able to stop for about 170 feet, which takes about 4 ½ seconds.

Your **total stopping distance**, then, at a speed of 55 mph, is about 290 feet (60 + 60 + 170 = 290). Drivers of vehicles with air brakes need to add another 32 feet to their total stopping distance because of brake lag, which you'll learn about in Chapter 6. Keep in mind that speed greatly affects total stopping distance. If you double your speed, it takes *four times longer* for your vehicle to stop, and in the event of a crash, your vehicle will have *four times the destructive power*. This is an important point to remember. Controlling your speed can make all the difference as to the damage caused by your CMV in an accident.

Vehicle weight is also a factor affecting total stopping distance. While a heavy vehicle will cause your brakes to work harder, the weight of the vehicle provides more traction in the event of a quick stop, which lessens both the stopping distance and the chance that your vehicle will skid. An empty vehicle will have a greater stopping distance and is much more likely to bounce, lock up its wheels, and skid. Don't forget that the brakes, tires, springs, and shock absorbers on a large vehicle designed to haul heavy cargo are engineered to work at their maximum potential when the vehicle is fully loaded. Always keep these factors in mind when operating your vehicle regardless of whether it's fully loaded.

If you're driving a CMV with air brakes, you need extra time to stop because the air needs time to go through the brake lines. This extra time is called **brake lag**. You'll learn more about brake lag in Chapter 6, "Air Brakes."

Speed and Road Surface

Road surface affects the amount of **traction** your vehicle will have, and this affects your steering and braking abilities. Traction is the friction between the tires and the road. The more traction your vehicle has, the faster you'll be able to stop, and the better you'll be able to steer, whether you're steering around a curve or into another lane.

A slippery road provides far less traction than a dry road. In fact, a wet road can actually *double* your stopping distance. Reduce your "dry-road speed" by one-third (i.e., from 55 mph to 35 mph) when driving on wet roads.

Packed snow also drastically changes the surface of the road. When driving on packed snow, reduce your "dry-road speed" by half or more. Icy roads call for you to drive as slowly as possible and to stop driving as soon as you can.

You should also slow down when you drive over the following:

- **Shaded areas.** If it appears that the ice on the roads has melted, slow down. Shaded areas allow slippery ice to remain on the road long after it has melted away from sun-exposed road surfaces.
- **Bridges.** Bridges always freeze before the rest of road surfaces. This can be tricky to determine when the temperature is around 32 degrees Fahrenheit, so be extra careful under these conditions.
- **Melting ice.** When ice begins to melt and becomes wet, the water on the surface of the ice increases the slipperiness of the road and drastically reduces traction. It's very difficult to regain control of your vehicle if you start to skid on melting ice, so use extreme caution.

- **Black ice.** Black ice is difficult to spot. Black ice is a layer of ice so thin and clear that the road appears wet rather than icy. If the temperature is below freezing and the road appears wet, be prepared to encounter black ice.

- **Vehicle icing.** One way to tell if the road is icy is to check the amount of ice on your vehicle. To do this, simply open the window and feel the antenna or the mirror and mirror support. If they're icy, chances are the road is becoming icy as well. You might also guess that ice is forming on the road when you notice that road spray is not coming off your vehicle or other vehicles.

- **Just after rain begins.** When rain first begins, the water mixes with oil on the road, and the road surface can become slippery. Lack of rain allows grease and oils to build up on the road surface. The longer it has been since it has rained, the more dangerous the road becomes after the rain starts. One way to tell that rain has caused the roadway to become slick is when a foamy substance appears on the road surface. Once it has rained for a while, the water washes the oil away.

- **Hydroplaning.** Sometimes water or slush collects on a road surface before it can drain or run off the road and hydroplaning can occur. Hydroplaning takes place when a vehicle's tires can't make contact with the road, resulting in a loss of traction. Think of it like waterskiing—your tires glide on the surface of the water instead of making contact with the road beneath it. Sometimes hydroplaning hinders your ability to brake or steer. Accelerating or braking may cause you to lose complete control of your vehicle.

The best way to regain control when you're hydroplaning is to release the accelerator and push in the clutch. This usually does the trick. If your drive wheels start to skid, push in the clutch, so they're able to turn freely.

Some drivers believe that hydroplaning can occur only when there's a lot of water on the road. Others think that hydroplaning won't occur at low speeds. Neither belief is true. Hydroplaning can occur when there's a small amount of water—such as a shallow puddle—on the road, so drivers must be alert and prepared to react when driving in these conditions. Hydroplaning can also occur at speeds as low as 30 mph, so be aware that driving slow won't necessarily prevent you from hydroplaning. Hydroplaning often occurs because of low tire pressure or worn treads. When treads are worn, the grooves in the tire aren't deep enough to carry the water away from the tire. Check your tires before driving in wet weather to ensure that they have good pressure and deep tread, and watch for signs of standing water on road surfaces, such as raindrops, tire splashes, and clear reflections.

Speed and Curves

Taking a curve too fast can result in one of two bad situations: (1) Your tires can lose traction and continue straight ahead, causing your vehicle to skid off the road, or (2) your tires may retain traction, but your vehicle may roll over. Adjust your speed when entering a curve. Drivers have rolled their CMVs even when following the posted speed limit for a curve because they didn't consider the vehicle's high center of gravity. (You learned in Chapter 1 that a tanker is a CMV with a high center of gravity.) Also, the speed limit signs are for smaller vehicles, so it's much safer for you to go slower than the posted speed limit for the curve.

Slow down *before* you enter the curve. If you use your brakes halfway through the curve, you run the risk of locking your wheels and causing your vehicle to skid. Don't go faster than the posted speed limit for a curve—that's asking for trouble. Once you're partway through the curve, you'll want to accelerate a little to help maintain control, so make sure you're in a gear that will allow you to do so.

Speed and Distance Ahead

Adjust your speed to make sure you'll be able to stop within the distance you see ahead. Fog, rain, and other elements can lessen your sight distance. Also, your sight distance decreases at night. Low beams allow you to see only about 250 feet ahead of you, while high beams allow you to see 350 to 500 feet ahead. Reduce your speed to compensate for the lack of sight distance at night. The rule of thumb is to drive at a speed that allows you to stop in the space illuminated by your headlights.

Speed and Traffic Flow

When driving in heavy traffic, driving at the speed of traffic is the safest way to go. Cars traveling in the same direction at the same speed aren't likely to collide. Driving too slow or too fast makes you a hazard to other drivers. As long as you're driving the legal speed limit and keeping a safe following distance, you're not creating a hazard.

Most people who drive fast do so because they think it will save them time. But increasing your speed doesn't save as much time as you might think, and it increases your chances of getting into an accident. Drivers who speed and pass driver after driver are more likely to collide with another vehicle. Speeding increases stress and therefore causes these drivers to

become tired sooner—an additional risk factor leading to a crash. Driving with the flow of traffic is much safer.

Speed on Downgrades

Gravity and the weight of your vehicle naturally increase your speed on downgrades. You must maintain a speed that is safe for the

- total weight of the vehicle and cargo
- length and steepness of the grade
- road conditions and weather

Never go faster than the posted speed limit on a downgrade—it's there for a reason. Sometimes you'll see signs specifying the length and steepness of the grade. The best way to slow down is to use the braking effect of the engine, which is greatest when it's near the governed RPM and the transmission is in the lower gears. Using the braking effect of the engine saves your brakes from unnecessary wear and tear. Keep in mind that your CMV must be in the proper gear for the downgrade. Use engine retarders when it's legal and safe to do so. Once you're in a lower gear, you can also use the snub braking technique to descend a steep downgrade. This technique consists of three steps:

1. Apply your brakes so that you feel a definite reduction in speed.
2. Reduce your speed by about 5 mph below the posted speed limit, and then release your brakes.
3. When your speed increases to the posted speed limit, repeat the first two steps. Do not fan the brakes—pressing and releasing the service brake in rapid succession—or you will bleed off the air supply for your air brake system. You'll learn more about braking on downgrades in the section "Driving in the Mountains" in Chapter 3.

Speed in Work Zones

Entering and traveling through work zones can be a dangerous situation for many reasons, which is why it requires increased awareness as a driver. As a CMV driver, you need to understand that many drivers want to enter the work zone ahead of you. Pay special attention to your mirrors to make sure no vehicles are trying to squeeze in front of you at the last second. Once you are in the work zone, approach it as you would any other adverse driving conditions. Follow these safety rules to drive through work zones without a problem:

- Maintain a safe distance between you and the vehicle ahead of you.
- Drive at or below the posted speed limit (as speed limits are normally reduced in work zones).
- Anticipate that other drivers will feel uncomfortable due to the reduced space in most work zones.
- Expect sudden stops because of high traffic volumes, construction vehicles entering the roadway, or many other issues that normally occur in work areas.

Many states have enacted laws to decrease accidents in work zones, such as doubling fines and requiring headlights to be on. Another important reason to be extra cautious is that four of every five fatalities in work zones are motorists. By being a defensive driver, you can avoid becoming a statistic.

▶ Managing Space

Safe drivers are always aware of the space around their vehicles, and constantly manage this space to ensure that they'll be able to avoid colliding with other vehicles during hazards. This is especially important for CMV drivers, because large vehicles take up more space and need more space to stop and turn.

Space Ahead

The space you're traveling into is the most important space around you. A common cause of accidents for CMVs is following too closely and not being able to stop in time to avoid a collision. It's important to remember that a smaller vehicle in front of you can probably stop a lot faster than your CMV can. Maintain enough space to ensure that you can come to a safe, sudden stop, if necessary.

The best way to manage space ahead of you is to count the seconds of space between you and the vehicle in front of you. At speeds below 40 mph, you need at least one second of space for every 10 feet of your vehicle length (i.e., 4 seconds of space for a 40-foot vehicle, 6 seconds of space for a 60-foot vehicle). At speeds above 40 mph, you should add one second (i.e., 5 seconds of space for a 40-foot vehicle, 7 seconds of space for a 60-foot vehicle).

How do you know how many seconds of space you have? This is very easy to measure. Pick a spot ahead of you such as a shadow on the road, a pavement marking, a sign, or some other clear landmark. When the vehicle in front of you passes that spot, begin counting like this: "One-thousand-one, one-thousand-two," and so on. Keep counting until you reach the same spot. Each "one-thousand" number represents a full second of space. Therefore, if you're driving a 60-foot vehicle at 55 mph and you reach only "one-thousand-three," you're driving *way too close*! Reduce your speed, drop back a bit, and count again until you're maintaining the appropriate amount of space. Periodically measure your space throughout your trip to make sure that you're constantly maintaining a safe distance from the vehicle in front of you. After a while, you'll be able to tell how many seconds of space you have without counting out loud. Don't forget to add a second when you're traveling over 40 mph. Also keep in mind that you need much more space to stop on slippery roads.

If another driver cuts into the space in front of you, don't slam on your brakes and swerve. You might cut off another driver, swerve into another lane, swerve off the road, or cause the driver behind you to crash into your vehicle or another vehicle. The best thing to do in this situation is to take your foot off the fuel pedal and attempt to regain a safe distance between you and the vehicle. To avoid overreacting, focus on what you can do to make the situation safer. Maintaining space in front of your vehicle allows you the room required for total stopping distance: perception, reaction, plus effective braking distance.

Space Behind

It's much more difficult to manage the space behind your vehicle. While it's true that you can't control the actions of drivers behind you, you can adjust your own driving to prevent some potentially dangerous situations.

Stay to the right. Vehicles carrying heavy loads often have trouble keeping up with traffic, especially when going uphill. This can cause other drivers to tailgate. If you're hauling a heavy load, stay to the right to allow other drivers to pass you. If you're driving behind a heavy vehicle that's going uphill, don't attempt to pass the vehicle until you know that you can do so quickly and safely.

Deal with tailgaters safely. When driving a large vehicle, it's sometimes hard to tell when you're being tailgated. Drivers often tailgate large vehicles that are traveling slowly. Drivers also tend to tailgate in bad weather, when it's difficult for them to see the road ahead. This can be dangerous for everyone, especially when the road surface is slippery and stopping distance is increased. Here are some tips to help you safely deal with tailgaters:

- Avoid quick lane changes and changes in speed. Signal drivers behind you before you slow down, and take care to slow down gradually. If you must change lanes, signal early and change lanes slowly.
- Increase your following distance. Give yourself enough room so that you can avoid quick changes in speed or direction. Making more room in front of your vehicle also gives tailgaters a place to go once they are able to get around you.
- Don't speed up. Speeding up most likely won't deter the tailgater from following too closely, and tailgating at high speeds can be very dangerous. Maintain a safe speed so you can control your vehicle no matter what happens.
- Avoid tricks. Don't try to discourage a tailgater by flashing your brake lights or turning on your tail lights.
- Ease off your fuel pedal to reduce your speed by one or two miles per hour to persuade tailgaters to pass.

Space to the Sides

Because CMVs are wide and take up a large portion of the road, it's often difficult for drivers to maintain the space to the sides of their vehicles. Always attempt to stay centered in your lane so that there's clearance on either side of your vehicle. Also, avoid traveling alongside other vehicles. This protects you from the possibility that another driver will suddenly change lanes and turn into you. It also prevents you from becoming trapped when you need to change lanes. Travel in a spot with open space on both sides. When this isn't possible due to heavy traffic, keep as much space as possible between you and the other vehicle. Pulling a bit ahead of the vehicle or dropping a bit behind it can make you more visible to the other driver.

Commercial drivers sometimes have trouble staying in a lane when winds are strong, especially when their vehicles are empty or when they're coming out of a tunnel. If you're traveling in strong winds, do your best to avoid driving alongside other vehicles.

Space Overhead

CMV drivers must be constantly aware of overhead clearance and avoid hitting objects above them. It's your responsibility to know your own clearance capabilities.

Don't assume that the clearance heights posted on bridges or overpasses are correct. Clearance can change due to circumstances such as repaving or packed snow. Clearance can also change due to the weight of your vehicle. A loaded vehicle is lower than an empty vehicle and can therefore clear more overhead obstacles. While you may have cleared a bridge with a loaded vehicle, this doesn't mean you'll be able to clear the same bridge when your vehicle is empty.

Also, keep in mind that some roads can cause vehicles to tilt. This might make it difficult to clear objects along the side of the road such as overhanging trees, signs, or bridge supports. If you encounter this situation, drive closer to the middle of the road to avoid overhead obstacles.

While some low bridges and underpasses may display warnings to drivers, many do not. If you're unsure of your clearance capabilities, go slowly until you're sure that you can make it. If you aren't sure, take a different route to avoid the overhead obstacle.

It's often difficult to see overhead obstacles when backing. Before you back into an area, get out of your vehicle and check the area for low-hanging trees, branches, or electric wires. Make sure you look for other hazards as well.

Space Below

You need to think about the clearance below your vehicle as well. Keep in mind that a loaded vehicle is much closer to the ground than an empty vehicle. Drivers must watch out for railroad tracks that stick up several inches, especially when the ground around the tracks is unpaved and has probably worn away a bit, exposing more of the track. Drainage channels can also cause a vehicle's end to drag, so they should be crossed with caution.

Space for Turns

CMVs need a lot of space around them to turn without hitting another vehicle. These vehicles make wide turns and must deal with **offtracking**, when a vehicle goes around a corner and its rear wheels follow a different path than its front wheels. You'll learn more about offtracking in Chapter 7.

Right turns. Right turns can be tricky because your view of what's happening to the right of your vehicle is limited. All turns should be executed slowly to give yourself and other drivers time to adjust if something goes wrong. There are two areas to pay particular attention to during a right turn: the left front corner of your vehicle and your right mirror. The left front corner is important because you need to make sure you're clearing objects in front of your truck. The right mirror indicates if you're missing objects to the rear, including vehicles that may try to pass on the right.

When driving a truck or a bus that can't make a right turn without swinging into another lane, turn wide as you *complete* the turn, making sure that the rear of your vehicle is close to the curb so that other drivers won't pass you on the right. Don't turn wide to the left as you start the turn because other drivers might assume that you're turning left. If a driver thinks that you're turning left and decides to pass you on the right, you could crash into the other vehicle when attempting to complete the turn.

If you must swing into the oncoming lane to complete a turn, be on the lookout for vehicles com-

ing toward you. Allow these drivers room to go around you or stop and wait for you. Don't back up to give them room, however, because you could hit a vehicle behind you.

Left turns. When making a left turn at an intersection, be sure you have reached the center of the intersection before you begin the turn, so that off-tracking doesn't cause you to hit another vehicle. If the intersection has two turning lanes, always start a left turn from the right-hand turn lane. Starting in the inside lane would be unsafe. Other drivers could pull next to you on the right, and it would be hard for you to see these drivers and avoid hitting them. Just like

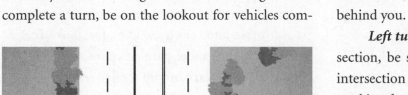

Figure 2.5. The Incorrect (top) and Correct (bottom) Ways to Make a Right Turn

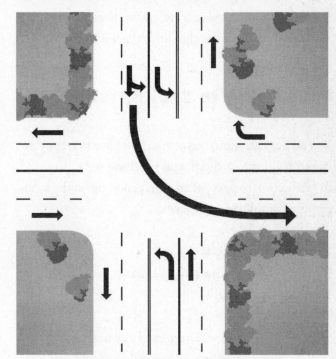

Figure 2.6. The Correct Way to Make a Left Turn

when making a right turn, watch two areas of your vehicle when turning: the right front corner and the left mirror. Again, watch the right front corner to make sure you're clearing objects in front of your vehicle. The left mirror shows that you have missed objects with the trailer, including vehicles sitting at or beyond the stop line.

Space to Cross or Enter Traffic

The size and weight of your CMV are important factors when crossing or entering traffic. A large CMV accelerates slowly, so you'll need to wait for a larger gap in traffic than a small truck would require. Also, a heavier load will delay acceleration. When crossing the road, be sure that you have enough time to get all the way across the road before traffic reaches you or the traffic light changes.

If you're approaching a stale green light or a yellow light, stop before you reach the stop line, so you don't block the intersection. Law enforcement officials in some areas will ticket drivers who cross an intersection after the light changes, while others will ticket drivers who are obstructing traffic because they are stopped in the intersection after the light changes.

▶ Learning to Spot Hazards

Not all hazards jump out at you. You have to train your eye to see some of them, and you have to be prepared to take action to prevent an emergency. Be on the lookout for the following hazards:

Road Hazards

If you see any of these road hazards, slow down, be alert, and drive safely.

- **Work zones.** Drive carefully near work zones. Reduce your speed to a legal and safe speed. Use your four-way emergency flashers or brake lights to warn drivers behind you of the work zone.
- **Pavement drop-off.** An uneven shoulder or drop-off near the edge of the road could cause your truck to tilt to the outside and hit objects near the road such as signs, tree limbs, and poles. Your truck might also be hard to steer or hang on the pavement edge if you drive off the shoulder of the road.
- **Foreign objects.** All sorts of things fall onto the road and can cause damage to your tires, brake lines, electrical lines, fuel tanks, fuel lines, and other parts of your CMV. Remain alert, so you can spot foreign objects early enough to avoid making sudden and unsafe moves.

Drivers Who Are Hazards

Sometimes other drivers cause hazards. It's important to recognize a hazard before it becomes a problem for you and your vehicle. Look out for the following while driving:

- **Distractions.** Drivers who aren't looking at the road can't see you. They may be unaware of who has the right of way.
- **Blocked vision.** Be observant of drivers with blocked vision such as those driving a van or a car packed with items so that the driver can't see out the rear or side windows or in the rearview mirror. Drivers may also have their view blocked by buildings, signs, parked cars, or other vehicles. Pedestrians, bicyclists, walkers, and joggers might also block the vision of those driving on the road.
- **Children.** Children tend to act quickly without checking traffic. Whenever you see a child near a roadway, slow down.
- **Road workers.** People working on the road may be so involved in their work that they aren't paying attention to nearby cars and trucks.
- **Disabled vehicles.** A disabled vehicle may have a person in it or near it who's trying to fix the vehicle or who's stranded.

- **Distracted drivers.** Distracted drivers are drivers who are not paying attention to the task of driving. They may be talking on a cell phone, changing stations on the radio, or upset about a life situation. Whatever the reason for their distraction, if you can tell that drivers aren't paying attention, attempt to avoid driving anywhere near them. Slow down or pull over to put space between your vehicle and theirs.
- **Drunk drivers.** Drunk drivers are similar to distracted drivers because the effect of the alcohol impairs a driver's ability to control a vehicle. You can encounter a drunk driver at any time of day, but be extra cautious in the early morning, after bars close.
- **Aggressive drivers.** Aggressive drivers are the bullies of the highway. Their tempers flare up any time another driver makes a mistake, whether it's real or imagined. They tailgate while flashing their lights in an effort to get you out of their way. Sometimes they get so aggressive that they run you off the road. When dealing with an aggressive driver, don't return the aggression. Attempt to diffuse the situation by allowing them to get around you. Do whatever you need to do to put distance between you and them.

- **Pedestrians and bicyclists.** Pedestrians and bicyclists can also be hazardous when crossing the roadway or failing to pay attention to what's going on around them.
- **Animals.** Animals can run in front of your vehicle, so it's important to watch out for animals alongside the road. Deer and other large animals can cause a great deal of damage to a vehicle. If an animal runs in front of your vehicle, don't swerve to avoid it; you could end up losing control of your vehicle.

As a professional driver, it's your responsibility to recognize hazards early enough to avoid an accident. By staying alert, you can observe many hazards and adjust what you're doing to compensate for the hazardous situation.

It's also important to have a plan as you drive in case something happens right in front of you and you don't have time to think it through. A plan can be as simple as changing lanes because you already know that the lane to your left is clear. It can be as difficult as choosing to leave the roadway rather than hitting another vehicle. Your plan needs to be in place before you're presented with a hazardous situation, for your own safety and for the safety of other drivers.

Chapter 2 Review Quiz

1–2: Write your answers on the lines below.

1. List four situations in which you should always check your mirrors.

a. _____

_____

_____

_____

b. _____

_____

_____

_____

c. _____

_____

_____

_____

d. _____

_____

_____

_____

2. What are the four main types of retarders?

a. _____

_____

_____

_____

b. _____

_____

_____

_____

c. _____

_____

_____

_____

d. _____

_____

_____

_____

3–13: Circle the correct answer.

3. When you execute an upshift with a manual transmission, what should you do after you push in the clutch and shift to the higher gear?
a. Release the accelerator.
b. Allow the engine gears to slow down.
c. Release the clutch.
d. Shift to neutral.

4. A layer of ice so thin and clear that the road appears wet rather than icy is called
   a. a shaded area.
   b. black ice.
   c. vehicle icing.
   d. wet ice.

5. A(n) _____ transmission has a gear select and a clutch that you use only to start and stop the vehicle.
   a. manual
   b. automated
   c. multi-speed
   d. automatic

6. What is an advantage of having curved mirrors on your CMV?
   a. You can see more.
   b. Images appear smaller.
   c. You can see very clearly.
   d. Images appear closer.

7. You should upshift with a manual transmission when your vehicle reaches the _____ number in its RPM range.
   a. bottom
   b. middle
   c. top
   d. middle or top

8. You should always turn off a retarder when
   a. driving on wet roads.
   b. you need more braking power.
   c. you have exceptional traction.
   d. driving on dry roads.

9. The distance your vehicle moves from the time your brain recognizes a hazard until your foot moves off the accelerator and pushes the brake pedal is called the _____ distance.
   a. total stopping
   b. perception
   c. braking
   d. reaction

10. What is your total stopping distance if you're traveling at 55 mph?
    a. 60 feet
    b. 170 feet
    c. 200 feet
    d. 290 feet

11. When you back up, what should you do before you put your CMV into reverse?
    a. Pull forward.
    b. Look at your path.
    c. Lean out your window.
    d. Turn toward the driver's side.

12. While turning, when should you cancel your turn signal?
    a. before the turn
    b. at the beginning of a turn
    c. in the middle of the turn
    d. after the turn

13. You should use your four-way emergency flashers when you
    a. make a turn.
    b. are driving under the speed limit.
    c. need to stop suddenly.
    d. are driving in the rain.

Check your answers on page 293.

CHAPTER

3 ▶ Driving Safely, Part 2

CHAPTER SUMMARY

In Chapter 2, you learned some of the basics about driving your CMV safely. This chapter expands on that information by explaining how to drive during bad weather and how to handle emergency situations.

You already know that you need to know how to drive your CMV safely to pass the General Knowledge Test, one of the knowledge tests you need to take and pass before you can get your CDL. In Chapter 2 of this book, "Driving Safely, Part 1," you learned why it's important to stay visually alert while driving. You also learned about shifting gears, backing safely, communicating with other drivers, and managing speed.

In this chapter, you'll expand your knowledge of driving safely and learn about driving in different conditions such as at night, in winter, in hot weather, in rain, in fog, and in the mountains. You'll also learn what to do in an emergency.

▶ Driving at Night

Driving at night can be dangerous for many reasons. Hazards aren't as visible at night, which means you have less time to react to avoid a crash. The factors that make it more difficult to drive at night can be grouped into three categories: driver factors, roadway factors, and vehicle factors.

Driver Factors

Driver factors include those that involve you, the driver. When you're driving at night, be aware of these driver factors:

Reduced Vision

It's harder to see at night or in dim lighting. Your eyes take longer to adjust in dim light, which delays your ability to understand what you're seeing. Keep this in mind when you're driving at night.

Glare

The high beams of an oncoming vehicle can be temporarily blinding when driving at night. Older drivers are especially sensitive to headlight glare. No matter what your age, however, it can take a few seconds before your vision fully recovers. Driving blind is as dangerous as it sounds, even if it lasts only for 2 or 3 seconds. If you're traveling at 55 mph when blinded by glare, in the 2 seconds that it takes for you to recover your vision, your vehicle will have traveled more than half the distance of a football field. That's a long way to drive without being able to see!

Instead of staring directly into bright lights ahead of you, look toward the right side of the road and watch the sidelines. If you're not driving in the right-hand lane, look at the lines of your specific lane. This technique will keep you safely on track when driving at night.

When an oncoming car has not dimmed its lights, don't flash your high beams to make the driver switch to low beams. Two blind drivers heading in opposite directions is an accident waiting to happen! Instead, look to the sidelines to help you follow the road.

Fatigue and Lack of Alertness

Many drivers of CMVs are required to drive at night when the body naturally wants to sleep. A person's level of alertness drops at night, especially after midnight. Fatigue also sets in when a driver has been on the road for a long time. Lack of alertness and fatigue can affect your ability to spot hazards and react quickly, which increases the likelihood that an accident will occur. If you're tired or are not alert while driving, get off the road and get some sleep. Though this might make your trip longer than intended, it might save your life or the life of another driver.

Roadway Factors

Roadway factors are just that—conditions on the road that make driving more difficult. Be on the lookout for these roadway factors:

Poor Lighting

Many roadways are poorly lit at night. Some areas are so dark that you have only your headlights to guide you. Hazards aren't as visible in poor lighting, especially people on the road, such as pedestrians, joggers, and bicyclists. Animals are even less visible and often become confused when they find themselves on a roadway. Their instinct is often to dart into traffic. Unfortunately, many accidents occur because drivers can't see well in poor lighting. When driving in areas with little light, be sure to drive slowly, so you can stop within your sight distance if necessary.

Drunk Drivers

Intoxicated drivers are an extreme hazard. Unfortunately, most cases of driving under the influence of alcohol or drugs occur at night, especially around the time when bars close. Be on the lookout for drunk drivers around this time, but keep in mind that different states require bars to close at different times. You probably already know how to spot a drunk driver.

Intoxicated drivers have a difficult time staying within a lane and maintaining a constant speed. They also exhibit other erratic driving behaviors, such as stopping for no apparent reason.

Vehicle Factors

Vehicle factors involve your CMV. Be aware of the following vehicle factors when you're driving:

Headlights

Headlights obviously don't provide as much light as you would have during the day, so your night vision will always be somewhat limited. Low beams normally provide about 250 feet of light, while high beams should give you about 300 to 500 feet of light. Use this knowledge to help you figure out your stopping distance and adjust your driving speed accordingly. Always drive at a speed that will allow you to stop within the distance of your headlights. If you drive too fast, you might not see a hazard outside of this range, and you might not be able to stop in time to avoid a collision.

Your range of sight will be more limited if your headlights are dirty, broken, or not adjusted correctly. And if your headlights aren't properly adjusted, you might be blinding other drivers.

A good rule to follow is to turn on your headlights 2 hours prior to sunset until 2 hours after sunrise. Many states have laws that require you to have your lights on if your wipers are on. So use your lights in any low-light condition, such as in rain, fog, or snow. Better yet, drive with your lights on at all times for ultimate safety.

Other Lights

Other lights on your vehicle should also be clean and in proper working order. This includes reflectors, markers and clearance lights, tail lights, and identifi-cation lights. If these lights don't work properly, it will be harder for other drivers to see you.

Turn Signals and Brake Lights

Your turn signals and brake lights are important tools that you need to communicate with other drivers. Make sure your turn signals and brake lights are clean and in working order.

Windshield and Mirrors

The glare from other vehicles' headlights can become worse if you're looking through a dirty window or dirty mirrors. Your windshield should be clean on the inside and outside.

Night-Driving Procedures

Follow these steps when driving at night:

1. Get ready.

First, consider your own ability to drive. If you're tired, make sure you sleep before you start driving. Even a couple hours of sleep can save lives! If you wear eyeglasses, make sure that the lenses are clean and free of scratches. If your eyeglasses are in poor shape, don't substitute prescription sunglasses. Never wear sunglasses while driving at night.

Check your vehicle before going on a night drive. Check all lights and reflectors on your vehicle, and clean the ones that are within your reach.

2. Use high beams whenever possible.

High beams are intended to increase your range of sight when driving at night. Use them to your advantage whenever it's safe to do so. A good rule is turn off your high beams when you're within 500 feet of an oncoming vehicle and when following another vehicle within 500 feet.

3. Avoid excessive light in your cab.

Keep in mind that the brighter it is in your cab, the harder it is for you to see outside. Keep your instrument lights low, but make sure they're bright enough for you to read the gauges. Also, don't leave your interior light on. Use it only when necessary.

▶ Driving in Winter

You'll face some of the worst driving conditions during the winter. It's harder to get good traction in snow and ice, and blowing snow can make it difficult to see. Find out about the driving conditions in areas where you'll be traveling beforehand, and prepare yourself and your CMV. How do you prepare yourself? Driving in winter conditions requires extra energy, so get lots of rest prior to a trip. Allow yourself extra time to reach your destination.

Vehicle Checks

Perform a series of vehicle checks to make sure that your vehicle will give you the best possible performance in winter conditions. Performing vehicle checks such as the following also ensures that you know where all the necessary equipment in your vehicle is located and how to operate it.

Coolant and Antifreeze

Check your cooling system to make sure that it's full. Also make sure that your vehicle has enough antifreeze to protect against freezing. You'll need a coolant tester for these checks.

Defrosting Equipment

Defrosters are absolutely necessary for safe winter driving, so make sure yours work before your trip. You don't want to find out in the middle of a winter storm that your defrosters are broken!

Heating Equipment

Check the operation of your main heater, as well as any secondary heaters such as mirror heaters, battery box heaters, and fuel tank heaters.

Wipers and Washers

Windshield wipers are a necessity when driving in the winter. Wiper blades should be in good condition. Keep in mind that you may have to replace wiper blades often in the winter. Check the operation of wipers to make sure that the blades make firm contact with the windshield, so they'll be able to clear snow from your field of vision. Fill the washer fluid reservoir, and make sure that the fluid comes out properly. You should also use washer fluid antifreeze to ensure that the fluid doesn't freeze. Frozen washer fluid won't be of much use when your windshield is covered with mud or grimy slush. If you encounter a problem with wipers or washers while you're driving and you can't see well enough to continue, stop and fix the problem.

Tires

Your tires should have enough tread to be able to cut through rain, snow, or a slushy mixture of both. Your **drive tires**—the tires that are powered, located on the rear of the tractor—provide the traction to push your vehicle through the water or snow, while your **steering tires**—the tires used to steer your vehicle, located at the front of the tractor—provide traction so you can steer. This is especially important in winter conditions. Use a tread gauge to make sure that your front tires have *at least* $4/_{32}$-inch tread depth in every major groove. Other tires must have *at least* $2/_{32}$-inch tread depth. The more tread depth you have, the better control you'll have in harsh winter conditions. Shoddy tires must be replaced.

Tire Chains

You may need tire chains in extreme winter conditions, so make sure you have enough chains and that your chains are in good condition. Your tire chains won't work properly if they have worn or broken hooks, cross links, or side chains. Stock your vehicle with extra cross links that fit your tires. It's also very important to know how to put chains on your tires before you have to do it in bad winter weather.

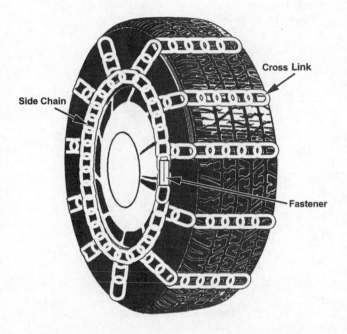

Figure 3.1. The Correct Way to Put Chains on Your Tires

Lights and Reflectors

Your lights and reflectors should be clean and in proper working order. They'll help you stay safe in dangerous winter conditions. In the winter, you'll need to clean lights and reflectors more often than in other seasons.

Windows and Mirrors

Use a windshield scraper, a snow brush, and a windshield defroster to clear snow and ice from your windows and mirrors before you set out on the road.

Hand Holds, Steps, and Deck Plates

Remove snow and ice from these surfaces so that you can enter your vehicle without slipping.

Radiator Shutters and Winterfront

Remove ice from the radiator shutters. Also make sure that the winterfront isn't closed too tightly. You don't want it to freeze because this could cause your engine to overheat and shut down.

Exhaust System

Make sure that your exhaust system isn't leaking and doesn't have any loose parts. Exhaust leaks are even more dangerous in the winter because your windows are closed. An exhaust leak that allows poisonous carbon monoxide to seep into your vehicle will make you sleepy and can even kill you if it's allowed to build up for too long.

Winter-Driving Tips

As you know, driving in the winter presents its own share of hazards. Keep the following in mind when driving your CMV in the north during the winter:

Slippery Surfaces

As you've learned, maintaining traction on slippery surfaces can be tricky. Always drive slowly, and know when the road is too slippery to drive on. If you determine that the road is too slippery to maintain safe control of your vehicle, stop at the first safe place you come across and wait for road conditions to improve.

- **Start slowly.** You should always get the feel of the road before feeling confident enough to drive at higher speeds. Don't rush on slippery roads. You might need to lock both drive axles by engaging the differential lock located on the dash, but don't allow the differential lock to be in the locked position for long distances or at high speeds. (Use the differential lock as it was intended to be used—for starting out in very slippery conditions or steep inclines that are wet or snow covered.) Some CMVs have alarms that sound to notify the driver that the differential lock is engaged.

- **Turning and braking.** Turn and brake gently, not suddenly or harder than necessary. Don't use the engine brake and speed retarder because they could cause your wheels to skid on slippery surfaces.

- **Adjust speed to conditions.** Always adjust your speed to winter conditions. Go slowly and avoid passing other vehicles unless it's absolutely necessary for safety reasons. Try to keep a steady speed without constantly slowing down or speeding up. Make sure you go slow around curves and avoid using your brakes while in curves. Keep in mind that when the temperature begins to rise, snow and ice will start to melt. This makes the road slippery, so you'll have to maintain a slow speed.

- **Adjust space to conditions.** Increase your following distance and avoid driving alongside other vehicles. Also, look far ahead to anticipate problems before you reach them. As soon as you see a problem ahead, such as a traffic jam or an accident, begin slowing down immediately and continue to slow down gradually.

Wet Brakes

When brakes get wet, they sometimes don't work as well. Water can cause brakes to weaken, apply unevenly, or grab. If this happens, you might lose braking power, experience wheel lockups, feel pulling to one side or the other, or undergo jackknifing, which occurs when a

vehicle towing a trailer skids and the trailer swings around so that it resembles the angle of a pocketknife.

Keep in mind that if roads are wet, your stopping distance doubles. Reduce your speed on wet roads.

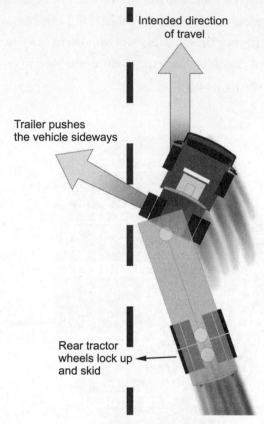

Figure 3.2. Jackknifing

To prevent your brakes from getting wet, try not to drive through large puddles or flowing water. If you can't avoid water ahead of you on the road, slow down and place your transmission in a low gear. Then, before entering the water, gently press your brakes. This will press linings against brake drums or discs, which will help keep mud, silt, and water from getting in your brakes. As you cross the water, increase engine RPM and keep light pressure on the brakes. Once you have driven through the water, keep light pressure on the brakes, so they heat up and dry out. Don't do this for too long, however, or your brake drums and linings may overheat. When you have room around you to test your braking capabilities, apply your brakes to make sure they're working. If not, continue to dry them out.

▶ Driving in Hot Weather

Your engine is more likely to overheat when the weather is very hot. When you're driving in hot weather, perform your normal pre-trip inspection, but pay attention to these factors as well:

Tires

Verify the tire mounting and air pressure in hot weather, and check the tires every 2 hours or every 100 miles. Air pressure can increase when the temperature is high. Don't let air out while tires are hot from running or the pressure will be too low when they cool. If a tire is too hot to touch, remain stopped until it cools. A tire that's excessively hot might blow or catch fire.

Oil

Engine oil keeps your engine cool and lubricated. Make sure that you have enough engine oil and that the temperature of the oil remains within the proper range. Check this regularly while you're driving.

Coolant

Before you begin driving in hot weather, check that you have enough water and antifreeze. You can find an explanation of the proper amount for your vehicle in the engine manufacturer's directions. Antifreeze is important in both hot and cold weather. Check the water and coolant temperature periodically while driving. These fluids should always remain in the normal temperature range. When climbing steep grades, the temperature of these fluids will rise, but they should return to normal when your vehicle is no longer under a hard pull. If your water and coolant temperatures exceed the highest safe temperature, stop driving

immediately and find out what's wrong. Many late model CMVs are set up to automatically shut down when coolant level is too low or when the temperature is too high. Your vehicle may be equipped with an override button that allows you 30 seconds to move the vehicle to a safe area before it shuts down once again.

Some vehicles have see-through coolant overflow containers that permit drivers to check the coolant level of a hot engine. If the container isn't part of the pressurized system, you can still remove the cap and add coolant when the engine is at operating temperature.

Never remove the radiator cap or any part of the pressurized system until the system has cooled. If you remove the cap while the pressurized system is still hot, you might suffer a severe burn from steam and boiling water. Don't remove the radiator cap until it has cooled to the point that you can remove it with your bare hand.

If you need to add coolant to a system that doesn't have a recovery or an overflow tank, turn off the engine and allow it to cool. Using gloves or a thick cloth, turn the radiator cap to the first stop. This releases the pressure seal. Step back and allow the pressure to escape from the cooling system. Once the pressure is released, press down and turn the cap until you can remove it. Look at the coolant level and add more coolant if necessary. When you finish, replace the cap and tighten it.

Belts

It's especially important to check the belts on your CMV during the summer because your water pump and fan won't work correctly if your belts are loose or broken, and your vehicle can overheat. Check for cracking, splitting, glazing, and fraying.

The fan belt is V-shaped, so it's called a **V-belt**. Check the tightness of the V-belt, and have it adjusted according to the specifications in your owner's manual.

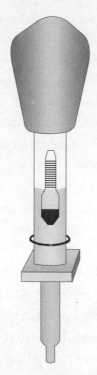

Figure 3.3. A Coolant Tester

Most newer CMVs have serpentine belts that drive all major engine components.

Hoses

Check to make sure that your coolant hoses are in good condition. Broken hoses can lead to fires or engine failure.

Other Precautions

You may need to drive slower in very hot weather. Driving fast creates more heat in the engine and tires. This can be especially dangerous in desert conditions.

Keep an eye out for bleeding tar. In very hot weather, the tar in pavement rises to the surface of the road. These bleeding tar spots can be very slippery.

▶ Driving in Rain

Be aware that roads are most slippery just as a rainstorm begins—even more so, in fact, than during a rainstorm. Driving during a rainstorm, however, has its own set of problems. Heavy rain can make your brakes wet, which can weaken them or cause them to work incorrectly. Wet brakes can cause your vehicle to jackknife or pull to one side among other problems.

▶ Driving in Fog

Some experts say you shouldn't drive in heavy fog. If you must drive, however, take these precautions:

- Obey all fog-related warning signs.
- Drive at a slower rate of speed.
- Turn on all lights and leave your headlights on low beams.
- Always be prepared to stop for an emergency.

▶ Driving in the Mountains

Imagine a large, heavy CMV going up a steep mountain. The CMV you're picturing is probably moving very slowly. Now imagine that same CMV traveling down the steep mountain. All that weight would make the CMV move much more quickly. When driving in the mountains, gravity plays an important role.

Your speed should also depend on your ability to come to a stop without the brakes becoming too hot and "fading." When your brakes fade, you must apply more and more pressure on them to stop. Travel at a speed that is slow enough for the brakes to hold you back without getting too hot. Hot brakes can fade. If you continue to overuse your brakes, they'll fade until you can't slow down your CMV at all.

You should use the braking effect of the engine as the primary way of controlling your speed. Never exceed the posted speed limit, and look for warning signs that show the length or degree of steepness factors.

Upgrades

Expect that your vehicle will slow down when going uphill. Keep in mind that the steeper the grade, the longer the grade, and the heavier the load, the slower your vehicle will move. You'll need to shift into a lower gear to climb a steep mountain. Turn on your four-way emergency flashers to warn other drivers of your slow speed if it's legal to do so.

Downgrades

When you're driving downhill, you'll need to slow down your vehicle as its speed increases. Move at a safe speed, use a low gear, and employ a safe braking technique. You can prepare for steep grades by talking to drivers who are familiar with certain routes before you attempt to drive them.

Before going downhill, shift your transmission into a lower gear. Don't wait until you build up speed to downshift. Trying to do this could result in your not being able to find a gear or seriously damaging the transmission.

Here's a rule that works best with older trucks: Use the same gear to go downhill as you would to go uphill. Newer trucks work better when drivers use a lower gear going downhill than would be required to go uphill. This is because newer trucks have more powerful engines and are built for better fuel economy. Know your vehicle well enough to determine its proper speed.

Your main way of controlling speed should be the braking effect of the engine. Your engine brakes best

when you brake according to RPM and when your transmission is in a lower gear. This is also an appropriate time to use a retarder if your vehicle is equipped with one.

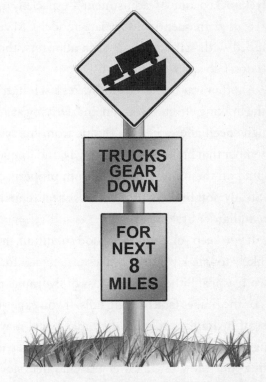

Figure 3.4. Some downgrades have signs warning commercial drivers to shift to a lower gear.

Fading Brakes and Brake Failure

When you use your brakes, the brake shoes or pads rub against the brake discs or drum to slow the vehicle. Brakes are built to handle heat, but excessive heat created by braking can cause your brakes to fade or fail. Improper braking will create excess heat, which will cause the brake lining to glaze and lose friction. Friction is why brakes work in the first place.

To keep brakes working properly, adjust them correctly. If brakes aren't adjusted correctly, they may stop working. Brakes that are out of adjustment will not do their share of the work of slowing or stopping the vehicle, and the brakes that are in adjustment will build heat faster because they're handling more of the braking. You already know that too much heat will cause brakes to fade and eventually fail. Also, brake linings will wear more quickly when they're hot. Check your brake adjustment frequently, because brakes are easily knocked out of adjustment—especially when they're used frequently. Most late model CMVs are equipped with self-adjusting slack adjusters, though these don't always work properly.

Another way to make your brakes last longer is to use the braking effect of your engine. Driving at a slow enough speed allows heat to escape from the brakes. Remember that brakes cool very slowly, and frequently stepping on them prevents them from properly cooling. Steady, soft braking produces less heat than intermittent, harder braking does.

If you keep your brakes in good condition, they're not likely to fail. Hydraulic brakes usually fail for one of two reasons: Either there's a loss of hydraulic pressure, or the brakes fade on long hills. If you experience a loss of hydraulic pressure, the brake pedal may feel spongy or go directly to the floor when you step on it. Putting your CMV into a lower gear may help slow the vehicle. Pumping the brake pedal should generate enough hydraulic pressure to slow the vehicle.

Also remember that the parking brake is separate from the hydraulic brake system. You can use the parking brake to slow the vehicle, but make sure to press the release lever at the same time you use the emergency brake, so that you can adjust the brake pressure and keep the wheels from locking up.

Snub Braking

If the vehicle is in the proper low gear, you can try snub braking, the proper technique for long, steep downgrades. When **snub braking**, first apply the brakes just enough to feel a definite slow down. When your speed changes to about 5 mph below your safe speed, release the brakes. When the speed returns to the safe speed, repeat the first two steps until you come to the end of the downgrade.

On downgrades, going slow and braking properly almost always prevents brake failure. If your brakes do fail, look for something outside of the vehicle to help you stop it. Escape ramps are designed to stop runaway vehicles without injuring drivers or passengers. An **escape ramp** consists of a long upgrade or a long bed of loose material such as gravel or both. If your brakes fail while you're driving on a downgrade, look for signs indicating an escape ramp. These signs are usually set up a few miles from the top of a downgrade. If you lose your brakes on a downgrade, using an escape ramp will help you avoid injury. If no escape ramp is available, pull off onto another escape route such as an open field or a side road.

As soon as you realize your brakes have failed, find an escape route. The longer you stay on a downgrade with no brakes, the faster your vehicle will go, and your vehicle will soon be out of control.

Signs for off-ramps have a speed posted on them. Be aware that this speed is for automobiles and not for CMVs. Don't drive this fast on an off-ramp in your CMV.

▶ Crossing Railroad Tracks

Crossing railroad tracks is dangerous for CMV drivers. Just because you don't hear a train doesn't mean that one isn't approaching. The noise in a cab often drowns out the sound of the train horn. Also, warning signals and gates might be out of order, so always double-check whether a train is coming with your own eyes. Often, railroad crossings feature double tracks, so be sure to check both directions before proceeding. After a train passes, make sure to check that no other trains are coming.

To stay safe, approach all railroad tracks as if a train is coming. Slow down as you approach and come to a complete stop, and don't resume driving until you're certain there isn't a train. Also keep in mind that a full stop is required when you're carrying certain types of cargo, such as hazardous materials or a bus with passengers. Some states require you to come to a complete stop before crossing railroad tracks.

Remember that determining the speed of a moving train is extremely difficult. Never attempt to beat a train to a crossing, and never shift gears while on the tracks. Also, don't stop your vehicle on the tracks. Be aware that railroad crossings with steep approaches can cause your unit to hang up on the tracks. Always make sure that traffic conditions won't cause you to have to stop on the tracks. Be sure that you can fully cross the tracks before attempting to cross them. Never shift gears while crossing the tracks.

MULTIPLE TRACKS

Figure 3.5. Be sure to look both ways when crossing multiple tracks.

▶ Skid Control and Recovery

When your vehicle's tires lose their grip on the road, it's called **skidding**. Several actions can cause your CMV to skid. Braking too hard and locking up the wheels can cause your vehicle to skid. If the road is slippery and you're using a speed retarder, your vehicle may skid. Turning the wheel more sharply than the vehicle can

handle is called **oversteering** and this, too, can cause skidding.

The most serious skidding occurs if you drive too fast for road conditions. Skids that occur while going too fast can usually be stopped by removing your foot from the accelerator. A **rear-wheel braking skid** occurs when the rear drive wheels lock and is most commonly caused by excessive braking or acceleration. Locked wheels have less traction than rolling wheels, so rear wheels will sometimes slide sideways in this situation. A rear-wheel braking skid can be changed if the driver correctly maneuvers the vehicle. The first way to fix a rear-wheel braking skid is to stop braking, which will allow the wheels to roll. If a vehicle begins to slide sideways, quickly turn the vehicle in the direction that you want to go. When you turn a vehicle back on course, it has the tendency to keep moving in that direction, so you need to **countersteer**, which means you turn the wheel back in the other direction. It's difficult to learn how to recover from a skid, so you should practice, if possible, on a large driving range or skid-pad in case you actually do skid.

Front-wheel skids usually occur when drivers are going too fast for the weather conditions, but they can also be caused by a lack of tread on the front tires or loading cargo so not enough weight is on the front axle. When a vehicle experiences a front-wheel skid, the front end usually goes in a straight line no matter how much you turn the steering wheel. The only way to stop a front-wheel skid is to let the vehicle slow down.

▶ Managing Emergencies

When two or more vehicles are about to collide, it's referred to as a **traffic emergency**. When tires, brakes, or other important parts of a vehicle fail, it's called a **vehicle emergency**. Your chances of avoiding a collision depend on how well you're prepared to take action in either type of emergency.

Steering to Avoid a Crash

You can steer away from an emergency more quickly than you can stop. Because of this, it's better to try to steer away from whatever you might collide with. Be careful when using this technique, however, if you're carrying a top-heavy load or multiple trailers, because they're more likely to flip over. Keep both hands firmly on the steering wheel when attempting to avoid a crash by steering away from it. To make sure that both of your hands are already on the steering wheel when an emergency occurs, make it a habit to keep them there.

Don't apply brakes while you're turning. Brakes are more likely to lock up while you're turning, and this could cause you to skid. And don't turn more than you have to. A sharp turn might cause you to skid. Also be prepared to countersteer. Do you remember how to do this? When you countersteer, you turn the wheel back in the other direction and return to the lane where you should be.

When steering to avoid a crash, it's better to steer to the right because the shoulder is more likely to be free of traffic than the left lane. Even if you're blocked on both sides, it's better to move to the right. Moving to the left could force someone in another lane into oncoming traffic.

If you do need to pull over to the shoulder, follow some of these safety rules:

Avoid braking if possible until your speed has slowed to about 20 mph. Harsh braking can cause you to skid on any loose material scattered on the sides of the road. Maintaining control is always easier if you keep at least one set of tires on the pavement.

If you pull onto the shoulder, stay there until you come to a complete stop. Signal and check your mirrors before returning to the road. If you must go back

to the road before you can come to a complete stop, turn sharply enough to get back onto the road safely.

Stopping Quickly

If you must stop quickly, make the stop as safe as possible. If you can, brake in a straight line. Whatever you do, don't jam on the brakes! Jamming on the brakes will lock up the wheels and cause you to skid, which means you won't be able to control the vehicle.

In **controlled braking**, you apply the brakes as hard as you can without locking up the wheels. Don't move the steering wheel too much when doing this. If you need to make a wide steering adjustment or if the wheels lock up, release the brakes and reapply them when you can.

In **stab braking**, you apply your brakes all the way and release them when they lock up. When your wheels begin to roll, apply the brakes all the way again—but be careful. If you reapply the brakes before the wheels start turning, the vehicle won't straighten.

If your vehicle is equipped with an antilock braking system (ABS), don't use the stab braking method. With ABS, the wheel that locks will automatically be released and reapplied by the braking system. With ABS brakes, apply the brake pedal and continue to apply pressure until your vehicle stops or you avoid the obstruction.

Caution: If your tractor has ABS brakes and the trailer doesn't, or vice versa, use the stab braking method to stop quickly.

Tire Failure

When a tire fails, you have only a few seconds to react. Because of this, it's important to know the signs of tire failure. A loud bang is one of the most obvious signs. You might not feel the change in your tire right away, but it has probably failed if you hear the bang. Your vehicle may thump or vibrate heavily if a tire has failed. If the failed tire is a rear tire, this vibration may be the only sign. Lastly, if steering the vehicle suddenly becomes more difficult, you may be experiencing a steering tire failure.

Should you experience tire failure, firmly hold onto your steering wheel with both hands at all times. Though you may want to use your brake, this could cause you to lose control. Instead, depress the accelerator and try not to use the brake until the vehicle slows down. Then gently apply your brake. After you come to a stop, check all your tires. The only way to know if a dual tire has failed is to get out and check it.

Accidents

No matter how many precautions you take, at some point you may be involved in an accident, so you need to know what to do if the unthinkable happens. Remember these three steps: (1) protect the area, (2) notify the authorities, and (3) care for any injured persons.

1. Protect the area.

The accident scene needs to be protected so that no more accidents occur. Do your best to get your CMV to the side of the road so that other traffic can move freely. If you aren't in the accident but are only stopping to help, park away from the accident. Use your four-way emergency flashers and put out reflective triangles to warn other vehicles of the accident.

2. Notify the authorities.

If you have a citizen's band (CB), put a call out over the emergency channel before getting out of your vehicle. If not, protect the scene of the accident and then use a phone to call the authorities. Determine your location so that you can give it to the person who answers the call.

3. Care for injured persons.

If you see an accident and paramedics have already arrived, stay out of their way so they can better help those who have been injured. If no qualified personnel are on the scene, follow basic first aid rules. Don't move an injured person unless the person is in danger of fire or being hit by oncoming traffic. If a person is bleeding heavily, apply pressure to the wound. Keep any injured persons warm until help arrives.

4. Additional steps.

In addition to the previous steps, there are other things you should do if you're involved in an accident:

Write down information regarding the other vehicle(s) involved, including vehicle license number, insurance information, make, model, color, and a description of the damage.

Write down information about other drivers and their passengers, including the driver's license information and a description of each person and his or her injuries.

Consider carrying a disposable camera in your CMV to take pictures of an accident scene. Pictures should show all vehicles, drivers, and passengers involved; road conditions; and anything else that will help tell the story of the accident. Don't take pictures of any severely injured people.

Make sure you contact your company and inform them of your involvement in an accident. They can give you instructions on what to do at the accident scene based on their policy. Many companies keep accident packets in their vehicles to assist drivers in obtaining important information at accident scenes.

Fires

Vehicle fires can be caused by fuel spills, improper use of flairs, underinflated tires, duals that touch, short circuits, loose fuel connections, and flammable cargo. To prevent fires, be sure to do the following:

- Before going on a trip, inspect fuel, cargo, electrical systems, and exhaust systems. Also, check that the fire extinguisher is charged.
- While on your trip, check tires, wheels, and the body of your CMV for signs of heat whenever you stop.
- Make sure to follow all safety procedures for fueling the vehicle, using the brakes, handling flares, and performing any other activities that could result in a fire.
- Check the instruments and gauges for signs of overheating and use the mirrors to look for smoke coming from the tires or vehicle.
- Use extra caution when you're handling any flammable materials.

You should learn how to properly fight a fire in case you should have one. If your CMV is on fire, pull off the road and park in an open area away from anything else that could catch fire. Never pull into a fueling station! Once you stop your vehicle, notify the police of your location and your problem.

Keep the fire from spreading. If your engine is on fire, turn off the engine as soon as possible. Don't open the hood if you don't have to. Shoot the fire extinguisher through louvers or the radiator or from the underside of the vehicle. If you experience a cargo fire, keep the doors of the van or box closed. Opening the van doors can make the fire worse.

If you're unsure how to fight the fire, wait for firefighters to arrive. Using the wrong method to fight a fire could make the fire worse. Study the instructions on your fire extinguisher and know how to use it. Don't wait until a fire occurs to learn how to use the fire extinguisher.

Chapter 3 Review Quiz

1: Write your answer on the line below.

1. List four precautions you should take when driving in fog.

a. _____
_____
_____
_____

b. _____
_____
_____
_____
_____

c. _____
_____
_____
_____

d. _____
_____
_____
_____

2–13: Circle the correct answer.

2. What should you do when driving up a mountain?
a. Apply your brakes.
b. Use a low gear.
c. Use a high gear.
d. Apply the parking brake.

3. Bleeding tar spots can be dangerous because they
a. are hot.
b. can wet brakes.
c. can damage tires.
d. are slippery.

4. Which hand or hands should you keep on the steering wheel when trying to avoid an accident?
a. your right hand
b. your left hand
c. both hands
d. either your right or left hand

5. What should you do if the glare from another vehicle's headlights makes it difficult for you to see?
a. Look toward the right side of the road.
b. Stare directly into the lights.
c. Look toward the left of the road.
d. Lightly tap your horn.

6. How often should you check your tires in hot weather?
a. every hour
b. every 2 hours
c. every 4 hours
d. once a day

7. What usually causes front-wheel skids?
a. countersteering
b. driving too fast
c. carrying heavy cargo
d. driving in the wrong gear

8. You should turn off your high beams when another vehicle is closer than _____ feet.
   a. 50
   b. 150
   c. 300
   d. 500

9. Which of these is a sign that your brakes might be wet?
   a. a loud bang
   b. pulling to one side
   c. overheating
   d. skidding

10. Which of the following is good tread depth for your steering tires when you're driving during winter?
   a. 1/32
   b. 2/32
   c. 3/32
   d. 4/32

11. What can cause your brakes to fade?
   a. heat
   b. overuse
   c. both a and b
   d. neither a nor b

12. When your vehicle's tires lose their grip on the road, it's called
   a. skidding.
   b. tire failure.
   c. locking up.
   d. jackknifing.

13. What should you do as soon as you realize that your brakes have failed?
   a. Stay on the downgrade.
   b. Call for help.
   c. Steer to the side of the road.
   d. Find an escape route.

Check your answers on page 293.

CHAPTER

4 ▶ Vehicle Inspection

CHAPTER SUMMARY

Learning how to inspect your vehicle is important to make certain that your vehicle is safe to drive. As part of the Skills Test, you'll be asked to conduct a pre-trip inspection of your vehicle for an examiner. The information in this chapter is important, so be sure to study it until you know it.

Vehicle problems aren't always obvious. Sometimes you have to do some detective work to uncover a problem before it causes a safety issue. When you inspect your vehicle, you're really trying to prevent a dangerous or costly problem, such as a breakdown or crash, from happening while you're on the road.

Inspecting your vehicle isn't only smart; it's also required by state and federal laws. These laws are sometimes enforced by local, state, and federal inspectors, who might randomly inspect your vehicle to make sure that it's safe. A driver can undergo a vehicle inspection at different locations and for different reasons. Many states conduct inspections at the weigh scales set up along the highway. An inspector may choose your vehicle at random or he or she may decide to inspect your CMV because your company's safety rating is not as good as it could be. Sometimes inspectors sit alongside the highway and pull over trucks that appear to be in disrepair. There are different levels of inspection, and each level requires that specific items be checked. It's important to be professional and follow the directions given by the inspector when your vehicle is the subject of an inspection.

If an inspector decides that your vehicle is unsafe, the inspector can put your vehicle **out of service**. This means that it can't be driven. Your vehicle will remain this way until either you or the vehicle owner has a certified mechanic fix the problems with the vehicle. The Federal Motor Carrier Safety Administration (FMCSA), a part of the U.S. Department of Transportation, has set rules about what a driver must inspect on a vehicle. These rules are outlined in the Federal Motor Carrier Safety Regulations (FMCSR; see parts 393 and 396 for more information about what drivers and inspectors must inspect), which you learned about in Chapter 1.

Though inspecting your CMV may seem like an enormous task, it's not so bad if you have an inspection routine. This way, you won't have to guess which steps you've already taken because you'll always do them in the same order. You'll also be able to move through your inspection quickly while still being careful and thorough. You'll learn more about how to establish an inspection routine or method later in this chapter.

If you do uncover a problem while inspecting your vehicle, you can make certain small repairs yourself. Your employer will tell which repairs you can make yourself and when you need to call a mechanic.

Before you can get your CDL, you'll need to know how to inspect your vehicle. You learned that once you pass the General Knowledge Test, you can take the Skills Test. You'll need to do a pre-inspection of your vehicle during the Skills Test.

During the Skills Test, you'll show the examiner that you know what to look for during an inspection. You'll point out parts of the vehicle and explain what you're looking for and how you know whether the vehicle is safe. This chapter will give you the tools you need to pass the pre-inspection on the Skills Test. You'll find more information on inspecting air brake systems, combination vehicles, tank vehicles, doubles and triples, passenger vehicles, and vehicles hauling hazardous materials in later chapters of this book.

▶ Who Inspects Your Vehicle

You aren't the only person who will inspect your vehicle. The motor carrier actually bears the main responsibility for vehicle inspection. Motor carriers must perform annual inspections of their vehicles, though your motor carrier may pass off the responsibility of routine pre- and post-trip inspections to you.

As you just learned, state or federal inspectors may also inspect your CMV. Additionally, a state police Motor Carrier Investigator or an employee of a large motor carrier may also inspect your vehicle. If you perform regular pre- and post-trip inspections on your CMV, you'll greatly reduce the chance that it will be put out of service during one of these unexpected inspections.

▶ When to Inspect

Responsible CMV drivers check their vehicles at the following points during a trip:

- before a trip (pre-trip inspection)
- while driving (en-route inspection)
- when making stops
- after a trip (after-trip or post-trip inspection and report)

A pre-trip inspection will help you make sure that you're heading onto the road in a vehicle that's safe to drive. Inspecting your CMV before a trip also limits your chances of breaking down or being involved in an accident. Though it takes time to inspect your CMV, most drivers agree that it's time well spent. Any problems you find should be fixed before you begin your trip.

Once you're on the road, paying attention to how your vehicle is operating becomes almost second nature. This includes watching your gauges for signs of trouble and using your senses to look, listen, smell, and feel for problems. Sometimes your own senses are more reliable than your CMV's instruments, which can stop working or provide you with the wrong information.

A stop during a trip is a perfect opportunity to see whether the state of your vehicle has changed since your last inspection. Always check the following:

- tires, wheels, and rims
- fluids leaking from the vehicle
- brakes
- lights and reflectors
- brake and electrical connections to the trailer
- trailer coupling devices
- cargo securement devices

You're required by law to inspect your vehicle 50 miles into a trip, though it's often a good idea to check cargo securement at 25 miles. After that, inspect it every 150 miles or 3 hours—whichever comes first.

Once you've completed your trip, you'll inspect your vehicle once again, and you'll also fill out an after-trip or post-trip inspection report, also called a driver's vehicle condition report (DVCR) or daily vehicle inspection report (DVIR). The report is really a list of any problems you find during your inspection. It lets the motor carrier know if something on the vehicle must be repaired before it's taken back onto the road.

▶ What You Need to Inspect

What exactly should you look for? The next few sections will tell you what to inspect to make sure that your vehicle is safe. Checking these things before, during, and after a trip will also help you avoid having your vehicle placed out of service if you have to go through a roadside inspection.

If you find a mechanical problem with your vehicle, follow company policy regarding who should complete the repair(s). Some minor, non-safety issues, such as replacing a burnt-out lightbulb, can usually be corrected by the driver. However, more complex repairs should be completed by a qualified mechanic. Most companies won't even allow their drivers to replace a bad tire, as this presents a safety concern.

What should you do if you experience a mechanical problem once you begin your trip? Most carriers require you to contact them with information about the equipment failure. The company will either contact a repair facility or will let you know whom to contact. Make sure you have as much information about the problem as possible before you make a phone call. For instance, if one of your tires is flat, you'll need to know the tire size and where the tire is located on the vehicle. You'll also need to give information about your location, so the mechanic can find you. Remember to know the breakdown policy of your company before you start your trip.

Tire Problems

Tire problems are a huge safety concern. If your tires are bad, you won't have full control of your vehicle. Also, your CMV will fail an inspection if you have bad tires. Look for the following tire problems when inspecting your vehicle:

- **Too much or too little air pressure.** An air leak in a tire will cause a flat. Some drivers bang on their tires with a device called a tire billy to check air pressure. This isn't the most reliable method for checking a tire's air pressure, however. The best way to check pressure is to use a tire pressure gauge. An underinflated tire is dangerous because it may allow dual tires to touch, which can create friction. Friction causes heat, which increases the chances of a tire fire, tread separation, or a blowout. An underinflated steer tire decreases your ability to steer and take corners smoothly. If you overinflate your tires, not as much of the tire surface will touch the road, and you'll have less control over your vehicle. An overinflated tire will also easily puncture or burst on impact. Either way, an improperly inflated tire quickly becomes weak. A weak tire is likely to have irregular tread wear, cuts, punctures, and bubbles. These problems can lead to sudden loss of tire tread (the "alligators" you've seen along the sides of the highway). Checking the air pressure in your tires can save you a lot of headaches and hassles in the end. Proper air pressure will also provide better fuel economy.

- **Bad wear.** Your front tires must have at least $4/_{32}$-inch tread depth in every major groove. Your other tires must have at least $2/_{32}$-inch tread depth. It's a good idea to measure your tread during your pre-trip inspection. When you look at your tires, you shouldn't be able to see any fabric (from the tire's body ply) or steel cords (from the tire's belts) showing through the tread or sidewall—this is a sign of a very unsafe tire. Also check for even wear across the tire treads. Uneven wear can be a sign of incorrect inflation, poor alignment, or mechanical defects.

- **Cuts or other damage.** A tire with a cut or other damage can quickly become flat or lead to a blowout—a tire burst while driving due to pressure or a weak spot.

- **Tread separation.** When the tread begins to separate from the body of the tire, the tire should be replaced. A driver who drives on tires with tread separation puts other drivers at risk. If your tire sheds its tread, you could lose control of your vehicle and crash into another driver. The loose tread is also dangerous. It might crash into another vehicle, causing an emergency or damage to the vehicle. This is another reason why checking your tires is so important.

- **Dual tires that come in contact with each other or parts of the vehicle.** If your tire is rubbing on another tire or a part of the vehicle, it will quickly develop a weak spot, putting it at risk of blowout. It could also cause a tire fire or might otherwise interfere with the way your vehicle normally operates.

- **Mismatched sizes or treads.** Mixing radial and bias-ply tires and mismatching tire treads or sizes on a vehicle will cause differences in traction and turning abilities. Mixing these same tires side by side as duals will cause one tire to carry more weight than the other, resulting in excessive tread wear, an overheated tire, and possibly a blowout from tread separation.

- **Cut or cracked valve stem.** The valve stems in your wheels and rims regulate the pressure of the air inside your tires. If your valve stems are cut or cracked, your tire pressure won't be right. Maintaining correct tire pressure helps you avoid many of the issues you've already learned about in this section. Also make sure that the valve stem is properly centered in the wheel and that it has a cap.

- **Regrooved, recapped, or retreaded tires.** It's illegal to put regrooved, retreaded, or recapped tires on the front wheels of a CMV.

Wheel and Rim Problems

Your wheels and **rims** (the outer part of the wheels to which the tires are attached) must be in good shape for your vehicle to run properly and smoothly. The following wheel and rim problems could create safety issues, so be sure to check these areas when you inspect your vehicle:

- **Damaged rims.** A rim that's cracked, broken, bent, or deformed in some other way may not be able to support a tire. If the rim is damaged in the area of the tire, it may prevent the tire from setting properly on the rim. Without a proper bead, the tire won't maintain air pressure. This is dangerous for obvious reasons.

- **Rust around lug nuts.** If you see rust around your lug nuts, it may be a sign that your lug nuts are loose. Sometimes lug nuts aren't properly tightened after a tire has been changed. If you find rust around your lug nuts, check the tightness of the nuts to make sure your wheel is securely fastened to your vehicle. If you've recently changed a tire, stop driving shortly after the tire change to check the tightness of the lug nuts. Lug nuts may be relatively small, but they play an important role in helping you maintain control of your CMV.

- **Missing clamps, spacers, studs, or lugs.** You don't want to drive a vehicle with missing clamps, spacers, studs, or lugs—this is very dangerous. Spacers and clamps are used in the assembly of Dayton rims, which are not usually found on late model equipment. Missing spacers or clamps could cause rims and tires to detach from the vehicle, ultimately resulting in serious damage to your vehicle and putting you at risk for an accident. Studs and lugs hold the tires and rims in place. Missing studs or lugs could also result in the loss of wheels from the vehicle. If an inspector finds that any of these elements are missing from your vehicle, he or she can put your vehicle out of service.

- **Mismatched or damaged lock rings.** Lock rings are found on Dayton wheel and hub assemblies; they hold the tire on the rim. The rim is placed inside the tire, a solid ring is added, the lock ring is hammered into place, and air is added to the tire. The assembled tire is placed on the hub, a spacer is added, the outside rim and tire are mounted, and finally, the wedges and lug nuts are secured. A damaged lock ring will allow the rims to slip on the hub or allow the tires to touch, creating the potential for a tire fire. It isn't difficult to see why lock rings must be in good condition and must be matched to the same rim they were removed from to assure they remain locked in place when the tire is fully inflated. Each wheel on your vehicle should be outfitted with matching lock rings. If lock rings on one or more of your wheels are cracked, bent, split, or otherwise damaged, they must be replaced. Driving with mismatched or damaged lock rings is dangerous.

- **Wheels or rims that have had welding repairs.** Making welding repairs to wheels or rims isn't safe because it reduces the tensile strength of the welded areas. (**Tensile strength** refers to a material's resistance against tearing.) This reduces the wheel's ability to undergo stress and can cause wheels or tires to fail. Damaged wheels and rims should be replaced, not repaired. If you see that welding repairs have been made to the wheels or rims of your vehicle, don't drive the vehicle until the repaired items have been replaced.

Bad Brake Drums or Shoes

Brake problems are an obvious safety concern. Brake shoes and brake drums work together to stop a vehicle when the brakes are applied. If either part on your vehicle is broken or has a problem that causes it to malfunction, you may lose the ability to stop your vehicle. Be sure to check for the following problems:

- **Cracked drums.** Brake drums should be checked for cracks. It's important to inspect them carefully before heading onto the road and during a trip.
- **Brake shoes and brake pads.** Brake shoes or pads that are contaminated with oil, grease, or brake fluid can cause your vehicle to pull to the side when the brakes are applied. Dirty brake shoes or pads might also cause your brakes to grab too quickly when only minimal pressure is applied. (This is sometimes referred to as having "touchy" brakes.) Contaminated brake shoes or pads should be either cleaned or replaced. Keep in mind that oil or grease on brake shoes or pads might indicate a problem, such as a leak, somewhere else on the vehicle.
- **Shoes or pads worn dangerously thin, missing, or broken.** Brake shoes or pads that are very thin or broken won't give you the same braking control that you would normally have. Of course, missing brake

components will guarantee even *less* control and are even *more* dangerous. Also look at your vehicle's brake pads or shoes for proper thickness. They shouldn't be thinner than ¼-inch at their thinnest point. If they're under ¼-inch thick, you can be sure that they won't work properly, so have them replaced before you start your trip.

Don't forget that air brakes are different from hydraulic brakes. You'll learn how to inspect air brakes in Chapter 6.

Steering System Defects

Your steering system has many components including the steering wheel, steering shaft, steering gear box, pitman arm, drag link, steering arm, tie rod, and steering tires. Any problem with your steering system is serious. You can avoid problems by checking for the following during an inspection:

- **Missing nuts, bolts, cotter keys, or other parts.** These smaller parts all help hold together the larger elements of the steering system. Check the entire system to make sure that no nuts, bolts, cotter keys (or cotter pins), or other parts are missing.
- **Bent, loose, or broken parts, such as steering column, steering gear box, or tie rods.** The steering column connects the steering wheel to the other elements of the steering system. If any of these elements—including the steering shaft, steering gear box, pitman arm, drag link, steering arm, or tie rods—are loose, bent, or broken, you won't be able to steer your vehicle properly.
- **If the vehicle is equipped with power steering, check hoses, pumps, and fluid level; check for leaks.** Your steering system needs

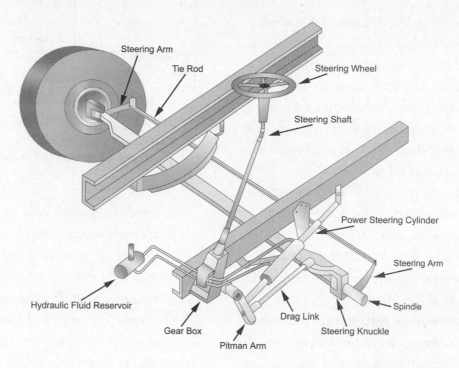

Figure 4.1. Parts of a Steering System

fluid to run properly. Allowing the fluid to leak from a broken hose, a faulty pump, or a bad connection can cause your steering system to fail and can lead to costly repairs to your vehicle or even an accident.

- **Check fluid levels, hoses, pumps, and connections to make sure that leaks don't occur.** Even if hoses aren't leaking at the time, twisted, kinked, or worn spots can cause problems later on. To be on the safe side, assume that problems will occur sooner rather than later. Though you may not be responsible for the cost of repairs, the time it takes to make these repairs could cost you valuable road time.
- **Steering wheel play.** Steering wheel play refers to how far you can turn your steering wheel before the wheels turn. Steering wheel play of more than 10 degrees (approximately 2 inches movement at the rim of a

20-inch steering wheel) can make it hard to steer and might indicate a problem in the steering system.

Suspension System Defects

The **suspension system** supports the vehicle and its load. It also keeps the axles in place. Because it's constantly working, its parts wear out easily, especially during long trips or when hauling heavy loads. Broken suspension parts can be extremely dangerous, so you'll want to check the following parts of your suspension system and look for these defects:

- **Spring hangers.** Spring hangers shouldn't be loose or bent. If they are, the leaf springs might move from their correct position (see Figure 4.2). Also make sure that spring hangers aren't cracked or broken.
- **Leaf springs.** Check for missing or broken leaves in any leaf spring (see Figure 4.3). If

one-fourth or more of your leaves are missing, your vehicle can be put out of service. Also, if leaves in a multi-leaf spring have shifted (especially when one or more are missing), they might be hitting a tire or interfering with another part of the vehicle.

- **Shock absorbers.** Look for leaking shock absorbers. A small amount of "weeping" fluid may be normal, but for the most part, shocks should not leak. Shocks that leak fluid are worn, and you'll have to make sure that they're replaced. Also check that rubber grommets at the top and bottom of shocks are in good condition.

- **Axle positioning parts.** Torque rod or arm, U-bolts, spring hangers, or other axle positioning parts that are cracked, damaged, or missing can cause problems. You'll want to replace any of these parts that are broken.

- **Air suspension systems.** Air suspension systems that are damaged, especially to the point where they're leaking, can cause problems. See Figure 4.4 for an illustration of key air suspension parts. Also check the air

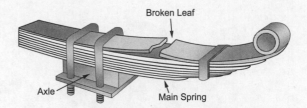

Figure 4.3. Broken Leaf in Leaf Spring

pressure regulator valve to make sure that it's working, and then check to make sure that the air suspension doesn't leak more than 3 psi within 5 minutes. Ideally, air suspension shouldn't leak at all.

- **Frame.** The frame includes left and right side frame rails and cross members connecting the frame rails. The frame is connected directly or indirectly to all parts of the truck. Loose, cracked, broken, bent, sagging, or missing frame members can be very unsafe. Make sure frame members are intact and attached in their proper places.

Exhaust System Defects

A broken exhaust system can allow poisonous fumes to seep into the cab or sleeper berth. This is extremely dangerous. No driver wants to get sick from exhaust fumes! Check the following parts of the exhaust system for defects:

- **Main exhaust system parts.** Look for loose, broken, or missing exhaust pipes, mufflers, tailpipes, or vertical stacks.

- **Leaking parts.** No part of the exhaust system should be leaking. If you hold your hand up to the exhaust manifold—being careful not to burn yourself—you may be able to feel air leaking from it. It's important not to simply patch an exhaust leak. This is

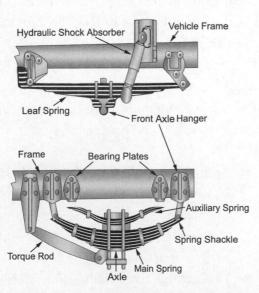

Figure 4.2. Basic Parts of a Suspension System

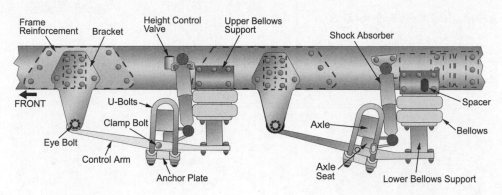

Figure 4.4. Basic Parts of an Air Suspension System

a serious safety defect that must be properly repaired.

- **Connecting parts.** Look for loose, broken, or missing mounting brackets, clamps, bolts, and nuts. Flawed connections can cause main parts to break or fail.

- **Rubbing parts.** Check for exhaust system parts that might be rubbing against tires, fuel system parts, or other moving parts of vehicle. Parts that are rubbing aren't in the proper position, which means that they can't function properly and might damage other parts of the CMV.

- **Leaking parts.** Exhaust system leaks are a big safety concern. Look for black streaks on the exhaust system because they can be a sign of an exhaust leak.

Emergency Equipment

Your vehicle must be equipped with the following emergency equipment:

- A fully charged fire extinguisher that's secured and easily accessible. Check the fire extinguisher's nozzle, ring pin, and pressure gauge to make sure that the extinguisher will work properly if you need it. The fire extinguisher must have a minimum rating

of 5 B:C or 10 B:C for vehicles hauling hazardous materials.

- Spare electrical fuses (unless your vehicle has circuit breakers)

- Warning devices for parked vehicles (such as three reflective warning triangles)

Cargo (Trucks)

Make sure that your cargo is balanced and secured. Also be sure that you haven't loaded too much cargo into your vehicle. Too much cargo may not only cause a variety of stresses and strains on your vehicle but can also put your CMV over legal weight limits or over the load capacity for your vehicle. If your cargo contains hazardous materials or wastes that require placarding, inspect for proper papers and placarding.

▶ The Pre-Trip Inspection Test

When you take the Skills Test, you'll perform a pre-trip inspection for the examiner. You might also have to answer questions about why it's important to inspect certain parts of your vehicle or when your vehicle is or isn't safe to drive. While this might seem like an intimidating task, it isn't so bad if you prepare ahead of time.

The best way to prepare for this part of the Skills Test is to practice inspecting your vehicle the same way

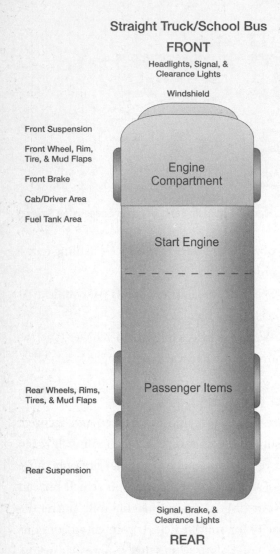

Straight Truck/School Bus
FRONT
Headlights, Signal, & Clearance Lights
Windshield
Front Suspension
Front Wheel, Rim, Tire, & Mud Flaps
Front Brake
Cab/Driver Area
Fuel Tank Area
Engine Compartment
Start Engine
Passenger Items
Rear Wheels, Rims, Tires, & Mud Flaps
Rear Suspension
Signal, Brake, & Clearance Lights
REAR

Figure 4.5. Straight Truck/School Bus

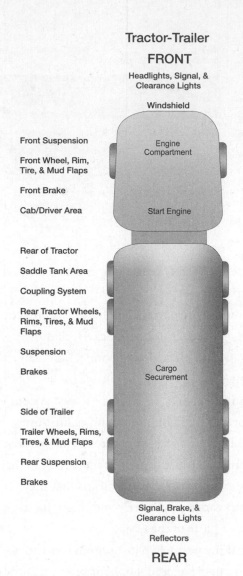

Tractor-Trailer
FRONT
Headlights, Signal, & Clearance Lights
Windshield
Front Suspension
Front Wheel, Rim, Tire, & Mud Flaps
Front Brake
Cab/Driver Area
Engine Compartment
Start Engine
Rear of Tractor
Saddle Tank Area
Coupling System
Rear Tractor Wheels, Rims, Tires, & Mud Flaps
Suspension
Brakes
Cargo Securement
Side of Trailer
Trailer Wheels, Rims, Tires, & Mud Flaps
Rear Suspension
Brakes
Signal, Brake, & Clearance Lights
Reflectors
REAR

Figure 4.6. Tractor-Trailer

each time so that it will become second nature to you. It might also be helpful to have a friend act as the examiner while you practice.

▶ The Seven-Step Pre-Trip Inspection Method

If you follow these same seven steps each time you do a pre-trip inspection, you'll be much less likely to forget to inspect something when you take the Skills

Test—and when you're working as a licensed CMV driver! Use the "cheat sheets" provided in Figures 4.5, 4.6, and 4.7 to help you remember the parts of each step when you practice your pre-trip inspection method.

Step 1: Vehicle Overview

During the vehicle overview, you'll approach the vehicle and check its general condition. You'll also have to look at the last vehicle inspection report.

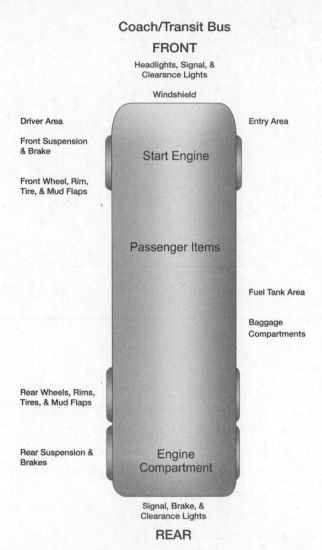

Coach/Transit Bus

FRONT

Headlights, Signal, & Clearance Lights

Windshield

Driver Area

Front Suspension & Brake

Front Wheel, Rim, Tire, & Mud Flaps

Entry Area

Start Engine

Passenger Items

Fuel Tank Area

Baggage Compartments

Rear Wheels, Rims, Tires, & Mud Flaps

Rear Suspension & Brakes

Engine Compartment

Signal, Brake, & Clearance Lights

REAR

Figure 4.7. Coach/Transit Bus

Approach the Vehicle

When you approach the vehicle to check its general condition, ask yourself questions such as these:

- Can I see damage on either side of the vehicle?
- Are lights amber to the front and red to the rear? Check clearance lights, marker lights, turn signal lights, and headlights.
- Is there a license plate on the front, and does it have a current registration?

- Is there a current inspection sticker?
- Does the vehicle lean to one side or the other? (This might mean a flat tire or shifted cargo. It could also indicate poor suspension.)
- When I look under the vehicle, do I see evidence of fresh oil, coolant, grease, or fuel leaks?
- Do I notice hazards (people, other vehicles, low-hanging wires, tree limbs, or other objects) anywhere around the vehicle that will get in the way if I move the vehicle?

Review the Last Vehicle Inspection Report

Most drivers are required to keep a daily vehicle inspection report (DVIR) about the condition of the vehicle. Drivers can note safety concerns, things that must be repaired, and repairs that were actually made to the vehicle that day. This helps drivers of shared vehicles make sure that the vehicle continues to run smoothly. It alerts a driver who is taking the vehicle on the road to potential problems.

If the previous driver noted any vehicle defects on the DVIR, you also need to check if the repairs were signed off by a mechanic, if necessary. As you do your pre-trip inspection, inspect any repairs noted on the inspection report to make sure that repairs were done properly. DVIRs come in different formats, so be sure to look over the form to determine how to complete it. Some forms have a check box to indicate no defects found, while others don't. All DVIRs require the driver to sign off regardless of whether defects are found. If you find any defects during your pre-trip inspection, note them on the DVIR and notify your dispatcher or mechanic of the problems. Many problems, even though they seem minor, must be repaired before you start your trip.

Pre-Trip Checklist

Bring these items with you for the pre-trip inspection on the Skills Test:

- a tire pressure gauge
- a tread depth gauge
- wheel chocks
- a rag to clean your lights
- gloves
- your driver's license
- your vehicle's registration
- proof of insurance
- any permits required in your state

Step 2: Check the Engine Compartment

Before you check the engine compartment, make sure of the following:

- The parking brake is on.
- The wheels are **chocked** (secured with a wedge).
- Articles in the cab are secured (so they don't fall and break something if you must tilt the cab to check the engine compartment).

To check the engine compartment, you might have to raise the hood, tilt the cab, or open the engine compartment door. Then, check the following:

- engine oil level
- coolant level (Check that the expansion tank is between minimum and maximum level. If there is no expansion tank or sight glass, remove the radiator cap and check the level.

Never remove the cap on the radiator when the engine is hot. Wait until it cools.)
- condition of all hoses and radiator
- power steering fluid level and condition of hoses (if the vehicle is equipped with power steering)
- windshield washer fluid level
- battery connections and tie downs unless the battery is located in another spot (Most batteries are maintenance free and do not require a check of the fluid level.)
- transmission fluid, if your vehicle has an automatic transmission (You might have to start the engine first.)
- tightness of and wear (not cracked, frayed, or glazed) on all belt-driven components (The more you conduct pre-trip inspections, the better you'll know how much "give" each belt should have when properly adjusted. Your owner's manual can help you figure out how much give or slack is appropriate for each belt.)

- leaks (fuel, coolant, oil, power steering fluid, hydraulic fluid, battery fluid, etc.) in the engine compartment
- loose or broken wires
- cracks, wear, and/or chafing of electrical wiring insulation
- corroded connections
- windshield (not cracked or damaged)
- windshield wipers (proper tension and good rubber)
- fan (no missing or damaged blades)
- water pump (properly mounted and not leaking)
- alternator (properly mounted)
- air compressor and governor (properly mounted, with no audible air leaks on air brake equipped vehicles)
- steering parts including steering shaft, universal joint, gear box, pitman arm, drag link, steering arm, and tie rod
- frame (no cracks, dents, or illegal welds)
- suspension (spring hangers, leaf springs not missing or shifted, U-bolts, shock absorbers not leaking, bushings not dry rotted)

When you're finished checking each part of the engine compartment, lower and secure the hood, cab, or engine compartment door.

Step 3: Start the Engine and Inspect the Inside of the Cab

Get in and start the engine.

First, make sure that the parking brake is on.

As you get into your vehicle, make sure that steps, deck plates, and handholds are free of ice, snow, water, and grease. This will show the examiner that you've got safety in mind!

Put the gearshift in neutral (or in park, if the vehicle has an automatic transmission) and check that the clutch has about 1 inch of free play.

Start the engine and listen for unusual noises such as banging, squealing, clicking, or rattling. (A rattling noise could indicate that the engine isn't getting any oil; squealing could indicate a problem with your belts.)

If the vehicle has an antilock braking system (ABS), make sure that the indicator light on the dashboard comes on and then goes off. If the light stays on, there's a problem with the ABS. If the vehicle has a trailer and the yellow light on the left rear of the trailer stays on, this is also a sign that the ABS isn't working the way that it should be.

Look at the gauges.

It's important to know the normal operating range for each gauge. This way you'll be able to tell if a gauge is letting you know that there's a problem with the vehicle. Figure 4.8 shows where each gauge is located. Keep in mind, however, that different manufacturers may place gauges in different locations than the ones shown here.

The oil pressure gauge should come up to normal within seconds of starting the engine. If the gauge is low or if it drops or fluctuates, turn off the engine immediately to avoid damaging it. Late model CMVs will shut down automatically if oil pressure is too low.

The **ammeter** and/or **voltmeter** (devices that measure electric current and voltage from your battery) should be within normal range(s).

The coolant temperature gauge will gradually rise to normal range.

The engine oil temperature gauge should begin its gradual rise to normal operating range when you start the engine.

Warning lights and buzzers for oil, coolant, and charging circuit should come on and then go off right

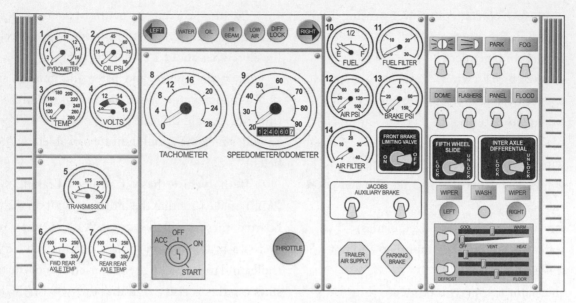

1. Exhaust Pyrometer
2. Engine Oil Pressure
3. Engine Oil Temperature
4. Volt Meter
5. Transmission
6. Forward Rear Axle Temperature
7. Rear Rear Axle Temperature

8. Tachometer
9. Speedometer/Odometer
10. Fuel Gauge
11. Fuel Filter Gauge
12. Air Pressure
13. Air Brake Application Pressure
14. Air Filter Restriction

Figure 4.8. A CMV Instrument Panel

away. If one of these lights or buzzers stays on after you start the vehicle, you'll know there's a problem.

Air pressure gauge(s) should begin a gradual rise to normal operating range when you start the engine. The low air pressure warning buzzer and/or light should go out once it reaches 60 psi.

Check the condition of the controls.

Make sure the following controls aren't loose, sticking, or damaged and their settings are correct:

- steering wheel (Again, make sure your steering wheel doesn't have more than 10 degrees of free play.)
- clutch (if the vehicle has a standard transmission; you should feel resistance after you push the clutch down an inch or two)
- accelerator (or "fuel pedal")

- brake controls, such as the foot brake, trailer brake (if the vehicle has one), parking brake, and retarder controls (if the vehicle has them)
- transmission controls
- interaxle differential lock (if the vehicle has one)
- horn(s)
- windshield wiper/washer control
- lights, such as headlights, dimmer switch, turn signals, four-way emergency flashers, and parking, clearance, identification, and marker switch(es)
- illumination of the dash (Make sure it allows you to view all gauges and instruments.)
- heater and defroster

Check the mirrors and windshield.

The mirrors and windshield shouldn't be dirty or cracked (though cracks smaller than $1/4$-inch are acceptable). They also shouldn't have illegal stickers or decals. Keep in mind that your cab-side windows can't have any stickers at all. Make sure the mirrors and windshield don't have other obstructions that would prevent you from seeing clearly. Adjust your mirrors now, too, so you know you'll have the best possible view and vision while driving.

Check the emergency equipment.

Some safety equipment is required, and some is optional. Check the vehicle to see what you have and to make sure that the vehicle contains all required safety equipment.

The following safety equipment is required:

- spare electrical fuses
- three red reflective triangles
- at least one properly charged and rated fire extinguisher
- seat belt (that works properly)

These are optional emergency safety items:

- tire chains (If you're driving in harsh winter conditions, you need tire chains; some state laws require you to use tire chains in the winter.)
- tire-changing equipment such as a hydraulic jack and tire wrenches or tire irons and a hammer
- a list of emergency phone numbers including dispatch, mechanic, or emergency road repair service
- an accident reporting kit/packet, which usually includes company accident procedures, an accident reporting form, witness cards or

list, and a disposable camera. (If your vehicle isn't equipped with an accident reporting kit, assemble your own. In an emergency situation, a kit helps you remember everything you need to do.)

Step 4: Turn Off the Engine and Check the Lights

First, check that the parking brake is set. Then turn off the engine and take the key with you so that no one else can start the vehicle. Turn on your headlights (low beams) and four-way emergency flashers before you exit the vehicle.

Step 5: Do a Walkaround Inspection

Since your headlights and four-way emergency flashers are already on, as soon as you get out of the vehicle, go to the front and make sure that your headlights, or low beams, work. Also check that both of your four-way emergency flashers are working on the front and rear of the vehicle and the trailer, if you have one.

Then, get back in the vehicle and push the dimmer switch so you can see if your high beams are working. If so, you can now turn off your headlights and four-way emergency flashers.

Now it's time to turn on your parking, clearance, side-marker, and identification lights. After that, turn on your right-turn signal and exit the vehicle to continue your walkaround inspection.

As you walk around the vehicle, make sure that everything you've turned on is working. Also, clean your lights, reflectors, and glass surfaces, even if they don't necessarily appear dirty. You'd be surprised how much dirt you'll wipe off without realizing that it's there. Dirt cuts down on the amount of light given off by your lights and on the reflective ability of your lights and reflectors.

Left Front Side:

Check that the glass in the driver's door is clean and make sure it goes up and down. Also check that door latches and locks work correctly.

Check the following parts of the left front wheel:

- The wheel and rim shouldn't have missing, bent, or broken studs, clamps, or lugs. The rim shouldn't be cracked or bent and the tire bead shouldn't be leaking. Also look for any signs of misalignment by checking for even wear across the tire treads.
- Tires should be properly inflated, should have good valve stems and caps, and shouldn't have serious cuts, bulges, or tread wear. Tread depth should be no less than $^4/_{32}$-inch on front tires.
- If you see rust around lug nuts, it could be an indication of looseness. Have it checked by a mechanic or tire personnel.
- Make sure that the level of hub oil is okay and that hub oil isn't leaking.
- Look at the left front suspension to make sure springs, spring hangers, shackles, U-bolts, and shock absorbers are in good condition.
- Check the condition of the left front brake drum or disc. (Keep in mind, though, that you won't be able to remove the wheel to check the disc, which is the only way to truly check the disc. If you know that the pads haven't been changed in awhile, listen for squealing when you apply the brakes while driving.) Also check the condition of hoses or lines on the left front brake. Make sure they aren't twisted, bent, or kinked. If the vehicle is equipped with air brakes, check the air lines, brake chambers, and slack adjusters.

- Check mud flaps to be sure they're properly attached and not torn or missing.

Front:

Check the condition of the front axle.

Note the condition of the steering system. The steering system shouldn't have loose, worn, bent, damaged, or missing parts. It's also a good idea to grab the steering mechanism to test for looseness.

Check the condition of the windshield. It shouldn't be damaged or dirty. If it's dirty, clean it before you continue. Also check the windshield wiper arms for proper spring tension and check the wiper blades for damage, "stiff" rubber, and secure attachment. Test the wipers to make sure they actually clean the windshield. Imperfect blades won't clear water, washer fluid, or dirt from the windshield very well. They'll sometimes leave a film of dirt or patches of moisture and dirt on the windshield, which can be dangerous—especially when it's right in the driver's line of sight or when it travels from one part of the windshield to another while you're driving.

Your lights and reflectors should be clean and in working condition. Check to see if parking, clearance, and identification lights—as well as reflectors—are the proper color. Front lights and reflectors should be amber. Also, make sure that the right front turn signal light works, is clean, and is the proper color (amber or white on signals facing forward).

Right Side:

For the right front of the vehicle, check all items that you looked at when inspecting the left front.

Make sure that primary and secondary safety cab locks are engaged (if the vehicle has a cab-over-engine [COE] design).

Check that the right fuel tank(s) are securely mounted and that they aren't damaged or leaking. Also, make sure that the fuel crossover line is secure. Though it's obvious that a tank should contain enough fuel, you check to make sure it doesn't have too much fuel. A fuel tank shouldn't be more than 95 percent full, so that fuel won't leak out if it expands. While checking the amount of fuel in the tank(s), also check that the gasket in the fuel cap is present. You also want to confirm the amount of fuel in the tanks against the gauge. If the gauge is showing full, but the tanks are only half full, you'll know the gauge isn't working properly. Also complete the following checks:

- Check the rear of the engine to make sure it isn't leaking.
- Check the transmission for leaks.
- Check that the exhaust system is secure and isn't leaking. Also make sure it isn't touching wires, fuel lines, or air lines.
- Look for bends or cracks in the frame and cross members.
- Make sure air lines and electrical wiring are secured to prevent them from snagging, rubbing, and wearing.
- Look for damage to the spare tire carrier or rack (if the vehicle has one). Also check that the spare tire and wheel are securely mounted in the rack. The spare tire and wheel should be the proper size and should be properly inflated.

For trucks, you'll also have to check cargo securement:

- Cargo should be properly blocked, braced, tied, or chained.
- If a header board is required, make sure that it's acceptable and secure.
- If the truck has side boards, make sure that the stakes are strong enough, free of damage, and properly set in place.

- If a canvas or tarp is required for cargo, check that it's properly secured so that it won't tear, billow, or block the mirrors.
- If the vehicle is carrying an oversized load, make sure all required signs (flags, lamps, and reflectors) are mounted safely and properly and you have all required permits.
- Curbside cargo compartment doors should be in good condition and should be securely closed, latched, or locked. Also, check that necessary security seals are in place and check the door ties that hold the door open during unloading to make sure they work.

Right Rear:

Check the condition of the wheels and rims to make sure spacers, studs, clamps, or lugs aren't missing, bent, or broken.

Make sure tires are properly inflated, valve stems and caps are okay, and tires don't have serious cuts, bulges, or tread wear. Also check that tires aren't rubbing each other and that nothing is stuck between them. Tires should be of the same size and type (meaning you can't mix radial and bias types). Make sure wheel bearings/seals aren't leaking.

Check the following elements of the suspension:

- Check the condition of the spring(s), spring hangers, shackles, and U-bolts.
- Make sure the axle is secure and the powered axle isn't leaking lube (gear oil).
- Check the condition of torque rod arms and bushings.
- Make sure shock absorber(s) are in good condition.
- If the vehicle has a retractable axle, check the condition of its lift mechanism. If it's air powered, check for leaks.

- Check the condition of the air-ride components.
- Make sure brakes are properly adjusted and brake drum(s) or discs are in good condition. Also make sure hoses don't show wear from rubbing and are otherwise in good shape. For air brake equipped vehicles check brake chambers, brake shoes, and slack adjusters.
- Check all lights and reflectors on the right rear. Make sure that side-marker lights are clean and operating and that they're the proper color. Side-marker lights and reflectors at the rear should be red. (Others should be amber.)

Rear:

Make sure that lights and reflectors in the rear of the vehicle are clean and operating and the proper color. Rear clearance lights, identification lights, reflectors, and tail lights should be red. The right rear turn signal should be red, yellow, or amber.

Check that the vehicle has license plate(s) and that it's clean, secured, and has current registration.

The vehicle should have splash guards or mud flaps. These shouldn't be damaged, dragging on the ground, or rubbing the tires. Also make sure splash guards are securely fastened. (If the state has laws on the way that mud flaps or splash guards are mounted, be sure to check that these laws are being followed.)

For trucks, check that cargo is secure in the rear of the vehicle (meaning it's properly blocked, braced, tied, or chained). Also check these items relating to cargo:

- Tailboards should be up and properly secured.
- End gates shouldn't be damaged and should be properly secured in stake sockets.

- If a canvas or tarp is needed, it should be properly secured to prevent it from tearing, billowing, or blocking either the rearview mirrors or the rear lights.
- Again, if the vehicle is over-length or over-width, make sure all signs and additional lights and flags are safely and properly mounted and you have all required permits in your possession.
- Make sure that the rear doors are securely closed and latched or locked. Also make sure that door ties are operational for doors that swing open. For roll-up doors, make sure the door ties are in good condition and the door goes up and down.

Left Side:

For the left side of the vehicle, check all items that you looked at when inspecting the right side, as well as these additional items:

- If they aren't mounted in the engine compartment, battery boxes should be securely mounted to the vehicle and should have secure covers.
- Batteries should be secured against movement and shouldn't be broken or leaking.
- Battery fluid should be at the proper level. (If the vehicle has maintenance-free batteries, you don't have to check this.)
- Cell caps should be on the battery and securely tightened. Vents in the cell caps shouldn't contain foreign material. (If the vehicle has maintenance-free batteries, you won't have to check these things.)

Step 6: Check the Signal Lights

Get in and turn off the lights.

Now it's time to get back into your vehicle and turn off all lights. After doing this, though, you'll turn on the vehicle's stop lights. (To do this, apply the trailer hand brake or have a helper put on the brake pedal.) Then turn on your left turn signal lights.

Get out and check the lights.

Make sure that the left turn signal lights and stop lights are clean, operating, and the proper color. First, check the left front turn signal, and then check the left rear turn signal. On the left front, turn signals facing the front should be amber or white. The left rear turn signal and both stop lights should be red, yellow, or amber.

Get in the vehicle.

Get in and turn off all lights that aren't needed for driving. Then make sure you have all required papers (trip manifests, permits, etc.) in the vehicle with you, as if you were about to take a trip. Make sure all loose articles in the cab are secure so that they don't interfere when you're operating the controls. (Also, if you were about to take a trip, loose articles could fly around the cab and hit you.) Then start the engine.

Step 7: Start the Engine and Check the Brake System

Test for hydraulic leaks.

If the vehicle has hydraulic brakes, pump the brake pedal three times. Then apply firm pressure to the pedal and hold it for 5 seconds. The pedal shouldn't move. If it does, this tells you that there might be a hydraulic leak, air in the lines, or another problem. You'll have to have someone diagnose and fix the problem before you can drive the vehicle. If the vehicle has air brakes, refer to Chapter 6 for the appropriate checks during a pre-trip inspection.

Test parking brake(s).

First, set the parking brake (for a power unit only). Then, release the trailer parking brake (if applicable) and place the vehicle into a low gear. Gently pull forward against the parking brake to test its ability to hold. Do the same for the trailer when the trailer parking brake is set and the power unit parking brakes are released (if applicable). If the parking brake doesn't hold, you'll know that you have to get it fixed before you can drive your vehicle. You could also put the vehicle in gear and allow it to move forward slowly before applying the parking brake. If the parking brake doesn't stop the vehicle, it's defective.

Since you're about to drive the vehicle, you'll impress your examiner if you put your seat belt on as soon as you get into the cab!

Test the service brake stopping action.

To test the service brake stopping action, put the vehicle in gear and allow it to go about 5 mph. Put both hands on the steering wheel and then put firm pressure on the brake pedal. If you feel "pulling" to one side or the other or if you feel anything else unusual when you put pressure on the brake pedal, there might be a problem with your brakes. Delayed stopping is also an indication of brake problems.

Additional Checks for Buses

In addition to the checks just mentioned, coach and transit bus drivers must also check the following to make sure they're safe and operating properly:

- passenger entry doors
- emergency exits
- seats
- bus interior

- baggage compartment
- fire extinguisher

Refer back to Figure 4.7 for a "cheat sheet" overview of what you should inspect on a coach or transit bus.

Anything you find during a pre-trip inspection that's considered unsafe must be fixed before you can drive your vehicle. Federal and state laws prohibit drivers from operating unsafe vehicles.

▶ Inspection During a Trip

You already know that you should inspect your vehicle during a trip. Here's a summary of things to check while you're on the road:

- instruments
- air pressure gauge (if your vehicle has air brakes)
- temperature gauges
- pressure gauges
- ammeter/voltmeter
- mirrors
- tires
- brakes (especially that they're not overheating)
- cargo doors, covers, and securement
- lights
- coupling devices (such as safety chains used for towing, tow bars, saddle mounts, and pintle hooks)

Use your senses of sight, smell, hearing, and touch to constantly monitor your vehicle for problems. If you see, smell, hear, or feel anything unusual or anything that might be a problem while you're driving, stop and check your vehicle. As you've learned, the gen-

eral rule is that CMV drivers should inspect their cargo within the first 50 miles of a trip. After that, drivers should do routine inspections every 150 miles or every 3 hours—whichever comes first.

▶ After-Trip Inspection and Report

As a driver of a CMV, you'll inspect your vehicle after each trip. This is called a **post-trip inspection**. You'll probably also have to create daily written reports on the condition of the vehicle(s) that you drove. Include in these reports any possible safety issues or repairs that should be made to the vehicle before another driver drives it. Leave a copy of your report in the vehicle for one day so the next driver can understand what problems the vehicle might have.

▶ State and Local Requirements

Some states have additional laws about equipment that a vehicle must have. The laws of each state are different, so be sure to read up on the laws of your own state, as well as the laws of each state that you'll pass through on a trip. Even if you're unaware of the laws, your vehicle can be put out of service if it doesn't meet the inspection requirements of another state.

Chapter 4 Review Quiz

1–8: Circle the correct answer.

1. Which of the following items must be inspected only on a coach bus?
   a. cargo securement
   b. emergency exits
   c. tire pressure
   d. steering system

2. Before you check the engine compartment, make sure the wheels are
   a. turned to the left.
   b. engaged.
   c. chocked.
   d. turned to the right.

3. Rust around wheel nuts most likely indicates that the wheel nuts are
   a. missing.
   b. loose.
   c. too large.
   d. too tight.

4. Which of the following safety equipment items is always required?
   a. spare electrical fuses
   b. an accident reporting kit
   c. tire-changing equipment
   d. tire chains

5. Which action should a driver perform first when inspecting the inside of a cab?
   a. Listen for unusual noises in the engine.
   b. Check the oil pressure gauge.
   c. Make sure the parking brake is on.
   d. Make sure the indicator light comes on.

6. Brake pads should not be thinner than _____ inch at their thinnest point.
   a. 1/8
   b. 1/6
   c. 1/4
   d. 1/2

7. How many red reflective triangles must a driver have in a CMV?
   a. two
   b. three
   c. five
   d. seven

8. A steering wheel should not have more than _____ degrees of play.
   a. 2
   b. 5
   c. 10
   d. 20

9–12: Indicate whether each statement is true or false.

_____ **9.** The only person responsible for inspecting a CMV is the CMV driver.

_____ **10.** Drivers shouldn't put tires with radial tread and bias-ply tread on wheels that share an axle.

_____ **11.** Drivers should replace rims with welding repairs even if the rims haven't caused tire problems yet.

_____ **12.** Left rear turn signals should always be amber.

Check your answers on page 294.

5 ▶ Transporting Cargo Safely

CHAPTER SUMMARY
The main reason companies employ commercial drivers is to haul cargo. In this chapter, you'll learn the basic rules for transporting different types of cargo safely to their destinations.

When you become a commercial driver, your main responsibility will be to transport cargo. Your employer will try to keep **deadhead miles**—miles driven without cargo—to a minimum, since transporting an empty trailer means a loss of revenue for the company. So you'll almost always transport some type of cargo while you're on the job.

In this chapter, you'll learn basic safety rules about transporting cargo, which you need to know to pass the General Knowledge Test for the CDL. CMV drivers haul many types of **cargo**, which is also called **freight**. The kind of cargo you haul depends on where you work. You might carry food products on pallets, building supplies, furniture, animals, paper products, vehicles, garbage, liquids in containers—you name it. The amount of cargo your CMV can safely haul is called the **load**.

You learned in Chapter 1 that you need endorsements on your CDL to transport some types of cargo. If you drive a bus, your passengers are your cargo. You need a passenger endorsement on your CDL to transport passengers. If your cargo is in a bulk tank, dry or liquid, you need a tanker endorsement, and if your cargo is hazardous materials requiring placards, you need a hazardous materials endorsement. Lastly, if you haul cargo in double and triple trailers, you'll need this type of endorsement on your CDL. You'll learn more about the tests required for these endorsements later in this book.

The cargo you transport must be secure and balanced. Cargo that isn't secure can be a hazard to you and other drivers. Suppose you're transporting cargo on a flatbed and the cargo comes loose and falls onto the highway. It might cause an accident. Loose cargo can also harm you if you have to stop suddenly.

Because gravity plays an important role in the safe transportation of cargo, you need to make sure that your cargo is balanced in the trailer of your CMV so that the weight is evenly distributed. Imagine that you're transporting very heavy cargo that's leaning to one side of your trailer. What might happen when you drive around a curve? Your CMV might tip or even roll over. This is less likely to happen if your cargo is balanced.

Federal, state, and local laws regulate the transportation of cargo—and these laws vary across the country. While one state might allow cargo of a certain weight or height, another might not. Normally, your gross combination vehicle weight is 80,000 pounds with a maximum height of 13′ 6″, but it's your responsibility to know the regulations in the areas in which you drive.

▶ Inspecting Cargo

As a CMV driver, you're responsible for your cargo even if you don't load and unload it yourself. Truck drivers often have to wait for dockworkers to load cargo onto their CMVs. Never take the word of others that your cargo is properly loaded and secure. It's part of your job to make sure your cargo is loaded safely. Keep in mind that cargo on a CMV is usually worth thousands of dollars. If something happens to it, it's your job that's on the line.

As you learned in Chapter 4, once your cargo is loaded and you begin driving, you're required by federal law to check your cargo within the first 50 miles of your trip. Make any necessary adjustments if your cargo isn't balanced or secure. After this, recheck your cargo every 3 hours or 150 miles and after every break you take from driving, such as when you stop at a truck stop to eat.

Check for Overloads

It's important to check for overloads. An **overload** simply means that your CMV is overloaded—you're carrying too much cargo. How do you know if you're overloaded?

As a driver, you should know the unladen, or empty, weight of your vehicle. Take your CMV to a certified scale located at many truck stops along the highway. Make sure that your fuel tanks are full when you weigh your vehicle. Fuel can weigh a lot. Knowing your unladen weight with full fuel tanks will help you determine how much freight you can load onto your vehicle, while traveling with full fuel tanks, and remain within legal limits. For example, if your unladen weight is 32,000 pounds with a legal weight limit of 80,000 pounds, you can load up to 48,000 pounds of cargo. If your paperwork indicates that the cargo weighs 50,000 pounds, your CMV and its cargo may be exceeding a weight limit. As you learned, legal weight limits depend on where you are. Review them in trucker's map books for the state in which you'll be driving. Then proceed to a certified scale to determine if you are within legal weight limits.

Overloading your CMV is not only illegal, but also makes driving your CMV much trickier. An overloaded CMV is difficult to drive. It's harder to steer, brake, and control speed. If your CMV is overloaded, it will go very slowly on upgrades and may gain too much speed on downgrades. Your stopping distance will increase. Because an overload forces your brakes to work too hard, your brakes might fade or fail. Too much cargo might also damage a CMV and the roadway.

To see if your vehicle is overloaded, check the state's maximum gross vehicle weights (GVWs), gross combination weights (GCWs), and axle weights. (See "Definitions Related to Weight" for the meaning of these terms.)

Your CMV's axle weight isn't the weight of its axle; it's how much weight the axle transmits to the ground.

Imagine that you're transporting pallets of bricks and cinder blocks—heavy cargo. Instead of placing the pallets so that they're evenly distributed and cover the bottom of your trailer, you stack them up on one side. What will happen when you try to drive your CMV? You might tip over because too much weight is on one part of your CMV. The same is true of bridges—they could be damaged or break if there's too much weight on any part. Because of this, many states have laws to protect bridges and the drivers traveling over them. These states determine their maximum axle weight— the maximum weight a bridge can withstand in one place—using a "bridge formula." According to this formula, the maximum allowed weight will be less for your CMV if it has two axles (tandem axles) that are closer together. You may be able to check the gross weight and axle weight of your CMV at some shippers' locations after loading or on a certified scale at a nearby truck stop.

Check Your Cargo's Height, Length, and Width

You just learned that federal, state, and local laws regulate the weight of a CMV and its cargo. Some laws also regulate the height, length, and width of a CMV. If you try to drive under an overhead structure and your CMV and its cargo are too high, you'll get stuck and the

Definitions Related to Weight

- **axle weight**. the weight transmitted to the ground by an axle or set of axles.
- **coupling device capacity**. coupling devices are rated for the maximum weight they can pull or carry.
- **gross combination weight (GCW)**. the total weight of a powered unit plus trailer or trailers and cargo.
- **gross combination weight rating (GCWR)**. the maximum GCW specified by the manufacturer for a specific combination of vehicles and its load.
- **gross vehicle weight (GVW)**. the total weight of a single vehicle and its load.
- **gross vehicle weight rating (GVWR)**. the maximum GVW, as specified by the manufacturer, for a single vehicle and its load.
- **suspension system**. a mechanical system of springs that supports the vehicle and its load and keeps the axles in place. A suspension system has a weight capacity rating set by the manufacturer.
- **tire load**. the maximum safe weight a tire can carry at a specified pressure. You can find this rating on the side of each tire.

overhead structure may be damaged. Too much height can also make a CMV unstable.

In addition to height, most states have laws specifying the maximum vehicle length and width. Vehicles that exceed these specifications are called **oversized vehicles**, and special laws apply to them. For example, you need to apply for special permits to drive an oversized vehicle. You may be allowed to drive it on roadways only during certain times of day when there's little traffic, or you may be asked to take an alternate route with less traffic. You may also be required to have a police escort.

Check for Balance

It's very important that the cargo in your CMV be balanced so its weight is evenly distributed. How do you balance your cargo? Seasoned truck drivers will tell you that you'll learn how to balance cargo quickly and easily once you gain some experience. When you're a beginner, however, keep an eye out to make sure the load within a trailer is divided evenly between the front and the back. Try to distribute the weight evenly over all axles, which are the strongest parts of your CMV. The following rules will also help you effectively balance your cargo:

- Don't load too much weight on the **steering axle**, which is the front axle on most CMVs. Too much weight on this axle will make your CMV difficult to turn. Too little weight on the steering axle will also cause steering difficulty.

- The **driving axle** is part of the drivetrain. If you load too little weight on the driving axle, you're **underloading** this axle. An underloaded drive axle could cause your tires to lose traction, and you might not be able to drive in bad weather.

If you have a single axle, the weight should be slightly forward of the centerline.

In the beginning of this chapter, you learned that maintaining the proper center of gravity is important when transporting cargo. A high center of gravity—which means your cargo is piled up very high or the heaviest cargo is at the top—can cause your CMV to tip over, especially when you're driving around sharp curves or if you have to swerve to avoid a hazard. If you're driving a flatbed, a high center of gravity might cause your cargo to shift to the side or to fall off. Your center of gravity should be as low as possible, which means you need to load the heaviest cargo under the lightest cargo.

Figure 5.1. Right and Wrong Ways to Balance Cargo

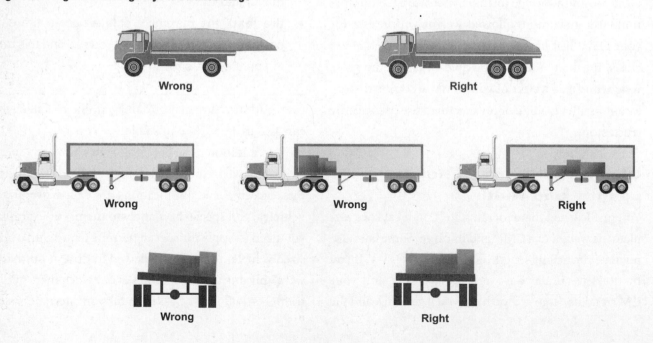

► Loading Cargo

Whether you load cargo yourself or whether someone will load it for you depends on where you work, the kind of cargo you're hauling, and your employer. Before loading any type of CMV, however, check the floor of the trailer for nails and splinters—remove anything that might damage the cargo. Remember that the cargo you're hauling is your responsibility and that it's your job to transport it safely to its destination.

Loading a Flatbed

You learned earlier that a flatbed is a trailer without sides. When you load a flatbed, load the heaviest items over the axles when possible, since these areas are the strongest. After you do this, distribute the rest of the cargo evenly in the front and back of the trailer. Don't load more than the maximum GVWR listed on the vehicle specifications sticker. Tie a red safety flag on any portion of the load that extends 4 feet or more behind the back bumper of the flatbed. Special warning devices such as flags and flashing lights may be required for loads that are over-length or over-width.

You can find the height requirements for CMVs by calling the state's transportation department.

Loading Vans

Before you begin loading a van, make sure the walls are clean and dry. When loading a van with boxes, pallets, or sacks, load the heaviest cargo on the bottom and work your way up to the lightest. Load the cargo using a tiered effect, as if you were laying bricks. This will prevent a column of cargo from falling on you when you open the doors of the van and will prevent the cargo from shifting while you drive.

Loading Refrigerated Vehicles

Check that refrigerated cargo is the correct temperature before you load it into a refrigerated vehicle, since the purpose of this vehicle is to maintain the temperature of cargo and not to cool like a refrigerator. Because a refrigerated vehicle needs air to circulate, you need to leave space between the top of the freight and the top of the trailer. Most refrigerated units will have a limit line to show how high you can load them.

► Securing Your Cargo

While loading your cargo properly will help it stay secure, proper loading usually isn't enough to keep your cargo from moving. Most of the time, you need to use cargo securement devices such as tie downs, header boards, covers, and blocks and braces to keep your cargo in one place.

Figure 5.2. Loading Cargo in a Tiered Manner in a Van

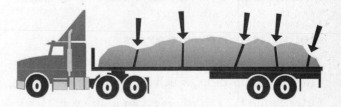

Figure 5.3. Tie Downs on Cargo on a Flatbed

Most cargo that needs to be covered is in a straight truck (often a dump truck) with an open bed or a flatbed with a front, back, and sides (open top trailer). Covers are usually tarps, which are very expensive, so care must be taken so they don't become ripped or damaged.

1. Lift the rolled-up tarp to the front rack and unroll it over the bars to the back of the trailer.
2. Pull it tightly—this is very important. If a tarp isn't tight enough, it will flap, which will eventually cause it to tear. Your tarp should be tight enough so that wind and rain don't get underneath it.
3. Tie the tarp to the cross bars on the rack.
4. Overlap the tarp in the front—as if you were wrapping a gift—to make it even tighter and stronger.

Figure 5.4. A Tarp Covering Cargo

Using Tie Downs

If you're driving a flatbed, you'll have to secure your cargo to keep it from falling off. You can use securement devices, called **tie downs**, to do this. Common tie downs include ropes, straps, chains, and tensioning devices such as winches, ratchets, and clinching components. Tie downs have to be the correct strength and type for the kind of cargo you're transporting—you can't keep a heavy load secure with thin rope or string. Tie downs need to be attached, or tied down, to your CMV with hooks, bolts, rails, or rings. Include at least one tie down per 10 feet of cargo, but no matter how small the cargo, secure it with at least two tie downs.

Using Header Boards

Your CMV may be equipped with header boards, also called headache racks, which keep cargo from moving forward into the cab where it can injure you. Header boards protect you in case you're involved in an accident or have to stop suddenly.

Figure 5.5. A Header Board

Using Covers

You might be required by state laws to cover your cargo to keep it from spilling. Drivers also cover cargo to protect it from the weather and to protect the public from spilled cargo. If you cover your cargo, check in the mirrors from time to time while you're driving to make sure the covers stay snug and aren't flapping. Covers that flap might tear loose and obstruct your view.

Bracing and Blocking

Bracing prevents cargo from moving within a trailer or cargo compartment. When you brace a load, you use securing elements—braces—to steady the load. Braces

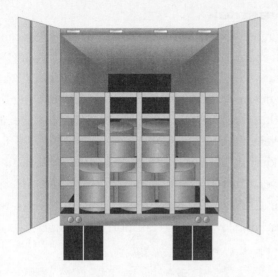

Figure 5.6. Blocking

are usually attached from the upper part of the cargo to the floor.

Blocking looks like fencing. Blocking is designed to fit snugly against cargo and may be used in the front, back, or sides of cargo.

Using Other Securing Devices

Load locks are long poles that extend from wall to wall within a trailer to prevent cargo from falling. One load lock is usually placed at the top of the cargo and another is placed halfway down. **Loading pallets** make sure pallets don't lean and fall. If possible, each pallet should be placed tightly against the one in front of it.

Securing Sealed and Containerized Loads

When freight is transported part of the way by ship or train, containers are often used. CMVs typically transport this type of cargo at the beginning or end of a trip. Some containers have their own tie-down mechanisms that are attached to a special chassis. Other containers must be loaded onto flatbeds and secured. Note that you can't open and inspect sealed containers. Sometimes you pick up a trailer that was loaded by the cus-

tomer and then sealed. Since you can't inspect the load, you should indicate on your paperwork "shipper loaded and sealed" and have the shipper sign off. If freight is shrink wrapped on pallets, you should note on the paperwork "shipper load and count" and have them sign off. This releases you, the driver, and your company from any claims that the correct number of pieces were not received.

While you're not allowed to open sealed containers or trailers to inspect them, it's still your responsibility to make sure you stay under the maximum weight for whatever state or states you're driving in.

Securing Logs

Because logs can be very dangerous if they come loose and slide off a CMV trailer, the Federal Motor Carrier Safety Administration (FMCSA) has very specific rules about transporting them. In general, logs must be **bundled**, which means they must be tied together in groups. All logs must be packed solid and logs on the outer bottom must rest against devices called stakes, bunks, bolsters, or standards. The center of the highest outside log on each side must be below the top of each stake, bunk, bolster, or standard.

Each log that isn't held into place by another log or the stakes, bunks, or standards must be held in place with a tie down, and tie downs should be used in any place where a log might slip or come loose.

Firewood, stumps, log debris, and short logs must be transported in a trailer or truck with sides and a front and rear—and these must be strong enough to contain them. This type of trailer is called a "dump body," and in most states, it must be covered with a tarp to prevent debris from blowing out and onto the highway.

Securing Metal Coils

Metal coils are very heavy, and since they are circular, they can roll. Like logs, they can be very dangerous if they should break loose and come off a CMV trailer. Because of this, the FMCSA also has specific rules about how metal coils must be tied down on a trailer. The center of a metal coil is called the "eye." During transportation, metal coils may be placed on a trailer so that the eyes are vertical, crosswise, or lengthwise. It isn't necessary for you to memorize how coils in each position must be tied down, but it helps to know that tie downs are used diagonally, over top, and sometimes through the opening in the center of the coil.

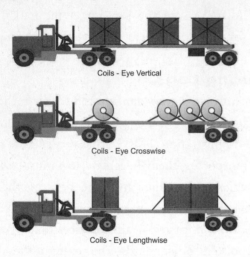

Coils - Eye Vertical

Coils - Eye Crosswise

Coils - Eye Lengthwise

Figure 5.7. Vertical, Crosswise, and Lengthwise Positioning of Metal Coils

▶ Transporting Special Kinds of Cargo

Some kinds of cargo need more attention than other kinds. While it's important to check state laws for requirements regarding the transportation of any type of cargo, it's especially important to do this for these kinds of cargo:

- livestock
- hanging meat
- dry bulk
- oversized loads

Livestock

Because livestock can move, transporting them can be challenging. Unconfined livestock can rock your CMV. Because of this, it's recommended that you use securing devices called false bulkheads when hauling livestock, as these devices group the livestock together and prevent their movement. Even with the use of false bulkheads, however, livestock are known to lean on curves, which shifts the center of gravity and can cause your CMV to tip. Because of this, you have to turn especially slowly when transporting livestock.

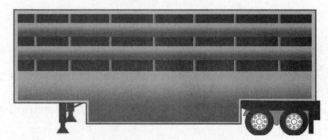

Figure 5.8. Livestock Transport

Hanging Meat

Earlier, you learned the dangers of transporting cargo with a high center of gravity—mainly that your CMV is more likely to roll over. Hanging meat is one type of cargo that has a high center of gravity. Hanging meat such as a side of beef hangs in a refrigerated trailer, dubbed a **reefer**, so it can swing, which makes it very unstable. When hauling hanging meat, you may need to drive slowly—under the speed limit—and take extra care on turns, on-ramps, and off-ramps.

Figure 5.9. Meat Trailer

Dry Bulk

Dry bulk tanks also have a high center of gravity, and the load can shift, so you must take curves slowly. When driving a dry bulk tank, be extremely cautious.

Figure 5.10. Dry Bulk Trailer

Oversized Loads

Earlier in this chapter, you learned that you need a special permit to drive a CMV hauling an oversized load.

Have you ever seen a CMV pulling a manufactured home? This is an oversized load. If you're hauling such a load, you might be asked to travel only during certain times of day and on alternate routes that aren't as heavily traveled. You might also need a police escort and an escort by special vehicles with warning signs and flashing lights. You need to drive very slowly when hauling an oversized load and take special care.

Figure 5.11. Oversized Vehicle with Oversized Load

Chapter 5 Review Quiz

1–8: Circle the correct answer.

1. The main reason that it's difficult to transport livestock is because livestock
   a. have a high center of gravity.
   b. are very heavy and tall.
   c. must be moved in a large trailer.
   d. can move and lean.

2. If you have too much cargo in your CMV, it's said to be
   a. over-axle.
   b. overloaded.
   c. unbalanced.
   d. overbulked.

3. Loading too little weight on your _____ axle will cause your drive tires to lose traction.
   a. driving
   b. steering
   c. single
   d. rear

4. _____ keep cargo from moving forward into the cab of your CMV.
   a. Tie downs
   b. Header boards
   c. Covers
   d. Tarps

5. Once you begin your trip, you should check your cargo within the first ____ miles.
   a. 10
   b. 25
   c. 50
   d. 150

6. The total weight of a powered unit plus a trailer or trailers and cargo is called
   a. gross combination weight.
   b. tire load.
   c. gross vehicle weight.
   d. axle weight.

7. Which type of load might require a special permit and a police escort?
   a. dry haul
   b. hanging meat
   c. oversized
   d. livestock

8. Load straps, chains, and tensioning devices are examples of
   a. tie downs.
   b. braces.
   c. load locks.
   d. coils.

9–12: Indicate whether each statement is true or false.

____ 9. When securing a load on a flatbed, you should use a tie down every 20 feet.

____ 10. Axle weight is the weight transmitted to the ground by an axle or set of axles.

____ 11. Federal, state, and local laws regulating the weight of CMVs vary across the country.

____ 12. To balance the cargo in a trailer, you should load the lightest cargo underneath the heaviest cargo.

Check your answers on page 294.

General Knowledge Practice Test 1

1. ⓐ ⓑ ⓒ ⓓ   11. ⓐ ⓑ ⓒ ⓓ   21. ⓐ ⓑ ⓒ ⓓ

2. ⓐ ⓑ ⓒ ⓓ   12. ⓐ ⓑ ⓒ ⓓ   22. ⓐ ⓑ ⓒ ⓓ

3. ⓐ ⓑ ⓒ ⓓ   13. ⓐ ⓑ ⓒ ⓓ   23. ⓐ ⓑ ⓒ ⓓ

4. ⓐ ⓑ ⓒ ⓓ   14. ⓐ ⓑ ⓒ ⓓ   24. ⓐ ⓑ ⓒ ⓓ

5. ⓐ ⓑ ⓒ ⓓ   15. ⓐ ⓑ ⓒ ⓓ   25. ⓐ ⓑ ⓒ ⓓ

6. ⓐ ⓑ ⓒ ⓓ   16. ⓐ ⓑ ⓒ ⓓ   26. ⓐ ⓑ ⓒ ⓓ

7. ⓐ ⓑ ⓒ ⓓ   17. ⓐ ⓑ ⓒ ⓓ   27. ⓐ ⓑ ⓒ ⓓ

8. ⓐ ⓑ ⓒ ⓓ   18. ⓐ ⓑ ⓒ ⓓ   28. ⓐ ⓑ ⓒ ⓓ

9. ⓐ ⓑ ⓒ ⓓ   19. ⓐ ⓑ ⓒ ⓓ   29. ⓐ ⓑ ⓒ ⓓ

10. ⓐ ⓑ ⓒ ⓓ   20. ⓐ ⓑ ⓒ ⓓ   30. ⓐ ⓑ ⓒ ⓓ

▶ General Knowledge Practice Test 1

Choose the correct answer. Mark the letter on the answer sheet on page 87.

1. What can happen if you drive too fast around a curve?
   a. Your vehicle might skid.
   b. Your tires can lose traction.
   c. Your vehicle may roll over.
   d. All of the above.

2. Which of the following is true about backing in a commercial vehicle?
   a. You should back to the right whenever possible.
   b. You should use a high reverse gear when backing.
   c. You should lean out the driver's window when backing.
   d. You should avoid backing whenever possible.

3. If you're traveling at 55 mph on dry pavement, what is your reaction distance?
   a. 60 feet
   b. 81 feet
   c. 390 feet
   d. 512 feet

4. How many reflective triangles should you have in your commercial vehicle?
   a. one
   b. two
   c. three
   d. none of the above

5. After you first stop and check your vehicle's cargo, how many miles can you drive before you must stop and check the cargo again?
   a. 50
   b. 75
   c. 150
   d. 300

6. Which of the following is true about hydroplaning?
   a. It occurs only when there is a lot of water on the road.
   b. It won't occur if you're driving at a slow speed.
   c. It often occurs because of low tire pressure.
   d. None of the above.

7. How many tie downs should you use for 20 feet of cargo?
   a. 1
   b. 2
   c. 5
   d. 10

8. When should you apply your brakes while driving around a curve?
   a. halfway through the curve
   b. before you enter the curve
   c. after the curve
   d. all of the above

9. When should you turn off your high beams?
   a. when an oncoming vehicle is within 500 feet
   b. when following another vehicle within 750 feet
   c. when an oncoming vehicle is within 750 feet
   d. when following another vehicle within 1,000 feet

10. Which of the following parts of the Skills Test must all drivers applying for a CDL take?
  a. Basic Control Skills
  b. Road Test
  c. Pre-Trip Inspection
  d. All of the above

11. If you're tested for alcohol while driving a commercial vehicle and your blood alcohol concentration (BAC) is 0.04 percent, what will happen?
  a. You'll be disqualified for 6 months.
  b. You'll be disqualified for 1 year.
  c. You'll be disqualified for 3 years.
  d. You'll be disqualified for life.

12. How much tread depth should your front tires have in every groove?
  a. 1/32-inch
  b. 2/32-inch
  c. 4/32-inch
  d. 5/32-inch

13. Which of the following is true about the oil pressure gauge in a commercial vehicle?
  a. It should reach the normal range within several seconds of starting the engine.
  b. It should gradually rise to the normal operating range after several minutes.
  c. It should drop or fluctuate several seconds after starting the engine.
  d. It should be within the normal range before you start the vehicle.

14. What can happen to brakes if they get wet?
  a. They might grab.
  b. They might fail.
  c. They can apply unevenly.
  d. All of the above.

15. The total weight of a single vehicle and its load is called the
  a. gross combination weight (GCW).
  b. gross vehicle weight (GVW).
  c. gross combination weight rating (GCWR).
  d. gross vehicle weight rating (GVWR).

16. What might happen if there is too little weight on the front axle?
  a. Your wheels might spin easily.
  b. You might be unable to drive in bad weather.
  c. Your vehicle might be hard to steer.
  d. You might not be able to steer safely.

17. If your engine is on fire, you should
  a. open the doors of the van or box.
  b. open the hood and shoot a fire extinguisher.
  c. shoot a fire extinguisher through louvers.
  d. all of the above.

18. How can you recover from a skid caused by driving too fast?
  a. Step hard on the brakes.
  b. Take your foot off the accelerator.
  c. Use a speed retarder.
  d. Turn your wheel in the opposite direction.

19. When you load cargo on a flatbed, you should
  a. put the heaviest items over the axles.
  b. load the cargo using a tiered affect.
  c. check the temperature before loading the cargo.
  d. load the heavier cargo near the header board.

20. Signs placed on the outside of a vehicle warning others of danger are called

   a. placards.

   b. endorsements.

   c. restrictions.

   d. none of the above.

21. What should you do if you're being tailgated while driving a commercial vehicle?

   a. Make room in front.

   b. Speed up.

   c. Change lanes.

   d. Turn on your tail lights.

22. When should you inspect your vehicle?

   a. before a trip

   b. while driving

   c. after a trip

   d. all of the above

23. What should you be aware of if your vehicle has curved mirrors?

   a. They don't allow you to see as much as flat mirrors.

   b. They make images appear small and far away.

   c. They cause your vehicle to have a blind spot.

   d. They don't allow you to look at your vehicle's tires.

24. When driving downhill, when should you shift your transmission into a lower gear?

   a. before you begin going downhill

   b. after using your brakes repeatedly

   c. after you build up speed

   d. none of the above

25. When crossing railroad tracks in a commercial vehicle, you should

   a. rely on your hearing to alert you of an oncoming train.

   b. approach railroad tracks as though a train is coming.

   c. shift into a lower gear while crossing railroad tracks.

   d. try to determine the speed of the train before crossing tracks.

26. Securing devices called false bulkheads are often used to haul

   a. livestock.

   b. logs.

   c. hanging meat.

   d. dry bulk.

27. When transporting metal coils, the coils can be placed so that the "eyes" are

   a. lengthwise.

   b. vertical.

   c. crosswise.

   d. all of the above.

28. To find your total stopping distance, add perception distance, reaction distance, and

   a. driving distance.

   b. braking distance.

   c. recognition distance.

   d. acceleration distance.

29. A long bed of loose material such as gravel you can use if your brakes fail is called an

   a. off-ramp.

   b. escape ramp.

   c. upgrade.

   d. emergency stop.

30. Applying the brakes all the way and releasing
them when they lock up is called
   a. fade braking.
   b. controlled braking.
   c. snub braking.
   d. stab braking.

▶ Answers and Explanations

1. **d.** If you take a curve too fast, your tires can lose traction and continue straight ahead, causing your vehicle to skid off the road, or your tires may retain traction, but your vehicle may roll over.

2. **d.** Because your view of your surroundings is very limited, backing is always dangerous. Avoid it whenever possible. Parking in an area where you can pull out straight is a better alternative.

3. **a.** Your reaction distance is the distance your vehicle moves from the time your brain recognizes the hazard until your foot moves off the accelerator and pushes the brake pedal. At 55 mph, your vehicle will travel an additional 60 feet before your foot hits the brakes.

4. **c.** You're required to have this safety equipment in your CMV: spare electrical fuses, three red reflective triangles, and at least one properly charged and rated fire extinguisher.

5. **c.** You're required by law to inspect your vehicle 50 miles into a trip. After that, inspect it every 150 miles or 3 hours, whichever comes first.

6. **c.** Hydroplaning often occurs because of low tire pressure or worn treads.

7. **b.** Include at least one tie down per 10 feet of cargo, but no matter how small the cargo, secure it with at least two tie downs. If you have 20 feet of cargo, you would need two tie downs.

8. **b.** You should apply your brakes before you enter a curve. If you use your brakes halfway through, you run the risk of locking your wheels and causing your vehicle to skid.

9. **a.** You should turn off your high beams when you're within 500 feet of an oncoming vehicle and when following another vehicle within 500 feet.

10. **d.** The Skills Test consists of three components: (1) Pre-Trip Inspection, (2) Basic Control Skills, and (3) Road Test.

11. **b.** You can lose your CDL for 1 year if you're tested for alcohol and your blood alcohol concentration (BAC) is 0.04 percent or more.

12. **c.** Your front tires should have at least $^4/_{32}$-inch tread depth in every major groove. Other tires must have at least $^2/_{32}$-inch tread depth.

13. **a.** The oil pressure gauge should come up to normal within seconds of starting the engine. If the gauge is low or if it drops or fluctuates, turn off the engine and have it checked.

14. **d.** Water can cause brakes to weaken, apply unevenly, or grab. If this happens, you might lose braking power, experience wheel lockups, feel pulling to one side or the other, or undergo jackknifing.

15. **b.** The total weight of a single vehicle and its load is the gross vehicle weight (GVW).

16. **d.** Too much weight on the front axle will make your CMV hard to steer. If you have too little weight on this axle, you won't be able to steer safely.

17. **c.** If your engine is on fire, turn it off and don't open the hood if you don't have to. Shoot the fire extinguisher through louvers, the radiator, or from the underside of the vehicle.

18. **b.** Skids that occur while going too fast can usually be stopped by removing your foot from the accelerator.

19. **a.** When you load a flatbed, load the heaviest items over the axles when possible, since these areas are the strongest. After you do

this, distribute the rest of the cargo evenly in the front and back of the trailer.

20. a. Placards are signs on the outside of a vehicle warning others of danger. If you're transporting hazardous material, you'll have placards on the outside of the front and rear of the vehicle and on both sides.

21. a. To safely deal with a tailgater, increase your following distance, so there's room in front of your vehicle. Making more room in front of your vehicle gives a tailgater a place to go if he wants to pass you.

22. d. Responsible CMV drivers check their vehicles before a trip (during pre-trip inspection), while driving (en-route inspection), whenever they make stops, and after their trip (or post-trip inspection).

23. b. Some large vehicles are equipped with curved mirrors, sometimes called convex, fisheye, bug-eye, or spot mirrors. These mirrors allow you to see more than flat mirrors do, but images in these mirrors appear smaller and farther away than they actually are, which is why it's important to look in both mirrors.

24. a. You should shift your transmission into a lower gear before going downhill. Don't wait until you build speed to downshift or you might not be able to find a gear and could seriously damage the transmission.

25. b. You can't rely on your hearing when crossing railroad tracks because the sounds of a commercial vehicle might drown out a train's horn. Since warning signals and gates might not work properly, always approach railroad tracks as though a train is coming.

26. a. Because unconfined livestock can rock a CMV, securing devices called false bulkheads are often used to group the livestock together and prevent their movement. Even with the use of false bulkheads, however, livestock are known to lean on curves, which shifts the center of gravity and can cause your CMV to tip. Because of this, you have to turn especially slowly when transporting livestock.

27. d. Metal coils are very heavy and circular shaped, so they can roll, which makes them more likely to break loose and fall off a trailer. Because of this, the FMCSA has specific rules about how metal coils must be tied down on a trailer. The center of a metal coil is called the "eye." During transportation, metal coils may be placed on a trailer so that the eyes are vertical, crosswise, or lengthwise

28. b. Three factors dictate stopping distance: perception distance, reaction distance, and braking distance. These factors are added together to determine total stopping distance. Air brake vehicles have one more factor called "brake lag."

29. b. Escape ramps are designed to stop runaway vehicles without injuring drivers or passengers. An escape ramp consists of a long upgrade, a long bed of loose material such as gravel, or both. If your brakes fail while you're driving on a downgrade, look for signs indicating an escape ramp.

30. d. In stab braking, you apply your brakes all the way and release them when they lock up. When your wheels begin to roll, apply the brakes all the way again.

General Knowledge Practice Test 2

1.	ⓐ	ⓑ	ⓒ	ⓓ	11.	ⓐ	ⓑ	ⓒ	ⓓ	21.	ⓐ	ⓑ	ⓒ	ⓓ
2.	ⓐ	ⓑ	ⓒ	ⓓ	12.	ⓐ	ⓑ	ⓒ	ⓓ	22.	ⓐ	ⓑ	ⓒ	ⓓ
3.	ⓐ	ⓑ	ⓒ	ⓓ	13.	ⓐ	ⓑ	ⓒ	ⓓ	23.	ⓐ	ⓑ	ⓒ	ⓓ
4.	ⓐ	ⓑ	ⓒ	ⓓ	14.	ⓐ	ⓑ	ⓒ	ⓓ	24.	ⓐ	ⓑ	ⓒ	ⓓ
5.	ⓐ	ⓑ	ⓒ	ⓓ	15.	ⓐ	ⓑ	ⓒ	ⓓ	25.	ⓐ	ⓑ	ⓒ	ⓓ
6.	ⓐ	ⓑ	ⓒ	ⓓ	16.	ⓐ	ⓑ	ⓒ	ⓓ	26.	ⓐ	ⓑ	ⓒ	ⓓ
7.	ⓐ	ⓑ	ⓒ	ⓓ	17.	ⓐ	ⓑ	ⓒ	ⓓ	27.	ⓐ	ⓑ	ⓒ	ⓓ
8.	ⓐ	ⓑ	ⓒ	ⓓ	18.	ⓐ	ⓑ	ⓒ	ⓓ	28.	ⓐ	ⓑ	ⓒ	ⓓ
9.	ⓐ	ⓑ	ⓒ	ⓓ	19.	ⓐ	ⓑ	ⓒ	ⓓ	29.	ⓐ	ⓑ	ⓒ	ⓓ
10.	ⓐ	ⓑ	ⓒ	ⓓ	20.	ⓐ	ⓑ	ⓒ	ⓓ	30.	ⓐ	ⓑ	ⓒ	ⓓ

▶ General Knowledge Practice Test 2

You have the option of taking this practice test online to see your score instantly. See the insert at the back of this book for details.

Choose the correct answer. Mark the letter on the answer sheet on page 95.

1. Which of the following is true of your stopping distance on wet roads?
   a. It's cut in half.
   b. It decreases by 10 percent.
   c. It increases by 25 percent.
   d. It doubles.

2. When you begin a trip, how many miles can you drive before you must stop and check your cargo?
   a. 25
   b. 50
   c. 75
   d. 150

3. You should use the mirrors on your vehicle to
   a. check your tires.
   b. make lane changes.
   c. turn safely.
   d. all of the above.

4. Which of the following is true about using the correct gear on a downgrade when driving a newer truck?
   a. You should use the same gear going downhill as uphill.
   b. You should use a lower gear going downhill than you use uphill.
   c. You should use a higher gear going downhill than you use uphill.
   d. None of the above.

5. If you're backing with a trailer and the trailer begins to drift, you should
   a. countersteer away from the direction of the drift.
   b. keep the tractor and trailer as straight as possible.
   c. turn the steering wheel in the direction of the drift.
   d. pull forward to reposition your vehicle.

6. While signaling a turn, when should you cancel the signal?
   a. once you've begun turning
   b. about 3 seconds into the turn
   c. right after you've completed the turn
   d. about 30 seconds after the turn

7. Which of these has a high center of gravity?
   a. dry bulk
   b. livestock
   c. hanging meat
   d. all of the above

8. The distance it takes for your vehicle to stop once your foot has pushed the brake is called
   a. total stopping distance.
   b. braking distance.
   c. perception distance.
   d. reaction distance.

9. When you're loading cargo into a van, you should
   a. load the heaviest cargo over the axles.
   b. leave space between the rows of cargo.
   c. use strong cargo securement devices.
   d. load the heaviest cargo on the bottom.

10. Which of these is a type of retarder?
   a. electric
   b. hydraulic
   c. engine
   d. all of the above

11. When a vehicle is driven around a turn and its rear wheels follow a different path than its front wheels, it's called
   a. offtracking.
   b. hydroplaning.
   c. skidding.
   d. poor traction.

12. When driving a CMV, about how many seconds should you look ahead of your vehicle?
   a. 5
   b. 10
   c. 12
   d. 20

13. If you're driving a vehicle with a manual transmission, you should shift up when your vehicle's tachometer
   a. is at the top number of its RPM range.
   b. is at the bottom number of its RPM range.
   c. reaches the minimum speed for a gear.
   d. reaches the maximum speed for a gear.

14. About how many feet of light do low beams provide?
   a. 100
   b. 250
   c. 300
   d. 500

15. In hot weather, you should check your tires every
   a. 2 hours.
   b. 3 hours.
   c. 5 hours.
   d. none of the above.

16. If your driving axle is underloaded, your
   a. tires could lose traction.
   b. vehicle might be hard to steer.
   c. cargo might shift or fall off.
   d. center of gravity will be too high.

17. When should you use snub braking?
   a. on wet roads
   b. when driving at night
   c. on long, steep downgrades
   d. when you change gears

18. What is the best way to regain control of your vehicle if it hydroplanes?
   a. Accelerate immediately.
   b. Brake slowly and consistently.
   c. Shift to a lower gear instead of braking.
   d. Release the accelerator and push in the clutch.

19. To test hydraulic brakes for a leak, pump the brake pedal 3 times and then apply firm pressure. Then hold for 5 seconds. How can you tell if there is a leak?
    a. The pressure will increase.
    b. The pedal will move.
    c. The pressure will decrease.
    d. The pedal will stay still.

20. If you see rust around wheel nuts, it may mean that the nuts are
    a. broken.
    b. loose.
    c. cracked.
    d. bent.

21. What should you do if a tire is too hot to touch?
    a. Let out air until it cools.
    b. Have it changed.
    c. Check the tread depth.
    d. Remain stopped until it cools.

22. Which of the following safety equipment is optional?
    a. spare electrical fuses
    b. a fire extinguisher
    c. tire chains
    d. none of the above

23. Which of the following can cause you to have a greater overhead clearance?
    a. packed snow
    b. a repaved road
    c. heavy cargo
    d. an empty trailer

24. Which is a sign that a parking brake is in need of repair?
    a. It stops the vehicle.
    b. It only slows the vehicle.
    c. It will not hold.
    d. It pulls to one side.

25. While inspecting your vehicle, what should you check for when you inspect wheel bearing seals?
    a. leaks
    b. looseness
    c. cracks
    d. none of the above

26. The total weight of the powered unit plus a trailer and its cargo is the
    a. axle weight.
    b. gross combination weight (GCW).
    c. gross vehicle weight (GVW).
    d. gross combination weight rating (GCWR).

27. What is the purpose of the suspension system?
    a. to support the vehicle
    b. to support the load
    c. to keep the axles in place
    d. all of the above

28. When inspecting brakes, you should inspect brake drums for
    a. leaks.
    b. contamination.
    c. tensile strength.
    d. cracks.

29. What is the minimum number of tie downs you can use to secure cargo loaded on a flatbed?
  a. 1
  b. 2
  c. 3
  d. 4

30. What is black ice?
  a. a thin layer of ice on pavement
  b. melting ice covering pavement
  c. shaded areas with slippery ice
  d. none of the above

► **Answers and Explanations**

1. d. A wet road can actually double your stopping distance. When driving on wet roads, reduce your "dry-road speed" by one-third (i.e., from 55 mph to 35 mph).

2. b. You're required by law to inspect your cargo (if it's not in a sealed container) 50 miles into a trip. After that, inspect it every 150 miles or 3 hours—whichever comes first.

3. d. You should always use your mirrors when making lane changes, merging, and turning. You should also use your mirrors in tight spaces and on congested roads to make sure you have enough room to drive without hitting anything. Look in your mirrors for any signs of tire trouble (loose or flapping tread, smoke, fire, or flats).

4. b. Newer trucks work better when drivers use a lower gear going downhill than they would use going uphill.

5. c. If your trailer does begin to drift, correct the drift immediately by turning the steering wheel in the direction of the drift.

6. c. When turning, signal several seconds before you turn. Don't remove your hands from the wheel to cancel a signal until you have completed a turn. If your vehicle doesn't have a self-canceling signal, turn off your signal once you've completed the turn.

7. d. Livestock stand tall, so they have a high center of gravity. Hanging meat and dry bulk are also types of cargo with a high center of gravity. All three types of cargo can shift, so when you're hauling this type of cargo, you need to drive very slowly around curves.

8. b. The braking distance is the distance it takes for your vehicle to stop once your foot has pushed the brake.

9. d. When loading a van, load the heaviest cargo on the bottom and work your way up to the lightest. It's safest to load the cargo using a tiered effect, as if you were laying bricks.

10. d. The four main types of retarders are (1) exhaust, (2) engine, (3) hydraulic, and (4) electric.

11. a. Your CMV needs a lot of space around it in order to turn without hitting another vehicle. You'll make wide turns and have to deal with offtracking (when your CMV goes around a corner and its rear wheels follow a different path than its front wheels).

12. c. Commercial drivers should look at least 12 to 15 seconds ahead of their vehicles. If you're driving at a lower speed, this is about one-eighth of a mile (one city block) ahead of your vehicle. If you're driving faster (highway speeds), it's about one-quarter of a mile.

13. a. If you're driving a manual transmission, shift up when your tachometer is at the top number of the range.

14. b. Low beams allow you to see only about 250 feet ahead of you. Reduce your speed when you must rely on low beams alone.

15. a. In hot weather, check your tires every 2 hours or every 100 miles. Air pressure can increase when the temperature is high.

16. a. If you load too little weight on the drive axle, you're underloading this axle. An underloaded driving axle could cause your tires to lose traction, and you might not be able to drive in bad weather.

17. c. Snub braking is the proper technique for long steep downgrades. When snub braking, first apply the brakes just enough to feel a definite slowdown. When your speed has been reduced to around 5 mph below the posted or safe speed, release the brakes. Let your speed increase back to the posted or safe speed and then repeat the procedure.

18. d. Accelerating or braking may cause you to lose complete control of your vehicle. The best way to regain control when you're hydroplaning is to release the accelerator and push in the clutch. This usually does the trick. If your drive wheels start to skid, push in the clutch, so they're able to turn freely.

19. b. To check hydraulic brakes for a leak, pump the brake pedal 3 times. Then apply firm pressure to the pedal and hold it for 5 to 30 seconds. The pedal shouldn't move. If it does, this tells you that there might be a hydraulic leak, air in the lines, or another problem.

20. b. If you see rust around your wheel nuts, it may be a sign that your wheel nuts are loose. Sometimes wheel nuts aren't tight enough after a tire has been changed. If you see rust around your wheel nuts, check the tightness of the nuts to make sure your wheel is fastened securely to your vehicle.

21. d. If a tire is too hot to touch, remain stopped until it cools. A tire that's excessively hot might blow or catch fire.

22. c. Spare electrical fuses, three red reflective triangles, and a fire extinguisher are required safety items that you must have in your CMV. Tire chains are optional, but some states require you to use them in the winter.

23. c. Heavy cargo will cause the height of your vehicle to be lower than it is when empty. Just because you were able to get under a bridge when you were loaded doesn't mean that you can clear that same bridge when you're empty.

24. c. To test the parking brake, put the vehicle in a low gear and gently pull forward against the parking brake. Do the same for the trailer when the trailer parking brake is set and the power unit parking brakes are released (if applicable). If the parking brake doesn't hold, you'll know that you have to get it fixed before you can drive your vehicle.

25. a. When you inspect your vehicle's wheels, you should check to make sure the wheel bearing seals aren't leaking.

26. b. Gross combination weight (GCW) is the total weight of a powered unit plus trailer or trailers and cargo.

27. d. The suspension system supports the vehicle and its load and keeps the axles in place.

28. d. Brake drums crack over time, so inspect them carefully before heading onto the road and during a trip.

29. b. You should include at least one tie down per 10 feet of cargo, but no matter how small the cargo, secure it with at least two tie downs.

30. a. Black ice is a layer of ice so thin and clear that the road appears wet rather than icy. If the temperature is below freezing and the road appears wet, be prepared to encounter black ice.

6 ▶ Air Brakes

CHAPTER SUMMARY

Many CMVs are equipped with air brakes. If you plan on operating one of these vehicles as a commercial driver, you must learn how they operate. The following chapter provides you with information about driving with air brakes and the components that make up the air brake system.

As you learned in Chapter 1, if you plan to drive a CMV with air brakes, you need to pass the Air Brakes Knowledge Test and the Air Brakes Skills Test. On the knowledge test, you'll have to show that you know about air brakes, and on the skills test, you'll have to show that you know how to use air brakes.

All Class A vehicles have air brakes, and most Class B vehicles have them. You may remember that you won't get an endorsement on your CDL for passing tests about air brakes. If you choose not to take the tests, however, or if you don't pass them, you get a restriction on your CDL. Your CDL will have the letter code L printed on it, which means, "Restricts the driver to vehicles not equipped with air brakes."

An air brake system is complicated, and understanding the way its many parts work is difficult. Fortunately, on the knowledge test, you'll be asked only about the major parts of an air brake system, how to use this system, and how it can fail.

▶ The Air Brakes Knowledge Test

On the Air Brakes Knowledge Test, there are 25 multiple-choice questions, and you'll have to answer 20 questions, or 80 percent, correctly to pass.

You learned earlier in this book that air brakes work using compressed air. They're a safe and effective way to stop a large and heavy vehicle—provided they're maintained properly and used correctly.

The Three Different Systems of Air Brakes

An air brake system is actually comprised of three different braking systems:

1. service brake system
2. parking brake system
3. emergency brake system

You use the **service brake system** during normal driving to apply the brakes by stepping on the brake pedal. This is the brake system you'll use most often. When you apply the parking brake, you use the **parking brake system**. Suppose your brakes fail. If you're in an emergency situation like this, the **emergency brake**

system will use parts of the service and parking brake systems to stop your vehicle.

Parts of an Air Brake System

You just learned that an air brake system is complicated, because it contains many parts. The major parts of an air brake system, the parts you need to know to pass the knowledge portion of the Air Brakes Test, are discussed in this chapter.

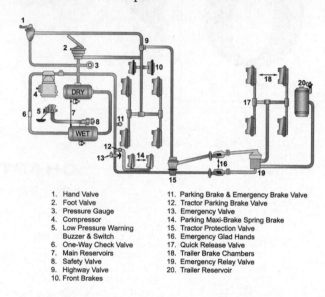

1. Hand Valve	11. Parking Brake & Emergency Brake Valve
2. Foot Valve	12. Tractor Parking Brake Valve
3. Pressure Gauge	13. Emergency Valve
4. Compressor	14. Parking Maxi-Brake Spring Brake
5. Low Pressure Warning	15. Tractor Protection Valve
Buzzer & Switch	16. Emergency Glad Hands
6. One-Way Check Valve	17. Quick Release Valve
7. Main Reservoirs	18. Trailer Brake Chambers
8. Safety Valve	19. Emergency Relay Valve
9. Highway Valve	20. Trailer Reservoir
10. Front Brakes	

Figure 6.2. The Components of an Air Brake System

Air Compressor

The air compressor pulls in the air around it and pumps this air into small storage tanks. When air is pumped into these tanks, it compresses, so pressure builds inside the tank.

Different types of air compressors have different types of cooling systems. Some are air-cooled, while others are cooled using the engine cooling system. The air compressor gets its power from the engine, so it's usually mounted on the side of the engine. Most are gear driven directly from the engine, but some may be belt driven. If your air compressor has V-belts, check to make sure they're in good condition before driving. They shouldn't have cracks in them. Some air com-

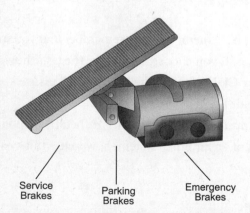

Service Brakes   Parking Brakes   Emergency Brakes

Figure 6.1. The Three Major Parts of an Air Brake System

pressors have their own oil supply, but most use the engine oil for lubrication. If your air compressor has its own oil supply, check the oil level before driving.

Air Governor

The **air governor** is located on the compressor. It "governs," or controls, the amount of air pressure in the system. When the air pressure rises, it reaches a **cut-out level**, usually between 120 and 130 psi, and the governor stops the compressor from pumping additional air. When the pressure is reduced and falls within a **cut-in level**, usually between 90 psi and 100 psi, the governor allows the compressor once again to pump air.

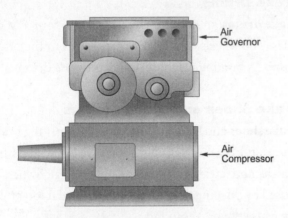

Figure 6.3. Air Compressor and Air Governor

Air Storage Tanks

The **air storage tanks** on a vehicle are also called **air tanks** or **air reservoirs**. These tanks hold enough air to stop your vehicle a few times—even if the air compressor stops working. The number and size of air tanks depend on your vehicle.

Air Tank Drains

Air tank drains are usually at the bottom of the tanks. Oil and water accumulate in the tanks, and this is bad for your air brake system. If the weather is cold, the oil and water may freeze, which can cause your brakes to fail.

The oil and water in air tanks have to be drained daily to keep your CMV working properly. If your air brakes have a manual drain, you have to turn a handle or pull a cord to drain the air tanks. You don't have to do anything if your air tanks have an automatic drain, but you'll hear the drain working each day. Some air tanks with automatic drains also have an electric heater, which offers additional protection by ensuring that the automatic drain doesn't freeze.

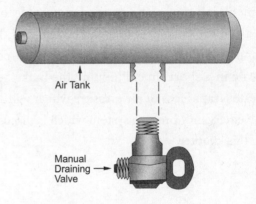

Figure 6.4. A Manual Air Tank Drain

Alcohol Evaporator

If ice forms inside your air brake system, it may stop working. Alcohol can prevent water from turning to ice, so some air brake systems have an alcohol evaporator that releases alcohol into the system as needed. If your air brake system has an alcohol evaporator, check the alcohol container and fill it when it's low—every day in very cold weather. Note that if you have a manual drain, you still have to release the water and oil each day even if your system has an alcohol evaporator.

Safety Release Valve

The first air tank that the air compressor pumps air into has a **safety release valve**, which protects the tank and the entire air brake system from too much pressure. The safety valve is usually set to open at 150 psi.

If your safety valve releases air, something is wrong and you need to call a mechanic.

Brake Pedal

The **brake pedal** is also called the **foot pedal**, the **foot brake**, or the **treadle valve**. When you apply pressure on the brake pedal, air is forced through the lines to the brakes. The harder you push down on the brake pedal, the harder you apply the brakes. When you let up the pressure on the brake pedal, you reduce the pressure and some air is let out of the system. It is possible to use all the air in the tanks before it can be replaced. This can happen if you push down on the brake pedal repeatedly in a short time. Pumping the brake pedal will create a rapid loss of air pressure which will activate the emergency braking system which is discussed later in this chapter.

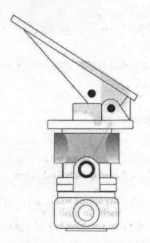

Figure 6.5. The Brake Pedal

S-Cam Drum Brakes

A **foundation brake** is at the end of each wheel. While there are several types of foundation brakes, the most common is the **s-cam drum brake**. You need to know the parts of this brake to pass your test.

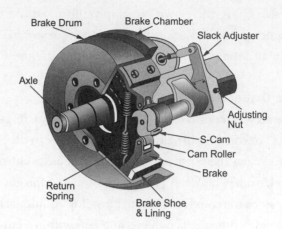

Figure 6.6. S-Cam Drum Brake

Brake Drums

Brake drums are located at each end of your CMV's axles. The wheels on the axles are bolted to the brake drums. A braking mechanism is inside the drum.

Brake Shoes and Brake Linings

Brake shoes and **brake linings** press against the brake drum and create friction, which slows or stops the vehicle and creates heat. Too much heat, which is caused by pushing down on the brake pedal too often, can cause the brakes to fail.

Other Parts

When you push down on the brake pedal, the system releases air into the brake chamber (See Figure 6.6). The air pressure pushes out a rod, called a **pushrod**, and moves the **slack adjuster**. One end of the slack adjuster is attached to the pushrod and the other end is attached to the brake camshaft. When the slack adjuster is moved, it twists the brake camshaft, which turns the s-cam. The s-cam forces the brake shoes away from each other and pushes them against the inside of the brake drum, creating friction. When you take your foot off the brake pedal, the s-cam turns back to its original place and a return spring pulls the brake shoes away from the drum. Then the brake is no longer applied and the wheels can turn freely again.

Wedge Brakes and Disc Brakes

Wedge brakes and **disc brakes** are two other types of foundation brakes. In wedge brakes, the chamber pushrod pushes a wedge between the ends of the brake shoes. Disc brakes are like s-cam brakes in that air pressure acts on a brake chamber and a slack adjuster. In disc brakes, however, a power screw is used instead of an s-cam, and the pressure of the brake chamber on the slack adjuster turns the power screw. The power screw clamps the disc or rotor between the brake lining pads of a **caliper**, which is similar to a large c-clamp.

Warnings and Pressure Gauges

It's extremely important to be able to stop your CMV when you need to. Because air brakes are so important, CMVs are equipped with numerous warnings and pressure gauges.

Supply Pressure Gauge

All vehicles with air brakes have a **supply pressure gauge** on the air tank, which tells you how much pressure is in the air tank. If your CMV has a dual air brake system, which you'll read about later in this chapter, it will have a gauge on each tank or a single gauge with two needles, one for each half of the system.

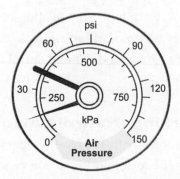

Figure 6.7. Supply Pressure Gauge

Low Air Pressure Warning Signal

All CMVs with air brakes must have a **low air pressure warning signal**. If your air pressure drops below 60 psi, or one-half the compressor governor's cut-out level on older vehicles, a warning light (usually red) will come on and a buzzer will sound.

Some older CMVs will also give you a warning called a **wigwag**. With this type of warning, a mechanical arm drops into your view if the pressure in the system drops below 60 psi. If the wigwag in your CMV is automatic, it returns to its normal position once the pressure rises to a safe level. If the wigwag is manual, however, you'll have to manually place it into the "out-of-view" position.

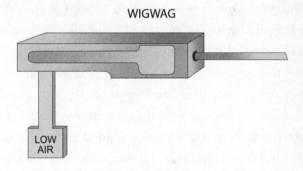

Figure 6.8. A Wigwag

Application Pressure Gauge

Some CMVs have an **application pressure gauge**, which shows how much air pressure you're applying to the brakes. If the pressure indicated on this gauge continues to increase to maintain the same speed, it could mean your brakes are fading, so you should slow down and use a lower gear.

Stop-Light Switch

If your CMV has an air brake system, an air-activated electric switch called a **stop-light switch** turns on your brake lights when you step on the brake pedal. This

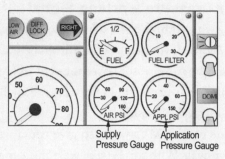

Figure 6.9. Application Pressure Gauge

switch warns drivers behind you that you're applying your brakes.

Front-Brake Limiting Valve

If you drive a CMV made before 1975, it may have a **front-brake limiting valve** and a control in the cab. This kind of valve was supposed to reduce the chances of skidding on slippery surfaces by reducing air pressure to the front brakes by half if the control was switched from "normal" to "slippery." This was found to actually reduce vehicle stopping power. Tests have shown that front wheel braking is good under all conditions. For these reasons, keep the front-brake-limiting valve in the "normal" position at all times. Many vehicles now have automatic front-wheel limiting valves that reduce air to front wheel brakes except during emergency braking.

Spring Brakes

You already learned that if you apply your brakes too often and/or too quickly, they might fail. To keep commercial drivers safe, tractors and buses are equipped with emergency brakes controlled by springs—in case all the air in the air tanks is released. **Spring brakes**, often called **fail-safe brakes**, are powerful springs held back by air pressure. When the air is released, the springs put on the brakes. On most tractors and buses, the spring brakes are emergency brakes and parking brakes.

Keep in mind that, in an emergency, when the air pressure drops to about 20–40 psi, the remaining air will be automatically released and the spring brakes will be fully applied. This is why warning signals come on when the pressure drops to about 60 psi. As soon as you see or hear these warning signals, find a place to stop to avoid your spring brakes locking up and while you can still control the brakes on your CMV.

Parking Brake Controls

To put on the parking brakes in a newer CMV, you pull a diamond-shaped yellow knob. When you push in the knob, the parking brake is released. In an older CMV, you might have to pull a lever to activate the parking brake.

Never push down on the brake pedal when the emergency brake or the parking brake—the spring brakes—are on. Your CMV's brakes may be damaged by the force of both brakes. While some CMVs are designed so you can't activate both the air brakes and the spring brakes, others aren't. It's a good idea, therefore, to remember not to press on the brake pedal when the spring brakes are on.

Modulating-Control Valve

A **modulating-control valve** is a control handle on the dashboard that allows you to gradually apply the spring brakes if the service brakes fail. The more you move the control handle, the harder the brakes come on. If you want to park a vehicle with a modulating-control valve, move the lever as far as it will go and lock it in position. Not all CMVs have a modulating-control valve, however.

Dual-Parking Control Valve

Some CMVs, mainly buses, have a separate air tank that you can use to supply air so you can release the spring brakes once they're applied and move the vehicle in an emergency. Vehicles with a separate air tank also have a **dual-parking control valve** in which one valve is used to put on the spring brakes (push-pull type) and another is used to release them. This valve is spring loaded in the out position and must be held in to release the brakes. Being able to do this is extremely beneficial. Suppose your spring brakes are applied and you're in the middle of a busy intersection. If your CMV has a dual-parking control valve, you can release the spring brakes, drive the vehicle, and park it in a safer place. The tank holds only enough air to do this a few times, however, so plan your movements carefully. Once the tank runs out of air and the spring brakes are activated, you'll be stuck in this place.

Antilock Braking Systems (ABS)

An **antilock braking system** (ABS) is a computerized system that keeps your wheels from locking up when you're braking hard. While it may not decrease your stopping distance, it does help you keep your vehicle under control. Truck tractors with air brakes built on or after March 1, 1997, and other vehicles with air brakes (trucks, buses, trailers, and converter dollies) built on or after March 1, 1998, are required to have ABS. To see if your CMV has ABS, check the certification label. Also, tractors, trucks, and buses with ABS will have yellow malfunction lamps on the instrument panels, so you can tell if something isn't working properly. Trailers will have yellow ABS malfunction lamps on either the front or the rear corner of the left side of the trailer. These lamps will be visible in the driver side mirror.

On newer vehicles, the malfunction lamp will come on for a bulb check when you start the CMV and then will quickly go out. On older vehicles, the lamp may stay on until you're driving over 5 mph. If the lamp doesn't go out fairly quickly or comes on again once you're driving at a normal speed, you may have lost ABS control in one or more wheels.

If one of the vehicles in your combination doesn't have ABS, use stopping methods for non-ABS vehicles.

Dual Air Brake Systems

A **dual air brake system** has two separate air brake systems—two air tanks, hoses, lines, and so on—and a single set of controls. Why do you need two separate air brake systems? Having two systems gives you greater protection when driving a heavy-duty CMV, because you're less likely to have complete brake failure. The primary air brake system controls the regular brakes on the rear axle or axles. The secondary air brake system controls the brakes on the front axle and sometimes also on one rear axle. Both the primary and the secondary air brake systems supply air to the trailer, if one is attached.

You learned earlier that a dual air brake system has an air gauge for each system, but may have one gauge with two needles, one needle for each system. If your vehicle has a dual air brake system, you have to allow the air compressor time to build pressure before driving. The pressure in both systems should be at least 100 psi before you begin driving the CMV.

Pay attention to the gauge or gauges, low air pressure warning light, and buzzer as you drive. The warning light and buzzer should come on before the air pressure drops below 60 psi in either system. Once the air pressure in the systems rises to more than 60 psi, the warning light and buzzer should shut off. Low pressure in an air brake system means it's not fully operating. Have the problem fixed before you continue driving.

Inspecting Air Brakes

Inspecting your air brakes to make sure they're working properly *before* you begin driving can save your life and the lives of others on the road. Follow these steps when inspecting air brakes:

1. **Check the air compressor drive belt (if equipped) to make sure that it's tight and in good condition.** The belt shouldn't be cracked.

2. **Check the slack adjusters on the s-cam brakes.** Drive your CMV onto level ground. Chock your CMV's wheels (use a wedge or block to steady them) to prevent them from moving. Turn off the parking brake. Wearing gloves, pull hard on each slack adjuster within your reach. A slack adjuster shouldn't move more than an inch where the pushrod attaches to it. If a slack adjuster moves more than this, it needs adjustment. Too much slack may make it difficult to stop your CMV.

   Be aware that vehicles built since 1991 have automatic slack adjusters. Automatic adjusters shouldn't have to be manually adjusted during routine inspections. The only time automatic adjusters should require manual adjustment is when a mechanic is performing maintenance on the brakes or is installing the slack adjusters. If your CMV has automatic adjusters and the pushrod stroke exceeds the legal brake adjustment limit, there may be a mechanical problem within the adjuster or the related foundation brake components or the adjuster may not have been properly installed.

   If you manually adjust an automatic adjuster to force the pushrod stroke within legal limits, you're not fixing the underlying problem. Also, doing this will cause the adjuster to prematurely wear out. If an automatic adjuster is out of adjustment, take your CMV to a repair facility as soon as possible.

   Different manufacturers make automatic slack adjusters, so the adjusters don't all operate the same way. Consult the service manual for the manufacturer of your slack adjusters if you think you have a problem with adjustment.

3. **Check the brake drums or discs, linings, and hoses.** If brake drums or discs have cracks, check their length. Cracks shouldn't be longer than one-half of the friction area. If they are, they're out of service and you shouldn't drive your CMV until they're repaired. You learned earlier that brake linings, along with brake shoes, press against the brake drum and create friction. Your brake linings shouldn't be soaked in oil or grease and they shouldn't be too thin.

   Check the air hoses connected to the brake chambers to make sure that they aren't cracked or worn and aren't rubbing against other hoses.

4. **Test the air leakage rate.** When your air system is fully charged—when the gauge reads about 125 psi—chock the wheels, turn off the engine, turn on the key, and release the parking brakes. After the initial drop in air pressure, time how long it takes the air pressure to drop. In a straight truck (a single vehicle), the air leakage rate should be less than 2 psi in 1 minute. In a combination vehicle, the leaking rate should be less than 3 psi in 1 minute. Then, use the brake pedal to apply 90 psi or more to the braking system. After the initial pressure drop, time the leakage rate again. With the service brake applied, a straight truck (single vehicle) should have a loss rate of less than 3 psi in 1 minute. In a combination vehicle, the leakage rate should be less than 4 psi in 1

minute. If the air leakage rate exceeds these guidelines, air is leaking too quickly and there may be an air leak. Have your CMV checked before you drive it to make certain your brakes don't fail while you're driving.

Straight Truck
Less than 2 psi per minute

Combination Truck
Less than 3 psi per minute

Figure 6.10. Air Leaking Rates

5. **Test the low air pressure warning signal.** You learned earlier that the low air pressure warning signal is usually a red light—sometimes accompanied by a buzzer—that comes on if your air pressure drops below 60 psi. To test the low air pressure warning signal, you will continue where you left off in step 4 with engine shut off, key on, wheels chocked, and brakes released. Fan down the brakes by stepping on and off the brake pedal. This will reduce the air tank pressure. The low air pressure warning signal should come on before the pressure drops to less than 60 psi. If your CMV has dual air brake systems, the low air pressure warning signal should come on in the tank with the lowest

air pressure. If it doesn't come on, get it repaired before driving.

6. **Check that your spring brakes come on automatically.** To check that your spring brakes will come on in an emergency, continue stepping on and off the brake pedal to reduce the pressure in the air tank. Pump the brakes until the parking brake control knob pops out. This usually happens between 20 and 40 psi, but check your manufacturer's specifications for your particular CMV.

7. **Check the rate of air pressure buildup.** Continuing from step 6, you'll start your vehicle and rev the engine between 1300 and 1500 RPM. The air pressure should start to build in the system. As the needles rise, the low air pressure warning light and buzzer should go off around 60 psi. As the engine is at operating RPM, the air pressure should build from 85 psi to 100 psi within 45 seconds. If the pressure doesn't build according to these guidelines, there's a problem.

8. **Check the air compressor governor cut-in and cut-out pressures.** In the beginning of this chapter, you learned that the air governor controls the amount of air in the system. You learned that when the air pressure reaches a cut-out level, usually between 120 and 130 psi, the governor stops the compressor from pumping additional air. Likewise, when the air pressure falls within a cut-in level, usually about 100 psi, the governor allows the compressor to pump air once again.

   To check that the governor is operating as it should, continue to run the engine at a fast idle as indicated in step 7, and check that the governor stops the air compressor at the cut-out level. Then, with the engine idling, step on and off the brake to reduce the air pressure between 90 and 100 psi. Check to make sure the compressor cuts in at the correct level. You will know that the governor cut in when the needles start to rise back to the cut-out level. (Note that the exact psi may vary from vehicle to vehicle, so you should check the manufacturer's specifications.) If your air governor doesn't work as it should, it may need to be repaired.

9. **Test your parking brake.** With your CMV stopped, apply the parking brakes, put your vehicle in a low forward gear, and ease up on the clutch to give a gentle tug. For a combination vehicle you need the parking brake (tractor) applied and the emergency brake (trailer) released. Put your vehicle into a low forward gear and ease up on the clutch to give a gentle tug. If the parking brake is working correctly, it will keep the CMV from moving.

10. **Test your emergency brakes.** With your CMV stopped, apply the emergency brake (trailer) and release your parking brake (tractor). Put your vehicle in a low forward gear and ease up on your clutch to give a gentle tug. If the emergency brake is working correctly, it will keep the CMV from moving.

11. **Test your service brakes.** Once air pressure has built up to a normal level, release the parking brake and move the vehicle ahead slowly at about 5 mph. Your hands should be on the steering wheel at the 3 o'clock and 9 o'clock positions. Then apply the brakes firmly. The brakes should stop your CMV

without delay and without pulling to one side.

Note that some truck tractors are equipped with a trailer brake on the dash, also known as a trolley brake. You will need to test this also by releasing your brakes, putting the transmission in a low forward gear, pulling down on the trolley brake, and then easing up on the clutch to give a gentle tug. If the brake is working properly, the vehicle won't move.

▶ Part 2: The Air Brakes Skills Test

You learned that you need to take and pass both a knowledge test and a skills test on air brakes to avoid having an air brake restriction on your CDL. In this section, you'll learn the skills you need to drive a CMV equipped with air brakes.

Making Normal Stops

For normal stops, push down the brake pedal smoothly and steadily so you come to a smooth, safe stop. If your CMV has a manual transmission, don't push in the clutch until the engine is nearly idling. When you come to a complete stop, select a starting gear.

Using an Antilock Braking System

If your CMV doesn't have ABS and you brake on a slippery surface, your wheels may lock up and you'll lose control of your steering. You might skid, jackknife, or spin your CMV. ABS helps you maintain control of your vehicle at all times. It is controlled by a computer, which senses when your brakes are about to lock up and then reduces the braking pressure so you can stay in control of your CMV.

Having ABS on your CMV doesn't necessarily mean that you can stop faster, but it will help you steer around a hazard or stop suddenly while braking.

You might not have ABS on your entire CMV. You might have it on only the tractor or on only the trailer. More rarely, you might have ABS on only one axle. Having ABS on any part of your CMV is better than not having ABS at all.

ABS on the trailer only. ABS on a trailer only requires you to drive and stop as if you have no ABS. However, if you lose control of the steering or start to jackknife, let up on the brakes.

ABS on the tractor only. If you have ABS on only the tractor, you should be able to maintain control with less chance of jackknifing. If the trailer begins to swing out, however, let up on the brakes.

ABS on a tractor-trailer combination. Follow these guidelines for braking when a tractor and trailer both have air brakes with ABS:

- Brake with firm, constant pressure. Do not pump the brakes.
- Brake only as much as you need to stop safely.
- During an emergency situation that requires you to stop quickly, apply brakes and hold. The ABS will automatically apply or release individual brakes to prevent lockup, which allows your vehicle to stop in a straight line. When the ABS is working, you may feel a pulsating effect in the vehicle. Do not release the pressure on the brake pedal unless you have avoided the emergency situation.
- When you slow down, keep an eye on both the tractor and trailer. Ease up on the brakes whenever it's safe to do so.

- If you're driving a straight truck or a combination vehicle with ABS on all axles, you can brake fully in an emergency situation.

Keep in mind that if your ABS doesn't work properly, you still have regular brakes, so you can safely drive to a service facility. However, you'll want to get them checked out as soon as possible.

Making Emergency Stops

Occasionally, you'll have to make emergency stops while driving to avoid hazards such as a vehicle pulling out in front of you or a fallen object on the roadway. When you have to stop because of an emergency, you need to brake so that you can keep your CMV in a straight line while leaving yourself room to turn if you have to. You can use either controlled braking or stab braking to do this.

Controlled braking. In controlled braking, you apply the brakes as hard as you can—without locking the wheels. Don't attempt to turn the wheels while applying the brakes. Release the brakes if you need to

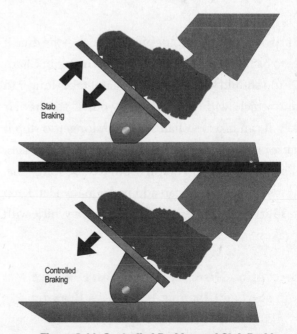

Figure 6.11. Controlled Braking and Stab Braking

Stopping Distance Chart						
Miles Per Hour	How Far CMV Will Travel in One Second	Driver Perception Distance	Driver Reaction Distance	Brake Lag Distance (only for CMVs with air brakes)	Vehicle Braking Distance	Total Stopping Distance
55 mph	81 feet	60 feet	60 feet	32 feet	170 feet	322 feet

Figure 6.12. Calculating Total Stopping Distance for a CMV with Air Brakes.

turn the wheels. Then apply the brakes again as soon as it's safe to do so.

Stab braking. In stab braking, you apply the brakes all the way and then release them when they lock up. (You learned about stab braking in Chapter 3.) As soon as the wheels start rolling—this can take up to a second—fully reapply the brakes. It's important not to apply the brakes before the wheels start rolling or your CMV won't straighten out.

▶ Stopping Distance

You learned about total stopping distance—the time it takes to bring your CMV to a complete halt—in Chapter 2. You should know, however, that it takes longer to stop a vehicle with air brakes. If your CMV has air brakes, it can take one-half second or longer to stop it because air has to flow through the lines to the brakes. While one-half second doesn't sound like a long time, in terms of distance, it can add up to many feet. Keep these four factors in mind when stopping a vehicle with air brakes:

> Perception Distance + Reaction Distance + Brake Lag Distance + Effective Braking Distance = Total Stopping Distance

If you're traveling at 55 mph, add about 32 feet to your stopping distance if your vehicle has air brakes and you're stopping on dry pavement. Your total stopping distance if you're traveling in a CMV with air brakes at 55 miles per hour is over 300 feet (see Figure 6.12).

▶ Avoiding Brake Fading or Failure

You learned earlier that air brakes are a great way to stop a CMV—if they are well-maintained and are used properly. Each time you apply your air brakes, brake shoes or pads rub against the brake drum or discs. This is what slows the vehicle. Each time this happens, however, heat is created. Air brakes are designed to withstand a lot of heat, but it's possible to overheat them. Excessive heat can cause your air brakes to fade because such high temperatures cause chemical changes in the brake lining, which reduces friction. So much heat also causes the brake drums to expand, which forces the brake shoes and linings to move farther apart to contact the drums, which once again reduces the force of contact. If you continue to overuse your brakes, they'll eventually fail.

If your brakes are out of adjustment, they're more likely to fail. (You learned about this in the section "Inspecting Air Brakes" in this chapter.) If some brakes on your CMV are out of adjustment, they won't work as well as those that are properly aligned. So the brakes that are adjusted properly will have to work extra hard, which can cause them to overheat and fade.

▶ Braking Properly

When you're driving down a steep downgrade, it's important to put your CMV in the correct lower gear, so you don't have to rely solely on your brakes. Then use the snub braking method to maintain the posted speed for the downgrade.

Follow these steps to brake properly once your vehicle is in the correct gear:

1. Apply the brakes. Don't apply the brakes harder than necessary. If you feel a definite slowdown, then you're applying them hard enough.
2. Release the brakes for about 3 seconds when your speed has been reduced to 5 mph below the posted safe speed.
3. When your speed increases to your safe speed, repeat steps 1 and 2.

Using Parking Brakes

Use your parking brakes whenever you park except when your brakes are very hot, such as when you've just

Figure 6.13. Signs That Prompt Drivers to Shift to a Lower Gear on Downgrades

driven down a steep downgrade, or if your brakes are very wet, such as in freezing temperatures. Let hot brakes cool before using parking brakes. If your brakes are wet, use the brakes lightly while driving in a low gear. This will heat and dry them. If necessary, use wheel chocks to hold the vehicle.

If your CMV doesn't have automatic air tank drains, drain the air tanks at the end of each day to remove moisture and oil. If you don't do this, you may not be able to release your parking brakes if the water and/or oil freezes.

Chapter 6 Review Quiz

1–7: Circle the correct answer.

1. What is the most common foundation brake found on CMVs?
   a. wedge
   b. s-cam
   c. disc
   d. chamber

2. Which braking system will you use most often?
   a. emergency
   b. parking
   c. safety release
   d. service

3. The part of the air brake system that pulls the air around it into the system is the
   a. air compressor.
   b. air governor.
   c. air storage tank.
   d. air tank drain.

4. The cut-out level for an air governor is usually about
   a. 60 psi.
   b. 90 psi.
   c. 100 psi.
   d. 125 psi.

5. What is the purpose of the alcohol evaporator?
   a. to reduce air pressure
   b. to keep water from turning to ice
   c. to soak up alcohol in the system
   d. to drain oil and water

6. What presses against the brake drum and creates friction?
   a. brake shoes
   b. brake linings
   c. both a and b
   d. neither a nor b

7. Which gauge shows how much pressure you're applying to the brakes?
   a. application pressure gauge
   b. low air pressure warning signal
   c. front-brake limiting valve
   d. supply pressure gauge

8–12: Indicate whether each statement is true or false.

_____ 8. A dual air brake system has a single set of controls.

_____ 9. In a dual air brake system, the secondary air brake system controls the regular brakes on the rear axle or axles.

_____ 10. The low air pressure warning signal comes on if your air pressure drops below 60 psi.

_____ 11. If your service brakes are working correctly, they'll pull your CMV to one side when you test them.

_____ 12. Having an ABS on only the tractor makes the trailer less likely to swing out.

Check your answers on page 294.

Air Brakes Endorsement Practice Test

1.	(a) (b) (c) (d)	11.	(a) (b) (c) (d)	21.	(a) (b) (c) (d)
2.	(a) (b) (c) (d)	12.	(a) (b) (c) (d)	22.	(a) (b) (c) (d)
3.	(a) (b) (c) (d)	13.	(a) (b) (c) (d)	23.	(a) (b) (c) (d)
4.	(a) (b) (c) (d)	14.	(a) (b) (c) (d)	24.	(a) (b) (c) (d)
5.	(a) (b) (c) (d)	15.	(a) (b) (c) (d)	25.	(a) (b) (c) (d)
6.	(a) (b) (c) (d)	16.	(a) (b) (c) (d)	26.	(a) (b) (c) (d)
7.	(a) (b) (c) (d)	17.	(a) (b) (c) (d)	27.	(a) (b) (c) (d)
8.	(a) (b) (c) (d)	18.	(a) (b) (c) (d)	28.	(a) (b) (c) (d)
9.	(a) (b) (c) (d)	19.	(a) (b) (c) (d)	29.	(a) (b) (c) (d)
10.	(a) (b) (c) (d)	20.	(a) (b) (c) (d)	30.	(a) (b) (c) (d)

▶ Air Brakes Endorsement Practice Test

Choose the correct answer. Mark the letter on the answer sheet on page 117.

1. Your spring brakes will be automatically applied at no less than
   a. 20 psi.
   b. 40 psi.
   c. 60 psi.
   d. 100 psi.

2. If your vehicle has s-cam drum brakes, what happens when you take your foot off the brake pedal?
   a. The brake shoes are forced away from each other.
   b. The brake shoes are pushed against the brake drum.
   c. The air pressure pushes out a pushrod.
   d. The s-cam turns back to its original position.

3. What do you have to do to drain your air tanks if you have a manual drain?
   a. Step on a treadle valve.
   b. Move a lever into the "down" position.
   c. Open a valve or pull a cord.
   d. Pull a diamond-shaped yellow knob.

4. What should you do instead of consistently applying your brakes on a steep downgrade?
   a. shift to a lower gear
   b. release the parking brake
   c. fully charge your system
   d. all of the above

5. In s-cam drum brakes, what moves the slack adjuster?
   a. brake linings
   b. a caliper
   c. the brake camshaft
   d. a pushrod

6. When you test your parking brakes, you stop your vehicle, apply the parking brake, and gently pull against it while in a lower gear. If your parking brakes are working correctly, your vehicle will
   a. move slowly.
   b. not move.
   c. pull to a side.
   d. not cut out.

7. Which of the following protects the air tank and the entire air brake system from too much pressure?
   a. an alcohol evaporator
   b. a modulating-control valve
   c. a stop-light switch
   d. a safety release valve

8. What is an advantage of a dual-parking control valve?
   a. It prevents your spring brakes from coming on unnecessarily.
   b. It allows you to gradually apply the spring brakes to better control your vehicle.
   c. It allows you to release the spring brakes and move the vehicle.
   d. It reduces the chances of skidding when driving on slippery surfaces.

9. What is the main advantage of a dual air brake system?
   a. better control
   b. greater protection
   c. a decreased stopping distance
   d. less chance of your wheels locking up

10. If you have an antilock braking system (ABS) on only the trailer and you start to lose control of your steering, what should you do?
   a. Ease up on the brakes.
   b. Apply your parking brake.
   c. Brake as you normally would.
   d. Employ stab braking.

11. When you apply the brakes as hard as you can without locking the wheels, it's called
   a. stab braking.
   b. press braking.
   c. controlled braking.
   d. none of the above.

12. If you're driving on dry pavement at 55 mph and your vehicle has air brakes, how many feet should you add to your stopping distance?
   a. 32
   b. 55
   c. 60
   d. 81

13. Which part of the air brake system controls the compressor?
   a. storage tank
   b. evaporator
   c. brake drum
   d. governor

14. What can happen if the oil and water in your air tank freezes?
   a. You will have to drain it immediately.
   b. Your brakes may fail.
   c. The pressure may build up.
   d. The compressor may stop working.

15. Where are brake drums located?
   a. at the end of each axle
   b. inside the brake mechanism
   c. at the end of each wheel
   d. none of the above

16. What happens when the air pressure in an air brake system is below 60 psi?
   a. The stop-light switch turns on.
   b. A warning light comes on.
   c. A wigwag goes out of view.
   d. The spring brakes are applied.

17. If you're checking the rate of air pressure buildup in a single air system (pre-1975), in 3 minutes the pressure should build from about 50 psi to
   a. 60 psi.
   b. 70 psi.
   c. 80 psi.
   d. 90 psi.

18. Which of the following is used to keep an air compressor cool?
   a. a V-belt
   b. an oil tank
   c. air or the engine cooling system
   d. all of the above

19. Why is there a brake lag distance in a vehicle with air brakes?

a. Air has to go through the lines to the brakes.

b. Pressure has to build up in the system.

c. The compressor needs to cut in at the correct level.

d. The low-pressure signal must turn off.

20. A slack adjuster needs adjustment if it moves more than

a. $1/2$ inch.

b. 1 inch.

c. 2 inches.

d. 6 inches.

21. You should brake fully in an emergency situation, if you are driving a

a. vehicle with ABS on only the trailer.

b. vehicle with ABS on only the tractor.

c. straight truck without ABS.

d. combination vehicle with ABS on all axles.

22. What holds back spring brakes during normal driving?

a. springs

b. air pressure

c. brake shoes

d. discs

23. When you test your service brakes, you should release the parking brake, drive slowly, and then apply the brakes. Which of the following indicates that there may be a problem?

a. a smooth stop

b. a release in pressure

c. an abrupt stop

d. a delay in stopping

24. If you have to make an emergency stop, you should brake

a. after you switch to a lower gear.

b. only as much as you need to stop safely.

c. so you can keep your vehicle straight and turn it, if necessary.

d. so you apply the brakes while turning the wheel.

25. Which is an example of stab braking?

a. releasing the brakes whenever you need to turn

b. applying the brakes hard without locking the wheels

c. turning the wheels sharply while applying the brakes

d. applying the brakes all the way and then releasing them

26. What do you have to do each day during cold weather if your air tanks have an automatic drain and an alcohol evaporator?

a. Check the alcohol container.

b. Turn on the electric heater.

c. Release the water and oil.

d. Turn on the safety release valve.

27. What should you do if your safety release valve releases air?

a. Activate the parking brake.

b. Pay attention to the gauges.

c. Call a mechanic right away.

d. Drive slowly in a lower gear.

28. What happens to the air pressure when you let up on the brake pedal?

a. It's reduced.

b. It's increased.

c. It's compressed.

d. none of the above

29. If the pressure in an air brake system has reached the cut-out level, the air compressor won't be allowed to pump air. In most systems, it will be allowed to pump air again once the pressure reaches a cut-in level of about

a. 60 psi.

b. 100 psi.

c. 120 psi.

d. 130 psi.

30. In a dual air brake system, the secondary air brake system controls the brakes on

a. all rear axles.

b. the front axle.

c. none of the above.

d. all of the above.

► **Answers and Explanations**

1. a. Your spring brakes will be automatically applied when the air pressure drops to no less than 20 psi and the remaining air is automatically released.

2. d. When you take your foot off the brake pedal, the s-cam turns back to its original position and a return spring pulls the brake shoes away from the drum. Then the brake is no longer applied and the wheels can turn freely again.

3. c. If your air brakes have a manual drain, you have to turn a handle or open a valve (petcock) to drain the air tanks; with an automatic drain, you don't have to do anything.

4. a. When you're driving down a steep downgrade, it's important to put your vehicle in a lower gear before starting down the hill so you don't have to rely solely on your air brakes, which can overheat and fade.

5. d. When you push down on the brake pedal, the system releases air into the brake chamber. The air pressure pushes out a rod, called a pushrod, and moves the slack adjuster.

6. b. To test your parking brakes, stop your vehicle, apply the parking brake, and gently pull against the brake in a lower gear. If the parking brake is working correctly, it will keep the vehicle from moving.

7. d. The safety release valve protects the tank and the entire air brake system from too much pressure. The safety valve is usually set to open at 150 psi.

8. c. A dual-parking control valve (usually found on buses) allows you to release the spring brakes that have been applied during an emergency, so you can move the vehicle.

9. b. A dual air brake system offers greater protection against brake failure. The primary air brake system controls the regular brakes on the rear axle or axles. The secondary air brake system controls the brakes on the front axle and sometimes also on one rear axle. Both systems supply air to the trailer, if there is one.

10. a. If you lose control of your steering when driving a vehicle with an antilock braking system (ABS) on only a trailer, let up on the brakes.

11. c. With controlled braking, you apply the brakes as hard as you can without locking the wheels.

12. a. If you're traveling at 55 mph on dry pavement, add about 32 feet to your stopping distance if your vehicle has air brakes. Your total stopping distance if you're traveling in a CMV with air brakes at 55 mph is over 300 feet.

13. d. The air governor is located on the compressor and governs, or controls, the amount of air pressure in the air tanks.

14. b. If the oil and water in your air tank freeze, they can cause your brakes to fail. This is why air tanks have drains at the bottom that allow you to release the oil and water. However, if the oil and water in the tank are frozen, you will not be able to drain the tank immediately.

15. a. Brake drums are located at each end of your CMV's axles. The wheels on the axles are bolted to the brake drums. A braking mechanism is inside the drum.

16. b. If your air pressure drops below 60 psi, or one-half the compressor governor's cut-out level on older vehicles, a red warning light comes on and a buzzer might sound.

17. d. In a single air system (pre-1975), the pressure should build from about 50 to 90 psi within 3 minutes. If the pressure doesn't build according to these guidelines, there's a problem.

18. c. Different types of air compressors have different types of cooling systems. Some are air-cooled; others are cooled by the engine cooling system.

19. a. It takes longer to stop a vehicle with air brakes because air has to flow through the lines to the brakes.

20. b. A slack adjuster shouldn't move more than 1 inch where the pushrod attaches to it. If it does, it most likely needs adjustment. Too much slack may make it difficult to stop your CMV.

21. d. If you're driving a combination vehicle or a straight truck with an antilock braking system (ABS) on all axles, you can brake fully in an emergency situation.

22. b. Spring brakes, often called fail-safe brakes, have powerful springs held back by air pressure.

23. d. When you test your service brakes, release the parking brake once air pressure has built up to a normal level and move the vehicle ahead slowly at about 5 mph. Then apply the brakes. If they're working properly, the brakes should stop your vehicle without any delay and without pulling to one side.

24. c. If you have to make an emergency stop, brake so that you can keep your vehicle in a straight line and allow you to turn if you have to. You can use either controlled braking or stab braking to do this.

25. d. With stab braking, you apply the brakes all the way and then release them when they lock up. Fully reapply the brakes as soon as the wheels start rolling.

26. a. If your air brake system has an alcohol evaporator, check the alcohol container and fill it when it's low. You'll have to fill it every day in very cold weather.

27. c. The safety valve is usually set to open at 150 psi. If your safety valve releases air, something is wrong and you need to call a mechanic.

28. a. When you let up the pressure on the brake pedal, you reduce the pressure and some air is let out of the system.

29. b. When the air pressure rises, it reaches a cut-out level, usually between 120 and 130 psi, and the governor stops the compressor from pumping additional air. When the pressure is reduced and falls within a cut-in level, usually around 100 psi, the governor allows the compressor once again to pump air.

30. b. The secondary air brake system controls the brakes on the front axle and sometimes also on one rear axle. Both the primary and the secondary air brake systems supply air to the trailer, if one is attached.

CHAPTER

7 ▶ Combination Vehicles

CHAPTER SUMMARY

Driving a combination vehicle is very different from driving a straight truck. This chapter will give you information about driving a combination vehicle safely and help you understand the special concerns that come with operating these vehicles.

A combination vehicle consists of a tractor or truck and a trailer that's used to haul cargo. Combination vehicles are longer and heavier than straight trucks are, and they're much more likely to roll over—you can't drive them like you would drive a straight truck or a car. Because of this, you need to pass a special knowledge test about combination vehicles before you can drive one. Be aware that you can't drive doubles and triples—very long tractor-trailers—by passing this test. You need to pass an additional test to drive doubles and triples. You'll learn about this test in Chapter 9.

On the Combination Vehicle Test, you'll be asked questions about:

- driving combination vehicles safely
- combination vehicle air brakes
- antilock braking systems
- coupling and uncoupling
- inspecting a combination vehicle

Of the 20 questions on the Combination Vehicle Test, you need to correctly answer 16, or 80 percent, to pass.

▶ Single-Unit Trucks

It's important to understand the difference between single-unit trucks and combination vehicles.

The cargo-carrying unit on a straight truck, or **single-unit truck**, is mounted on the same chassis as the engine, the cab, and the drive train. Single-unit trucks include trash trucks, dump trucks, and tank trucks, which are often called tankers. Single-unit trucks typically have two or three axles and aren't combination vehicles.

Specialized hauling vehicles (SHVs) are very common single-unit trucks. SHVs are designed to haul very heavy cargo that can't be divided into parts. They usually transport material such as ready-mix cement, grain, milk, gravel, and construction materials over short distances within one state.

▶ Conventional Combination Vehicles

A **combination vehicle**, on the other hand, is most often used to haul cargo over long distances across one or more states. A combination vehicle has two or more parts hooked—or coupled—together, and the cargo is hauled in a trailer attached to the truck or tractor. Combination vehicles come in many shapes and sizes, but most have five or six axles. You'll learn about some of the most common combination vehicles in this chapter.

A **tractor-trailer combination** consists of a tractor pulling a semitrailer or a semitrailer and one or two full trailers. A semitrailer is a trailer that can't stand on its own because the front must be attached to the tractor using the fifth wheel on the tractor and the kingpin on the semitrailer. (You'll learn more about these parts later in this chapter and in Chapter 9, "Doubles and Triples.") A semitrailer has axles only in the rear. A tractor-trailer combination consisting of a tractor and a semitrailer has five axles and is the most common type of combination vehicle.

A **full trailer**, on the other hand, is attached to a semitrailer, a straight truck, or another full trailer. A full trailer has axles in the front and rear and can stand without support. Both semitrailers and full trailers come in different lengths.

A **truck-trailer combination** is less common than a tractor-trailer combination. It consists of a straight truck pulling a full trailer.

Combination Vehicle Names

Some combination vehicles have informal names used within the trucking industry. Following are some of these names and their definitions:

- **big-rig**. a combination vehicle.
- **bobtail tractor**. a tractor without trailers attached to it.
- **double**. a tractor with two trailers attached to it, also called a double-trailer rig.
- **pup trailer**. a short semitrailer with a single axle.
- **semi**. a semitrailer.
- **single**. a tractor pulling a semitrailer.
- **triple**. a tractor with three trailers attached to it, also called a triple-trailer rig.

Single Unit Trucks

Truck-Trailer Combinations

Tractor-Semitrailer Combinations

STAA Double-Trailer Combination

Double-Trailer Combinations

Triple-Trailer Combination

Figure 7.1. Types of Combination Vehicles

The Approximate Distribution of Trucks on the Road				
Single-unit trucks	Truck-trailer combinations	Tractor-semitrailor combinations (primarily with five axles)	Double-trailer combinations	Triple-trailer combinations
68%	4%	26%	2%	less than 1%

► Driving Combination Vehicles Safely

Staying safe while driving a combination vehicle means knowing what could go wrong and how to prevent it from happening. It also means keeping the word *slow* in mind at all times. Whenever you're in doubt about what to do when driving a combination vehicle, consider slowing down. It could save your life and the lives of others.

Know Rollover Risks

More than half of all truck-driver deaths in crashes are from rollovers. Combination vehicles are much more likely to roll over than straight trucks because cargo piled high in trailers causes them to have a high center of gravity. In fact, if a fully loaded rig crashes, it's 10 times more likely to roll over than an empty rig.

You can do your best to prevent rollovers by following two important safety rules:

1. **Keep cargo as close to the ground and centered as possible.** Though this is an important rule for straight trucks, it's even more important for combination vehicles. Keeping cargo low and centered brings your vehicle's center of gravity closer to the road and reduces the chance that your load will shift and cause your vehicle to lean or roll over. Your vehicle will be sturdier if your load is properly distributed. Refer back to Chapter 5 if you need to refresh your memory about loading and transporting cargo.

2. **Drive slowly around turns.** Turning too quickly is the most common cause of rollovers. Take your time around turns, especially when navigating on-ramps and off-ramps.

Steer Gently

Because they're longer and heavier, combination vehicles react differently to the steering techniques you might use when driving a straight truck. Have you ever heard of the "crack-the-whip effect"? It gets its name from an old children's game called "Crack the Whip." To play the game, one player is chosen to be the whip while the others form the tail. The whip holds hands with another player, who holds hands with another player, and so on, until a long whip is formed.

The whip runs in different directions and makes sharp turns, which directs a great deal of force to the children who make up the end of the tail. These children often fall—and have a lot of fun in the process.

This same "crack-the-whip" effect applies to combination vehicles. If the tractor makes a sharp turn, the trailer or trailers are whipped and might tip and fall. In other words, the force you use to steer increases as it travels through the trailers you're pulling, causing the rear trailer to tip over. This is called **rearward amplification**. It often occurs when a driver changes lanes too quickly; the trailer might tip on its side. In many cases, the trailer turns over, but the truck remains upright. This kind of situation is a major headache, to say the least!

Some vehicles are more prone to rearward amplification than others are. Figure 7.2 lists rearward amplification for each type of combination vehicle. On this chart, rearward amplification of 2.0 means that during a quick lane change, the rear trailer is twice as likely as the tractor to roll over. The less rearward amplification, the safer the vehicle is.

Even if the rearward amplification is low, however, it doesn't mean it's safe to make a quick lane change in a 5-axle tractor with a 45-foot trailer. No matter what you're pulling, it's important to steer gently. Any sudden movement of the steering wheel could cause your trailer to tip over. Follow these tips to avoid having to make sudden movements:

- Follow far enough behind other vehicles that you can gradually change lanes or slow down if you need to. Count off at least 1 second for every 10 feet of your vehicle's length, as well as an additional second if you're traveling over 40 mph, to maintain a good distance from the vehicle in front of you.

- Look far down the road so you won't be surprised if you have to react to a situation ahead. Make sure you have enough time to react, so you don't have to react suddenly.

- At night, your headlights will limit your range of vision. Drive slowly enough at night that your headlights allow you to see a problem up ahead without having to make a sudden lane change or come to an immediate stop.

Figure 7.2. Influence of Combination Type on Rearward Amplification

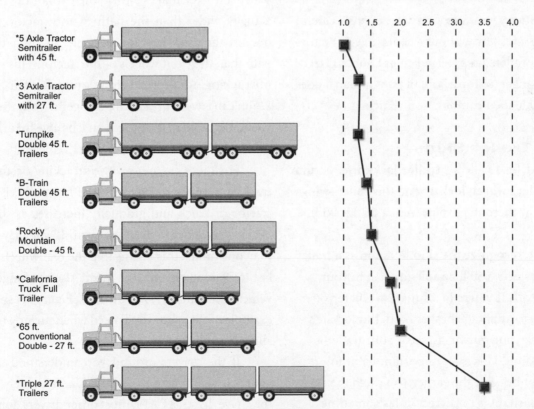

- Reduce your speed before you go into a turn.

Brake Early

Though you should always drive at a safe speed, it's helpful to remember that an empty combination vehicle will take more time to stop than a fully loaded one. It's also easier to lock up the wheels when making a sudden stop in an empty or lightly loaded CMV. This is partly because a light load doesn't engage the stiff suspension springs. It also happens because the vehicle's brakes are powerful enough to stop a much heavier vehicle, so the overcompensation of the brakes causes poor traction in a lightly loaded vehicle. If your wheels lock up, your trailer might swing into another lane and could crash into another vehicle. Locking up your wheels also creates a situation where your tractor might suddenly jackknife. You can see an example of a tractor jackknife, as compared to a trailer jackknife, in Figure 7.3.

Surprisingly, you also have to be extra careful when driving a tractor without a semitrailer. Tractors without semitrailers are referred to as "bobtail" tractors. It takes longer to stop a bobtail tractor than it does to stop a fully loaded combination vehicle.

Prevent Trailer Skids

A **trailer skid**, also called a **trailer jackknife**, occurs when the trailer's wheels lock up and the trailer swings around. Follow these steps to prevent a trailer skid:

- **First, recognize the skid.** As soon as a trailer skid starts, you'll be able to see it in your mirrors. If you're in a situation where you have to apply the brakes hard, immediately check your mirrors to see if your trailer is skidding. This is an important habit to adopt because the earlier you catch the skid, the easier it is to correct it. It's sometimes

very difficult to regain control once your trailer has skidded into another lane.

- **Then, release the brake pedal.** Taking your foot off the brake will help you regain the traction you need to get your vehicle back under control. Drivers sometimes mistakenly think that they can correct a skid by using the hand brake, which can make the situation worse, since the trailer brakes are what caused the skid to begin with. If you can regain traction by letting up on the brake, the trailer wheels will be able to grip the road and the trailer will begin to follow the tractor's path once again.

Note that a combination vehicle that's equipped with ABS is less likely to jackknife.

Turn Wide

When a tractor makes a turn, the path of the trailer is actually wider than the path of the tractor. This is because the rear wheels of the trailer follow a different path than the front wheels of the tractor. This is called **offtracking**. You learned about offtracking in Chapter 2. You can't avoid offtracking altogether, but the better you understand it, the easier you'll be able to turn when you're sharing the road with other vehicles.

First, let's examine *why* offtracking occurs. Offtracking actually begins with the front wheels of the tractor or truck and gradually increases as the connected trailers complete the turn. If you have more than one trailer, this means that the rear wheels on the last trailer will offtrack the most. Also the longer your vehicle is, the more it will offtrack. Figure 7.4 shows an example of the space you'll need when turning to safely allow for offtracking.

If the drivers around you understood all this, your job would be a lot easier! Unfortunately, unless they have driven a CMV, most other drivers don't real-

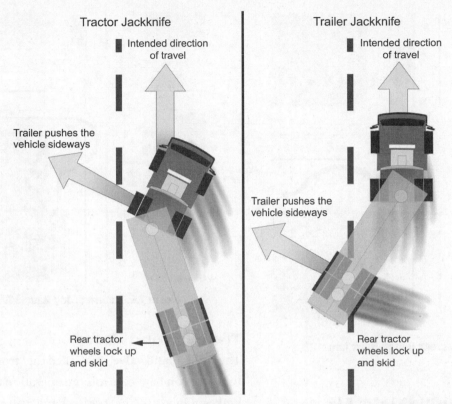

Figure 7.3. The Difference Between a Tractor Jackknife and a Trailer Jackknife

ize how much space you need to make a turn. They might try to pass you because they don't realize that you're setting yourself up to turn. Other drivers create dangerous situations without realizing it. That's why it's sometimes your job to prevent them from putting themselves—and you!—in a dangerous situation. This sounds difficult, but it really isn't if you keep these tips in mind:

- Steer the front end of the vehicle wide enough around a corner so that the rear end doesn't run over a curb or injure a pedestrian.
- Keep the rear of your vehicle close to the curb so that other drivers can't pass you on the right.
- Sometimes you won't be able to complete a turn without moving into another traffic

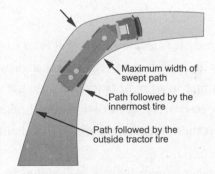

Figure 7.4. Offtracking on a 90-Degree Turn

lane. If this is the case, turn wide as you complete the turn. It's better to swing wide into another lane as you complete the turn (called a **button-hook turn**; see Figure 7.5) than it is to swing left when you start (called a **jug-handle turn**; see Figure 7.6). Swinging left might encourage other drivers to try to pass you on the right, which could result in a collision when you turn.

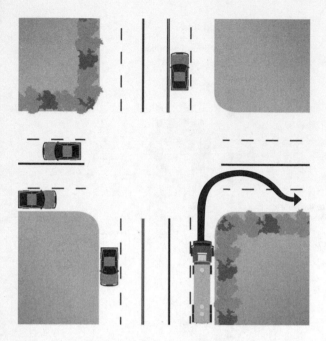

Figure 7.5. Correct: Button-Hook Turn

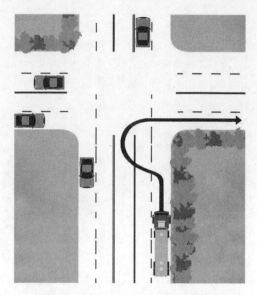

Figure 7.6. Incorrect: Jug-Handle Turn

▶ Combination Vehicle Air Brakes

You've already learned about air brakes in Chapter 6. Air brakes in combination vehicles are slightly different from those in straight trucks because the braking system also has parts to control the trailer brakes. You'll learn about these additional parts in this chapter:

- trailer hand valve (also called the "trolley valve" or "Johnson bar")
- tractor protection valve
- trailer air supply control valve
- trailer air lines
- hose couplers (glad hands)
- trailer air tanks
- shut-off valves
- trailer service, parking, and emergency brakes

Trailer Hand Valve

The **trailer hand valve**, also called the "trolley valve" or the "Johnson bar," controls the operation of the trailer brakes. Only use the trailer hand valve to test the brakes, however. Using the trailer hand valve while you're driving could cause a trailer skid or jackknife. Instead, use the foot brake while driving. The foot brake delivers air to all the brakes on the vehicle, including the trailer's brakes. It's a much safer way to slow down your vehicle.

Avoid using the hand valve for parking as well. Using the hand valve for parking could cause the air to leak out. In trailers without spring brakes, the loss of air would cause the brakes to unlock. Instead, use the parking brake for parking. If your vehicle doesn't have spring brakes, you'll have to chock the wheels as well.

Tractor Protection Valve

If your trailer happens to break away or develop a bad air leak, the **tractor protection valve** will keep air in the brake system of the tractor or truck, so you can still control the vehicle's brakes. You can use the trailer air supply control valve in the cab, which you'll learn about next, to open and shut the tractor protection valve. Note, however, that it will automatically close if the pressure drops too low (from 20 to 45 psi). This stops any air from escaping from the tractor and lets air out of the trailer emergency line. If this happens, your emergency brakes will come on, and if you're not careful or prepared, you could lose control of the vehicle. You'll learn more about emergency brakes later in this chapter.

Trailer Air Supply Control Valve

The **trailer air supply control valve** controls the air supply in the trailer. On more modern vehicles, it's a red, eight-sided knob that's pushed in to supply the trailer with air and pulled out to shut off the air and engage the emergency brakes. If the air pressure falls within the range of 20 to 45 psi, the knob will pop out on its own, closing the tractor protection valve. On an older vehicle, you might notice that the trailer air supply control valve is a lever rather than a knob. The lever should be in the "normal" position when towing a trailer and should be moved to the "emergency" position when shutting off the air and engaging the emergency brakes.

Trailer Air Lines

Every combination vehicle has two air lines that run between each part of the vehicle (tractor → trailer → dolly → second trailer):

- **The service air line.** Also called the **control line** or **signal line**, the service air line carries air from the tractor to the trailer(s). The pressure of the air in the service line is controlled by the amount of pressure applied to the foot brake or the trailer hand valve. The service line is connected to **relay valves**, which connect the trailer air tanks to the trailer air brakes. This allows the trailer brakes to be applied very quickly when

needed. Services lines are often colored blue to distinguish them from emergency lines.

- **The emergency line.** Also called the **supply line**, the emergency line has two functions: (1) It supplies air to the trailer air tanks and controls the combination vehicle's emergency brakes; and (2) if the air pressure in the emergency line drops, it allows the emergency brakes to come on. As you've learned, loss of air pressure can occur if the trailer breaks free of the tractor and tears apart the emergency air hose. It can also happen if a hose, metal tube, or other part breaks and releases the air. Loss of pressure in the emergency line will cause the air supply knob to pop out and the tractor protection valve to close. Emergency lines are often colored red to distinguish them from service lines.

Hose Couplers (Glad Hands)

Coupling devices called **glad hands** are used to connect the service and emergency air lines from the tractor or truck to the trailer. Before connecting the glad hands, clean the couplers and the rubber seals, which prevent air from escaping. To connect the glad hands, press the two seals together, making sure that the couplers are at a 90-degree angle. Then turn the glad hand attached to the hose to join and lock the couplers.

When you connect the lines, make sure that you're connecting the proper lines. These lines are often color-coded (red for emergency/supply lines, blue for service lines). Sometimes they're marked with metal tags. If you cross the air lines, air will go to the service line instead of going to charge the trailer air tanks. This means that you won't be able to release the trailer spring brakes (or parking brakes) when you push the trailer air supply control. If you find that you can't release the trailer spring brakes, check the air line connections.

If you cross the lines on older trailers without spring brakes and the air in the trailer air tank has previously leaked away, you won't have emergency brakes and the wheels will roll freely. This could be very dangerous because you won't have trailer brakes. Before you drive away, always test the trailer brakes with the hand valve or by pulling gently against the tractor protection valve control while your vehicle is in a low gear.

Have you ever seen "dummy" or "dead-end" couplers on a vehicle? Hoses should be attached to these couplers when they're not in use. This helps keep the coupler and the air lines free of water or dirt when they aren't connected to a trailer. This is important because you don't want any foreign matter to obstruct the flow of air when they're connected. If the vehicle doesn't have dummy couplers, the glad hands can sometimes be locked together to keep the coupler and air lines clean.

Trailer Air Tanks

The air tanks on a trailer and converter dolly are filled by the emergency (supply) line that comes from the tractor. The relay valves send air pressure from the air tanks to the brakes. The pressure in the services lines (which is controlled by the brake pedal and the trailer hand brake) lets the relay valves know how much pressure to send to the trailer brakes.

Allowing water and oil to build up in the air tanks may cause brake failure, so it's very important to drain the tanks every day. Even if your tanks have automatic drains, you should still open the drain valves to be safe.

Shut-Off Valves

Each trailer used to tow another trailer with air brakes has shut-off valves for the service and air supply lines, so that the air lines can be closed when the trailer isn't towing another trailer. Shut-off valves are located at the

back of a trailer that's used to tow another trailer. Make sure all shut-off valves are in the open position except for the ones at the back of the last trailer, which should be closed.

Trailer Service, Parking, and Emergency Brakes

Since 1975, all trailers and converter dollies have been equipped with spring brakes. Before this time, trailers weren't required to have spring brakes. Many older trailers have only emergency brakes, which work from air stored in the trailer air tank. They come on when the air pressure in the emergency line drops, such as when the air supply knob is pulled, the trailer is disconnected, or a major air leak develops in the emergency line (which, in turn, causes the tractor protection valve to close). Keep in mind, though, that the emergency brakes will hold only as long as there is air pressure in the trailer air tank. Once the air leaks away entirely, the trailer won't have brakes at all. This makes chocking the wheels very important when you park trailers without spring brakes.

You won't always know that the service line has a major air leak until you try to use the brakes. If the service line has a major leak, putting on the brakes will cause the pressure in the air tank to drop very quickly. If the pressure drops low enough, the emergency brakes will come on.

▶ Antilock Braking Systems

An antilock braking system (ABS) will help prevent your trailer from swinging out during hard braking. All vehicles manufactured on or after March 1, 1998, are required to have an ABS. Many older vehicles have been voluntarily outfitted with an ABS because of its skid-shortening benefits.

Vehicles with ABS still have normal braking abilities. In fact, ABS doesn't affect your normal brake usage. ABS won't necessarily prevent your trailer from swinging out, and it may not shorten your stopping distance, but it will make it easier for you to get your trailer under control if it does swing into another lane. ABS activates only *right before* your wheels would normally lock up. How does this work? When you apply the brakes quickly, ABS adjusts the braking pressure to a safe level, preventing your wheels from locking up. Even if you have ABS only on the trailer—even if only on one axle—you'll still have more control over the vehicle when you brake. If you do lose steering control or begin to jackknife, again, as long as it's safe to do so, release the brakes until you regain control. Antilock brakes work best when you hit the brake pedal and hold it down. If your ABS fails, you'll still have normal brakes, but you should get the system fixed as soon as you can.

How do you know if a trailer has ABS? If you look at the outside of a trailer with ABS, you'll see an ABS malfunction light on the left front or rear corner. However, it's not as easy to spot ABS on trailers manufactured before March 1, 1998. On older trailers, you'll have to look under the vehicle for the electronic control unit (ECU) and the wheel speed sensor wires coming from the back of the brakes.

▶ Coupling and Uncoupling

Coupling means attaching tractors and trailers or trailers and other trailers, and **uncoupling** means taking them apart. The procedures for coupling and uncoupling differ slightly depending on the vehicle, so check the manufacturer's specifications for the vehicle you're driving. The basic steps, however, are the same for all vehicles.

Coupling Tractor-Semitrailers
Step 1: Inspect the Fifth Wheel

- Check for damaged or missing parts.
- Check to see that the mounting to the tractor is secure. Check for cracks in the frame.
- Make sure the fifth-wheel plate is greased as required. If you don't keep it lubricated, you might have steering problems due to friction between the tractor and the trailer. The fifth-wheel plate shouldn't be overgreased, though. Overgreasing a fifth-wheel plate can hide problems such as cracks and missing bolts.
- Make sure the fifth wheel is in the proper position for coupling. The correct position is as follows:

  - The fifth wheel should be tilted down toward the rear of the tractor.
  - Make sure the jaws are open.
  - The safety release handle should be in the automatic lock position.
  - If you have a sliding fifth wheel, make sure that it's locked.
  - Make sure the trailer kingpin isn't bent or broken. The kingpin is in the center of the front of a semitrailer and is used to attach the semitrailer to the tractor.

Step 2: Inspect the Area and Chock the Wheels

- Make sure the area around the vehicle is clear. Remove any debris such as boards and glass that might harm the vehicle.
- Be sure that the trailer wheels are chocked and that the spring brakes are on.
- If you have cargo, check that it's secure and won't move while you're coupling.

Step 3: Position the Tractor

- Move the tractor right in front of the trailer. Don't ever back under the trailer at an angle—you could push the trailer sideways and break the landing gear.
- Check your position by using your mirrors to look down both sides of the trailer.

Step 4: Back Slowly

- Back until the fifth wheel just touches the trailer.
- Make sure you don't hit the trailer with the tractor.

Step 5: Secure the Tractor

- Put on the parking brake.
- Put the transmission in neutral. Exit the cab.

Step 6: Check the Trailer Height

- The trailer should be low enough that it rises slightly when the tractor backs under it. You might need to raise or lower the trailer. You don't want the trailer to be too low because the tractor could hit it and damage the trailer nose. If it's too high, it might not couple correctly.
- Make sure the kingpin and the fifth wheel are aligned.

Step 7: Connect the Air Lines to the Trailer

- Check the glad hand seals, and connect the tractor emergency air line to the trailer emergency air line.

- Check the glad hand seals, and connect the tractor service air line to the trailer service air line.

Step 8: Supply Air to the Trailer

- From the cab, push in the red trailer air supply knob or move the tractor protection valve control from the "emergency" to the "normal" position. This will supply air to the trailer brake system.
- Wait until the air pressure is normal.
- Check the brake system for crossed air lines.
- Shut off the engine, so you can hear the brakes.
- Apply and release the trailer brakes and listen for sounds of the trailer brakes being applied and released. You should be able to hear the brakes move when they're applied and hear the air escape when they're released.
- Check the air brake system pressure gauge to make sure that there aren't any signs of major air loss.
- When you're sure that the trailer brakes are working, start the engine.
- Make sure the air pressure is at a normal level.

Step 9: Lock the Trailer Brakes

- Pull out the trailer air supply knob or move the tractor protection valve control from "normal" to "emergency."

Step 10: Back under the Trailer

- Release the tractor parking brake.
- Use the lowest reverse gear.

- Back the tractor slowly under the trailer to avoid hitting the kingpin too hard.
- Stop when the kingpin is locked into the fifth wheel.

Step 11: Check the Connection for Security

- Pull the tractor *gently* forward while the trailer brakes are still locked to check that the trailer is locked onto the tractor.

Step 12: Secure the Vehicle

- Put the transmission in neutral.
- Put the parking brakes on.
- Shut off the engine, and take the key with you so that someone else can't move the truck while you're under it.

Step 13: Inspect the Coupling

- Use a flashlight, if you need one.
- Make sure there isn't space between the upper and lower fifth wheel. If there's space, something is wrong. (The kingpin might be sitting on top of the fifth-wheel jaws, which would allow the trailer to come loose very easily.)
- Get under the trailer and look into the back of the fifth wheel. Make sure the fifth-wheel jaws have closed around the shank of the kingpin (see Figure 7.7).
- Check that the locking lever is in the "lock" position.
- Check that the safety latch is in position over the locking lever. (On some fifth wheels, the catch must be put in place by hand.)

- If the coupling isn't right, don't drive the coupled unit until it's coupled correctly.

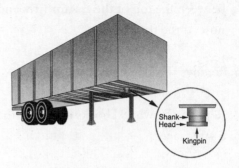

Figure 7.7. Trailer Kingpin

Step 14: Connect the Electrical Cord and Check Air Lines

- Plug the electrical cord into the trailer and fasten the safety catch.
- Check both air lines and the electrical line for signs of damage.
- Make sure the air and electrical lines won't hit any moving parts of the vehicle.

Step 15: Raise the Front Trailer Supports (Landing Gear)

- Use the low gear range (if it's equipped) to start raising the landing gear. Once it's free of weight, switch to the high gear range.
- Raise the landing gear all the way up. (Never drive with the landing gear only partway up. It could catch on railroad tracks or other things below the trailer and cause major damage.)
- After raising the landing gear, safely secure the crank handle.
- When the full weight of the trailer is resting on the tractor, check for enough clearance between the rear of tractor frame and the landing gear. (When the tractor turns

sharply, it must not hit the landing gear.) Check that there's enough clearance between the top of the tractor tires and the nose of the trailer.

Step 16: Remove the Trailer Wheel Chocks

- Remove the wheel chocks and store them in a safe place.

Uncoupling Tractor-Semitrailers

Follow these steps to uncouple safely:

Step 1: Position the Rig

- Make sure the surface of the parking area can support the weight of the trailer.
- Check that the tractor is lined up with the trailer. (If you pull out at an angle, you can damage the landing gear.)

Step 2: Ease the Pressure on the Locking Jaws

- Shut off the trailer air supply (pull out the red knob) to lock the trailer brakes.
- Back up gently to ease the pressure on fifth-wheel locking jaws. (This will help you release the fifth-wheel locking lever.)
- Put on the tractor parking brakes (pull out the yellow knob) while the tractor is pushing against the kingpin. (This will hold the rig with pressure off the locking jaws.)

Step 3: Chock the Trailer Wheels

- Chock the trailer wheels if the trailer doesn't have spring brakes or if you're not sure. (The air could leak out of the trailer air

tank, releasing its emergency brakes, and without chocks, the trailer could move.)

Step 4: Lower the Landing Gear

- If the trailer is empty, lower the landing gear until it makes firm contact with the ground.
- If the trailer is loaded, after the landing gear makes firm contact with the ground, turn the crank a few extra turns in low gear. This will lift some weight off the tractor. (Don't lift the trailer off the fifth wheel.) This will make it easier to unlatch the fifth wheel and couple next time.

Step 5: Disconnect the Air Lines and the Electrical Cable

- Disconnect the air lines from the trailer. Connect air line glad hands to dummy couplers at the back of the cab or couple them together.
- Hang the electrical cable with the plug down to prevent moisture from entering it.
- Make sure the lines are supported, so they won't be damaged while you're driving the tractor.

Step 6: Unlock the Fifth Wheel

- Raise the release handle lock.
- Pull the release handle to the "open" position.
- Keep your legs and feet clear of the rear tractor wheels. If you don't, you could be seriously injured if the vehicle moves.

Step 7: Pull the Tractor Partially Clear of the Trailer

- Pull the tractor forward until the fifth wheel comes out from under the trailer.
- Stop with the tractor frame under the trailer. (This prevents the trailer from falling to the ground if the landing gear collapses or sinks.)

Step 8: Secure the Tractor

- Apply the parking brake.
- Put the transmission in neutral.

Step 9: Inspect the Trailer Supports

- Make sure the ground is supporting the trailer.
- Make sure the landing gear isn't damaged.

Step 10: Pull the Tractor Clear of the Trailer

- Release the parking brakes.
- Check the area, and then drive the tractor forward until it clears.

Inspecting a Combination Vehicle

You'll use the same seven-step inspection procedure you learned about in Chapter 4 to inspect your combination vehicle. Keep in mind, however, that there's more to inspect on a combination vehicle than on a single vehicle (such as tires, wheels, lights, reflectors, etc.).

Additional Checks During a Walkaround Inspection

Check the following when inspecting a combination vehicle:

Coupling System Areas

- Check the lower fifth wheel.
- Make sure the fifth wheel is mounted securely to the frame.
- Look for missing or damaged parts. Have them replaced before driving the vehicle.
- Make sure the fifth-wheel plate is properly greased.
- Make sure there isn't visible space between the upper and lower fifth wheel.
- Check that the locking jaws are around the shank—not the head—of the kingpin.
- Make sure the release arm is properly seated and that the safety latch/lock is engaged.
- Check the upper fifth wheel.
- Check that the glide plate is mounted securely to the trailer frame.
- Make sure the kingpin isn't damaged.
- Check the air and electric lines to the trailer.
- Make sure the electrical cord is firmly plugged in and secured. ·
- Check that the air lines are properly connected to the glad hands, with no air leaks. Air lines should be properly secured with enough slack for turns.
- Make sure none of the lines are damaged.
- Check the sliding fifth wheel.
- Make sure the slide isn't damaged and that it doesn't have missing parts.
- Check that the sliding fifth wheel is properly greased.
- Confirm that all locking pins are present and locked in place.

- If it's air powered, make sure there aren't any air leaks.
- Check that the fifth wheel isn't so far forward that the tractor frame will hit the landing gear during turns. Also make sure the cab won't hit the trailer during turns.
- Check the landing gear.
- Make sure the landing gear is fully raised, isn't missing parts, and isn't bent or otherwise damaged.

- Check that the crank handle is in place and is secured.
- If it's power operated, make sure there aren't air leaks or hydraulic leaks.
- Adding these important checks to your walkaround inspection will help ensure that you have a safe ride in your combination vehicle.

Chapter 7 Review Quiz

1–8: Circle the correct answer.

1. When coupling a tractor and semitrailer, what should you do right after you secure the tractor?
   a. Supply air to the trailer.
   b. Chock the wheels.
   c. Check the height of the trailer.
   d. Check the position of the fifth wheel.

2. "Johnson bar" is another name for the
   a. emergency line.
   b. trailer hand valve.
   c. glad hands.
   d. trailer air valve.

3. When traveling 35 mph, you should follow another vehicle no closer than
   a. 1 second for every 10 feet of vehicle length.
   b. 1 second for every 20 feet of vehicle length.
   c. 3 seconds for every 3 feet of vehicle length.
   d. 5 seconds for every 15 feet of vehicle length.

4. Which part connects the trailer air tanks to the trailer air brakes?
   a. glad hands
   b. relay valves
   c. locking jaws
   d. fifth wheel

5. The "crack-the-whip effect" can occur when a driver changes lanes too quickly, causing the trailer to
   a. skid.
   b. turn over.
   c. come loose.
   d. jackknife.

6. A tank truck is classified as a
   a. specialized hauling vehicle.
   b. triple trailer.
   c. turnpike double.
   d. semitrailer.

7. Tractors without semitrailers attached are referred to as
   a. California trucks.
   b. bobtail tractors.
   c. kingpins.
   d. singles.

8. When you swing wide into another lane as you complete a turn, it's called
   a. a button-hook turn.
   b. a jug-handle turn.
   c. rearward amplification.
   d. offtracking.

9–13: Indicate whether each statement is true or false.

____ **9.** All trailers and converter dollies are equipped with spring brakes.

____ **10.** Service air lines are often blue, while emergency air lines are red.

____ **11.** Offtracking occurs when the rear wheels of a trailer follow a different path than the front wheels of a tractor.

____ **12.** It's best to back a tractor at an angle when coupling it to a trailer.

____ **13.** When making a wide turn, it's better to swing wide into another lane as you complete the turn than it is to swing left when you start the turn.

Check your answers on page 294.

Combination Vehicles Practice Test

1.	ⓐ	ⓑ	ⓒ	ⓓ		11.	ⓐ	ⓑ	ⓒ	ⓓ		21.	ⓐ	ⓑ	ⓒ	ⓓ
2.	ⓐ	ⓑ	ⓒ	ⓓ		12.	ⓐ	ⓑ	ⓒ	ⓓ		22.	ⓐ	ⓑ	ⓒ	ⓓ
3.	ⓐ	ⓑ	ⓒ	ⓓ		13.	ⓐ	ⓑ	ⓒ	ⓓ		23.	ⓐ	ⓑ	ⓒ	ⓓ
4.	ⓐ	ⓑ	ⓒ	ⓓ		14.	ⓐ	ⓑ	ⓒ	ⓓ		24.	ⓐ	ⓑ	ⓒ	ⓓ
5.	ⓐ	ⓑ	ⓒ	ⓓ		15.	ⓐ	ⓑ	ⓒ	ⓓ		25.	ⓐ	ⓑ	ⓒ	ⓓ
6.	ⓐ	ⓑ	ⓒ	ⓓ		16.	ⓐ	ⓑ	ⓒ	ⓓ		26.	ⓐ	ⓑ	ⓒ	ⓓ
7.	ⓐ	ⓑ	ⓒ	ⓓ		17.	ⓐ	ⓑ	ⓒ	ⓓ		27.	ⓐ	ⓑ	ⓒ	ⓓ
8.	ⓐ	ⓑ	ⓒ	ⓓ		18.	ⓐ	ⓑ	ⓒ	ⓓ		28.	ⓐ	ⓑ	ⓒ	ⓓ
9.	ⓐ	ⓑ	ⓒ	ⓓ		19.	ⓐ	ⓑ	ⓒ	ⓓ		29.	ⓐ	ⓑ	ⓒ	ⓓ
10.	ⓐ	ⓑ	ⓒ	ⓓ		20.	ⓐ	ⓑ	ⓒ	ⓓ		30.	ⓐ	ⓑ	ⓒ	ⓓ

▶ Combination Vehicles Practice Test

Choose the correct answer. Mark the letter on the answer sheet on page 145.

1. What is the first thing you should do if you're forced to brake hard?
   a. Count the seconds between you and the vehicle in front of you.
   b. Use the trailer hand valve to slow down your vehicle.
   c. Look in your mirrors to see if the trailer is skidding.
   d. Listen for an air leak from the trailer air supply control.

2. How can you tell if you've crossed the service and emergency lines on a newer trailer?
   a. You won't be able to move the trailer air supply control valve.
   b. You won't be able to release the trailer spring brakes.
   c. You won't be able to lock the glad hands together.
   d. You won't be able to change the position of the shut-off valves.

3. Why should you grease the fifth-wheel plate?
   a. to reduce friction between the tractor and the trailer
   b. to make it easier for you to chock the wheels
   c. to reduce the noise of the trailer landing gear
   d. to make it easier for you to pull the release handle

4. After pushing the trailer air supply knob, you don't hear air escape when you release the trailer brakes. What is most likely the cause?
   a. The kingpin might not be locked into the fifth wheel.
   b. The brake system air lines might be crossed.
   c. The transmission might not be in neutral.
   d. The trailer might not be locked onto the tractor.

5. Which type of vehicle would most likely be used to deliver a large load of gravel to a construction site?
   a. a double-trailer rig
   b. a tractor with a bobtail trailer
   c. a specialized hauling vehicle
   d. a tractor with a pup trailer

6. When connecting the glad hands, at what angle should the couplers be placed before coupling?
   a. 45 degrees
   b. 90 degrees
   c. 180 degrees
   d. 240 degrees

7. Why is it important to keep cargo low to the ground and centered?
   a. to prevent your vision from being obstructed
   b. to keep the vehicle's center of gravity close to the road
   c. to help you test for pulling and brake problems while driving
   d. to shield you from the tractor protection valve

8. In which of these situations would your tractor protection valve close?
   a. if your trailer breaks away or develops a bad air leak
   b. if your emergency brakes fail to work
   c. if your spring brakes have failed when the trailer is parked
   d. if your semitrailer is too low when you're coupling

9. What happens when all of the air leaks out of the trailer air tank of a pre-1975 trailer without spring brakes?
   a. The trailer loses all braking ability.
   b. The vehicle can no longer run.
   c. The hose couplers become unhooked.
   d. All of the above.

10. When does a vehicle's antilock braking system (ABS) activate?
   a. every time the driver puts a foot on the brakes
   b. only when the driver is able to brake slowly
   c. right before the wheels would normally lock up
   d. only when the transmission is in neutral

11. Which of the following has the least amount of rearward amplification?
   a. a triple with 27-foot trailers
   b. a B-train double
   c. a 3-axle tractor-semitrailer
   d. a conventional double

12. When should you stop backing underneath a trailer?
   a. when the locking jaws of the fifth wheel lock around the shank of the kingpin
   b. when the tractor hits the trailer bed
   c. when the cargo is as close to the ground as possible
   d. when the tractor has traveled at least 45 feet

13. Which of the following statements is true?
   a. A vehicle with a heavier load will lock up more easily than one with a lighter load.
   b. It takes a bobtail tractor longer to stop than it takes a fully loaded tractor-semitrailer.
   c. A Rocky Mountain double has less rearward amplification than a turnpike double.
   d. Combination vehicles are more common on the road than single-unit trucks.

14. What is the first step when uncoupling a tractor-semitrailer?
   a. Chock the trailer wheels.
   b. Lower the landing gear.
   c. Secure the tractor.
   d. Position the rig.

15. What should you do to secure a CMV?
   a. Put the transmission in neutral, and put the parking brake on.
   b. Pull the tractor gently forward while the trailer brakes are locked.
   c. Make sure that the air pressure reads at a normal level.
   d. Remove the wheel chocks, and store them in a safe place.

16. After coupling with a semitrailer, how should the landing gear be positioned before you begin to drive the coupled vehicle?
a. partway up, without the crank handle
b. all the way up, with the crank handle secured
c. fully extended, without the crank handle
d. partway up, with the crank handle loose

17. How should you use the trailer hand valve?
a. in place of the foot brake
b. to help you with parking
c. to test the trailer's brakes
d. in the middle of a skid

18. What should you do if your trailer begins to skid while you're driving?
a. Remove your foot from the brake.
b. Use the trailer hand valve.
c. Release the parking brake.
d. Pull the emergency brake.

19. After coupling a tractor-semitrailer, you see space between the upper and lower fifth wheel. What could be the cause?
a. The cargo might be causing the vehicle to lean.
b. The landing gear might not be raised up all the way.
c. The air supply lines might be kinked or crossed.
d. The kingpin might be on top of the fifth-wheel jaws.

20. When might the trailer air supply control valve knob pop out on its own?
a. when the air in the trailer becomes too hot
b. when the air pressure becomes too low
c. when the trailer hand valve fails to engage
d. when the trailer's emergency brakes fail to work

21. What is the standard color for service air lines?
a. black
b. red
c. green
d. blue

22. What position must the safety catch for the fifth-wheel locking lever be in before driving a coupled vehicle?
a. over the locking lever
b. beneath the kingpin
c. tilted toward the front
d. aligned with the glad hands

23. Locking jaws should close around which part of the kingpin?
a. the base
b. the head
c. the shank
d. the back

24. What is the first step when coupling a tractor-semitrailer?
a. Secure the tractor.
b. Inspect the fifth wheel.
c. Supply air to the trailer.
d. Check the trailer height.

25. Which of the following is another name for glad hands?

a. shut-off valves

b. service lines

c. hose couplers

d. trolley valves

26. When a tractor makes a turn, the rear wheels of the trailer follow a different path than the wheels of the tractor. What is this called?

a. offtracking

b. skidding

c. jackknifing

d. none of the above

27. When coupling a tractor-semitrailer, what might happen if the trailer is too low?

a. The air pressure might not be normal.

b. The trailer nose might be damaged.

c. The trailer brakes might not lock.

d. The cargo might not be secure.

28. What is the main concern when a trailer's cargo is too high?

a. The tractor might be too light to pull it.

b. The trailer's brakes might not work.

c. The vehicle might lean or roll over.

d. The tractor might suddenly jackknife.

29. When completing a wide right turn, what is the main reason you should keep the rear of your vehicle close to the curb?

a. so pedestrians will know to stay out of your way

b. so your vehicle won't tip over

c. so other drivers can't pass you on the right

d. so your cargo won't shift too much

30. What is the best way to slow down a combination vehicle?

a. with the foot brake

b. with the trolley valve

c. with the emergency brake

d. with the spring brakes

▶ Answers and Explanations

1. c. Braking hard puts you at risk for a trailer skid. The first step in preventing a trailer skid is to recognize the skid. As soon as a trailer skid starts, you'll be able to see it in your mirrors. If you're suddenly forced to brake hard, check your mirrors immediately to see if your trailer is skidding because the earlier you catch the skid, the easier it will be for you to correct it.

2. b. On a newer trailer, if you cross the service and emergency air lines, air will travel through the service line instead of supplying the trailer tanks with air. The service line is usually connected to relay valves, which connect the trailer air tanks to the trailer air brakes. If the lines are crossed, the trailer air tanks won't receive air, and you won't be able to release the trailer brakes when you push the trailer air supply control valve.

3. a. The fifth wheel on a tractor is used to couple the tractor with a trailer. It's very important to grease the fifth-wheel plate to reduce friction between the tractor and the trailer while you're on the road. Friction can cause dangerous steering problems.

4. b. Pushing the trailer air supply knob inside the tractor allows air to flow to the trailer brake system. Once the pressure has reached a normal level, the next step is to check the brake system to make sure that you haven't crossed the air lines. You can do this by listening closely to the noises the trailer brakes make when you apply and release them. If your air lines aren't crossed, you should be able to hear the brakes move when they're applied and hear air escape when they're released. If you don't, you've probably crossed air lines between the tractor and trailer.

5. c. A specialized hauling vehicle (SHV) is designed to haul heavy cargo—such as gravel, ready-mix cement, and other construction materials—over short distances within one state.

6. b. Glad hands are coupling devices that connect the service and emergency air lines running from the truck or tractor to the trailer. These devices have rubber seals that prevent air from escaping when they're connected. If they're not placed at a 90-degree angle before turning and locking them together, the seals won't press together when connected and the couplers won't lock properly.

7. b. Keeping cargo low and centered brings a vehicle's "center of gravity" closer to the road, which is important because it reduces the chance that the load will shift and cause the vehicle to lean and/or roll over. A vehicle is sturdier when its load is distributed properly. This is one of two rollover-prevention safety rules.

8. a. The tractor protection control valve is designed to ensure that your tractor's brakes have enough air to keep working in an emergency situation such as a trailer breakaway or an excessive air leak. This valve closes when air pressure drops too low, to prevent air from escaping from the tractor, and to let air flow out of the trailer emergency line, engaging the trailer emergency brakes.

9. a. When the air leaks out of the air tank of a trailer built before 1975 without spring brakes, the drop in pressure in the emergency line causes the emergency brakes to come on. The emergency brakes can only work as long as some pressure is coming from the trailer air tank, though. If the tank is empty, the emergency brakes won't work, and the trailer won't have any emergency brakes at all.

10. c. ABS doesn't affect your normal braking abilities and usage. ABS is activated only when you slam on your brakes hard enough to signal the system that the braking pressure is unsafe. Slamming on your brakes normally causes your wheels to lock up. ABS senses this before it happens and adjusts braking pressure to a safe level.

11. c. Rearward amplification, or the "crack-the-whip effect," refers to the effect of reckless steering that makes the rear trailer of a combination vehicle more likely to tip over while the truck remains upright. On a double or triple, the force a driver uses to steer increases as it passes through the trailers, possibly causing the last trailer to turn over. Since a 3-axle tractor-semitrailer combination has only one trailer, it has less rearward amplification than doubles and triples.

12. a. When the locking jaws of the fifth wheel lock around the shank of the kingpin, the tractor and trailer are connected, so there's no reason to continue backing. In fact, if you continued backing past this point, you might end up

causing major damage to the tractor and trailer, especially if the connection isn't secure or if you crash into an object with the trailer.

13. b. A bobtail tractor, a tractor without semitrailers, can't stop as quickly as a fully loaded tractor-semitrailer can because the bobtail tractor doesn't have as much weight. Because of this, its wheels don't have as much traction, meaning they can't grip the road as well and might cause the tractor to skid.

14. d. Before you can uncouple a vehicle, you must make sure that it's in a good position that will allow you to separate the tractor from the trailer (or a trailer from another trailer) without damaging them. This includes making sure that you're on a flat surface and that the tractor and trailer are in a straight line.

15. a. When uncoupling, once you've pulled the tractor partially clear of the trailer and you've stopped, you can secure the tractor by applying the parking brake and putting the transmission in neutral.

16. b. A driver should never drive the vehicle with the landing gear down. After coupling, you should raise the landing gear slightly off the ground while you're checking that the connection is secure. This way, if it's not secure and the tractor isn't supporting the trailer, the landing gear will provide support for the trailer. But it's very important to fully raise the landing gear before you drive so that you don't damage it or another part of the vehicle.

17. c. The trailer hand valve, which controls the operation of the trailer brakes, should only be used to test the trailer brakes. Using it while you're driving could cause the trailer to skid or jackknife. Never use the hand valve for parking because it could vibrate to the released position. You can use the foot brake for driving and the parking brake for parking, but don't use the trailer hand valve in place of the foot brake or the parking brake.

18. a. If your trailer begins to skid while you're driving, take your foot off the brake to allow your wheels to regain traction, so you can get control of your vehicle. Using the trailer hand valve could make the skid even worse.

19. d. The main connection between a coupled tractor and trailer is the connection between the tractor's fifth wheel and the trailer's kingpin. When you're coupling, if the fifth-wheel jaws don't close around the kingpin, the tractor and trailer won't be properly or safely connected. If you check the connections and see space between the upper and lower fifth-wheel jaws, the kingpin might be sitting on top of the fifth wheel rather than between the jaws.

20. b. The trailer air supply control valve controls the tractor protection valve, which keeps air in the tractor's air lines (so that the tractor's brakes will still work) if the trailer breaks away or develops a bad leak. The trailer air supply control valve on the dash allows the driver to open and close the tractor protection valve; however, it will close automatically if the pressure drops to the range of 20 to 45 psi.

21. d. Service air lines are usually colored blue, while emergency/supply air lines are usually colored red. This is a standard for most vehicles to help drivers avoid crossing the lines.

22. a. The fifth-wheel locking lever should lock the fifth-wheel jaws around the trailer's kingpin to keep the coupling secure. The safety latch should go over the locking lever to help ensure that the coupling remains secure.

23. c. Locking jaws are designed to close around the shank of the kingpin. If they only close around the head of the kingpin, the vehicle isn't properly coupled and should be adjusted.

24. b. The fifth wheel is the part that actually attaches to the trailer's kingpin to couple a tractor and trailer. This makes it one of the most important aspects of coupling a vehicle. If it's damaged, in the wrong position, or otherwise unfit for coupling, you won't be able to complete the coupling. This is why it's the first thing that should be checked before attempting to couple a tractor-semitrailer.

25. c. Glad hands are also called "hose couplers" because they're coupling devices that connect the service and emergency air lines from the tractor or truck to the trailer.

26. a. When turning, the wheels of the trailer follow a different path than the front wheels of the tractor. You can think of the trailer wheels as being "off the track" that is set by the front wheels of the tractor. This might help you remember the definition for the term "off-tracking."

27. b. When coupling a tractor-semitrailer, check the trailer height to make sure it's not too high or too low. If it's too high, it might not couple correctly because the fifth-wheel locking jaws won't meet the kingpin shank in the right position. If it's too low, the tractor might hit the trailer and damage the trailer nose.

28. c. When cargo is piled high in a truck, it can cause the truck to lean (due to its high center of gravity), which can make the truck roll over. You learned that a fully loaded rig is 10 times more likely to roll over than an empty rig is. Keeping cargo low to the ground and centered in the middle of the truck or trailer makes the cargo less likely to shift and cause the vehicle to lean or roll over.

29. c. When you're making a wide right turn, keep the rear of your vehicle close to the curb so other drivers can't pass you on the right, putting you both at risk for a crash. To another driver, it may look like you intend to move to the left. Impatient drivers—especially those who have been driving behind you for a while and are anxious to go faster than your vehicle will allow them to—might try to hurry past you without realizing that you're actually making a right turn.

30. a. Using the foot brake is the safest way to slow down your vehicle. Using the trailer hand valve will only engage the trailer brakes, which could cause a skid or a jackknife. The emergency brakes could do the same. The foot brake engages the brakes on the tractor and the trailer at the same time. If you apply them gently enough and have enough time to slow down, you shouldn't have to worry about a trailer skid or a jackknife.

CHAPTER

8 ▶ CDL Skills Test

CHAPTER SUMMARY

This chapter will help you prepare to take the Skills Test, a test that you need to pass to get your CDL. The Skills Test is made up of three smaller tests: the Pre-Trip Inspection Test, the Basic Vehicle Control Skills Test, and the Road Test.

You read about the CDL Skills Test in Chapter 1. You learned that on a skills test, you show what you can *do*, whereas on a knowledge test, you show what you *know*. All drivers applying for a CDL must take the General Knowledge Test and the Skills Test—in that order. You need to take and pass the General Knowledge Test before you can take the Skills Test. The Skills Test is actually made up of three smaller tests:

1. Pre-Trip Inspection Test
2. Basic Vehicle Control Skills Test
3. Road Test

To take the Skills Test, you need to make an appointment at your local Department of Motor Vehicles (DMV). When you contact the DMV, ask where the test will be conducted and how much it will cost to take it. Some states hire trucking companies or trucking schools to give the Skills Tests, so the location will vary. The cost of the test varies by state.

It's not easy to pass the Skills Test. You have to know what you're doing. To avoid letting your nerves get the best of you, practice, practice, and practice until you can easily complete the exercises on this test.

Bring the following items with you when you take the Skills Test:

- a tire pressure gauge
- a tread depth gauge
- wheel chocks
- a rag to clean your lights
- gloves
- your driver's license
- your vehicle's registration
- proof of insurance
- any permits required in your state

▶ 1. The Pre-Trip Inspection Test

The Pre-Trip Inspection Test is the first test you'll take. You learned how to complete a pre-trip inspection of your vehicle in Chapter 4. While the most important information is repeated in this chapter, study Chapter 4 before taking the Pre-Trip Inspection Test.

During the test, your examiner will request that you conduct a complete and thorough inspection of your vehicle. Your examiner will tell you to point to the items you're inspecting and explain what you're looking for while inspecting them.

If you skip an item during your pre-trip inspection, you won't receive any credit for that item. This is why it's important to practice inspecting your vehicle before the actual test. If you develop a routine, you're less likely to skip an item during the test. It should take you about 45 minutes to an hour to complete your pre-trip inspection.

Your examiner will most likely ask you to perform your inspection in this order:

1. Inspect the engine compartment.
2. Start the engine, and perform the in-vehicle checks.
3. Shut off the engine and perform the external inspection.

As you perform your pre-trip inspection, call out what you're inspecting, and explain what you're looking for. For example, you might say, "I'm checking the tread depth on the steering tires. They must have at least $4/32$-inch tread depth in every major groove."

Review the Seven-Step Pre-Trip Inspection Method

You learned the seven-step pre-trip inspection method in detail in Chapter 4. Here's a summary of this method:

Step 1: Approach the Vehicle

As you approach the vehicle, look for signs of damage. Check for leaks, and make sure the vehicle isn't leaning. Check the area around the vehicle for hazards.

Step 2: Check the Engine Compartment

To check the engine compartment, you might have to raise the hood, tilt the cab, or open the engine compartment door. Then check all the components such as fluid levels, belts, hoses, wiring, front brakes, tires, rims, and steering controls.

Step 3: Start the Engine and Inspect Inside the Cab

If your transmission is manual, put it in neutral. If the transmission is automatic, put it in park. Apply the brakes, depress the clutch, and start the engine. Check all the gauges and controls. Check that you have the required emergency equipment, and make sure you have your vehicle's registration. Check the mirrors and the windshield, including wipers and washers.

Step 4: Turn Off the Engine and Check the Lights

First, check that the parking brake is set. Then turn off the engine and take the key with you, so no one else can start the vehicle. Check your headlights, both low and high beams. Check your four-way emergency flashers. Turn off your headlights and flashers. Check your right turn signal.

Step 5: Do a Walkaround Inspection

Begin with the driver's side of the cab and check all items such as wheels, lights, coupling devices, the suspension, air lines, air line connections, brakes, mirrors, and doors. Check that the tires are properly inflated, and inspect each axle thoroughly.

Step 6: Check Signal Lights

Get back into your vehicle and turn off all lights. Turn on the brake lights and the left turn signal. Get out and check that they're working properly. Make sure the left turn signal lights and brake lights are clean and the proper color.

Step 7: Start the Engine and Check Brake System

Test the brakes. If you have air brakes, turn off your engine and turn the key before pumping the brakes to check the low air pressure warning. Check the parking brake.

Note that for more information on how to inspect air brakes, review Chapter 6. You'll learn how to inspect buses in Chapter 12. Also refer to Figures 4.5, 4.6, and 4.7 for pre-trip inspection "cheat sheet" overviews of what to inspect on a straight truck or school bus, a tractor-trailer, and a coach or transit bus.

▶ 2. The Basic Vehicle Control Skills Test

The Basic Vehicle Control Skills Test comes after the Pre-Trip Inspection Test and before the Road Test. The exercises in this test are designed to measure whether you have basic control of your vehicle. Depending on your state and your examiner, you may be asked to perform only a few of the exercises discussed in this chapter or all of them.

Most of the time, the Basic Vehicle Control Skills Test is given on a course designed for this purpose. At some sites, however, an examiner will ask you to start the road test and will have you complete the exercises in this test along the way.

Exercises

The typical exercises you may be asked to perform during the Basic Vehicle Control Skills Test are discussed in this section. Most examiners ask you to do the easier exercises first and lead up to the harder ones.

Right Turn

Your examiner may ask you to simulate a right turn at an intersection. The goal of this exercise is to measure your ability to position your vehicle for making and completing a right turn. You'll start about 30 to 50 feet from a cone, line, or marker. You'll drive forward and make a right turn around a cone. You'll be asked to bring the right rear wheel(s) of your vehicle as close to the cone as you can without hitting it.

Here are some hints:

- Don't turn too wide. In some states, it's an error if your rear wheel is more than 6 inches from the cone.

- After turning, keep driving forward until your vehicle is straight. Then wait for further instructions from your examiner.
- Remember to watch your right mirror to see where your trailer is.

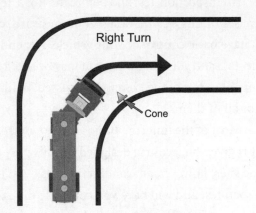

Right Turn

Cone

Figure 8.1. Making a Right Turn

Straight Line Backing

In a **straight line backing** exercise, you back your vehicle in a straight line between lines or cones without touching or crossing over these boundaries. Crossing over the boundaries with any part of your vehicle is an **encroachment**, which will result in a loss of points. You'll read about encroachments and other errors later in this chapter.

Here are some hints:

- Go slowly when you pull forward.
- Keep your vehicle straight, centered, and between the boundaries.

- Back slowly and watch your mirrors for trailer drift.
- Stop gently.

Offset Back/Right

When you're asked to back into a space that's to the right rear of your vehicle, it's called an **offset back/right** exercise. To complete this exercise, you need to first drive straight forward, and then back your vehicle into a space to the right without striking boundaries marked by cones. You need to park your entire vehicle in this space.

Here are some hints:

- When you drive forward, stop your vehicle within 2 feet of the stop line.
- Check your path and clearance while backing. Use your mirrors! Don't lean out the window or open the door to get a better view.
- Bring your vehicle to a smooth stop.

Offset Back/Left

When you're asked to back into a space that's to the left rear of your vehicle, it's called an **offset back/left** exercise. As in an offset back/right exercise, you'll begin by driving forward, and then back your vehicle into a space to your left without striking any cones. Once again, you need to park your entire vehicle in this space.

Figure 8.2. Straight Line Backing

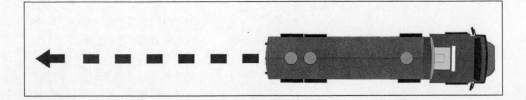

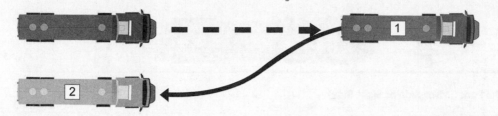

Figure 8.3. Offset Back/Right

Here are some hints:

- When you drive forward, stop your vehicle within 2 feet of the stop line.
- Check your path and clearance while backing. Use your mirrors! Don't lean out the window or open the door to get a better view.
- Bring your vehicle to a smooth stop.

Parallel Park (Driver Side or Sight Side)

If you're asked to parallel park in a space to your left, you've been asked to complete a **parallel park (driver side or sight side)** exercise. To complete this exercise, drive past the parking space and back into it. Bring the rear of your vehicle as close as you can to the rear of the space without crossing boundaries, which will be marked by cones or lines. If you're driving a straight truck, you must maneuver your entire vehicle into the space. If you're driving a tractor-trailer combination, you need to get the trailer into the space without jackknifing the tractor.

Here are some hints:

- The space you need to park in will be 15 feet longer than your trailer and 12 feet wide.
- You need to get your vehicle within 18 inches of the stop line and as close as possible to the "curb" (which will actually be a line).
- You must not place the tractor in a jackknife position unless you're asked to parallel park the trailer only.
- Don't go over the rear boundary.

Parallel Park (Conventional or Blind Side)

If you're asked to parallel park in a space to your right, your examiner has asked you to complete a **parallel park (conventional or blind side)** exercise. As with the previous exercise, pull past the parking space and back into it. Bring the rear of your vehicle as close as possible to the rear of the space without crossing any boundaries. If you're driving a straight truck, you must maneuver your entire vehicle into the space. If you're driving a tractor-trailer combination, you need to get

Figure 8.4. Offset Back/Left

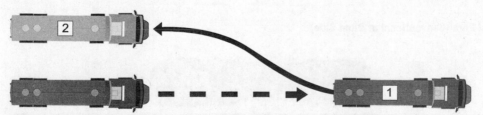

Figure 8.5. Parallel Park (Driver Side or Sight Side)

the trailer into the space without jackknifing the tractor.

Here are some hints:

- The space you need to park in will be 15 feet longer than your trailer and 12 feet wide.
- You need to get your vehicle within 18 inches of the stop line and as close as possible to the "curb" (which will actually be a line).
- You must not place the tractor in a jackknife position unless you're asked to parallel park the trailer only. Don't go over the rear boundary.

Alley Dock

For this exercise, your examiner will ask you to drive by the entrance to an alley with the alley on your left side. Then your examiner will ask you to maneuver your vehicle into a 45-degree angle and back into the alley without crossing side or rear boundaries, which are marked by cones or lines. You need to get your vehicle completely into the alley and within 2 feet of the stop line.

Here are some hints:

- When the middle of your vehicle passes the entrance, turn the steering wheel hard to the right.
- Go slowly and brake softly.
- Use the lowest reverse gear.
- When the rear of your vehicle passes the clearance line, you're 2 feet from the stop line.

If you think you're going to hit a cone, stop and reposition your vehicle. This is a pull-up, which is an error, but it's better than hitting a cone.

Remember you must pass the Pre-Trip Inspection Test and the Basic Vehicle Control Skills Test before you can move on to the Road Test.

Scoring

You'll lose points for each of these errors:

- encroachments (crossing boundaries)
- pull-ups
- final position

Encroachments

You learned earlier in this chapter that any time you touch a boundary, such as a cone or a line, with any

Figure 8.6. Parallel Park (Conventional or Blind Side)

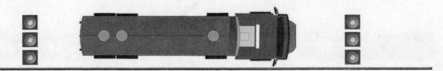

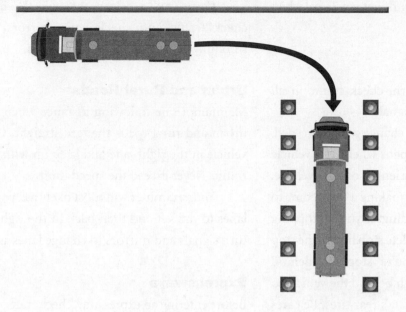

Figure 8.7. Alley Dock

part of your commercial vehicle, it's called an encroachment. Each encroachment counts as an error.

Pull-Ups

As you learned, any time you stop and reverse direction to get into a better position, it's referred to as a pull-up. In some states, you may not be penalized for a few pull-ups, but an excessive number of pull-ups will count as errors. However, in other states, such as North Carolina, each and every pull-up counts as an error. Note that if you stop without changing direction, it's not considered a pull-up.

Final Position

It's important to finish each exercise exactly as you've been instructed. If your vehicle isn't in the final position as described by your examiner, you'll be penalized or you may fail the Basic Vehicle Control Skills Test.

▶ 3. The Road Test

The goal of the Road Test is to measure your ability to drive a CMV responsibly and safely in real-life situations. Your examiner will most likely select a route with a variety of traffic situations that will require you to make right and left turns, cross railroad tracks, drive on country roads, and drive on interstate highways. If a traffic situation isn't available on your route, your examiner might ask you to simulate this situation. This means that your examiner will ask you questions about what you would do in a particular situation.

While you're driving, your examiner will complete an evaluation form. Expect the Road Test to last about 35 to 40 minutes.

Don't panic if you make a mistake or two on the Road Test. Your examiner won't fail you because of a few minor errors.

Driving Maneuvers

Study the guidelines in this section to perform the driving maneuvers on the Road Test—and practice. The more you practice, the more confident you'll feel when you take the test.

Turns

Whenever you're asked to turn, check traffic in all directions and use your turn signals.

Slow down smoothly and change gears as needed. Don't coast unsafely. This happens when your vehicle is out of gear for more than the length of your vehicle.

If you have to stop before making a turn, come to a smooth stop and avoid skidding. If you're stopping for a stop sign, come to a complete stop before the stop sign and/or stop line. If you're stopping behind another vehicle, stop far enough behind the vehicle so that you're able to see the vehicle's rear tires. Be careful not to let your vehicle roll and keep your front wheels aligned and straight.

When you're ready to turn, keep both hands on the steering wheel. Don't change gears during the turn, and use your mirrors to make sure your vehicle isn't going to hit anything on the inside of the turn.

Finish your turn in the correct lane. Turn off your turn signal and get up to the speed of traffic. If you're not in the right lane, move into it as soon as it's safe to do so.

Intersections

When you approach an intersection, check traffic in all directions. Slow down gently and brake smoothly. Change gears when necessary. Come to a complete stop before stop signs, sidewalks, stop lines, or signals. Keep a safe following distance between your vehicle and the one in front of you.

Continue to check traffic, and check your mirrors as you drive through the intersection. Slow down for pedestrians. Avoid changing lanes or shifting gears while driving through an intersection. Keep both hands on the wheel.

Once you've driven through the intersection, check traffic and check your mirrors. Accelerate smoothly, and change gears as needed.

Urban and Rural Roads

Maintain a safe following distance when driving on urban and rural roads that are straight. Center your vehicle in the right lane and keep up with the flow of traffic. Never exceed the speed limit.

Your examiner will most likely ask you to change lanes to the left and then back to the right. Use your turn signals and mirrors to change lanes smoothly.

Expressways

Before entering an expressway, check traffic in all directions, and use your turn signals. Merge smoothly into the proper lane. Once you're on the expressway, pay attention to vehicle spacing and speed. Monitor traffic in all directions. When your examiner tells you to change lanes, be sure to check traffic, and use your turn signal.

When your examiner tells you to get off the expressway, once again check traffic, and use your turn signal. Smoothly reduce your speed and stay within lane markings on the exit ramp.

Stops and Starts

Your examiner will ask you to pull your vehicle over to the side of the road and stop as though you were going to check something on your vehicle. Your examiner may ask you to stop on a grade. Before stopping, check traffic, and move into the right lane.

When you're getting ready to stop, check traffic, and turn on your right turn signal. Smoothly reduce your speed and brake evenly. If necessary, change gears. Bring your vehicle to a full, gentle stop. Make sure your vehicle is parallel to the shoulder of the road and safely out of the way of traffic. Make sure your vehicle won't be blocking driveways or fire hydrants.

Once you've stopped, cancel your turn signal, activate your four-way emergency flashers, and set your parking brake. Move your gear shift to neutral or park and remove your feet from the brake and clutch pedals.

When your examiner tells you to resume driving, use your mirrors to check traffic. Turn off your four-way emergency flashers, and active your left turn signal. When you're ready to pull back onto the road, release your parking brake. Don't turn the wheel before your vehicle moves. Pay close attention to traffic on the left. Accelerate smoothly and get into the proper lane. Cancel your left turn signal once you're back into the flow of traffic. Activate your four-way emergency flashers until you're up to speed, and then cancel them.

Curves

When you're approaching a curve, use your mirrors to check the traffic around you. Reduce your speed before you enter the curve to avoid having to brake heavily and shift during the curve. Keep your vehicle within the lane, and use your mirrors to check traffic.

Railroad Crossings

Your examiner may choose a route that requires you to cross railroad tracks. Before you reach a railroad crossing, slow down, brake smoothly, and shift gears if necessary. Look and listen for oncoming trains and check traffic in all directions. Never stop, change gears, change lanes, or pass another vehicle while any part of your commercial vehicle is on the crossing.

If you're driving a vehicle placarded for hazardous materials, a bus, or a school bus, follow this procedure when crossing railroad tracks:

- Activate your four-way emergency flashers when you approach a railroad crossing.
- Stop your vehicle within 50 feet, but not less than 15 feet, from the nearest track.

- Listen and look in both directions for approaching trains, and watch for signals indicating that a train is on the way. If you're driving a bus, you might also be required to open the window and door before you cross the tracks.
- Keep your hands on the steering wheel as you cross the tracks.
- Don't stop, change gears, or change lanes while any part of your vehicle is on the tracks.
- Deactivate your four-way emergency flashers once you've crossed the tracks, and your vehicle is up to speed.

Note that when you stop 15 to 50 feet from the nearest rail, some states require you to set your parking brake and roll down your window in order to hear a train.

Overpasses and Bridges

After you have driven under an overpass, your examiner may ask you to recall the posted height or clearance, so take note of this early on. After you drive over a bridge, your examiner may ask you to recall the posted weight limit, so pay close attention to signs offering this information. If your route doesn't have an overpass, your examiner might ask you to explain the meaning of another traffic sign. (Study the traffic signs in Chapter 1 to refresh your memory as to their meaning.)

Your General Driving Behavior

In addition to evaluating your skills, your examiner will evaluate your general driving behavior, which simply means he or she will note whether you're a responsible driver. Be sure to do the following:

- Wear your seat belt.
- Obey all traffic signs.
- Complete the test without a moving violation or an accident.

Your Overall Driving Performance

Your examiner will rate your overall driving performance. Follow these guidelines for a good score:

Clutch Usage (for Manual Transmission)

If your vehicle has a manual transmission, always use the clutch to shift. Double-clutch if your vehicle has a nonsynchronized transmission. Don't rev or lug the engine or ride the clutch to control your speed. Don't "pop" the clutch.

Gear Usage (for Manual Transmission)

Don't grind or clash your gears. Select gears that don't rev or lug your engine. Avoid shifting while turning and crossing intersections.

Brake Usage

Don't ride or pump your brakes, and don't brake harshly. Brake smoothly while applying steady pressure.

Lane Usage

Be careful not to drive your vehicle over curbs, sidewalks, or lane markings. Stop behind lines, crossways, and stop signs. When you complete a turn, get into the correct lane. When you complete a right turn, stay in the right lane. Unless a lane is blocked, always move to the right lane.

Steering

Avoid under- or oversteering your vehicle. Unless you're shifting, both of your hands should be on the steering wheel.

Regular Traffic Checks

Check traffic and check your mirrors periodically. Check your mirrors before, during, and after you drive through an intersection. Keep an eye on traffic in busy areas and areas where there are pedestrians.

Use of Turn Signals

Always use your turn signals at appropriate times and cancel them after a turn or lane change.

Chapter 8 Review Quiz

1–4: Circle the correct answer.

1. When you're asked to back into a space that's to the right rear of your vehicle, it's called a(n) _____ exercise.
   a. offset back/right
   b. straight line backing
   c. alley dock
   d. offset back/left

2. When completing the right turn exercise on the Basic Vehicle Control Skills Test, your right wheel shouldn't be more than _____ inches from the cone.
   a. 2
   b. 4
   c. 6
   d. 8

3. Whenever you touch a boundary with your CMV during the Basic Vehicle Control Skills Test, it's called a(n)
   a. pull-up.
   b. encroachment.
   c. final position.
   d. offset

4. The _____ exercise requires you to maneuver your vehicle into a 45-degree angle and then back it into a space.
   a. alley dock
   b. straight line backing
   c. offset back
   d. parallel park (conventional or blind side)

5–8: Indicate whether each statement is true or false.

____ **5.** When completing the offset back/left exercise, you should lean out your window to get a good view of your vehicle.

____ **6.** When parallel parking (driver side or sight side) in a straight truck, you must pull the entire truck into the space.

____ **7.** During the Road Test, it's okay to change gears when making a turn.

____ **8.** During the Road Test, you should spend most of your time in the right lane.

Check your answers on page 295.

CHAPTER

9 ▶ Doubles and Triples

CHAPTER SUMMARY

Doubles and triples are combination vehicles with a tractor and two or three semitrailers. This chapter will help you understand the special concerns associated with safely driving doubles and triples to prepare for the various exams you'll have to pass to operate these vehicles.

I n Chapter 7, you learned that a combination vehicle consists of a tractor or truck and a trailer used to haul cargo. You learned about two types of trailers: semitrailers and full trailers. A **semitrailer** has only rear axles and can't stand on its own. It's attached to the tractor using the fifth wheel on the tractor and the kingpin on the semitrailer. The most common combination vehicle consists of a tractor and semitrailer. A **full trailer**, on the other hand, has both front and rear axles and can stand on its own. A full trailer is most often connected to a semitrailer but may also be connected to a straight truck. Both semitrailers and full trailers come in different lengths.

Doubles and triples are even longer and heavier than the combination vehicles you learned about in Chapter 7. A **double**, also called a **double-bottom rig**, usually consists of a tractor, a semitrailer connected to the tractor, and a second semitrailer connected to the first. Two trailers together are often called **twins** or **twin trailers**. A **triple**, also called a **triple-bottom rig**, usually consists of a tractor, a semitrailer connected to the tractor, a second semitrailer connected to the first, and a third semitrailer connected to the second. Because they're difficult to drive and take up a lot of space on highways, triples aren't allowed in some states.

Becoming licensed to drive doubles and triples isn't easy. For starters, you need to take the General Knowledge Test and the Skills Test that everyone applying for a CDL must take, but you need to take your Skills Test in a combination vehicle. You also need to take a knowledge test about combination vehicles and a knowledge test about doubles and triples—and you aren't finished yet! Since a combination vehicle is a Class A vehicle and all Class A vehicles have air brakes, you need to take both a knowledge test and a skills test about air brakes. Once you pass all of these tests, you'll receive a "T" endorsement letter code on your CDL, which means you're qualified to drive doubles and triples.

On the Doubles and Triples Test, you may be asked questions about:

- pulling doubles and triples
- coupling and uncoupling doubles and triples
- inspecting doubles and triples

The Double and Triples Test contains 20 multiple-choice questions, and you must correctly answer 16, or 80 percent, to pass.

▶ Types of Doubles and Triples

Doubles and triples of different lengths have different names, and these names are commonplace within the trucking industry.

Figure 9.1. Double and Triple Trailers

STAA Double-Trailer Combination

An **STAA double-trailer combination** consists of a tractor pulling two 28-foot trailers. STAA stands for Surface Transportation Assistance Act, which was

Tests You Need to Take to Drive Doubles and Triples	
General Knowledge Test	50 questions (40 must be answered correctly)
Skills Test (in a combination vehicle)	
Combination Vehicles Test	20 questions (16 must be answered correctly)
Air Brakes Test	25 questions (20 must be answered correctly)
Air Brakes Skills Test (in a vehicle with air brakes)	

passed in 1982 to allow longer trucks to travel on a certain network of federal highways referred to as the National Network (the NN). Note that a single-trailer STAA truck can be from 48 to 53 feet long.

Longer Combination Vehicles (LCVs)

Longer combination vehicles (LCVs) include double-trailer combinations where at least one trailer is longer than 28 feet, as well as triple-trailer combinations.

One type of LCV is a **Rocky Mountain double (RMD)**. This is a tractor pulling a 40- to 48-foot trailer and a 26- to 29-foot trailer.

A **turnpike double (TPD)** is a tractor pulling two trailers, each of which are generally 40 to 48 feet long.

Triple-trailer combinations usually consist of three 28-foot-long trailers.

Each state has different restrictions about the types of LCVs allowed on certain roadways, and each requires different permits to drive certain LCVs.

▶ Pulling Doubles and Triples

You just learned that pulling doubles and triples is more difficult than pulling only one trailer. It's extremely important to plan ahead when pulling so many trailers to make sure you have enough time and space to change lanes when necessary. Keep the following in mind when driving doubles and triples:

Avoid Rollovers

Turning too quickly is the main cause of a rollover. Therefore, when driving a double or a triple, steer gently. Go slowly while driving around corners and curves and when traveling on-ramps and off-ramps. Keep in mind that a safe speed for a single tractor-trailer combination is usually too fast for a double or a triple.

A fully loaded trailer is much more likely to roll over than an empty one because the center of gravity is much higher in a loaded trailer. Keep the cargo as close to the ground as possible, and try to make sure the load is centered. A load that's leaning to one side will cause the trailer to lean, which makes it more likely to tip.

Avoid the "Crack-the-Whip" Effect

The last trailer in a triple is 3.5 times more likely to turn over because of the "crack-the-whip" effect—and the more trailers you're pulling, the greater the odds that the last trailer will roll over. You read about this effect in Chapter 7. To understand the crack-the-whip effect better, imagine a group of children holding hands while roller-skating around a turn. The force is greater for those at the end of the line than it is for those closer to the center of the rink. The children at the end of the line are "whipped" around the corner and are more likely to fall. To avoid your rear trailer tipping over from the crack-the-whip effect, steer gently and slowly.

If your trailer whips or swerves and you haven't steered abruptly, slow down immediately and stop as soon as you can. Then try to determine the cause of the swerve. You may have a flat tire, your brakes may be dragging, or your load may have shifted.

Look Far Ahead

In Chapter 2, you learned that you should look about 12 to 15 seconds ahead of your vehicle, a distance of about one-eighth of a mile (or one city block) at slower speeds or one-quarter of a mile at faster (highway) speeds. When you're driving a double or a triple, look even farther ahead than this. Keep a close eye on the upcoming road to make sure you have enough time and space to slowly change lanes when necessary, so you can avoid rolling over or jackknifing.

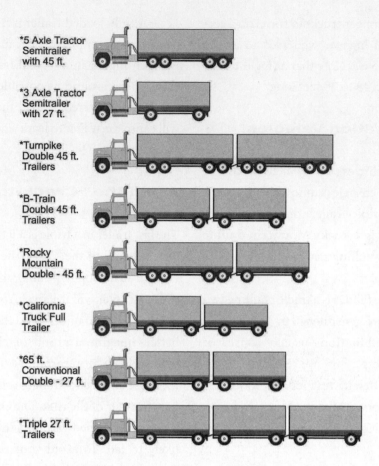

Figure 9.2. Influence of Combination Type on Rearward Amplification

Manage Space Appropriately

Doubles and triples take up a lot of space on highways—much more than other commercial vehicles. Because of this, motorists usually aren't happy to see them. It takes a lot longer to pass a double or a triple. Such long vehicles also block entrance and exit ramps, making it difficult for motorists to get on and off highways.

Try to understand motorists' frustrations and take extra care not to cut off motorists when changing lanes in a double or a triple. Allow a safe following distance and make sure you have sizable gaps before and after your vehicle when getting on or off highways.

▶ Drive Carefully in Adverse Conditions

Adverse conditions are unfavorable driving conditions. Use extra care when driving doubles and triples in adverse conditions such as snow, ice, rain, and fog and when driving at night or in the mountains. Be aware that you're much more likely to skid in adverse conditions when driving a double or a triple because your length is greater and you have to pull more **dead axles**, or axles that aren't connected to the drive train. Follow these guidelines when driving doubles and triples in adverse weather conditions:

Allow More Following Distance

Allow a greater following distance when pulling two or more trailers. Allow one second for every 10 feet of your vehicle's length. Add an additional second when you're driving over 40 mph. For example, a 100-foot double traveling at 35 mph would need 10 seconds following distance. The same vehicle traveling at 45 mph would need 11 seconds.

Maintain Traction

If you're driving on slippery roads, don't use the engine brake or the speed retarder. They can cause your CMV to lose traction and skid. Losing traction can also cause your CMV to jackknife. If a set of wheels on one of your trailers skids, the trailer might jackknife.

Recover from Skids

The most common kind of skid is the drive-wheel skid, which is usually caused by accelerating on ice or snow.

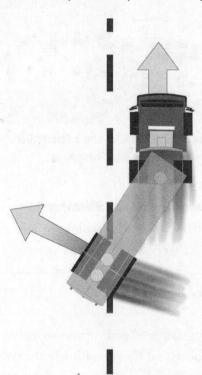

Figure 9.3. A drive-wheel skid might cause the trailer to push the tractor sideways, causing a jackknife.

Taking your foot off the accelerator is sometimes enough to stop a drive-wheel skid. If it's very slippery and you're on ice, push in the clutch. This will let the wheels roll freely until they can regain traction. If your CMV begins to slide sideways, steer quickly in the direction that you want your vehicle to go. **Counter-steering**—turning the steering wheel quickly in the other direction after steering to correct a skid—can also help you recover from a skid and restore traction to the tires.

Brake Correctly

It's especially important to correctly apply brakes when driving doubles and triples in bad weather, since these vehicles are extremely long and heavy. Follow these guidelines:

- Slow to a safe speed before driving around a curve. Accelerate slightly during the curve.
- Go slowly on long downgrades using the right gear and the proper braking method (snub braking) to keep your speed from increasing.
- When your trailer is empty, bouncing can cause your wheels to lose traction and lock up, which can cause the trailer to swing around and jackknife. Also keep in mind that an empty truck takes longer to stop than a loaded truck.
- If you have to brake in an emergency, use controlled or stab braking to stop your CMV. (Turn back to Chapter 3 if you need to review these methods of braking.) These braking methods work very well when stopping doubles and triples because they allow you to stop your vehicle in a straight line and avoid jackknifing.

Change Lanes Carefully

You already know that you need to steer gently when driving doubles and triples, especially in adverse conditions. Use your mirrors to help you safely change lanes. Look in your mirrors when you signal a lane change, when you're making the change, and after you make the lane change. Avoid changing lanes near on-ramps, off-ramps, and intersections.

▶ Parking Doubles and Triples

As you can imagine, parking doubles and triples is tricky. Always park in a spot where you can pull straight through, meaning you don't have to back or turn to get out of your parking space. Scan parking lots to find a good place to park before you pull into them.

▶ Coupling and Uncoupling Doubles and Triples

As you learned in Chapter 7, **coupling** means backing the tractor so it's close to the trailer and then attaching the trailer to the tractor air supply. Once you attach the tractor and trailer, you need to supply electricity to the trailer so its lights work. If the trailer has air brakes, you need to supply a line to the trailer for air. **Uncoupling** means detaching the tractor and trailer.

Position the more heavily loaded trailer in the first position behind the tractor. The lightest trailer should be last.

Coupling and uncoupling trailers isn't difficult, but getting it right is very important. Incorrect coupling or uncoupling can be dangerous since it could result in serious damage or an accident. Note that while there are other ways of coupling and uncoupling the many different types of tractor-trailer and truck-trailer combinations, the most common methods for doubles

and triples are discussed here. These are the methods most likely to appear on your test.

Coupling Doubles

Be aware that not all rigs are the same. Check the specifics for your particular rig before coupling trailers. Before you begin, walk around the tractor and the trailers. Make sure the path is clear of anything that could damage the tractor and trailers. Be aware that boards lying on the ground are a hazard, because they may pop up if you run over them. They might also have nails in them that could damage a tire.

Learn the parts of your tractor and trailers that are involved in coupling and uncoupling. Study the list of parts on this page. Look at Figure 9.4 so you can see where each part is located.

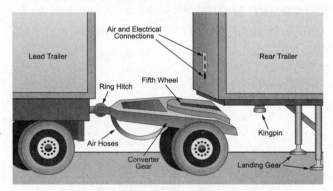

Figure 9.4. The Parts of a Tractor and a Semitrailer Involved in Coupling and Uncoupling

Attach the Tractor to the Semitrailer

While you learned how to attach a semitrailer to a tractor in Chapter 7, we'll review these steps here.

Step 1: Inspect the Fifth Wheel

- Check for damaged and/or missing parts.
- Check to see that the mounting to the tractor is secure, and check for cracks in the frame.
- Make sure the fifth wheel plate is greased.

Parts Involved in Coupling and Uncoupling

- **air tank petcock**. a valve on an air tank that, when turned, releases air.
- **apron**. a surface for resting the trailer on the fifth wheel.
- **converter dolly**. an assembly, or group of parts, with one or more axles and a fifth wheel, which is used to convert a semitrailer to a full trailer; sometimes called **converter gear**, converter dollies are used to create doubles and triples.
- **drawbar**. a bar, usually made of metal, that connects a truck and a trailer; sometimes called the tongue of the trailer.
- **fifth wheel**. a locking device used to connect a semitrailer to a tractor.
- **full trailer**. a trailer with axles in the front and rear and can stand without support (unlike a semitrailer); full trailers are coupled to straight trucks and to the rear of semitrailers or full trailers by a drawbar (also called a tongue); full trailers are seldom used alone with tractors and are more often attached to semitrailers.
- **kingpin**. attaches the semitrailer to the tractor; it's always in the center of the trailer apron in front of the semitrailer.
- **pintle hook**. hook on the rear of a truck used to tow trailers.
- **semitrailer**. a trailer that can't stand alone (the front part rests on a tractor). A semitrailer is coupled to a tractor using the fifth wheel on the tractor and the kingpin on the semitrailer.

- Make sure the fifth-wheel is in the proper position for coupling. The correct position is as follows:

  - The fifth wheel should be tilted down toward the rear of the tractor.
  - Make sure the jaws are open.
  - The safety unlocking handle should be in the automatic lock position.
  - If you have a sliding fifth wheel, make sure it's locked.
  - Make sure trailer kingpin isn't bent or broken.

Step 2: Chock the Wheels

- Be sure the trailer wheels are **chocked** (secured with a wedge) and the spring brakes are on.
- Check that the cargo (if you have any) is secure, so it won't move when you're coupling.

Step 3: Position the Tractor

- Move the tractor right in front of the trailer. Never back under the trailer at an angle because you might push the trailer sideways and break the landing gear.
- Check your position by using your mirrors to look down both sides of the trailer.

Step 4: Back Slowly

- Back until the fifth wheel just touches the trailer.
- Make sure you don't hit the trailer with the tractor.

Step 5: Secure the Tractor

- Put on the parking brake.
- Put the transmission in neutral.

Step 6: Check the Trailer Height

- The trailer should be low enough that it rises slightly when the tractor backs under it.
- If you need to adjust the height of the trailer, crank the landing gear up or down.
- Make sure the kingpin and fifth wheel are aligned.

Step 7: Connect the Air Lines to the Trailer

- Check the **glad hand seals** (air hose brake system connections between a tractor and a trailer) and connect the tractor emergency air line to the trailer emergency air line.
- Check the glad hand seals and connect the tractor service air line to the trailer service air line.

Step 8: Supply Air to the Trailer

- From the cab, push in the air supply knob or move the tractor protection valve control from the "emergency" to the "normal" position. This will supply air to the trailer brake system.
- Wait until the air pressure is normal.
- Check the brake system for crossed air lines.
- Shut off the engine so you can hear the brakes.

  - Apply and release the trailer brakes and listen for sounds of the trailer brakes being applied and released. You should be able to hear the brakes move when

they're applied and hear the air escape when they're released.

- Check the air brake system pressure gauge to make sure there aren't any signs of major air loss.

- When you're sure the trailer brakes are working, start the engine.
- Make sure the air pressure is at a normal level.

Step 9: Lock the Trailer Brakes

- Pull out the air supply knob or move the tractor protection valve control from "normal" to "emergency."

Step 10: Back under the Trailer

- Use the lowest reverse gear.
- Back the tractor slowly under the trailer to avoid hitting the kingpin too hard.
- Stop when the kingpin is locked into the fifth wheel.

Step 11: Check the Connection for Security

- Raise the trailer landing gear (the trailer supports) *slightly* off the ground.
- Pull the tractor *gently* forward while the trailer brakes are still locked to check that the trailer is locked onto the tractor.

Step 12: Secure the Vehicle

- Put the transmission in neutral.
- Put the parking brakes on.

- Shut off the engine and take the key with you so no one else can move the truck while you're under it.

Step 13: Inspect the Coupling

- Use a flashlight, if you need one.
- Make sure there isn't space between the upper and lower fifth wheel. If there is space, something is wrong. (The kingpin might be sitting on top of the closed fifth-wheel jaws, which would allow the trailer to come loose very easily.)
- Get under the trailer and look into the back of the fifth wheel. Make sure the fifth-wheel jaws have closed around the shank of the kingpin.
- Check that the locking lever is in the "lock" position.
- Check that the safety latch is in position over the locking lever. (On some fifth wheels, the catch must be put in place by hand.)
- If the coupling isn't right, don't drive the coupled unit until it's fixed.

Step 14: Connect the Electrical Cord and Check the Air Lines

- Plug the electrical cord into the trailer and fasten the safety catch.
- Check the air lines and the electrical line for signs of damage.
- Make sure the air and electrical lines won't hit any moving parts of the vehicle.

Step 15: Raise the Front Trailer Supports (Landing Gear)

- Use the low gear range (if it's equipped) to start raising the landing gear. Once it's free of weight, switch to the high gear range.
- Raise the landing gear all the way up.
- After raising the landing gear, secure the crank handle safely.
- When the full weight of the trailer is resting on the tractor:

  - Check for enough clearance between the rear of tractor frame and the landing gear. (When the tractor turns sharply, it must not hit the landing gear.)
  - Check that there's enough clearance between the top of the tractor tires and the nose of the trailer.

Attach the Second Trailer
Step 1: Get Ready

- Once you've attached the tractor to the first semitrailer, it's time to attach the second trailer. If the second trailer doesn't have spring brakes, drive the tractor (with the semitrailer attached) close to it. Then connect the emergency line, charge the trailer's air tank, and then disconnect the emergency line. If the slack adjusters are properly adjusted, this will set the trailer's emergency brakes. If you have any doubt as to whether the emergency brakes are set, chock the wheels.

Step 2: Position the Converter Dolly in Front of the Second Trailer

■ As you learned, the converter dolly is a coupling device with one or two axles and a fifth wheel. Converter dollies are used to couple a semitrailer to the rear of a tractor-trailer combination. Before you can couple a second semitrailer, you need to position the converter dolly in front of it. To do this, follow these steps:

• Release the converter dolly's brakes by opening the air tank petcock. If the converter dolly has spring brakes, use its parking brake control.
• If the converter dolly is fairly close to the second trailer, you can wheel the dolly into position by hand so it's in line with the kingpin. Another option is to use the tractor and first trailer to pick up the converter dolly. To do this, follow these steps:

   - Position the tractor-trailer combination as close as possible to the converter dolly.
   - Move the dolly to the rear of the first trailer and couple it to the trailer.
   - Lock the pintle hook.
   - Secure the dolly support in a raised position.
   - Pull the dolly into position—as close as possible to the nose of the second trailer.
   - Then lower the dolly support.
   - Unhook the dolly from the first trailer.

   - Wheel the converter dolly into position in front of the second trailer so that the converter dolly is in line with the kingpin.

Step 3: Connect the Converter Dolly to the Front Trailer

■ To begin this step, back the first semitrailer into position in front of the tongue of the converter dolly.
■ Hook the converter to the front semitrailer.
■ Lock the pintle hook.
■ Secure the converter gear support so it's in a raised position.

Step 4: Connect the Converter Dolly to the Rear Trailer

■ Before connecting the converter dolly to the rear trailer, make sure the trailer's brakes are locked. If you have any doubt, chock the wheels.
■ Check the height of the trailer. The trailer should be slightly lower than the center of the fifth wheel. The trailer should be raised slightly when the converter dolly is pushed underneath it.
■ Once you're sure that the height of the trailer is correct, back the converter dolly underneath the rear trailer.
■ Raise the landing gear slightly off the ground, so it's not damaged if the trailer moves.
■ The trailer should be coupled. Test it by pulling against the kingpin.
■ Check to make sure there isn't any space between the upper and lower fifth wheel.

As you learned, you need to couple and uncouple trailers correctly to avoid being injured. These are some common errors and their resulting hazards:

Error	Result
If the trailer isn't secure . . .	the brake lines may be damaged.
If the ground isn't firm where you're coupling . . .	a trailer might tip over.
If the jaws aren't securely fastened on the kingpin . . .	a trailer might break loose while you're driving.

Make sure the locking jaws are closed on the kingpin.

- If everything seems okay, connect the safety chains, the air hoses, and the light cords.
- Close the converter dolly's air tank petcock and the service and emergency shut-off valves at the rear of the second trailer.
- Open the shut-off valves at the rear of the first trailer and on the converter dolly, if the dolly has them.
- Completely raise the landing gear.
- Push the air supply knob in to charge the trailer's brakes. Then check for air at the rear of the second trailer. To do this, open the emergency line shut-off. There should be air pressure. If there isn't air pressure, something is wrong and the brakes won't work.

Attach the Third Trailer

Attaching a third trailer is just like attaching a second. Repeat the steps in the section, "Attach the Second Trailer."

▶ Uncoupling a Tractor and a Semitrailer

You learned how to uncouple a tractor and semitrailer in Chapter 7. These steps are repeated here for easy reference and to help you understand how to uncouple double and triple trailers.

Step 1: Position the Rig

- Make sure the surface of the parking area can support the weight of the trailer.
- Check that the tractor is lined up with the trailer. (If you pull out at an angle, you can damage the landing gear.)

Step 2: Ease the Pressure on the Locking Jaws

- Shut off the trailer air supply to lock the trailer brakes.
- Back up gently to ease the pressure on the fifth-wheel locking jaws, which will help you release the fifth-wheel locking lever.
- Put on the parking brakes while the tractor is pushing against the kingpin, which will

hold the rig with pressure off the locking jaws.

Step 3: Chock the Trailer Wheels

- Chock the trailer wheels if the trailer doesn't have spring brakes or if you're not sure whether the trailer's brakes are set.

Step 4: Lower the Landing Gear

- If the trailer is empty, lower the landing gear until it makes firm contact with the ground.
- If the trailer is loaded, after the landing gear makes firm contact with the ground, turn the crank in low gear a few extra turns. This will lift some weight off the tractor and will make it easier to unlatch the fifth wheel and couple again in the future.

Step 5: Disconnect the Air Lines and the Electrical Cable

- Disconnect the air lines from the trailer. Connect air line glad hands to dummy couplers at the back of the cab or couple them together.
- Hang the electrical cable with the plug down to prevent moisture from entering it.
- Make sure the lines are supported so they won't be damaged while you're driving the tractor.

Step 6: Unlock the Fifth Wheel

- Raise the release handle lock.
- Pull the release handle to the "open" position.

- Keep your legs and feet clear of the rear tractor wheels. If you don't, you could be seriously injured if the vehicle moves.

Step 7: Pull the Tractor Partially Clear of Trailer

- Pull the tractor forward until the fifth wheel comes out from under the trailer.
- Stop with the tractor frame under the trailer. This prevents the trailer from falling to the ground if the landing gear collapses or sinks.

Step 8: Secure the Tractor

- Apply the parking brake.
- Put the transmission in neutral.

Step 9: Inspect the Trailer Supports

- Make sure the ground is supporting the trailer.
- Make sure the landing gear isn't damaged.

Step 10: Pull the Tractor Clear of the Trailer

- Release the parking brakes.
- Check the area and then drive the tractor forward until it clears.

▶ Uncoupling Twin Trailers

Follow these steps to uncouple the rear trailer in a double:

- Park the double so the tractor and trailers are straight and on firm, level ground.
- Apply the parking brakes.

- If the second trailer doesn't have spring brakes, chock its wheels.
- Lower the second trailer's landing gear just enough to take some weight off the converter dolly.
- Close the air shut-offs on the second trailer and on the converter dolly, if it has them.
- Disconnect all air and electrical lines connected to the converter dolly and secure them.
- Release the converter dolly's brakes.
- Release the converter dolly's fifth-wheel latch.
- Slowly pull the tractor, the first semitrailer, and the converter dolly forward. This will pull the dolly out from under the rear of the semitrailer.

▶ Uncoupling a Converter Dolly

Follow these steps to uncouple a converter dolly:

- Lower the converter dolly's landing gear.
- Disconnect its safety chains.
- Apply the dolly's spring brakes or chock its wheels.
- Release the pintle hook on the first semi-trailer.
- Slowly drive and pull away from the dolly.

Never unlock the pintle hook while the dolly is still underneath the rear trailer. If you do this, the drawbar may fly up and injure you. It will also make it difficult for you to recouple the trailer.

▶ Inspecting Doubles and Triples

In Chapter 4, you learned the importance of inspecting your CMV. You learned that problems with your vehicle aren't always obvious and that sometimes you have to do some detective work to uncover them. You learned to inspect your vehicle at the following points during a trip:

- before a trip (pre-trip inspection)
- while driving (en-route inspection)
- when making stops
- after a trip (post-trip inspection)

The Seven-Step Inspection Procedure

- Step 1: Vehicle Overview
- Step 2: Check Engine Compartment
- Step 3: Start Engine and Inspect Inside of Cab
- Step 4: Turn Off Engine and Check Lights
- Step 5: Do a Walkaround Inspection
- Step 6: Check Signal Lights
- Step 7: Start the Engine and Check the Brake System

You also learned the seven-step inspection procedure you should use during pre-trip inspections. You should follow these same seven steps when inspecting a double or a triple. Be aware, however, that you have more of some items to inspect on a double or a triple. For instance, doubles and triples have more tires, wheels, lights, and reflectors. They also have some additional items in need of inspection. Check for the following additional items when inspecting a double or a triple:

Coupling System Area

Check the lower fifth wheel to make sure

- it's securely mounted to the frame
- it doesn't have missing or damaged parts
- it has enough grease
- there is not visible space between the upper and lower fifth wheel
- the locking jaws are around the shank (stem or leg) of the kingpin and not the head
- the release arm is properly seated and the safety lock is engaged

Check the upper fifth wheel to make sure

- the glide plate is securely mounted to the trailer frame
- the kingpin isn't damaged

Check the air and electrical lines to the trailer to make sure

- the electrical cord is firmly plugged in and secure
- the air lines are properly connected to the glad hands
- the air lines are free of leaks
- the air lines have enough slack for turns
- all lines are free of damage

Check the sliding fifth wheel to make sure

- the slide isn't damaged
- no parts are missing
- the slide is properly greased
- all locking pins are there and are locked in place
- it doesn't have air leaks if it's air powered

- it isn't so far forward that during turns the tractor frame will hit the landing gear or the cab will hit the trailer

Check the landing gear to make sure

- it's fully raised
- it isn't missing any parts
- its parts aren't bent or damaged
- the crank handle is in place and secure
- it's free from air or hydraulic leaks if it's power operated

Check double and triple trailers to make sure

- the shut-off valves are as follows:

  - rear of front and middle trailer: open
  - rear of last trailer: closed
  - converter dolly air tank drain valve: closed

- all air lines are supported and glad hands are properly connected
- the spare tire, if equipped, is secure on the converter dolly
- the pintle eye of the converter dolly is in place in the pintle hook of the trailer
- the pintle hook is latched
- safety chains to trailer(s) are secure
- light cords are firmly in sockets on trailers

▶ Doubles and Triples Air Brakes Check

As you learned, doubles and triples are Class A vehicles, which means they have air brakes. Check the air brakes as you would on a tractor-trailer combination vehicle.

Follow the procedure for inspecting air brakes on combination vehicles in Chapter 7. In addition, check for the following when inspecting air brakes on doubles or triples:

Check That Air Flows to All Trailers

- Secure the tractor by applying the parking brake and chocking the wheels.
- When the air pressure reaches normal, push in the red "trailer air supply" knob. This supplies air to the emergency supply lines.
- Use the trailer's hand brake to supply air to the service line.
- Open the emergency line shut-off valve at the rear of the last trailer.
- Listen for air escaping, which means the entire system is charged.
- Close the emergency line valve. Open the service line valve to check that air pressure goes through all trailers and then close the valve. Note that if you don't hear air escaping from both lines, check that the shut-off valves on the trailers and converter dollies are in the "open" position. In order for your brakes to work, you must have air all the way to the back of the rig.

Test the Tractor Protection Valve

- Charge the trailer's air brake system by building up normal air pressure and then pushing in the air supply knob.
- Shut off the engine.
- Step on and off the brake pedal several times. This reduces the air pressure in the tanks. The trailer air supply control should pop out or go from the "normal" to the

"emergency" position when the air pressure falls into the pressure range specified by the manufacturer. For most CMVs, this is within the range of 20 to 40 psi.

- If the tractor protection valve doesn't work properly, a leak in an air hose or trailer brake could drain all the air from the tractor, which would cause the emergency brakes to come on.

Test the Trailer Emergency Brakes

- Charge the trailer air brake system and check that the trailer rolls freely.
- Stop and pull out the trailer air supply control, which is also called the tractor protection valve control or the trailer emergency valve, or place it in the emergency position. Use the tractor to pull gently on the trailer to make sure the trailer emergency brakes are on.

Test the Trailer Service Brakes

- Check for normal pressure, release the parking brakes, and move the vehicle ahead slowly.
- Use the hand control, if there is one, to apply the trailer brakes. You should feel the brakes come on, which lets you know that the brakes are connected and are working properly.

Chapter 9 Review Quiz

1–4: Circle the correct answer.

1. A tractor pulling a 40- to 53-foot trailer and a
    26- to 29-foot trailer is called a
    a. triple-trailer combination.
    b. turnpike double.
    c. Rocky Mountain double.
    d. California truck full trailer

2. Which of these is a locking device used to con-
    nect a semitrailer to a tractor?
    a. converter dolly
    b. fifth wheel
    c. ring hitch
    d. kingpin

5–6: Write out your answer.

5. How do you release a converter dolly's brakes?

    a. _____
    _____
    _____
    _____

    b. _____
    _____
    _____
    _____

    c. _____
    _____
    _____
    _____

    d. _____
    _____
    _____

3. What kind of trailer has only rear axles and can't
    stand on its own?
    a. a semitrailer
    b. a tandem trailer
    c. a full trailer
    c. an axle trailer

4. A hook on the back of a tractor that's used to
    tow trailers is called a _____ hook.
    a. pintle
    b. drawbar
    c. petcock
    d. dolly

6. How can you tell if a trailer is the right height
    before you connect it to a converter dolly?

    a. _____
    _____
    _____

    b. _____
    _____
    _____

    c. _____
    _____
    _____

    d. _____
    _____

7–12: Indicate whether each statement is true or false.

_____ **7.** If you're driving on slippery roads, you should use the speed retarder.

_____ **8.** Countersteering can help you recover from a drive-wheel skid.

_____ **9.** You should use controlled braking to slow down a double or a triple in an emergency.

_____ **10.** The heaviest trailer should be positioned behind the tractor.

_____ **11.** When you inspect the lower fifth wheel after coupling, you should check to make sure the kingpin isn't damaged.

_____ **12.** The "crack-the-whip" effect usually affects only the first trailer in a double or a triple.

Check your answers on page 295.

Doubles and Triples Endorsement Practice Test

1. ⓐ ⓑ ⓒ ⓓ
2. ⓐ ⓑ ⓒ ⓓ
3. ⓐ ⓑ ⓒ ⓓ
4. ⓐ ⓑ ⓒ ⓓ
5. ⓐ ⓑ ⓒ ⓓ
6. ⓐ ⓑ ⓒ ⓓ
7. ⓐ ⓑ ⓒ ⓓ
8. ⓐ ⓑ ⓒ ⓓ
9. ⓐ ⓑ ⓒ ⓓ
10. ⓐ ⓑ ⓒ ⓓ

11. ⓐ ⓑ ⓒ ⓓ
12. ⓐ ⓑ ⓒ ⓓ
13. ⓐ ⓑ ⓒ ⓓ
14. ⓐ ⓑ ⓒ ⓓ
15. ⓐ ⓑ ⓒ ⓓ
16. ⓐ ⓑ ⓒ ⓓ
17. ⓐ ⓑ ⓒ ⓓ
18. ⓐ ⓑ ⓒ ⓓ
19. ⓐ ⓑ ⓒ ⓓ
20. ⓐ ⓑ ⓒ ⓓ

21. ⓐ ⓑ ⓒ ⓓ
22. ⓐ ⓑ ⓒ ⓓ
23. ⓐ ⓑ ⓒ ⓓ
24. ⓐ ⓑ ⓒ ⓓ
25. ⓐ ⓑ ⓒ ⓓ
26. ⓐ ⓑ ⓒ ⓓ
27. ⓐ ⓑ ⓒ ⓓ
28. ⓐ ⓑ ⓒ ⓓ
29. ⓐ ⓑ ⓒ ⓓ
30. ⓐ ⓑ ⓒ ⓓ

▶ Doubles and Triples Endorsement Practice Test

Choose the correct answer. Mark the letter on the answer sheet on page 185.

1. When you check the lower fifth wheel after coupling, you should make sure the
   a. release arm is properly seated.
   b. glide plate is securely mounted.
   c. air lines are properly connected.
   d. electrical cord is firmly plugged in.

2. What should you do to set the emergency brakes on a second trailer before coupling?
   a. Connect the emergency line.
   b. Charge the trailer air tank.
   c. Disconnect the emergency line.
   d. All of the above.

3. Which of the following is true about looking ahead when driving doubles and triples?
   a. You should look about 12 to 15 seconds ahead of your vehicle.
   b. You should look about 10 seconds ahead of your vehicle.
   c. You should look at least 16 seconds ahead of your vehicle.
   d. None of the above.

4. Which part involved in coupling and uncoupling allows a semitrailer to become a full trailer?
   a. the drawbar
   b. the apron
   c. the fifth wheel
   d. the converter dolly

5. If you're uncoupling a loaded trailer, what should you do after the landing gear makes contact with the ground?
   a. Unlatch the fifth wheel.
   b. Pull the release handle to "open."
   c. Turn the crank in low gear a few times.
   d. Check that the tractor is lined up with the trailer.

6. How do you check to make sure the trailer height is correct before coupling?
   a. The kingpin should be lower than the fifth wheel.
   b. The trailer should be slightly raised when the tractor or dolly backs under it.
   c. The trailer should be higher than the center of the fifth wheel.
   d. The glad hand seals should easily reach the air line.

7. Which long combination vehicle (LCV) consists of a tractor pulling two trailers that are each 40- to 48-feet long?
   a. a triple-trailer combination
   b. a Rocky Mountain double
   c. a turnpike double
   d. an STAA double-trailer

8. What is the main cause of a rollover in a double or a triple?
   a. an uneven load
   b. turning too quickly
   c. dragging brakes
   d. none of the above

9. How much following distance is required for a 90-foot triple traveling at 50 mph?
   a. 9 seconds
   b. 9.5 seconds
   c. 10 seconds
   d. 18 seconds

10. A valve on an air tank that releases air when you turn it is called
    a. an air tank petcock.
    b. an air tank apron.
    c. a pintle hook.
    d. a pintle eye.

11. What do you need to do before you couple a second semitrailer?
    a. Lock the pintle hook.
    b. Close the locking jaws on the kingpin.
    c. Position the converter dolly in front of it.
    d. Raise the landing gear.

12. On a long downgrade, you should apply your brakes
    a. barely at all, unless you are in traffic.
    b. hard enough to bring you to a complete stop.
    c. only as hard as necessary and then release.
    d. none of the above.

13. You're checking to make sure that air is flowing to all trailers in a triple. After you open the service and emergency line valves at the rear of the last trailer, you should hear air escaping from
    a. only the emergency line.
    b. only the service line.
    c. both the emergency line and service line.
    d. neither the emergency line nor the service line.

14. When inspecting the coupling area on a triple, which shut-off valve(s) should be open?
    a. the valves at the rear of the front and middle trailers
    b. the valves at the rear of the last trailer
    c. the converter dolly air tank drain valve
    d. none of the above

15. When uncoupling twin trailers, what should you do if the second trailer doesn't have spring brakes?
    a. Lock its pintle hook.
    b. Chock its wheels.
    c. Use the emergency brake.
    d. Use the dolly's brake.

16. If you're changing lanes, you should check your mirrors
    a. before you signal the lane change.
    b. after you change lanes.
    c. right after you start to change lanes.
    d. all of the above.

17. Which of these statements is true about empty trailers?
    a. They have a higher center of gravity than full trailers.
    b. They're more likely to lose traction than full trailers.
    c. They move faster on downgrades than full trailers.
    d. They're easier to control than full trailers.

18. If you're driving twin trailers on a slippery roadway and your drive wheels skid and your vehicle begins to slide sideways, you should
  a. take your foot off the accelerator.
  b. push in the clutch.
  c. steer in the direction you want to go.
  d. all of the above.

19. When inspecting the pintle hook, you should check to make sure that it's
  a. released.
  b. locked.
  c. raised.
  d. greased.

20. Where is the fifth wheel located?
  a. on the dolly's apron
  b. on the front of the trailer
  c. on the front of the dolly
  d. on the rear of the tractor frame

21. You're driving a double and you must use your brakes to avoid an upcoming emergency. You should
  a. use the emergency brake.
  b. apply the brakes fully and hold.
  c. apply the brakes lightly.
  d. use controlled or stab braking.

22. If you're coupling a second trailer that doesn't have spring brakes, you should first
  a. use safety chains.
  b. drive the tractor close to it.
  c. connect the emergency line.
  d. charge the trailer's air tank.

23. To supply air to the trailer brake system, move the tractor protection valve control from "emergency" to
  a. "normal."
  b. "air supply."
  c. "lock."
  d. "low."

24. A fifth wheel that's in the proper position for coupling will have jaws that are
  a. closed.
  b. tilted.
  c. open.
  d. none of the above.

25. The "crack-the-whip" effect is most likely to occur when you're driving a
  a. a long, straight truck.
  b. a tractor-semitrailer combination.
  c. a tractor-twin trailer combination.
  d. a tractor-triple trailer combination.

26. Which of these might cause you to lose traction when driving on wet roads?
  a. using the engine brake
  b. using a speed retarder
  c. pulling an empty trailer
  d. all of the above

27. When you inspect the air lines to a trailer, you should check that the air lines are
  a. plugged in and secure.
  b. connected to the glad hands.
  c. tight and don't move.
  d. none of the above.

28. What should you do to secure a tractor before coupling it to a trailer?
   a. Apply the parking brake and put the transmission in neutral.
   b. Connect the tractor service air line.
   c. Back under the trailer at an angle.
   d. Align the kingpin and the fifth wheel.

29. When checking the air supply to a trailer, there may be major air loss if
   a. the trailer air supply control knob does not pop out on its own.
   b. the air brake pressure system gauge isn't at a normal level.
   c. the tractor protection valve control is in the emergency position.
   d. you can hear the brakes being applied and released.

30. An axle that's not connected to the drive train is called
   a. a rear axle.
   b. a trailer axle.
   c. an extra axle.
   d. a dead axle.

► Answers and Explanations

1. a. When you check the lower fifth wheel after coupling, make sure it's securely mounted to the frame, has no missing or damaged parts, and has enough grease. Also make sure there's no visible space between the upper and lower fifth wheel, the locking jaws are around the shank (and not the head) of the kingpin, the release arm is properly seated, and the safety lock is engaged.

2. d. If the second trailer doesn't have spring brakes, drive the tractor (with the semitrailer attached) close to it. Then connect the emergency line, charge the trailer's air tank, and then disconnect the emergency line. If the slack adjusters are properly adjusted, this will set the trailer's emergency brakes.

3. c. If you're driving a straight truck, a tractor-trailer combination, or a truck-trailer combination, you should look about 12 to 15 seconds ahead of your vehicle, a distance of about one-eighth of a mile at slower speeds or one-quarter of a mile at faster speeds. When you're driving a double or a triple, look even farther ahead than this. Therefore, looking at least 16 seconds ahead of your vehicle is appropriate when driving a double or triple.

4. d. A converter dolly is an assembly, or group of parts, with one or more axles and a fifth wheel, which is used to convert a semitrailer to a full trailer.

5. c. If a trailer is empty, you should lower the landing gear until it makes full contact with the ground. You should follow the same procedure for a full trailer, except you should turn the crank in low gear a few extra times to lift some weight off the tractor.

6. b. If the trailer is at the correct height before coupling, it's low enough to rise slightly when the tractor backs under it and the kingpin and fifth wheel are aligned.

7. c. A turnpike double is a type of long combination vehicle (LCV) in which a tractor pulls two trailers, each of which are 40- to 48-feet long.

8. b. The main cause of a rollover in a double or triple is turning too quickly.

9. c. When determining following distance, allow one second for every 10 feet of your vehicle's length. Add an additional second when you're driving over 40 mph. Therefore, for a 90-foot triple, you would need 9 seconds at 40 mph. Since you're driving at 50 mph, you would add one second for a total of 10 seconds.

10. a. The air tank petcock is a valve on an air tank that releases air when you turn it.

11. c. Because a converter dolly is used to couple a semitrailer to the rear of a tractor-trailer combination, you need to move the converter dolly in front of the trailer before you couple it.

12. c. On long downgrades, you should use the snub braking technique. This requires you to apply just enough pressure to the brake as necessary to slow you down, and then release the brakes and repeat both steps as necessary.

13. c. In order for your brakes to work, air must be able to travel to the back of the rig. If the air is flowing to all trailers, including the trailer in the back, you should hear air escaping from both the emergency line and the service line. If you don't hear air escaping from both of these lines, check that the shut-off valves on the trailers and converter dollies are in the "open" position. If they are, you have an air flow problem and your brakes won't work properly.

14. a. When you check the shut-off valves on a double or a triple, the shut-off valves in the rear of the front and middle trailers should be open, the shut-off valves in the rear of the last trailer should be closed, and the converter dolly air tank drain valve should be closed.

15. b. If the second trailer doesn't have spring brakes, chock its wheels to be sure that it's secure.

16. d. Because doubles and triples are very long and heavy, you need to exercise great care when changing lanes. Look into your mirrors before you signal a lane change, right after you start to change lanes, and then again after you change lanes.

17. b. When your trailer is empty, bouncing can cause your wheels to lose traction and lock up, which can cause the trailer to swing around and jackknife.

18. d. A drive-wheel skid is most often caused by driving too fast on ice or snow. Taking your foot off the accelerator may be enough to stop a drive-wheel skid. If it's not, push in the clutch. This will let the wheels roll freely until they can regain traction. If your CMV begins to slide sideways, steer quickly in the direction that you want your vehicle to go. Countersteering, turning the steering wheel quickly in the other direction, may also help you recover from a skid and restore traction to the tires.

19. b. When you inspect the coupling area, check to make sure the pintle hook is latched. Also check to make sure the valves are in the correct position, all air lines are supported, glad hands are properly connected, safety chains are secure, and light cords are firmly in sockets on trailers.

20. d. The fifth wheel is a coupling device located at the rear of the tractor's frame.

21. d. If you have to brake in an emergency, use controlled or stab breaking to stop your vehicle. These braking methods work very well when stopping doubles and triples because they allow you to stop your vehicle in a straight line and avoid jackknifing.

22. b. If the second trailer doesn't have spring brakes, drive the tractor close to it, connect the emergency line, charge the trailer air tank, and disconnect the emergency line.

23. a. To supply air to the trailer brake system, push in the "trailer air supply" knob or move the tractor protection valve control from the "emergency" position to the "normal" position.

24. c. A fifth wheel ready for coupling should have open jaws. The fifth wheel should also be tilted down toward the rear of the tractor and its safety unlocking handle should be in the automatic lock position.

25. d. The force is greater for the trailer at the end of a long line of trailers. In this case, it would be greatest for the last trailer in a tractor-triple trailer combination.

26. d. If you're driving on slippery roads, using the engine brake or the speed retarder can cause your vehicle to lose traction and skid. If you're pulling an empty trailer, it is more likely to lose traction and skid than a fully loaded one.

27. b. When you check the air lines going to a trailer, make sure that these lines are connected to the glad hands. Also make sure they're free of leaks, have enough slack for turns, and are free of damage.

28. a. To secure a tractor before coupling it to a trailer, put on the parking brake and put the transmission in neutral.

29. b. You may have a major loss of air in the air supply to the trailer if the air brake system pressure gauge isn't at a normal level.

30. d. Dead axles are axles that aren't connected to the drive train. You're more likely to skid in adverse conditions if you're pulling dead axles.

CHAPTER

10▶ Tank Vehicles

CHAPTER SUMMARY

Driving tank vehicles used to haul liquid or liquid gases is especially challenging for commercial drivers because of the increased risk of a rollover. This chapter addresses safety concerns when operating tank vehicles and prepares you to take the Tank Vehicles Test.

As you've already learned, you must take and pass the Tank Vehicles Test if you plan to haul liquid or liquid gas in a permanently mounted cargo tank (which includes vehicles with collapsible containers called **bladder bags**) or a portable tank that holds 1,000 or more gallons. Tankers present unique driving knowledge and skills, mainly because of the tanker's high center of gravity and because the liquid in the tank moves as you drive.

The questions on the Tank Vehicles Test are about

- inspecting tank vehicles
- driving tank vehicles
- safe driving rules

Of the 20 multiple-choice questions, you need to correctly answer 16, or 80 percent, to pass. If you pass, you'll receive an endorsement on your CDL that allows you to drive tank vehicles.

▶ What Are Tank Vehicles?

All tank vehicles carry either a fixed (permanently mounted) cargo tank, which includes bladder bags, or a portable tank of 1,000 gallons or more. Some vehicles or combinations carrying smaller fixed tanks (those that hold more than 119 gallons) are also considered tank vehicles because you need a CDL or **placards** (the diamond-shaped signs that identify the type of hazardous material being hauled) to drive them. Portable tanks are loaded with cargo while they're off the vehicle and are then loaded onto the vehicle once the cargo is in the tank.

Dry bulk tankers carry dry cargo such as fly, ash, cement, and other dry materials. Keep in mind that the liquids and gases hauled in tank vehicles aren't always hazardous materials (HAZMAT or HM for short). Some tankers carry nonhazardous liquids such as milk.

If you want to haul hazardous materials, you'll need another special endorsement on your license, so you'll have to take an additional written test. You'll learn more about hazardous material hauling in Chapter 11. You might also consider taking special HAZMAT training courses, which may be offered by your employer or by a local university, training institution, or association.

▶ Inspecting Tank Vehicles

If you're going to drive a tank vehicle, always inspect it before you start driving. Since tank vehicles come in many different types and sizes, it's a good idea to read your vehicle's operator manual to become familiar with the setup and components of your specific tank vehicle. This will help you know exactly what to inspect. Tank vehicles vary—especially depending on the type of liquid or gaseous material being hauled. It's very important to make sure that your tank vehicle is safe to drive.

Leaks

The first thing you'll do when inspecting a tank vehicle is check for leaks. Carrying cargo in a leaking tank isn't only dangerous—it's also illegal! If you're caught carrying cargo in a leaking tank, you'll be cited and prevented from driving any farther on your trip. You may also be responsible for the costs of cleaning up the spilled cargo. To prevent a legal hassle, and to help ensure that your trip is the safest it can be, thoroughly inspect your vehicle for the following:

- Make sure there aren't dents or leaks in the tank's body or shell.
- Check the intake, discharge, and cut-off valves. These valves should always be in the correct position before the vehicle is loaded, unloaded, or moved. Don't ever drive a tank vehicle with open valves.
- Check the pipes, connections, and hoses for leaks, especially around joints.
- Make sure manhole covers close correctly and have gaskets. Don't ever drive a tank vehicle with open manhole covers. Keep the vents clear, so they can operate correctly.

Special-Purpose and Emergency Equipment

Each tank vehicle has special-purpose equipment that's unique to the operation of tank vehicles. In addition to the emergency equipment that's required in other CMVs, tank vehicles also require additional emergency equipment.

First, check the special-purpose equipment in the vehicle, make sure it works properly, and make sure you know how to use it. Special-purpose equipment includes

- vapor recovery kits
- grounding and bonding cables
- emergency shut-off systems
- built-in fire extinguisher

Then check that your vehicle has the required emergency equipment for that vehicle. (Check state and local laws and regulations to find out exactly what equipment is required.) Also make sure the emergency equipment works and that you know how to use it. You don't want to be stuck in an emergency situation with equipment that doesn't work, with equipment that you're not sure how to use, or without the equipment that you need!

▶ Driving Tank Vehicles

Tank vehicles present CMV drivers with unique situations that require these drivers to have special skills. Drivers must be prepared for a variety of situations that they normally wouldn't encounter when driving a regular straight truck or a combination vehicle.

High Center of Gravity

Although a high center of gravity is a rollover concern for other CMV drivers, drivers of tank vehicles must be especially concerned because liquid tankers are even more at risk of rolling over. Tankers can roll over even when traveling at the speed limits posted for curves. This means that when you're driving a tank vehicle, you should always drive around curves—both highway and on-ramp and off-ramp curves—much slower than the posted speed limit suggests.

Some tankers are low-profile tankers, meaning they're shorter and wider and have a lower center of gravity. While this improves the center-of-gravity issues, it doesn't eliminate the problem altogether.

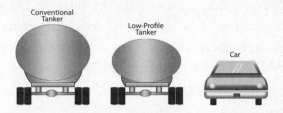

Figure 10.1. This shows the high center of gravity on a conventional tanker, the lower center of gravity of a low-profile tanker, and the low center of gravity of a car.

Danger of Liquid Surge

When a tank is only partially filled with liquid, the liquid has room to move around in the tank, which can cause handling problems for the driver. This is called **liquid surge**. Have you ever tried to walk quickly with a cup of water—or worse yet, a bowl of hot soup? You might have slowed down because the soup was sloshing around in the bowl and was threatening to spill. If you picture the movement of the soup in the bowl (which increases or decreases with your own speed), you can understand how liquid moves back and forth when it's contained in a tank attached to a moving vehicle. See Figure 10.2 for a better understanding of liquid surge.

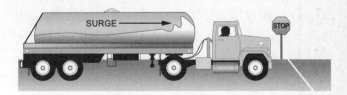

Figure 10.2. Side View of Liquid Surge within a Tanker

Drivers of liquid tankers must be aware that the liquid inside the tank can have a dramatic impact on the vehicle. When a driver comes to a stop, the liquid in the tank can still move around within the tank and will surge back and forth (referred to as **forward-and-backward surge**) while the vehicle is stopped. If the driver has stopped suddenly, the wave of liquid can hit the end of the tank so hard that it will actually push the stopped vehicle in the direction of the wave. This can be especially dangerous if the vehicle is on ice or another slippery surface. It can also be hazardous if a vehicle stopped at an intersection is then pushed into the intersection by the force of the surging liquid in the tank.

Keep in mind that the slower you turn, shift, accelerate, and stop, the less the liquid inside the tank will move around. Keep your movement smooth and gradual to avoid the dangers of liquid surge. The more experienced you become, the easier time you'll have driving a liquid tanker.

The density of the specific liquid you're hauling will also affect the liquid surge. Denser liquids don't surge as much as free-flowing, lightweight liquids do. For instance, gasoline is lighter than corn syrup, so when it surges in a tank, it will create a stronger wave of liquid than corn syrup. This is because free-flowing lightweight liquids can move faster than thicker ones can.

Bulkheads

Bulkheads are wall-like structures that can be used to divide large liquid tanks into several smaller tanks. These tanks can be loaded and unloaded separately. They can also be filled with different liquids that will be transported at the same time. Bulkheads reduce the impact of forward-and-backward liquid surge because they slow down the movement of the liquid and reduce the amount of space in which the liquid can move.

It's important to pay attention to weight distribution when loading and unloading the smaller tanks, so you don't put too much weight in the front or rear of the vehicle. Also remember that some liquids are heavier—or denser—than others. It's best to keep the heaviest liquids in the center of the vehicle to keep it stable.

Figure 10.3. Side View of a Tank with Bulkheads

Baffled Tanks

The compartment walls in **baffled tanks** have holes in them so that the liquid in the tank can flow through the tanks. Though the liquid can move through the whole tank rather than smaller compartments of a tank, the baffles slow its movement, which reduces the impact of the forward-and-backward surge. Baffled tanks don't have as much effect in reducing **side-to-side surge**, though, which puts the driver at risk for a rollover. That's why it's important to take turns and curves slowly when driving a liquid tanker.

Figure 10.4. Side View of a Baffled Tank

Unbaffled Tanks

Unbaffled tanks, also called **smooth bore tanks**, are long cylindrical tanks with no divisions inside. Because these tanks don't have bulkheads or baffles, the liquid inside can move freely without any obstructions to slow it down or reduce the force of its impact. As you can imagine, this causes a strong forward-and-backward surge, so drivers must drive slowly and carefully—especially when starting and stopping—to keep the vehicle under control.

Smooth bore tanks are usually used to transport food products, such as milk. Drivers can't transport food products in baffled tanks because it's prohibited by sanitation regulations. This is because they're hard to clean. Imagine how hard it would be to clean milk residue from the baffles of a tanker! Other nonfood products, such as corrosive liquids, can also be transported in smooth bore tanks.

Figure 10.5. Side View of an Unbaffled or Smooth Bore Tank

Outage

Liquid expands as it gets warmer. This means that cold liquid that's loaded into a tanker will take up more room if it gets warm. This is called **outage**, and it's the main reason that drivers can't load full cargo tanks. A driver should always leave room in a tank to allow the liquid to expand. Keep in mind, though, that liquids don't all expand the same amount. You'll have to find out the outage requirements for the specific liquid you're transporting before you load the tank.

How Much Should You Load?

Though filling a tank reduces liquid surge, it also increases the weight of the vehicle. If a vehicle is too full, it might exceed legal weight limits. The amount of liquid you can load into a tank depends on the following three factors:

1. the amount the liquid will expand in transit (outage)
2. the weight of the liquid
3. the legal weight limits

Tankers carrying heavier liquids should be either more or less than 80 percent full. Tanks that are 80 percent full are very unstable, which is dangerous. Leaving 20 percent of the tank empty gives heavy liquid too much room to move around, which can create major surge problems. If a tank is less than 80 percent full, the liquid will still have room to move, but it won't be as

heavy, which will reduce the impact of the surge. Also, though the liquid in a tank that's more than 80 percent full (say, 90 percent—remember to leave room for outage) will be heavier, it will also have less room to move, which will also reduce the impact of surge.

▶ Safe Driving Rules

Though you've already learned a bit about driving a tank vehicle safely, here's a review of some of the most impotant safe driving rules:

- **Drive smoothly.** The movements of your vehicle should be smooth when you start, slow down, and stop. You can make this easier to accomplish by driving slowly enough that you can ease your way into stops and by reminding yourself to be gentle when starting.

- **Braking.** Some situations are more difficult to plan for than others. If you find that you're forced to make a quick stop to avoid a crash, use stab braking or controlled braking to slow down your vehicle quickly. You learned about stab braking in Chapter 3. In stab braking, you apply your brakes all the way and release them when they lock up. When your wheels begin to roll, apply the brakes all the way again. Don't forget to be careful not to reapply the brakes before the wheels start turning. If you do this, the vehicle won't straighten.

- **Curves.** The best way to avoid a rollover when going around a curve is to slow down before the curve and then speed up just a little bit as you go through the curve. Remember that tank vehicles can't take curves as fast as other CMVs can, so the posted speed limit for a curve is too fast for a tank vehicle.

- **Stopping distance.** Remember that you'll need a certain amount of space to be able to stop your vehicle. You learned about stopping distance in Chapter 2. Here's a quick review of the three factors that dictate stopping distance:

Perception Distance + Reaction Distance + Braking Distance = Total Stopping Distance

In Chapter 2, you also learned about **perception distance**, which is the distance your vehicle moves from the time that your eyes spot a hazard until your brain recognizes it. At 55 mph, your perception distance will be 60 feet. **Reaction distance** is the distance your vehicle moves from the time your brain recognizes the hazard until your foot moves off the accelerator and pushes the brake pedal. At 55 mph, your vehicle will travel an additional 60 feet before your foot hits the brakes. Your **braking distance** is the distance it takes for your vehicle to stop once your foot has pushed the brake. A truck traveling 55 mph on a dry road with good brakes won't be able to stop for about 170 feet, which takes about 4½ seconds. In Chapter 6, "Air Brakes," you learned that a vehicle with air brakes will add 32 feet to your total stopping distance due to brake lag. So at 55 mph in an air brake equipped CMV, your total stopping distance will be 322 feet.

Remember, too, that an empty tanker will take longer to slow down than a full one. Also, stopping distance doubles when you're trying to stop on a wet road. Review Chapter 2 for more information about stopping distance and safe driving practices.

- **Skids.** Skidding occurs when drivers oversteer, overaccelerate, or overbrake. Avoid these unsafe driving practices to avoid skidding, which is especially dangerous in a tank vehicle. When your drive wheels or trailer wheels start to skid, the vehicle often jackknifes, which can be very dangerous for all drivers on the road. If your vehicle starts to skid, you'll have to let up on the brakes to regain traction. Review driving techniques for regaining control during a skid in Chapters 4 and 7.

Chapter 10 Review Quiz

1–6: Circle the correct answer.

1. An unbaffled tank is also called a
   a. dry cargo tank.
   b. smooth bore tank.
   c. bulkhead tank.
   d. conventional tank.

2. The posted speed for a curve may be _____ for a tank vehicle.
   a. too fast
   b. exactly right
   c. too slow
   d. nearly right

3. Outage refers to the _____ of liquid as its temperature increases during transit.
   a. movement
   b. force
   c. expansion
   d. freezing

4. Which of the following is considered "special-purpose equipment"?
   a. cut-off valves
   b. grounding and bonding cables
   c. manhole covers and vents
   d. bulkheads

5. Liquid surge results from the movement of liquid in _____ tanks.
   a. smooth bore
   b. several smaller
   c. partially filled
   d. low-profile

6. What is the most important item to check for when inspecting a tank vehicle?
   a. dents
   b. leaks
   c. fire extinguishers
   d. shut-off systems

7–11: Indicate whether each statement is true or false.

____ **7.** High center of gravity means that much of the load's weight is carried high up off the road.

____ **8.** The amount of liquid a driver puts in a tank depends on only the weight of the liquid.

____ **9.** Wet roads usually triple the normal stopping distance.

____ **10.** Oversteering can result in a trailer jackknife.

____ **11.** The best way to control liquid surge is to drive slowly and gently.

Check your answers on page 295.

Tank Vehicles Endorsement Practice Test

1.	ⓐ	ⓑ	ⓒ	ⓓ
2.	ⓐ	ⓑ	ⓒ	ⓓ
3.	ⓐ	ⓑ	ⓒ	ⓓ
4.	ⓐ	ⓑ	ⓒ	ⓓ
5.	ⓐ	ⓑ	ⓒ	ⓓ
6.	ⓐ	ⓑ	ⓒ	ⓓ
7.	ⓐ	ⓑ	ⓒ	ⓓ
8.	ⓐ	ⓑ	ⓒ	ⓓ
9.	ⓐ	ⓑ	ⓒ	ⓓ
10.	ⓐ	ⓑ	ⓒ	ⓓ

11.	ⓐ	ⓑ	ⓒ	ⓓ
12.	ⓐ	ⓑ	ⓒ	ⓓ
13.	ⓐ	ⓑ	ⓒ	ⓓ
14.	ⓐ	ⓑ	ⓒ	ⓓ
15.	ⓐ	ⓑ	ⓒ	ⓓ
16.	ⓐ	ⓑ	ⓒ	ⓓ
17.	ⓐ	ⓑ	ⓒ	ⓓ
18.	ⓐ	ⓑ	ⓒ	ⓓ
19.	ⓐ	ⓑ	ⓒ	ⓓ
20.	ⓐ	ⓑ	ⓒ	ⓓ

21.	ⓐ	ⓑ	ⓒ	ⓓ
22.	ⓐ	ⓑ	ⓒ	ⓓ
23.	ⓐ	ⓑ	ⓒ	ⓓ
24.	ⓐ	ⓑ	ⓒ	ⓓ
25.	ⓐ	ⓑ	ⓒ	ⓓ
26.	ⓐ	ⓑ	ⓒ	ⓓ
27.	ⓐ	ⓑ	ⓒ	ⓓ
28.	ⓐ	ⓑ	ⓒ	ⓓ
29.	ⓐ	ⓑ	ⓒ	ⓓ
30.	ⓐ	ⓑ	ⓒ	ⓓ

▶ Tank Vehicles Endorsement Practice Test

Choose the correct answer. Mark the letter on the answer sheet on page 203.

1. Liquid surge is most dangerous when a vehicle
   a. stops on an icy road.
   b. is hauling a dense liquid.
   c. has a baffled tank.
   d. has a low center of gravity.

2. When approaching a curve in a tank vehicle, a driver should
   a. keep an even speed when entering the curve and then slow down through the curve.
   b. slow down before the curve and then coast through the curve.
   c. keep an even speed before the curve and then coast through the curve.
   d. slow down before the curve and then accelerate slightly through the curve.

3. When stab braking, reapply the brakes right after
   a. the brakes lock up.
   b. you feel the vehicle begin to slow down.
   c. the wheels start turning again.
   d. you notice the possibility of collision.

4. Why is it important for a driver to know the outage requirements for the specific liquid being hauled?
   a. to let the driver know how to unload the liquid
   b. to tell the driver what kind of liquid it is
   c. to let the driver know how much room to leave in the tank
   d. to tell the driver what kind of tank is needed

5. How do baffles affect liquid surge?
   a. They reduce side-to-side surge.
   b. They increase overall surge.
   c. They reduce front-to-back surge.
   d. They create top-to-bottom surge.

6. When should you use the most caution in driving a smooth bore tanker?
   a. when driving up a large hill
   b. when starting and stopping
   c. when sitting at an intersection
   d. when driving at night

7. Unbaffled tankers are most often used to transport cargo such as
   a. gasoline.
   b. ash.
   c. milk.
   d. tar.

8. Which kind of tanker presents the least problem with backward-and-forward surge?
   a. a smooth bore tanker
   b. a conventional tanker with bulkheads
   c. a baffled tanker
   d. a low-profile tanker without bulkheads

9. When hauling liquid cargo, which is an issue that only drivers of tank vehicles with smaller tanks must think about?
a. weight distribution
b. backward-and-forward surge
c. side-to-side surge
d. skidding

10. Which of the following best describes outage?
a. the process of removing cargo from a tank
b. the movement of liquid in a partially filled tank
c. the failure of a tanker to stop at an intersection
d. the expansion of liquid as it gets warm

11. Which of the following is the name for the tank dividers with holes that allow liquid to flow through?
a. baffles
b. borders
c. bulkheads
d. bores

12. All tank vehicles carry either a fixed cargo tank or a portable tank of _____ gallons or more.
a. 100
b. 1,000
c. 10,000
d. 100,000

13. Which is another name for stab braking?
a. hit braking
b. controlled braking
c. puncture braking
d. none of the above

14. Before driving a tanker, always inspect your vehicle for _____ and make sure it contains emergency equipment.
a. placards
b. endorsements
c. leaks
d. hoses

15. Drivers of tankers must take special care when driving because of liquid surge and because of the vehicle's
a. high center of gravity.
b. small hauling capacity.
c. wall-like structures.
d. legal weight limits.

16. Which of the following percentages of liquid is considered safest for a tanker to haul?
a. 20
b. 60
c. 80
d. 100

17. Which of the following is considered "special-purpose equipment"?
a. outage requirements
b. baffle holes
c. portable tanks
d. vapor recovery kits

18. The lighter weight a liquid is, the _____ its surge when in a tank.
a. longer
b. quieter
c. stronger
d. safer

19. The three main factors to consider when loading liquid into a tank are the outage requirements, the total weight limit allowed by law, and the
   a. weight of the liquid.
   b. distance being driven.
   c. flammability of the liquid.
   d. sanitation regulations.

20. Once a driver has applied the brakes, an empty tanker will take _____ to slow down than a full one will.
   a. a few seconds
   b. more time
   c. less time
   d. a few miles

21. What kind of surge do baffles have the least effect on?
   a. horizontal
   b. front-to-back
   c. top-to-bottom
   d. side-to-side

22. Which of the following is considered a tank vehicle?
   a. a 115-gallon fixed tank containing water
   b. a 500-gallon portable tank containing corn syrup
   c. an 800-gallon portable tank containing water
   d. a 120-gallon fixed tank containing diesel

23. What is a placard?
   a. a part of a baffled tank that's removed in order to fill the tank with hazardous cargo
   b. a diamond-shaped sign that shows what type of hazardous material is being hauled
   c. a piece of emergency equipment that all tank vehicle drivers are required to have
   d. a training course that drivers must take if they want to haul hazardous materials

24. When is a tank vehicle at the biggest risk for a rollover?
   a. when traveling around a curve
   b. when driving on wet roads
   c. when carrying heavy liquids
   d. when coming to a quick stop

25. Which three valves should you check when inspecting a tank vehicle for leaks?
   a. shut-off, internal, and discharge
   b. uptake, cut-off, and retest
   c. intake, discharge, and cut-off
   d. discharge, uptake, and shut-off

26. Why would a tank vehicle driver try to maintain minimal liquid movement in a tank?
   a. to make sure the liquid doesn't escape
   b. to make the vehicle easier to control
   c. to make the load feel lighter in the tank
   d. to make a roadside inspector happy

27. Which of the following statements is true?

    a. Heavier liquids should be loaded onto the front of a vehicle.

    b. Tank vehicle drivers should always follow the posted speed for curves.

    c. Drivers can't transport food products in baffled tanks.

    d. A fast stop won't affect the impact of liquid surge on a tank.

28. What is perception distance?

    a. The distance it takes for a vehicle to stop once the driver's foot has pushed the brake.

    b. The distance a vehicle moves from the time the driver sees a hazard until the driver's brain recognizes it.

    c. The distance a vehicle moves from the time the driver's brain recognizes a hazard until the driver's foot moves off the accelerator and pushes the brake pedal.

    d. The distance a driver looks ahead to see upcoming hazards on the road.

29. Which of the following statements is false?

    a. Skidding can occur when drivers oversteer.

    b. Skidding can occur when drivers overaccelerate.

    c. Skidding is especially dangerous in a tank vehicle.

    d. Skidding can be corrected by pumping the brakes.

30. If a truck with good brakes is traveling 55 mph on a wet road, how far will the truck travel from the time the driver presses the brake until the truck actually stops moving?

    a. 170 feet

    b. 230 feet

    c. 340 feet

    d. 460 feet

▶ Answers and Explanations

1. a. Though liquid surge can be dangerous while driving, its force is greatest when a driver comes to a stop, especially when the driver has been driving fast and stops suddenly. The liquid can surge forward and hit the end of the tank so hard that it can push the stopped vehicle forward. This is especially dangerous if the road is wet or icy because the vehicle can slide faster and the driver will have a harder time regaining control of the vehicle.

2. d. Since tank vehicles are especially prone to rollovers, the best way to take a curve in a tank vehicle is to slow down before the curve and then accelerate slightly as you go through the curve. Drivers should also remember that posted speed limits for curves may still be too fast for tank vehicles.

3. c. When drivers use stab braking, they apply their brakes all the way and then release the brakes when they lock up. They then reapply the brakes when the wheels start rolling again. A driver who reapplies the brakes before the wheels begin to turn again won't be able to straighten out the vehicle.

4. c. The term outage refers to the expansion of liquid as it warms. Liquid cargo usually gets warmer as it's hauled, so drivers loading liquid cargo must remember to leave room for the liquid to expand. Since all liquids don't expand the same amount, it's important for drivers to pay attention to the outage requirements for the specific liquid they'll haul before they load the tank.

5. c. Baffles are tank compartment walls that have holes in them to allow the liquid in the tank to flow throughout the tank. Baffles slow the movement of the liquid, so that even though the liquid can flow through the whole tank, the forward-and-backward surge doesn't have as much impact as it would in an unbaffled tank (or "smooth bore tanker").

6. b. Smooth bore tankers experience more forward-and-backward surge than any other tanker. Since smooth bore tankers don't have baffles, the liquid can move very fast, especially when starting or stopping. Drivers of smooth bore tankers should take the most caution when starting or stopping to reduce the effect of the liquid surge.

7. c. Sanitation regulations prohibit drivers from transporting food products—such as milk—in baffled tanks because they're hard to clean. Instead, drivers must transport liquid food products in unbaffled tankers.

8. b. Because bulkheads don't have holes like baffles do, the liquid contained within each compartment can't move outside of that compartment, so it can't build up as much force as liquid that moves freely throughout a tank can. This makes forward-and-backward surge much less of a problem in a conventional tanker with bulkheads than in any other type of tank.

9. a. Most drivers who haul liquid cargo don't have to think about weight distribution because the liquid they're hauling can freely move back and forth. It isn't stationary, so it's weight distribution is constantly changing.

Drivers of tank vehicles with smaller tanks do have to think about weight distribution, though. Each tank should be placed in such a way that it doesn't throw off the stability of the vehicle. These drivers should also remember that tanks may weigh different amounts if they contain different liquids.

10. d. Liquids expand as they get warm, which happens when they're being transported in a tank. This expansion is referred to as outage.

11. a. The tank dividers with holes that allow liquid to flow through are called "baffles."

12. b. A tank vehicle carries either a fixed cargo tank or a portable tank of 1,000 gallons or more.

13. d. With stab braking, you fully apply the brakes then release them when the wheels lock. With controlled braking, you apply the brakes with steady pressure just short of locking the wheels.

14. c. The first thing you'll do when inspecting a tank vehicle is check for leaks because it's both illegal and dangerous to carry cargo in a leaking tank. If an inspector sees that you're driving with a leaking tank, you'll be cited, your vehicle will be put out of service, and you might have to pay the costs of cleaning up the spilled cargo as well.

15. a. The two major concerns for drivers of tank vehicles are the dangers of liquid surge and the vehicle's high center of gravity, both of which can cause a rollover.

16. b. Tankers carrying heavier liquids should be either more or less than 80 percent full, but not less than 20 percent full. Tanks that are 80 percent full are very unstable, and leaving 20 percent of a tank empty gives heavy liquid too much room to move around, making liquid surge very dangerous. A tank that is 100 percent full has no room for outage, which can also be dangerous.

17. d. In addition to the emergency equipment that's required in other CMVs, tank vehicles have additional emergency equipment—or special-purpose equipment—that's also required. Special-purpose equipment includes vapor recovery kits, grounding and bonding cables, emergency shut-off systems, and built-in fire extinguishers.

18. c. The lighter a liquid is, the stronger it surges inside a tank. As you learned, gasoline is lighter than corn syrup, so when it surges in a tank, it creates a stronger wave of liquid than corn syrup. This is because lighter weight liquids can move faster than heavier ones.

19. a. The amount of liquid you can load into a tank depends on the amount the liquid will expand in transit (outage), the legal weight limits, and the weight of the liquid.

20. b. An empty tanker has increased stopping distance. This means it takes longer for an empty tanker to stop once the driver has applied the brakes.

21. d. Baffled tanks slow the forward-and-backward movement of liquid surge, but they don't have much effect in reducing side-to-side surge, which puts the driver at risk for a rollover.

22. d. Some vehicles or combinations carrying smaller fixed tanks (those that hold more than 119 gallons) are also considered tank vehicles if you need a CDL or placards (indicating a hazardous material) to drive them. A tank vehicle, however, includes any commercial vehicle with fixed or portable tanks of a capacity of 1,000 gallons or more.

23. b. Placards are diamond-shaped signs on a tank that identify the type of hazardous material being hauled.

24. a. A rollover is a special concern for tank vehicle drivers because liquid tankers are more at risk for a rollover than any other vehicle due to liquid surge. When traveling around a curve, side-to-side surge can cause a tanker to roll even when it's traveling at the posted speed limit for curves. Tankers should be driven much slower around curves than is suggested by the posted speed limit.

25. c. Drivers should always check to make sure that the intake, discharge, and cut-off valves are in the correct position before the vehicle is loaded, unloaded, or moved. The valves should never be open while driving a vehicle.

26. b. The slower a driver turns, shifts, accelerates, and stops, the less the liquid inside the tank will move around and the easier it will be to control the vehicle. Keeping vehicle movement smooth and gradual helps drivers avoid liquid surge, which makes the vehicle difficult to control.

27. c. As you know, it's against the law for drivers to transport food products in baffled tanks because they're hard to clean. Food products must be transported in unbaffled tankers.

28. b. Perception distance is the distance your vehicle moves from the time that your eyes spot a hazard until your brain recognizes it.

29. d. Using the brakes while skidding can make the skid worse, putting you and others in a dangerous position. To correct a skid, let up on the brakes until your wheels regain traction.

30. c. A truck traveling 55 mph on a dry road with good brakes won't be able to stop for about 170 feet. Since wet roads double stopping distance, this same truck would need 340 feet to stop on a wet road.

11 ▶ Hazardous Materials

CHAPTER SUMMARY

Hazardous materials are dangerous. For this reason, as a commercial driver, you must obtain a hazardous materials endorsement on your CDL. This chapter will help you study for the Hazardous Materials Test and will help you understand the dangers associated with hazardous materials, so you can transport them safely.

As you've already learned, if you want to haul hazardous materials, you need a special hazardous materials endorsement on your license. To get this endorsement, you'll have to take a written knowledge test, the Hazardous Materials Test.

You won't have to take this test in a vehicle containing hazardous materials—that would be illegal! Instead, you'll be tested on your knowledge of these subjects:

- federal HAZMAT regulations and requirements
- the intent of the regulations
- who does what during hazardous materials transportation
- communication rules
- loading and unloading
- bulk packaging marking, loading, and unloading
- driving and parking rules when transporting hazardous materials
- emergencies

Of the 30 questions on this test, you must correctly answer 24, or 80 percent, to pass. You can take the test as many times as necessary until you pass. Once you pass the test required for the hazardous materials endorsement, a letter code—an "H" in many states—will be added to your CDL. Many states combine the hazardous materials endorsement and the tank vehicles endorsement by using the letter code "X."

Hazardous materials (often abbreviated HAZMAT or HM in government regulations) are materials that pose a risk to people, property, and the environment. This includes explosives, some gases, certain solids, and flammable and combustible liquids. Because these materials are dangerous, and because handling these materials is often very risky, the government regulates the way in which hazardous materials are handled and transported. This ensures that these materials are handled in the safest, most responsible manner possible—and for good reason. You certainly wouldn't want to share the road with an unskilled driver hauling explosives!

The section of the Code of Federal Regulations (CFR) that addresses these issues is called the Hazardous Materials Regulations (HMR). It's found in parts 171 to 180 of title 49 of the CFR (referred to as 49 CFR 171–180). This section of the regulations contains a table listing many of the hazardous materials that must be **placarded**, meaning that vehicles hauling these materials must display diamond-shaped, "square-on-point," warning signs to let others know what type of hazardous materials are being hauled. These signs are displayed on the front, rear, and both sides of the vehicle.

However, this list doesn't contain all the hazardous materials. It's often up to the shipper to classify a material as hazardous based on its characteristics and on the details of the regulations.

As is true in other areas of government, the CFR is constantly changing. This chapter will teach you the basic knowledge you need to pass the Hazardous Materials Test. Once you do, it's part of your job to stay updated on the constant changes to the regulations. Your employer may provide you with a copy of the 49 CFR, or you might seek one on your own. The regulations are also available online. You can view an electronic version of the regulations at the Government Printing Office Web site (http://www.gpoaccess/ECFR) or the Federal Motor Carrier Safety Administration Web site (http://www.fmcsa.dot.gov/rules-regulations/administration/fmcsr/fmcsrguide.htm).

Many states have their own requirements about the handling of hazardous materials. These requirements are strictly enforced, so it's important to know the requirements for each state in which you'll be hauling hazardous materials.

▶ Licensing Requirements: Endorsement and Beyond

Background Check

You already know that before you can drive a vehicle requiring hazardous material placarding, you must have a valid CDL with a hazardous materials endorsement. All applicants also undergo a federal background record check and threat assessment.

The USA PATRIOT Act requires that all drivers applying for a new, renewed, or transferred hazardous materials endorsement on their CDL undergo a background check and threat assessment to ensure the driver doesn't pose a security risk. In most states, this check is conducted by the Transportation Security Administration's (TSA) Hazardous Materials Endorsement Threat Assessment Program. (In others, it's conducted by the state's licensing agency.) It consists of the following steps:

- **Application/Renewal/Transfer.** Drivers applying for a new hazardous materials endorsement should apply for the program before they take the Hazardous Materials Test, since their state won't be able to issue the endorsement until the security threat assessment is complete. However, in some states you must pass the Hazardous Materials Test before you can start the security threat assessment process. Drivers applying for a renewal of an existing hazardous materials endorsement should apply for the program no later than 30 days before the CDL expires. (Keep in mind, though, that drivers who've already undergone the assessment and want to transfer their endorsement to another state can do so without going through another assessment as long as the new state can issue an endorsement that expires within 5 years of the last assessment.)

- **Assessment.** Drivers are fingerprinted either at their DMV or at a TSA agent site (only in participating states; to find out if your state participates, go to www.hazprints.com). Once you pay the required fee, your fingerprints will be sent to the Federal Bureau of Investigation (FBI) to check for a past criminal record. The results will then be sent to the TSA or to your state's DMV, and the security threat assessment will begin.

- **Results.** If you pass, you're eligible for a hazardous materials endorsement. If you don't pass because you have one or more disqualifying criteria or because you've been classified as an imminent threat to transportation security, you won't be eligible for a hazardous materials endorsement. If you already have one, it will be taken away for

the time being. You can appeal the decision, but you won't be able to hold a hazardous materials endorsement until state and federal governments decide that you're not a true safety threat.

Life of the Endorsement

The renewal period for your hazardous materials endorsement will vary depending on the state in which you're licensed. In some states, the HAZMAT endorsement must be renewed every 5 years, while others require renewal every 4 years. You'll have to take a written recertification test before your endorsement expires. About 7 months before your endorsement expires, you'll get a notice in the mail reminding you that it's time to renew. At this time, you'll have to undergo another background check. You have to take the written recertification test again either prior to the background check or after, depending upon the state. Check with your local DMV for specific details about your state's threat assessment process.

If you take the written test three times and don't pass, or if your CDL expires before you pass, your CDL will be renewed without the hazardous materials endorsement. If you need the hazardous materials endorsement, you'll have to apply for a HAZMAT Learner's Permit and take the written Hazardous Materials Test again.

If the results of the security threat assessment make you ineligible for hazardous materials endorsement, your endorsement will be revoked.

Continuous Training

According to federal regulations, all drivers working with hazardous materials must be trained and tested at least once every 2 years. Regulations also state that employers or other designated representatives must provide that training and testing. Employers have to keep records of each driver's training for as long as that driver works with hazardous materials and for 90 days afterward.

Drivers who transport highway route controlled materials such as certain flammable gases or radioactive materials need special training; so do drivers who transport cargo tanks and portable tanks. Employers must provide their employees with this training.

Permits

Some states or local areas require drivers to get special permits when they're transporting certain kinds of explosives, bulk hazardous wastes, or other hazardous materials such as rocket fuel. Some states also make drivers follow special routes when transporting hazardous materials. It's a good idea to find out what special circumstances you might encounter in the different areas you'll be driving through, so you can be prepared to follow the rules.

Other Concerns

The laws for transporting hazardous materials in passenger vehicles are different. Passengers sometimes carry hazardous materials such as acetone, battery acid, and hydrogen peroxide onto buses. These usually aren't a problem in small amounts, but they can become dangerous in larger amounts. You'll learn more about hazardous materials in passenger vehicles in Chapter 12.

▶ Intent of the Regulations

The federal government established the regulations so all drivers would know how to do three things:

1. **Contain the material.** The regulations let shippers know how to safely package hazardous materials for transport. They also tell drivers how to safely load, transport, and unload hazardous materials. These laws, or containment rules, are meant to protect everyone and everything—including you, those around you, and the environment—from injury, death, or contamination.

2. **Communicate the risk.** The regulations require shippers to let drivers and others know about the hazards of the material. This is why shippers must put warning labels on packages. They must also provide proper shipping papers (ones that clearly describe the risk involved), emergency response information, and placards. These precautions let everyone (the shipper, the carrier, and the driver) know what's being transported. If an accident, spill, or leak occurs, it's a driver's responsibility to let others know what has spilled and what risks are involved.

3. **Ensure safe drivers and equipment.** To get your hazardous materials endorsement, you'll have to pass the Hazardous Materials Test. To do this, you'll have to know how to

   - identify hazardous materials
   - safely load shipments
   - properly placard your vehicle
   - safely transport shipments

The rules are in place for a reason. They were created to protect you and those around you, so it's very important that you follow them. Failure to follow the rules could have disastrous results including fines, injury, death, or jail time.

Responsible drivers inspect their vehicles before and during every trip. Not only is this a good safety precaution to adopt as a habit, but it's also a good way to keep yourself out of trouble. You could be stopped by law enforcement officers who will want to inspect your entire vehicle, including placards and shipping papers. They may also want to look at your license to make sure you have a legal hazardous materials endorsement. Law enforcement officers know a lot about hazardous materials, and they might even want to test your own personal knowledge! It's best to be prepared for any situation you might encounter.

▶ Hazardous Materials Transportation: Who Does What

The three main players in hazardous materials transportation are the shipper, the carrier, and the driver.

The Shipper

The shipper's duties are to

- send the products from one place to another in a truck, a train, a ship, or an airplane
- review hazardous materials regulations and use them to determine the following information about the product:

    · proper shipping name
    · hazard class and division
    · identification number
    · correct packaging
    · correct label(s) and markings
    · correct placards

- package, mark, and label the hazardous materials
- prepare the shipping papers
- provide emergency response information
- supply placards
- provide written certification that the shipment has been prepared safely and lawfully

(unless you're pulling cargo tanks supplied by you or your employer)

The Carrier

The carrier's duties are to

- check that the shipper has properly described, marked, labeled, and prepared the shipment (before transporting it)
- refuse improper shipments
- take proper shipments from the shipper to their destinations
- report accidents and other negative situations involving hazardous materials to the proper government agency

The Driver

You—as the driver—also have important duties and responsibilities. As a driver transporting hazardous materials, you'll have to

- check the shipment again to make sure the shipper has properly identified, marked, and labeled the hazardous materials
- refuse leaking packages and shipments that aren't properly prepared
- placard your vehicle when loading it, if it's required
- safely transport the shipment without delay
- follow all special rules about transporting hazardous materials
- keep shipping papers and emergency response information in the proper place

▶ Communication Rules

You might be familiar with some of the terms relating to hazardous materials, but some of these terms have very

		Hazardous Materials Hazardous Class/Division Table	
Class	Division	Name of Class or Division	Example
1	1.1 1.2 1.3 1.4 1.5 1.6	Mass Explosives Projection Hazards Mass Fire Hazards Minor Hazards Very Insensitive Extremely Insensitive	Dynamite Ammunition, Incendiaries, Flares Display Fireworks Ammunition Blasting Agents Explosive, Detonating Devices
2	2.1 2.2 2.3	Flammable Gas Nonflammable Gases Poisonous/Toxic Gases	Propane Helium Fluorine, Compressed
3	—	Flammable Liquids	Gasoline
4	4.1 4.2 4.3	Flammable Solids Spontaneously Combustible Dangerous When Wet	Ammonium Picrate, Wetted White Phosphorus Sodium
5	5.1 5.2	Oxidizers Organic Peroxides	Ammonium Nitrate Organic Peroxide Type B, Solid
6	6.1 6.2	Poison (Toxic Material) Infectious Substances	Potassium Cyanide Infectious Substances Effecting Animals, Anthrax Virus
7	—	Radioactive	Uranium
8	—	Corrosives	Battery Fluid
9	—	Miscellaneous Hazardous Materials	Polychlorinated Biphenyls (PCB)
None	—	ORM-D (Other Regulated Material - Domestic)	Food Flavorings, Medicines
None	—	Combustible Liquids	Fuel Oil

Figure 11.1. Hazardous Materials Class/Division Table

different meanings when they're used in reference to hazardous materials. You might see these terms on your test, so it's important to learn their definitions. While some are listed here, don't forget that there's a glossary at the end of this chapter that will help you understand other terms you may or may not be familiar with.

Hazardous materials are categorized by one of nine different **hazard classes**, and some classes have separate divisions. Each division describes what type of material it is and what risks are associated with it. The nine different classes of hazardous materials are listed in Figure 11.1.

These terms are often used on shipping papers, which describe the hazardous materials being transported. Figure 11.2 shows an example of a shipping paper. Shipping papers include shipping orders, bills of lading, and manifests.

Imagine what would happen after a crash, spill, or leak if an injured driver couldn't tell those around him or her about the dangers of the hazardous material being transported. This could be a disastrous situation! Firefighters and other rescue personnel can do more to contain a bad situation and reduce the amount of damage done to people and to the environment if

Proper shipping name from Column 2 of Hazardous Materials Table

ID Number from Column 4 of the Hazardous Materials Table

"RQ" means that this is a reportable quantity

Hazard Class from Column 3 of the Table

SHIPPING PAPER

Page 1 of 1

TO: Party Time Balloons
      652 Burnside Avenue
      Athens, GA 30601

FROM: Noonan Corporation
        80 Poplar Street
        Macon, GA 30201

QTY	HM	DESCRIPTION	WEIGHT
1 cyl	RQ	Phosgene, 2.3, UN1076, Poison, Inhalation Hazard Zone A	25 lbs.

- -

This is to certify that the above named materials are properly classified, described, packaged, marked, labeled and placarded and are in proper condition for transportation according to the applicable regulations of the Department of Transportation.

Shipper: Noonan Corp.
Per: Shift
Date: 9/13/08

Carrier: Rodale Inc.
Per:
Date:

SPECIAL INSTRUCTIONS: 24-hour Emergency Contact, Emily Shift, 1-800-555-5555

Figure 11.2. Example of a Shipping Paper for Hazardous Materials

Figure 11.3. Examples of HAZMAT Labels

they know what kind of hazardous material they're dealing with. One way they can find this information is by looking at shipping papers. The faster they can locate these papers, the better off everyone in the area will be. That's why the following rules about shipping papers were created:

- Shippers must describe hazardous materials correctly. They must also include emergency response numbers on shipping papers.
- Carriers and drivers must put tabs on hazardous materials shipping papers or keep them on top of other shipping papers. They must also keep emergency response information with the papers. These rules help others find your shipping papers when you can't.

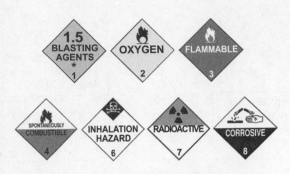

Figure 11.4. Example of HAZMAT Placards

Hazardous material identification numbers may be displayed on placards or orange panels.

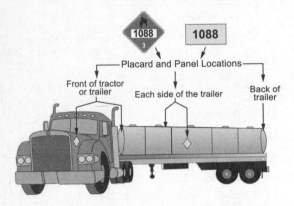

Figure 11.5. Placement of HAZMAT Placards on a CMV

- Drivers must keep shipping papers in one of three places so that they're easy to find:

1. in a pouch on the driver's door

2. in clear view and within immediate reach when the driver is wearing a seat belt

3. on the driver's seat when the driver isn't in the vehicle

Package Labels

Shippers use diamond-shaped labels that resemble placards to mark packages containing hazardous materials. The shape of the label lets others know that the package contains a hazardous material, while the text and pictures on the label let others know what kind

of risk the material presents. Some oddly shaped or very small packages have HAZMAT tags or decals rather than labels. See Figure 11.3 for examples of HAZMAT labels.

Lists of Regulated Products

Placards are placed on the outside of a vehicle to warn others that the vehicle is hauling hazardous materials. A placarded vehicle must have at least four identical placards: one in the front, one in the rear, and one on each side of the vehicle. They're placed in this way so that others can read the warning no matter which side of the vehicle they happen to be on. Figure 11.4 shows what placards look like, and Figure 11.5 shows where each placard should be placed.

Placards are always at least $10^3/_4$ inches square. They're always diamond-shaped, square-on-point signs. They show others what material is being transported and contain the identification number of the material as well. This identification number is usually a four-digit code that first responders (emergency personnel) use to identify specific hazardous materials. Some materials may share the same four-digit code but will be distinguished by a letter code that precedes the four numbers, either "NA" or "UN." The U.S. Department of Transportation published a guidebook containing all the identification numbers assigned to different chemicals. You'll learn more about identification numbers shortly.

Shippers, carriers, and drivers use three main lists from the Hazardous Materials Regulations to identify hazardous materials. You'll want to consult all three of these lists before you haul any type of hazardous material. Some lists are more comprehensive than others, meaning not all materials will be found on every list. These lists are

- Section 172.101, the Hazardous Materials Table

49 CFR 172.101 Hazardous Materials Table								
Symbols	Hazardous Materials Description & Proper Shipping Names	Hazard Class or Division	Identification Numbers	PG	Label Codes	Special Provisions §172.101	Packaging (173. ***)		
							Exceptions	Non Bulk	Bulk
(1) A	(2) Acetaldehyde ammonia	(3) 9	(4) UN1841	(5) III	(6) 9	(7) IB8, IP6	(8A) 155	(8B) 204	(8C) 240
	Acetylene (liquefied)	Forbidden							
G	Alcoholates solution, n.o.s., *in alcohol*	3	UN3274	II	3, 8	IB2	150	202	243
	Alkylsulfuric acids	8	UN2571	II	8	B2, IB2, T8, TP2, TP12, TP13, TP28	154	202	242
D	Aluminum, molten	9	NA9260	III	9	IB3, T1, TP3	None	None	247

Figure 11.6. Examples from the Hazardous Materials Table

- Appendix A to Section 172.101, the List of Hazardous Substances and Reportable Quantities
- Appendix B to Section 172.101, the List of Marine Pollutants

The Hazardous Materials Table

The Hazardous Materials Table lists hazardous materials shipping information. The first column lists symbols that tell which shipping mode the entry affects, as well as other shipping information. Each of these codes is explained in this chapter. The other five columns list the material's proper shipping name, its hazard class or division, its identification number, its packaging group, and the type of label required to ship it. Figure 11.6 shows examples of materials listed in this table. Look at these examples as you read about what kind of information appears in each part of the table.

Column 1. The following six symbols can appear in Column 1 of the Hazardous Materials Table:

(+) This symbol shows the proper shipping name, hazard class, and packing group. These classifications are used even if the material doesn't meet the hazard class definition.

(A) This symbol means that the hazardous material described in Column 2 is subject to the HMR only when offered or intended for transport by air, unless it's a hazardous substance or hazardous waste.

(W) This symbol means that the hazardous material described in Column 2 is subject to the HMR only when offered or intended for transport by water, unless it's a hazardous substance, hazardous waste, or marine pollutant.

(D) This symbol means that the proper shipping name is appropriate for describing materials for domestic transportation, but may not be proper for international transportation.

(I) This symbol identifies a proper shipping name that's used to describe materials in international transportation. A different shipping name may be used when only domestic transportation is involved.

(G) This symbol means that the hazardous material described in Column 2 is a generic shipping name. When a generic shipping name is used on a shipping paper, it must be accompanied by a technical name. A **technical name** is a recognized chemical or microbiological name that's used in scientific and technical handbooks, journals, and texts. It reveals what specific chemical makes the product hazardous.

Column 2. The second column lists the proper shipping names and descriptions of regulated materials. The names in this column have been alphabetized to make it easier for you to quickly find the name of a specific material. In this column, proper shipping names are listed in regular type, while common or "generic" names have been printed in italics. Remember that your shipping paper must show the material's proper shipping name.

Column 3. The number listed in Column 3 represents the hazard class or division of the material listed in Column 2. (You learned about hazard class and division earlier in this chapter.) Sometimes the word "forbidden" appears in this column in place of a number. This means that this particular material can't be transported. As a responsible driver, don't ever transport a material that's been classified as forbidden.

The information in this chapter will help you placard shipments. Before you can choose the correct placard, you'll need to know three things:

1. the material's hazard class
2. the amount of the material being shipped
3. the amount of all hazardous materials of all classes on your vehicle

Column 4. This column lists the **identification number**, also referred to as the **UN/NA identification number**, for the material's proper shipping name. Notice that the letters "UN" or "NA" come before each number. "UN" stands for "United Nations," indicating that this proper shipping name is internationally recognized. "NA" stands for "North America," meaning that this proper shipping name is used only in the United States and Canada.

The identification number should also appear in the description section of the shipping paper (see Figure 11.2) and on the package. It should also be displayed on cargo tanks and bulk packaging. In case of an emergency, a firefighter or police officer should be able to quickly locate this number to identify the type of hazardous material being transported.

Column 5. Each material is assigned to a packing group, which indicates the degree of danger it presents. The shipper is responsible for assigning a packing group number to the material, which is indicated in this column by a Roman numeral indicating a high danger (I), medium danger (II), or low danger (III). Note that packing groups aren't assigned for Class 2 materials, Class 7 materials, and ORM-D materials.

Column 6. Column 6 tells the shipper what kind of hazard warning label(s) to put on a package. Some materials present more than one type of hazard, so shippers must mark these materials with more than one hazard warning label. If the word "none" appears in this column, no hazard warning label is needed.

Column 7. Some materials require special provisions to make sure that the material is properly contained. This code is listed in Column 7 of the Hazardous Materials Table. For instance, look at the entry for "alcoholates solution, n.o.s., in alcohol" in Figure 11.6. In the code "IB2" in Column 7, the "IB" refers to a special provision for the transportation of materials in IBCs, or intermediate bulk containers, which are used to transport and store bulk fluids and other materials. The "2" in the code lets shippers, handlers, and drivers know that the material is a gas that's poisonous by inhalation, and that the gas has been assigned to "Hazard Zone B" (one of four hazard zones used to indicate the inhalation toxicity of gases).

You can find the meanings of each special provisions code by referring to 49 CFR 172.102.

Column 8. Column 8 is a three-part column showing the section numbers covering the packaging requirements for each hazardous material.

Columns 9 and 10. These two columns don't apply to highway transportation, so they aren't included here.

List of Hazardous Substances and Reportable Quantities (Appendix A to 49 CFR 172.101)

If a spill occurs while a hazardous substance is being transported, you or your employer will have to report the spill to the Department of Transportation (DOT) or the Environmental Protection Agency (EPA). See Figure 11.7 for an example of the List of Hazardous Substances and Reportable Quantities. This list is available in Appendix A to 49 CFR 172.101. You can also find a complete list by visiting the DOT or EPA Web sites. It's the shipper's responsibility to mark packages with the letters "RQ" (reportable quantity) when packages contain this amount or greater of a particular substance. These letters should also appear on the shipping paper (see Figure 11.2).

If the shipping paper and package contain the words INHALATION HAZARD, you'll have to display the POISON INHALATION HAZARD or POISON GAS placards, as well as any other placards that might be required due to the material's hazard class. Even when you're transporting only small amounts of an inhalation material, you're still required to display the

Figure 11.7. Example of the List of Hazardous Substances and Reportable Quantities

List of Hazardous Substances and Reportable Quantities		
Hazardous Substances	**Synonyms**	**Reportable Quantity (RQ) Pounds (Kilograms)**
Phenyl mercaptan®	Bensinethiol Thiophenol	100 (45.4)
Phenylmercuric acetate	Mercury, (acetato-O) Phenyl	100 (45.4)
N-Phenylthiourea Phorate	Thiourea, phenyl Phosphorodithioic acid, O, O-diethyl S-(ethylthio), methylester	100 (45.4) 10 (4.54)
Phosgene	Carbonyl Chloride	10 (4.54)
Phosphine Phosphoric acid	Hydrogen Phosphide	100 (45.4) 5000 (2270)
Phosphoric acid, diethyl 4-nitrophenyl ester	Diethyl-p Nitrophenyl Phosphate	100 (45.4)
Phosphoric acid, lead salt	Lead Phosphate	1 (0.454)

hazard class placard and POISON INHALATION HAZARD placards.

List of Marine Pollutants (Appendix B to 49 CFR 172.101)

Appendix B to 49 CFR 172.101 contains a list of chemicals that are toxic to marine life. This list applies only to highway transportation when they're being transported in a container that can carry 119 gallons or more without a placard label, as is stated in the HMR.

If you're transporting a bulk package of Marine Pollutants, the package must be marked with a marine pollutant marking. See Figure 11.8 for an example of what a marine pollutant marking looks like. Even though this marking isn't actually a placard, it must still be displayed on the outside of a package containing a marine pollutant and on the outside of the vehicle transporting the pollutant. On the shipping papers, the description of the material should also contain the words "marine pollutant."

Figure 11.8. Marine Pollutant Marking

Shipping Papers

You've already learned a little about shipping papers (see Figure 11.2 for an example). A shipping paper for hazardous materials must include the following:

- page numbers, if it's more than one page; the first page should show the total number of pages (e.g., "Page 1 of 1" or "Page 1 of 3")
- a proper shipping description for each hazardous material

- a shipper's certification, signed by the shipper, stating that the shipment was prepared according to the rules

The Item Description

A shipping paper will often contain descriptions of both hazardous and nonhazardous materials. If this is the case, the hazardous materials will be either described first, highlighted in a contrasting color, or identified by an "X" before the shipping name in the "HM" column. A shipper might use the letters "RQ" instead of the "X" to note a reportable quantity of a hazardous material.

The description should contain the following:

- the proper shipping name (not abbreviated, unless authorized in HMR)
- the hazard class or division (not abbreviated, unless authorized in HMR)
- the identification number (not abbreviated, unless authorized in HMR)
- the total quantity and unit of measure
- the letters "RQ," if it's a reportable quantity
- the name of the hazardous substance (if the letters "RQ" appear)
- the technical name of the hazardous material (if the letter "G" for "Generic" appears in Column 1, or if a poisonous material hasn't been identified by its technical name)
- an emergency response telephone number (at the responsibility of the shipper)

If there's a spill or a fire, emergency responders can call the emergency response telephone number to find out more information about the hazardous material. This is required for some—but not all—hazardous materials. The regulations contain a list of the materials that require an emergency response telephone number to be included on the shipping papers.

Shippers are also responsible for providing the motor carrier with emergency response information for each hazardous material they're shipping. This information should tell the motor carrier how to safely handle emergency incidents involving the material (while away from the vehicle) and should also include information such as the shipping name of the hazardous material, the health risks associated with the material, the risks of fire or explosion, and methods for the initial handling of the spill, fire, or leak until the proper authorities arrive. Shippers might also include a description of preliminary first aid information to protect the people involved in the emergency.

Sometimes shippers, motor carriers, or drivers have an Emergency Response Guidebook (ERG) that tells drivers what to do in the event of an emergency. It's the driver's responsibility to provide emergency response information to federal, state, or local authorities investigating or responding to a HAZMAT incident.

The total quantity must also be listed either before or after the item description, often with the packaging type and unit of measurement abbreviated as follows:

10 ctns. Paint,
3, UN1263,
PG II, 500 lbs.

If the shipper is shipping hazardous waste, the word "waste" must appear before the proper shipping name on the shipping paper, such as the following:

Waste Acetone,
3, UN1090,
PG II, 500 lbs.

If the hazardous material is a mixture of two or more hazardous materials, the shipper must enter the technical names of the two most hazardous materials in the mixture, such as the following:

Flammable liquid, corrosive, n.o.s., 3,
Un2924,
PG I, (contains Methanol, Potassium hydroxide)

A shipper should never assign a hazard class or identification number to a nonhazardous material. This could be very confusing to anyone who has to look at the shipping paper.

Shipper's Certification

The **shipper's certification** is a promise that the shipper has prepared the package according to the rules and that the package—as it is when it leaves the shipper— is safe for others to handle. The only time a shipper isn't required to provide certification is when the shipper also acts as a carrier transporting its own product, or when the package is provided by a carrier (e.g., a cargo tank).

Although you'll have to find out what rules your employer has about accepting packages, in general, you can accept a package with a shipper's certification unless you see something that makes you think that the package is unsafe (such as if it's leaking) or that it doesn't comply with the HMR. It's also important to find out if the carrier has its own additional rules about transporting HAZMAT.

Package Markings and Labels

Some shippers print package markings directly onto the package, while others attach labels or tags to the package. Packages should be marked or labeled with the following information:

- the proper shipping name of the hazardous material (this should match the name on the shipping paper)

- the identification number of the hazardous material
- the name and address of the shipper or **consignee** (the person or company that the goods are being shipped to)
- the required labels (which will always indicate the class of the hazardous materials being transported)

Keep in mind that requirements will be different depending on the material and the size of the package. If necessary, the shipper must mark the package with "RQ" or "INHALATION HAZARD." Packages containing liquids will also have "package orientation markings," or arrows that show which direction is upright. When a package has multiple labels, they should be placed close together near the proper shipping name.

Recognizing Hazardous Materials

The easiest way you can figure out whether a package contains hazardous materials is to look at the shipping paper and ask yourself the following questions:

- Does the shipping paper contain an entry listing a proper shipping name, hazard class, and identification number?
- Does the shipping paper contain a highlighted entry?
- Does the shipping paper contain an entry with an "X" or "RQ" in the hazardous materials column?
- What business is the shipper in? Does the shipper deal or supply hazardous materials (such as paint, chemicals, scientific materials, pest control supplies, agricultural supplies, explosives, munitions, or fireworks)?
- Do I see containers with diamond labels or placards anywhere on the premises?

- Is the package being shipped one that typically contains hazardous materials, such as a drum or cylinder?
- Is there a hazard class label, proper shipping name, or identification number on the package?
- Can I find any handling precautions on the package?

Hazardous Waste Manifest

A Uniform Hazardous Waste Manifest is a form that accompanies hazardous wastes throughout the delivery process. Figure 11.9 shows what this form looks like and what information must be added to it. The names and EPA registration number of the shipper, carrier(s), and destination point must be recorded on the form, and a copy of the most recent signed and dated form must be left at each site as the hazardous waste travels to its final destination (which must be a registered disposal or treatment facility). This form is basically a shipping paper for hazardous waste.

First, the shipper prepares the manifest, dates it, and signs it by hand. Then the shipper gives it to the carrier, who must also sign it by hand. Each carrier who handles and transports the waste must sign the manifest. When you deliver the waste, make sure the consignee signs and dates the manifest. Keep your copy of the manifest even after you've delivered it—it's a very important document. If for some reason you can't deliver the shipment to the destination listed on the manifest, you'll have to contact the shipper for instructions.

Certain states have their own regulations for reporting the transport of hazardous waste, so check with your state(s) to see if you'll have to fill out any additional forms when transporting HAZMAT.

A Uniform Hazardous Waste Manifest is a very important document. Make sure each carrier who handles and transports the waste signs and dates the

Please print or type. (Form designed for use on elite (12-pitch) typewriter.)   Form Approved. OMB No. 2050 0039

UNIFORM HAZARDOUS WASTE MANIFEST	1. Generator ID Number	2. Page 1 of	3. Emergency Response Phone	4. Manifest Tracking Number

5. Generator's Name and Mailing Address   Generator's Site Address (if different than mailing address)

Generator's Phone

6. Transporter 1 Company Name	U.S. EPA ID Number

7. Transporter 2 Company Name	U.S. EPA ID Number

8. Designated Facility Name and Site Address	U.S. EPA ID Number

Facility's Phone

9a. HM	9b. U.S. DOT Description (including Proper Shipping Name, Hazard Class, ID Number, and Packing Group (if any))	10. Containers		11. Total Quantity	12. Unit Wt./Vol.	13. Waste Codes
		No.	Type			
	1.					
	2.					
	3.					
	4.					

14. Special Handling Instructions and Additional Information

15. **GENERATOR'S/OFFEROR'S CERTIFICATION:** I hereby declare that the contents of this consignment are fully and accurately described above by the proper shipping name, and are classified, packaged, marked and labeled placarded, and are in all respects in proper condition for transport according to applicable international and national governmental regulations. If export shipment and I am the Primary Exporter, I certify that the contents of this consignment conform to the terms of the attached EPA Acknowledgment of Consent.
I certify that the waste minimization statement identified in 40 CFR 262.27(a) (if I am a large quantity generator) or (b) (if I am a small quantity generator) is true.

Generator's/Offeror's Printed/Typed Name	Signature	Month	Day	Year

16. International Shipments   ☐ Import to U.S.   ☐ Export from U.S.   Port of entry/exit: _____
Transporter signature (for exports only)   Date leaving U.S.:

17. Transporter Acknowledgment of Receipt of Materials

Transporter 1 Printed/Typed Name	Signature	Month	Day	Year
Transporter 2 Printed/Typed Name	Signature	Month	Day	Year

18. Discrepancy

18a. Discrepancy Indication Space   ☐ Quantity   ☐ Type   ☐ Residue   ☐ Partial Rejection   ☐ Full Rejection

Manifest Reference Number

18b. Alternate Facility (or Generator)	U.S. EPA ID Number

Facility's Phone

18c. Signature of Alternate Facility (or Generator)	Month	Day	Year

19. Hazardous Waste Report Management Method Codes (i.e., codes for hazardous waste treatment, disposal, and recycling systems)

1.	2.	3.	4.

20. Designated Facility Owner or Operator: Certification of receipt of hazardous materials covered by the manifest except as noted in Item 18a

Printed/Typed Name	Signature	Month	Day	Year

EPA Form 8700-22 (Rev 3-05) Previous editions are obsolete.   **DESIGNATED FACILITY TO DESTINATION STATE (IF REQUIRED)**

Figure 11.9. Environmental Protection Agency, "Uniform Hazardous Waste Manifest,"
http://www.epa.gov/epaoswer/hazwaste/gener/manifest/pdf/newform.pdf (accessed August 15, 2008).

GENERATOR

INT'L

TRANSPORTER

DESIGNATED FACILITY

Placard Table 1 Any Amount	
IF YOUR VEHICLE CONTAINS ANY AMOUNT OF . . .	**PLACARD AS . . .**
1.1 Mass Explosives	Explosives 1.1
1.2 Projection Hazards	Explosives 1.2
1.3 Mass Fire Hazards	Explosives 1.3
2.3 Poisonous/Toxic Gases	Poison Gas
4.3 Spontaneously Combustible When Wet	Dangerous When Wet
5.2 (Organic Peroxide, Type B, liquid or solid, Temperature Controlled)	Organic Peroxide
6.1 (Inhalation hazard zone A & B only)	Poison
7 (Radioactive Yellow III label only)	Radioactive

Figure 11.10. Placard Table 1—Any Amount

manifest. Keep your copy of the manifest even after you've delivered it.

Placarding

Before you transport hazardous wastes in your vehicle, you'll have to attach the proper placards to your vehicle. The only time you're allowed to drive (or even move) an improperly placarded vehicle is during an emergency to protect life or property.

When choosing the correct placard(s), you'll need to know

- the hazard class of the materials
- the amount of hazardous materials being shipped
- the total amount of all classes of hazardous materials being shipped

When you're deciding which placards to use, check the shipping paper to make sure the basic description is correct. You're responsible for affixing the right placards to your own vehicle. If you're unsure about the shipper's description, or if you're unfamiliar with the material, contact the shipper for clarification or ask the shipper to contact your office.

Placards must appear on both sides and both ends of the vehicle (see Figure 11.5). Here are some additional rules to follow when placarding. Placards must be

- easily seen from the direction that each one faces
- placed so the words and numbers are level from left to right
- placed at least 3 inches (76.2 mm) away from any other markings
- kept clear of attachments or devices such as ladders, doors, and tarpaulins
- clean and undamaged so the color, format, and message are easily seen
- affixed to a background of a contrasting color so the color, format, and message are easily seen

Placard Tables

Drivers can use one of two placard tables to help them placard correctly. Table 1—seen in Figure 11.10—shows materials that must be placarded whenever they're transported, no matter what amount is being transported.

Table 2—seen in Figure 11.11—lists the materials that need to be placarded only if the total amount you're transporting is over 1,000 pounds. Before you make this decision, you'll have to add the amounts of each Table 2 product you're transporting from all shipping papers for those materials.

Placard Table 2 1,000 Pounds or More	
Category of Material (Hazard class or division number and additional description, as appropriate	**Placard Name**
1.4 Very insensitive	Explosives 1.4
1.5 Extremely insensitive	Explosives 1.5
1.6	Explosives 1.6
2.1 Flammable Gases	Flammable Gas
2.2 Nonflammable Gases	Flammable
3 Flammable Liquids	Combustible*
Combustible Liquid	Flammable Solid
4.1 Flammable Solids	Spontaneously Combustible
5.1 Oxidizers	Oxidizer
5.2 (other than organic peroxide, Type B, liquid or solid, Temperature Controlled)	Organic Peroxide
6.1 (other than inhalation hazard zone A or B)	Poison
6.2 Infectious Substances	(None)
8 Corrosives	Corrosive
9 Miscellaneous Hazardous Materials	Class 9**
ORM-D	(None)
*FLAMMABLE may be used in place of COMBUSTIBLE on a cargo tank or portable tank.	
** Class 9 Placard is not required for domestic transportation.	

Figure 11.11. Placard Table 2—1,000 Pounds or More

Note that you're allowed to use DANGEROUS placards instead of separate placards for each hazardous material listed in Table 2 if (1) you have over 1,000 pounds of two or more Table 2 hazard classes that would normally require different placards, and (2) you don't have over 5,000 pounds of any Table 2 hazard class material at any one place. (But you must use the specific placard of this material!) Remember, though, that this is an option—not a requirement.

► Loading and Unloading

General Loading Requirements

Follow these rules to make sure you safely load your cargo:

- Make sure you protect HAZMAT containers at all costs! Don't use any tools or hooks that could damage the containers or other packaging during loading.
- Set the parking brake before you load or unload.

- Load HAZMAT away from heat sources, as some materials become even more hazardous when they're exposed to heat.
- Pay attention to the condition of the containers you're loading. They shouldn't be damaged or leaking. A popular saying is "LEAKS SPELL TROUBLE!" Don't load leaking packages into your vehicle, as they could be very dangerous for you, your truck, and others on the road.
- Brace containers in the following classes so they don't move while you're transporting them: Class 1 (explosives), Class 2 (gases), Class 3 (flammable liquids), Class 4 (flammable solids), Class 5 (oxidizers), Class 8 (corrosives), and Division 6.1 (poisons).

No Smoking

Keep all hazardous materials away from fire, and *don't smoke* or allow others to smoke near your vehicle when you're hauling hazardous materials. Remember, you should never smoke within 25 feet of the following classes of materials:

- Class 1 (explosives)
- Class 3 (flammable liquids)
- Class 4 (flammable solids)
- Class 5 (oxidizers)
- Division 2.1 (flammable gas)

Secure Against Movement

Brace all containers so that they won't slide, fall, or bounce while you're transporting them. As you're loading containers, make sure that all valves or other fittings are in place.

Once you've loaded your vehicle, don't open any packages or transfer materials from one container to another during your trip. Don't empty any package other than a cargo tank during your trip.

Cargo Heater Rules

Cargo heaters (including automatic cargo heater/air conditioner units) are usually forbidden when you're transporting the following materials:

- Class 1 (explosives)
- Class 3 (flammable liquids)
- Division 2.1 (flammable gas)

Though specific rules sometimes allow it, unless you've read all the rules and are sure you've interpreted them correctly, it's best to simply avoid loading these materials in a heated cargo space.

Use Closed Cargo Space

The following materials must be transported in a closed cargo space (meaning they can't be hauled with overhang or as tailgate loads) unless they're contained in packages that are fire resistant and water resistant or they're covered with a fire- and water-resistant tarp:

- Class 1 (explosives)
- Class 4 (flammable solids)
- Class 5 (oxidizers)

Precautions for Specific Hazards

Class 1 (Explosives) Materials

Before you load or unload your vehicle, make sure that your engine is off. Then check the cargo space by performing the following tasks:

- Disconnect cargo heater power sources and drain cargo heater fuel tanks to disable the cargo heaters entirely.
- Make sure there aren't sharp points that might damage the cargo (such as bolts, screws, nails, broken side panels, and broken floorboards) in the cargo space.

- Use a floor lining with Division 1.1, 1.2, or 1.3 (Class A or B Explosives). The floors must be tight and the liner must be either a nonmetallic material or a nonferrous metal.
- Be very careful to protect explosive materials from anything that might cause damage, including other cargo. Don't ever use hooks or other metal tools to load explosives. Also, take care not to drop, throw, or roll packages containing explosives as you're loading them.
- The only time you should transfer a Division 1.1, 1.2, or 1.3 (Class A or B Explosives) from one vehicle to another on a public roadway is during an emergency. If you have to do an emergency transfer for safety reasons, set out red warning reflectors, flags, or electric lanterns to warn others on the road to stay back.
- Never transport damaged packages of explosives or accept a package that's damp or has oily stains.
- Don't transport Division 1.1 or 1.2 (Class A Explosives) in triples or in vehicle combinations if there's a marked or placarded cargo tank in the combination and the other vehicle in the combination contains

  - Division 1.1 A (Initiating Explosives)
  - packages of Class 7 (Radioactive) materials labeled "Yellow III"
  - Division 2.3 (Poisonous Gas) or Division 6.1 (Poisonous) materials
  - hazardous materials in a portable tank, on a DOT Spec 106A, or 110A tank

Class 4 (Flammable Solids) and Class 5 (Oxidizers) Materials

Class 4 materials are solids that react (including catching fire and exploding) to water, heat, and air or even react spontaneously. Class 4 and 5 materials must be completely enclosed in a vehicle or covered securely. These materials become unstable when they get wet, which can lead to very dangerous situations. Keep Class 4 and 5 materials dry while in transit and during loading and unloading. If you're transporting materials that are subject to spontaneous combustion or heating, make sure your vehicle has sufficient ventilation.

Class 8 (Corrosive) Materials

If you're loading by hand, load breakable containers of corrosive liquid one by one, making sure they're right-side up and being careful not to drop or roll the containers. Make sure the containers are standing on an even floor surface. Stack carboys only if the lower tiers can safely bear the weight of the upper tiers. Don't load nitric acid above any other product.

Load charged storage batteries right-side up, so their liquid won't spill. Make sure other cargo can't fall against them or short-circuit them.

It's very important never to load corrosive liquids next to or above the following materials:

- Division 1.4 (Explosives)
- Division 2.3, Zone B (Poisonous Gases)
- Division 4.1 (Flammable Solids)
- Division 4.3 (Dangerous When Wet)
- Class 5 (Oxidizers)

It's also important never to load corrosive liquids with these materials:

- Division 1.1 or 1.2 (Explosives A)
- Division 1.2 or 1.3 (Explosives B)
- Division 1.5 (Blasting Agents)

- Division 2.3, Zone A (Poisonous Gases)
- Division 4.2 (Spontaneously Combustible Materials)
- Division 6.1, PGI, Zone A (Poison Liquids)

Class 2 (Compressed Gases) Including Cryogenic Liquids

Some vehicles don't have racks to hold cylinders. If your vehicle doesn't have cylinder racks, you can transport cylinders only if the cargo space floor is flat and the cylinders are held upright in racks attached to the vehicle or in boxes that will keep them from turning over. You can load cylinders only in a horizontal position (lying down) when it's designed so the relief valve is in the vapor space.

Division 2.3 (Poisonous Gas) or Division 6.1 (Poisonous) Materials

Never transport poisonous materials in containers with interconnections. Also, never load a package labeled POISON or POISON INHALATION HAZARD in the driver's cab or sleeper or with food materials that will be consumed by humans or animals. You need special training and must follow special, strict rules before you can legally load and unload Class 2 materials in cargo tanks.

Class 7 (Radioactive) Materials

Some packages of Class 7 (Radioactive) materials are marked with a number called the "transport index." The shipper labels these packages with either Radioactive II or Radioactive III and prints the package's transport index on the label.

The problem with radioactive materials is that radiation surrounds each package and then passes through all nearby packages. There are established controls to deal with this problem. First, you're allowed to load only a certain number of packages, based on the transport index of each package. Second, you have to keep these packages within a certain distance of people, animals, and unexposed film.

The transport index tells the degree of control needed during transportation. The total transport index of all packages in a single vehicle must not exceed 50. Radioactive Separation Table A (see Figure 11.12) shows you the rules for each transport index in terms

Figure 11.12. Radioactive Separation Table A

TOTAL TRANSPORT INDEX	Radioactive Separation Table A MINIMUM DISTANCE IN FEET TO NEAREST UNDEVELOPED FILM					TO PEOPLE OR CARGO COMPARTMENT PARTITIONS
	1–2 Hr.	2–4 Hrs.	4–8 Hrs.	8–12 Hrs.	Over 12 Hrs.	
None	0	0	0	0	0	0
0.1 to 1.0	1	2	3	4	5	1
1.1 to 5.0	3	4	6	8	11	2
5.1 to 10.0	4	6	9	11	15	3
10.0 to 20.0	5	8	12	16	22	4
20.1 to 30.0	7	10	15	20	29	5
30.1 to 40.0	8	11	17	22	33	6
40.1 to 50.0	9	12	19	24	36	

Do Not Load Table	
Do Not Load	**In the Same Vehicle With**
Division 6.1 or 2.3 (POISON or POISON INHALATION HAZARD labeled material)	Animal or human food unless the poison package is over packed in any approved way. (Foodstuffs are anything you swallow; however, mouthwash, toothpaste, and skin creams are not foodstuffs.)
Division 2.3 (Poisonous) gas Zone A or Division 6.1 (Poison) liquids, GI, Zone A	Division 1.5 (Oxidizers), Class 3 (Flammable Liquids), Class 8 (Corrosive Liquids), Division 5.2 (Organic Peroxides), Division 1.1, 1.2, 1.3 (Class A or B) Explosives, Division 1.5 (Blasting Agents), Division 2.1 (Flammable Gases), Class 4 (Flammable Solids)
Charged storage batteries	Division 1.1 (Class A Explosives)
Class 1 (Detonating primers)	Any other explosive unless in authorized containers or packages

Division 6.1 (Cyanides or cyanide mixtures)	Acids, corrosive materials, or other acidic materials that could release hydrocyanic acid; for example
	    Cyanides, Inorganic, n.o.s.
	    Silver Cyanide
	    Sodium Cyanide

Nitric acid (Class B)	Other materials unless the nitric acid isn't loaded above any other material

Figure 11.13. "Do Not Load" Table

of how close you can load Class 7 (Radioactive) materials to people, animals, or film. For example, you can't leave a package with a transport index of 1.1 within 2 feet of people or cargo space walls.

Don't leave Radioactive Yellow-II or Yellow-III labeled packages near people, animals, or film longer than is stated in Figure 11.12.

Mixed Loads

Some materials can't be loaded with other materials in the same cargo space. Figure 11.13 gives some examples of products that can't be loaded together. You can consult the regulations (the Segregation and Separation Chart) for a more comprehensive list of materials that must be kept apart.

▶ Bulk Packaging Marking, Loading, and Unloading

The term **bulk packaging** refers to packaging other than a vessel or barge, but including a transport vehicle or freight container, that hazardous materials are loaded into with no intermediate form of containment. To be considered bulk packaging, the packaging must also meet one or more of the following requirements:

- a maximum capacity of over 119 gallons (450 L) as a receptacle for liquid
- a maximum net mass of more than 882 pounds (400 kg) or a maximum capacity

greater than 119 gallons (450 L) as a receptacle for a solid

- a water capacity greater than 1,000 pounds (454 kg) as a receptacle for gas as defined in Section 173.115

Cargo tanks are bulk packaging permanently attached to a vehicle. Cargo tanks are stationary, meaning they remain on the vehicle when you load and unload them. There are many types of cargo tanks, but the most common are MC306 for liquids and MC331 for gases. Portable tanks are bulk packaging not permanently attached to a vehicle. Portable tanks are removed from the vehicle, so they can be loaded and unloaded and are then put on a vehicle for transportation.

Markings
The identification numbers of the hazardous materials in portable tanks and cargo tanks and other bulk packaging (such as dump trucks) must be displayed. You can find identification numbers in Column 4 of the Hazardous Materials Table. To display identification numbers, you must use black, 100 mm (3.9 inch) numbers on orange panels, on placards, or on a white, diamond-shaped background (if placards aren't required). Specific cargo tanks must also show retest date markings.

Portable tanks must also display the lessee or owner's name and the shipping name of the contents. This information should appear on two opposing sides of the tank. On portable tanks with capacities of more than 1,000 gallons, the letters of the shipping name must be at least 2 inches tall. On portable tanks with capacities of less than 1,000 gallons, the letters of the shipping name must be at least 1 inch tall.

The identification number must also appear on each side and each end of a portable tank or other bulk packaging that holds 1,000 gallons or more and on two opposing sides, if the portable tank holds less than 1,000 gallons. You must be able to see the identification numbers when the portable tank is on the CMV. If they aren't visible, you must display the identification number on both sides and ends of the CMV.

Intermediate bulk containers (IBCs) are bulk packages, but they aren't required to have the owner's name or shipping name.

Tank Loading
The person in charge of loading and unloading a cargo tank must make sure a qualified person is always watching and supervising. This supervising person must

- be alert
- be within 25 feet of the cargo tank
- have a clear view of the cargo tank
- be educated on the hazards of the materials involved
- know emergency procedures
- be authorized to move the cargo tank and be able to do so

There are special attendance rules for cargo tanks transporting propane and anhydrous ammonia.

Before you move a tank of hazardous materials, close all manholes and valves to prevent leaks, no matter how small the amount in the tank or how short the distance you're moving it. It's illegal to move a cargo tank with open valves or covers unless it's empty, according to 49 CFR 173.29.

Flammable Liquids
Turn off your engine before loading or unloading any flammable liquids, unless you need it to operate a pump. Ground a cargo tank correctly before filling it through an open filling hole. Ground the tank before

you open the filling hole, and maintain the ground until after you close the filling hole.

Compressed Gas

Keep liquid discharge valves on a compressed gas tank closed except when you're loading and unloading. Unless you need your engine to run a pump for product transfer, turn it off when loading or unloading. If you do need the engine to run a pump, turn it off after product transfer, before you unhook the hose.

Unhook all loading/unloading connections before coupling, uncoupling, or moving a cargo tank.

Also, make sure you always chock trailers and semitrailers to prevent them from moving when they're uncoupled from the power unit.

▶ Hazardous Materials—Driving and Parking Rules

You've already learned that hauling hazardous materials requires great attention to detail. The following driving and parking rules are designed to help protect you and other drivers from danger and make your journey go as smoothly as possible. While these rules are designed to help keep you and other drivers safe, they're only the basics. It's important to understand the dangers that the materials you're hauling pose to people. Most of all, it's important to use common sense when driving and parking a vehicle with hazardous materials.

Parking with Division 1.1, 1.2, or 1.3 (Class A or B) Explosives

When driving a vehicle that's hauling Division 1.1, 1.2, or 1.3 (Class A or B) explosives follow these rules:

- Never park within 5 feet of the traveled part of the road.

- Don't park within 300 feet of any structure such as a bridge, tunnel, or building; in a place where people are gathered; or near a spot with an open fire. The only exception to this rule is during the time needed for vehicle operation necessities, such as fueling.
- Don't park your vehicle on private property unless the owner knows of the danger. Always watch your parked vehicle. It's appropriate to allow someone else to watch the vehicle only if you're parked on the shipper's, carrier's, or consignee's property.
- You can leave your vehicle unattended in only approved safe havens. **Safe havens** are areas, authorized by local authorities, where it's considered safe to park an unattended vehicle loaded with explosives.

Parking a Placarded Vehicle Not Transporting Division 1.1, 1.2, or 1.3 (Class A or B) Explosives

The rules for parking a placarded vehicle that's not carrying explosives are less strict. For example, you can park your vehicle within 5 feet of the traveled part of the road. Park the vehicle for only a brief period to do your job or to fuel the vehicle. Always watch your vehicle when it's parked on a public roadway or on the shoulder. Never leave your vehicle unattended in a public area. Don't uncouple a trailer with hazardous materials and leave it on a public street. People often don't understand the danger associated with these materials, so it's best to keep members of the public away. Be sure to keep your vehicle at least 300 feet away from any area with an open fire. The best way to prevent a problem is to remember the danger that these materials present to the public. Being serious about safety is the best way to avoid danger.

Attending to Parked Vehicles

If your vehicle is parked and being attended to by another person, this person is required to have knowledge of the materials in the vehicle and be able to perform certain tasks in an emergency. This person must

- be awake, be inside (not in the sleeper berth) or within 100 feet of the vehicle, and have it within clear view at all times
- be aware of the types of hazardous materials being transported and the dangers they present
- know what to do in the event of an emergency
- be able to move the vehicle

Using Stopped Vehicle Signs

Imagine that you're hauling hazardous materials and your vehicle breaks down on the side of the road. The best way to alert other drivers of your presence is to use reflective triangles or red electric lights. Though it may seem like common sense, it's extremely important that you remember never to use burning signals, like flares or fuses, anywhere near a tank used to haul Class 3 (Flammable Liquids) or Division 2.1 (Flammable Gas). Even if the tank is completely empty, never use burning signals around the vehicle. You should also avoid using burning signals near a vehicle transporting Division 1.1, 1.2, or 1.3 (Class A or B) explosives.

No Smoking

For the same reasons you wouldn't use a burning signal near a vehicle hauling hazardous materials, you must also ensure that there's no smoking near the vehicle. It's important that you don't smoke or carry a lit cigarette, cigar, or pipe within 25 feet of any vehicle that contains Class 1 (Explosives), Class 3, (Flammable Liquids), Class 4 (Flammable Solids), or Class 5 (Oxidiz-ers) materials. Make sure no one else smokes around the vehicle. If someone is smoking nearby, keep that person as far away from the vehicle as possible to ensure the safety of everyone in the area.

Route Restrictions

If you're transporting a vehicle with hazardous materials across state or county lines, it's important that you're aware of the approved routes on which you can travel. Some areas require special permits to transport hazardous material or wastes. Part of your job as a driver is to find out if you'll need permits for the area you're traveling through or if there are special routes designated for vehicles hauling hazardous materials. Your trip will go much more smoothly if you get all the papers and information you need before you start out.

If you work for a carrier, contact your dispatcher about route restrictions or permits for the area you're traveling through. If you work independently, you can find the information you need by contacting state agencies in the states where you plan to travel. When speaking to a state representative, be sure to ask if there are any restrictions on transporting hazardous materials through tunnels, over bridges, or across other roadways. This will help you plan accordingly to avoid any problems or confusion while driving.

When planning your route, try to avoid heavily populated areas, narrow streets, and tunnels. Even if the route is inconvenient and takes longer, it's important to remember that your safety and the safety of others is your top priority when transporting hazardous materials.

When transporting Division 1.1, 1.2, or 1.3 (Class A or B) explosives, you're required to have a written route plan with you and to follow that plan. Carriers will often prepare a route plan in advance and give you a copy. If you're given the task of preparing the route plan, do it in advance and be sure you always have a copy with you. Remember, always choose the safest route—not the fastest—when you create your route.

Other Important Rules

No matter what type of hazardous material you're transporting, you'll want to follow a few other rules to ensure everyone's safety:

- Turn off the engine when fueling. Make sure someone is always at the pump to control the flow of the fuel.
- *Always* have a properly charged and rated fire extinguisher. The power unit of a placarded vehicle must have a fire extinguisher with a UL rating of 10-B:C or more, and it must be charged. Check to make sure your vehicle has this equipment.
- Make sure your tires are properly inflated. Check the tires using a pressure gauge during your pre-trip inspection and each time you stop. Don't drive with a flat or leaking tire. Replace damaged tires as soon as possible.
- Keep shipping papers and emergency response papers within your reach. Never accept a hazardous materials shipment without properly prepared shipping papers. It's important that people can find these papers in the event of an emergency or accident. Keep them where they can be found quickly, either in the pouch on the door, within easy reach with your seat belt on, or on the seat when you're out of the vehicle.
- When transporting Division 1.1, 1.2, or 1.3 (Class A or B) explosives, a carrier must provide you with a copy of the Federal Motor Carrier Safety Regulations (FMCSR), Part 397 and written instructions on what to do in case of an accident or emergency.

These instructions must include the names and telephone numbers of people to contact in case of an emergency (including carrier agents and shippers), the nature of the explosives being transported, and the precautions you should take in emergencies such as fires, accidents, or leaks. You'll be required to sign a receipt for these documents. Always have your shipping papers, emergency instructions, written route plan, and a copy of FMCSR, Part 397.

- If you're driving a vehicle that contains chlorine in the cargo tanks, be sure there's an approved gas mask in the vehicle. You must also have an emergency kit to repair any leaks in dome cover plate fittings on the cargo tank.
- Always stop before railroad crossings when driving a placarded vehicle or carrying any amount of chlorine. Stop between 15 and 50 feet from the nearest rail, and proceed only when you're certain that there's no train coming. Do not use the clutch or shift gears while crossing the tracks.

▶ Hazardous Materials— Emergencies

Though no one likes to think about it, it's extremely important to plan for the worst case scenario when transporting hazardous materials. The best way to prepare is to understand the different types of emergencies that might arise while you're hauling hazardous materials and how to deal with them. Although there are some general guidelines for dealing with hazardous materials emergencies, more specific rules focus on the exact materials you're transporting. You already learned that shippers, motor carriers, or drivers sometimes have an ERG (Emergency Response Guidebook) that tells them what to do in the event of an emergency. The DOT's ERG comes in handy during emergencies. This reference tells firefighters, police, and industry workers how to protect themselves and the public from hazardous materials. The ERG is indexed by proper shipping name and the hazardous materials identification number. During an accident, emergency workers will look for these identifiers on your shipping paper. This is why it's so important to make sure you have the proper shipping name, identification number, labels, and placards during your pre-trip inspection. This helps authorities deal with an emergency situation quickly and properly, so damage to property is minimal and there are as few injuries as possible.

Accidents: The Driver's Job

While accidents are frightening and difficult to deal with, it's important for professional drivers who are transporting hazardous materials to remain calm and follow proper procedure. If you're involved in an accident, the first thing you'll do is assess your own physical condition. After this, you must attend to specific tasks as quickly as possible to ensure your safety and the safety of people around you:

- If you have a driving partner, make sure that person is okay.
- Send for help. Communicate the danger of the hazardous materials you're carrying to the emergency response personnel.
- Warn anyone near the accident of the danger. Keep people as far away from the scene of the accident as possible. Keep them upwind of the vehicle to ensure that any leaking material isn't carried in the wind.
- If you can safely do so, limit the spread of the material according to the instructions

supplied by your employer. If you can't do this safely, do your best to secure the scene.
- When emergency personnel arrive, provide them with the shipping papers and emergency response information provided by your employer.

Fires and Leaks

Dealing with hazardous materials fires and leaks is extremely dangerous. Only specially trained emergency response personnel are qualified to deal with these emergencies. You can follow certain procedures in these situations, however.

Fires

As you've already learned, special training and equipment are required to fight hazardous materials fires safely. *Never* try to battle a fire on your own. Instead, immediately send for help! Grab your shipping papers, and keep them with you at all times. The shipping papers will help the emergency responders understand how to battle this particular blaze. If the fire is contained in the truck, you can use your fire extinguisher to keep it from spreading to the cargo before firefighters arrive on the scene. You might be able to tell if the fire has spread to the cargo area by feeling the trailer doors. Don't open the doors if they feel hot! Opening the doors will allow air in, which will fuel the fire. If you know the fire has spread to the cargo area, don't attempt to fight the fire. Stay as close to your vehicle as you safely can, and keep people away from your vehicle. Give the firefighters your shipping papers as soon as they arrive.

Leaks

It's easy to injure yourself in the event of a hazardous materials leak. *Never* touch any leaking materials. Don't try to identify the source of a leak by smelling it. Breathing a hazardous gas can severely injure or even kill you. The first thing you should do in the event of a leak is get your vehicle safely off the road and away from areas where people are gathered. Remember that your employer is responsible for cleaning up any leaking material. This can become expensive very quickly, so move your vehicle only as far as safety requires. Once you've stopped, remember to grab your shipping papers from the cab and begin securing the area. Emergency personnel will need the shipping papers to identify the hazardous materials leaking from your vehicle. Even though it might sound like a good idea to run for help, at this point you'll have to send someone else for help. *Never* leave a leaking vehicle! Provide the person you're sending for help with this information:

- a description of the emergency
- your exact location and the direction of travel
- your name, the carrier's name, and the name of the community or city where your terminal is located
- the proper shipping name, hazard class, and identification number of the hazardous materials

This is a lot of information for someone to remember, so you should write it down for the person. It's very important that emergency responders get the correct information as soon as possible, so they can deal with the leak in a timely manner. Remember, unless you have special training and the proper equipment to deal with leaks, you should always allow properly trained personnel to deal with the materials. This is the best way to ensure your safety.

Responding to Specific Hazards

The information you've just learned is important general knowledge for dealing with accidents when hauling hazardous materials. However, you need to be aware of some special concerns associated with specific materials.

Class 1 (Explosives)

If you break down while hauling explosive materials, warn others of the danger and keep them as far away as possible. Don't ever let anyone smoke or have an open fire of any kind near your vehicle. In the event of a collision, remove all explosives before separating the vehicles involved in the collision. Keep the removed explosives at least 200 feet away from the vehicles and any occupied buildings.

Class 2 (Compressed Gases)

If you discover a gas leak coming from your vehicle, immediately stop the vehicle, and park it safely away from the road and from any populated areas. Warn others of the danger and allow only emergency responders close to the vehicle. You must notify the shipper if compressed gas is involved in any accident.

Class 3 (Flammable Liquids)

If you have an accident, or if you break down while transporting flammable liquids, get off the road as soon as you can. Warn people of the danger, keep them away from the scene, and don't allow them to smoke. Call for help as soon as you can. Don't transfer flammable liquids from one vehicle to another on a public roadway—it's too dangerous!

Class 4 (Flammable Solids) and Class 5 (Oxidizing Materials)

If you experience a problem while hauling flammable solids or oxidizing materials, warn people of the fire danger, and keep them away from your vehicle. If you can safely remove unbroken packages from the vehicle, you can do this, but only to decrease the chance of fire. Never open smoldering packages—you could be seriously injured!

Class 6 (Poisonous Materials and Infectious Substances)

If you're involved in an accident while transporting poisonous material, the most important thing is to ensure your safety and the safety of others. Warn all nearby people of the danger, and keep them away from your vehicle. Many poisonous materials are also flammable, so take extra precautions if you think that a material may start a fire.

Immediately contact emergency personnel to help you deal with a poisonous material leak. Highly trained emergency professionals will have to check your vehicle for leaking poisons before you can take it back on the road. If a package carrying Division 2 (Infectious Substances) is damaged in transit, you must contact your supervisor immediately. Never accept packages containing this material if those packages appear damaged.

Class 7 (Radioactive Materials)

Notify your dispatcher or supervisor immediately if radioactive material is involved in a leak or is in a broken package. If a radioactive material spills, or if you suspect an internal container might be damaged, don't touch or inhale the material. Your vehicle will have to be cleaned and thoroughly checked with a survey meter before it can be used again.

Class 8 (Corrosive Materials)

As with other hazardous materials, the most important concern is to prevent any leaking corrosive materials from injuring yourself or others. If it's unsafe to drive with the leaking container, pull off the road and call for help. Contain any liquid leaking from your vehicle only if it's safe to do so. Any exposed part of your vehicle must be thoroughly washed with water.

▶ The National Response Center and the Chemical Transportation Emergency Center (CHEMTREC)

When an accident involving hazardous materials occurs, two agencies work together to assist industry professionals and emergency personnel. The National Response Center helps coordinate emergency response efforts and acts as a resource for police and firefighters. This agency has a 24-hour, toll-free hotline (800-424-8802). In certain instances, you're required to report an incident involving hazardous materials to this agency. You or your employer must call the National Response Center if any of the following occur because of any accident involving hazardous materials:

- There's a fatality.
- A person involved in the incident requires hospitalization.
- The damage to property exceeds $50,000.
- The incident causes one or more major transportation arteries to close for 1 hour or more.
- The incident involves fire, breakage, spillage, or suspected radioactive contamination.
- Fire, breakage, spillage, or suspected contamination occur involving etiologic agents (bacteria or toxins).
- The situation poses a continuing danger to life or property that the carrier believes should be reported.

When contacting the National Response Center, be prepared to provide your name, the name and address of the carrier you work for, and a phone number where you and the carrier can be reached. You also need to provide the date, time, and location of the incident as well as the classification, name, and quantity of the hazardous materials involved in the incident. Be prepared to describe the nature of the incident (e.g., collision, leakage), and explain whether there's any continuing danger to life or property. Injuries should also be reported at this time. This information is also extremely important to your employer. All carriers are required to submit detailed reports within 30 days of an incident.

The National Response Center works closely with the Chemical Transportation Emergency Center (CHEMTREC). This agency provides emergency personnel with vital information about the types of hazardous materials they're dealing with. CHEMTREC also has a 24-hour, toll-free hotline (800-424-9300). When you contact either the National Response Center or CHEMTREC, these agencies will quickly get in touch with each other, when appropriate, to offer the best possible response to any hazardous materials incident.

▶ Hazardous Materials Glossary

It can be very difficult to keep straight all the terms involved in the transportation of hazardous materials. Here are some key terms you'll need to know:

- **bulk packaging**. packaging, other than a vessel or barge, including a transport vehicle or freight container, that hazardous materials are loaded into with no intermediate form of containment and that has one or more of the following:

  - a maximum capacity greater than 119 gallons (450 L) as a receptacle for a liquid;

  - a maximum net mass greater than 882 pounds (400 kg) or a maximum capacity greater than 119 gallons (450 L) as a receptacle for a solid;
  - a water capacity greater than 1,000 pounds (454 kg) as a receptacle for a gas as defined in Section 173.115.

- **carboy**. a bottle or rectangular container, made of glass, plastic, or metal and cushioned in a wooden box that holds between 5 and 15 gallons of liquid.
- **cargo tank**. a bulk packaging that

  - is a tank intended primarily for the carriage of liquids or gases and includes appurtenances, reinforcements, fittings, and closures;
  - is permanently attached to or forms a part of a CMV, or isn't permanently attached to a CMV but that, by reason of its size, construction, or attachment to a CMV, is loaded or unloaded without being removed from the motor vehicle;
  - isn't fabricated under specification for cylinders, portable tanks, tank cars, or multiunit tank car tanks.

- **carrier**. a person engaged in the transportation of passengers or property by land or water as a common, contract, or private carrier or by civil aircraft.
- **consignee**. the business or person to whom a shipment is delivered.
- **division**. a subdivision of a hazard class
- **EPA**. abbreviation for the Environmental Protection Agency.
- **FMCSR**. abbreviation for the Federal Motor Carrier Safety Regulations.

- **freight container.** a reusable container having a volume of 64 cubic feet or more, designed and constructed to permit being lifted with its contents intact and intended primarily for containment of packages (in unit form) during transportation.

- **fuel tank.** a tank, other than a cargo tank, used to transport flammable or combustible liquid or compressed gas for the purpose of supplying fuel for propulsion of the transport vehicle that it's attached to, or for the operation of other equipment on the transport vehicle.

- **gross weight or gross mass.** the weight of a packaging plus the weight of its contents.

- **hazard class.** the category of hazard assigned to a hazardous material under the definitional criteria of Part 173 and the provisions of Section 172.101 Table B (see Figure 11.14). A material may meet the defining criteria for more than one hazard class but be assigned to only one hazard class. Hazardous materials are categorized into nine major classes and additional categories for consumer commodities and combustible liquids.

- **hazardous materials.** substances or materials that have been determined by the secretary of transportation to be capable of posing an unreasonable risk to health, safety, and property when transported in commerce and that have been so designated. The term includes hazardous substances, hazardous wastes, marine pollutants, elevated temperature materials, materials designated as hazardous in the Hazardous Materials Table of Section 172.101, and materials that meet the defining criteria for hazard classes and divisions in Section 173.

- **hazardous substance.** a material, including its mixtures and solutions, that (1) is listed in Appendix A to Section 172.101; (2) is in a quantity, in one package, that equals or exceeds the reportable quantity (RQ) listed in Appendix A to Section 172.101; and (3) when in a mixture or solution, for radionu-

Figure 11.14. Hazard Class Definitions—Table B

Hazard Class Definitions		
Table B		
Class	Class Name	Example
1	Explosives	Ammunition, Dynamite, Fireworks
2	Gases	Propane, Oxygen, Helium
3	Flammable	Gasoline Fuel, Acetone
4	Flammable Solids	Matches, Fuses
5	Oxidizers	Ammonium Nitrate, Hydrogen Peroxide
6	Poisons	Pesticides, Arsenic
7	Radioactive	Uranium, Plutonium
8	Corrosive	Hydrochloric Acid, Battery Acid
9	Miscellaneous	Formaldehyde, Asbestos
None	ORM-D (Other Regulated Material - Domestic)	Hair Spray or Charcoal
None	Combustible Liquid	Fuel, Lighter Fuel

Hazard Substance Concentrations		
RQ Pounds (Kilogram)	**Concentration by Weight**	
	Percent	PPM
5,000 (2,270)	10.000	100,000
1,000 (454)	2.000	20,000
100 (45.4)	0.200	2,000
10 (4.54)	0.020	200
1 (0.454)	0.002	20

Figure 11.15. Hazardous Substance Concentrations Table

clides, conforms to paragraph 7 of Appendix A to Section 172.101 and, for substances other than radionuclides, is in a concentration by weight that equals or exceeds the concentration corresponding to the RQ of the material (see Figure 11.15).

- **hazardous waste.** any material that's subject to the Hazardous Waste Manifest Requirements of the U.S. Environmental Protection Agency specified in 40 CFR Part 262.

- **intermediate bulk container (IBC).** a rigid or flexible portable packaging, other than a cylinder or portable tank, that's designed for mechanical handling. Standards for IBCs manufactured in the United States are set forth in subparts N and O Section 178.

- **marking.** the descriptive name, identification number, instructions, cautions, weights, specification, or UN marks or combinations thereof, required on outer packaging of hazardous materials.

- **mixture.** a material composed of more than one chemical compound or element.

- **name of contents.** the proper shipping name as specified in Section 172.101.

- **non-bulk packaging.** a packaging that has

  - a maximum capacity of 450 L (119 gallons) or less than a receptacle for a liquid;
  - a maximum net mass of 400 kg (882 pounds) or less and a maximum capacity of 450 L (119 gallons) or less as a receptacle for a solid;
  - a water capacity greater than 454 kg (1,000 pounds) or less as a receptacle for a gas as defined in 49 CFR Section 173.115.

- **N.O.S.** not otherwise specified.

- **outage or ullage.** the amount that a tank of liquid falls short of being filled by, usually expressed in percent by volume.

- **portable tank.** bulk packaging (except a cylinder having a water capacity of 1,000 pounds or less) that's designed primarily to be loaded onto, or on, or temporarily attached to a transport vehicle or ship and equipped with skids, mountings, or accessories to facilitate handling of the tank by mechanical means. It doesn't include the cargo tank or trailer carrying 3AX, 3AAX, or 3T cylinders.

- **proper shipping name.** the name of the hazardous materials shown in Roman print (not italics) in Section 172.101.

- **p.s.i. or psi**. pounds per square inch.
- **p.s.i.a. or psia**. pounds per square inch absolute.
- **reportable quantity (RQ)**. the quantity specified in Column 2 of the Appendix to Section 172.101 for any material identified in Column 1 of the Appendix.
- **RSPA**. the Research and Special Programs Administration, U.S. Department of Transportation, Washington, D.C. 20590.
- **shipper's certification**. a statement on a shipping paper, signed by the shipper, saying he or she prepared the shipment properly according to law.
- **shipping paper**. a shipping order, bill of lading, manifest, or other shipping document serving a similar purpose and containing the information required by Section 172.202, 172.203, and 172.204.
- **technical name**. a recognized chemical name or microbiological name currently used in scientific and technical handbooks, journals, and texts.
- **transport vehicle**. a cargo-carrying vehicle such as an automobile, van, tractor, truck, semitrailer, tank car, or rail car used for the transportation of cargo by any mode. Each cargo carrying body (trailer, rail car, etc.) is a separate transport vehicle.
- **UN standard packaging**. a specification packaging conforming to the standards in the UN recommendations.
- **UN**. abbreviation for United Nations.

Chapter 11 Review Quiz

1–8: Circle the correct answer.

1. The purpose of placards is to
    a. show that you're certified to haul a hazardous material.
    b. warn others that you're hauling a hazardous material.
    c. let carriers know what kind of material you're transporting.
    d. protect your employer from liability suits regarding hazardous materials.

2. One of the shipper's most important jobs is to
    a. correctly mark and label packages.
    b. refuse improper shipments.
    c. take the shipment to its destination.
    d. carefully unload the shipment.

3. On the Hazardous Materials Table, if the symbol "D" appears in Column 1, this indicates that the shipment is appropriate for _____ transportation.
    a. marine
    b. domestic
    c. international
    d. overseas

4. What type of hazard is described by Class 6?
    a. oxidizers
    b. gases
    c. poisons
    d. corrosives

5. In most states, the agency that conducts the background checks that take place before a driver can receive a hazardous materials endorsement is the
    a. Transportation Security Administration (TSA).
    b. Environmental Protection Agency (EPA).
    c. Department of Environmental Protection (DEP).
    d. Federal Bureau of Investigation (FBI).

6. Which of the following isn't included in the item description on the shipping paper?
    a. the material's weight
    b. the material's color
    c. the material's quantity
    d. the material's description

7. If you're transporting mass fire hazards, what placard should you use?
    a. Explosives 1.1
    b. Explosives 1.2
    c. Explosives 1.3
    d. Explosives 1.4

8. Which class of hazardous materials must be transported in a closed cargo space?
    a. Class 1
    b. Class 2
    c. Class 4
    d. Class 6

9–15: Indicate whether each statement is true or false.

____ **9.** The consignee is the person who delivers the shipment.

____ **10.** An intermediate bulk container (IBC) isn't a form of portable packaging.

____ **11.** A material's technical name is its recognized chemical or microbiological name.

____ **12.** The abbreviation "UN" stands for "unclassified."

____ **13.** A driver is allowed to refuse a HAZMAT package that appears to be damaged or leaking.

____ **14.** The Hazardous Waste Manifest must be signed by all shippers, carriers, and an agent at the destination.

____ **15.** A driver needs to know the reportable quantity (RQ) of the material being transported only when it's delivered to its destination.

Check your answers on page 295.

Hazardous Materials Endorsement Practice Test

1.	ⓐ	ⓑ	ⓒ	ⓓ	11.	ⓐ	ⓑ	ⓒ	ⓓ	21.	ⓐ	ⓑ	ⓒ	ⓓ
2.	ⓐ	ⓑ	ⓒ	ⓓ	12.	ⓐ	ⓑ	ⓒ	ⓓ	22.	ⓐ	ⓑ	ⓒ	ⓓ
3.	ⓐ	ⓑ	ⓒ	ⓓ	13.	ⓐ	ⓑ	ⓒ	ⓓ	23.	ⓐ	ⓑ	ⓒ	ⓓ
4.	ⓐ	ⓑ	ⓒ	ⓓ	14.	ⓐ	ⓑ	ⓒ	ⓓ	24.	ⓐ	ⓑ	ⓒ	ⓓ
5.	ⓐ	ⓑ	ⓒ	ⓓ	15.	ⓐ	ⓑ	ⓒ	ⓓ	25.	ⓐ	ⓑ	ⓒ	ⓓ
6.	ⓐ	ⓑ	ⓒ	ⓓ	16.	ⓐ	ⓑ	ⓒ	ⓓ	26.	ⓐ	ⓑ	ⓒ	ⓓ
7.	ⓐ	ⓑ	ⓒ	ⓓ	17.	ⓐ	ⓑ	ⓒ	ⓓ	27.	ⓐ	ⓑ	ⓒ	ⓓ
8.	ⓐ	ⓑ	ⓒ	ⓓ	18.	ⓐ	ⓑ	ⓒ	ⓓ	28.	ⓐ	ⓑ	ⓒ	ⓓ
9.	ⓐ	ⓑ	ⓒ	ⓓ	19.	ⓐ	ⓑ	ⓒ	ⓓ	29.	ⓐ	ⓑ	ⓒ	ⓓ
10.	ⓐ	ⓑ	ⓒ	ⓓ	20.	ⓐ	ⓑ	ⓒ	ⓓ	30.	ⓐ	ⓑ	ⓒ	ⓓ

▶ Hazardous Materials Endorsement Practice Test

Choose the correct answer. Mark the letter on the answer sheet on page 247.

1. The rules that shippers must follow when packaging hazardous materials are called _____ rules.
   a. suppression
   b. labeling
   c. containment
   d. packaging

2. Why are drivers required to placard their vehicles when transporting hazardous materials?
   a. to prove that they can legally transport hazardous materials
   b. to communicate the risk and hazardous nature of the materials
   c. to show that they know what materials they're transporting
   d. to tell carriers the identification number of the hazardous materials

3. An area that's authorized by local authorities as a safe place to park an unattended vehicle loaded with explosives is called a
   a. HAZMAT container.
   b. consignee's property.
   c. safe haven.
   d. containment area.

4. What should a driver do when getting ready to transport a chemical that is toxic to marine life?
   a. Write the word "waste" on the shipping paper.
   b. Put a "MARINE DANGER" placard on the vehicle.
   c. Call the shipper for specific handling instructions.
   d. Affix a "marine pollutant" marking to the vehicle.

5. If you're parking a vehicle transporting Division 1.1 explosives, how close can you park to a structure such as a bridge, tunnel, or building?
   a. 5 feet
   b. 50 feet
   c. 100 feet
   d. 300 feet

6. What is the first step in loading a vehicle?
   a. Look for leaking containers.
   b. Set the parking brake.
   c. Turn off the cargo heater.
   d. Secure containers.

7. What is the ideal way to load cylinders?
   a. confined in racks
   b. lying on their sides
   c. standing on the floor
   d. secured to a tailgate

8. Which three classes should not be loaded into a trailer with a heating/air conditioning unit?
   a. Class 2, Class 4, and Class 5
   b. Class 1, Class 5.1, and Class 8
   c. Class 1, Class 2.1, and Class 3
   d. Class 4.1, Class 4.3, and Class 6.1

9. If your vehicle is parked and another person is attending to your vehicle, this person must
   a. be able to move the vehicle.
   b. stay at least 200 feet away from the vehicle.
   c. have a hazardous materials endorsement.
   d. none of the above.

10. Which of the following materials can't be loaded with corrosive liquids?
   a. Division 1.5 materials
   b. Division 2.3, Zone B materials
   c. Division 4.1 materials
   d. all of the above

11. Where should a driver keep hazardous material shipping papers when the driver isn't in the vehicle?
   a. in the driver's pocket
   b. under the driver's seat
   c. on the driver's seat
   d. on the vehicle's dashboard

12. How far away must you stay from a vehicle that contains Class 1, Class 3, Class 4, or Class 5 materials while you're smoking or carrying a lit cigarette, cigar, or pipe?
   a. 15 feet
   b. 25 feet
   c. 50 feet
   d. 75 feet

13. If you're in an accident involving hazardous materials and there's a fire, breakage, spillage, or suspected contamination involving bacteria or toxins, you or your employer must
   a. keep people at least 15 feet away from the area.
   b. show the area to the local emergency crews.
   c. clean the area and check it with a survey meter.
   d. contact the National Response Center.

14. Imagine you're stopped at a rest stop. You discover that your hazardous materials shipment is slowly leaking from the vehicle, but there's no phone around. Which of the following should you do?
   a. Leave your vehicle and go for help.
   b. Drive your vehicle to the next rest stop.
   c. Stay with your vehicle and send someone for help.
   d. Open the shipment and look for the leaking material.

15. If you're in a vehicle transporting Class 1 (Explosives) and you're involved in a collision, you should remove all explosives before separating the vehicle involved. How far away from the vehicles and from occupied buildings should you keep the removed explosives?
   a. no more than 15 feet
   b. at least 150 feet
   c. at least 200 feet
   d. more than 500 feet

16. A shipper who is filling out shipping papers for a hazardous material mixture must enter an item description for the mixture. Which name(s) should the shipper enter in the item description?

   a. the names of the two most hazardous materials in the mixture

   b. the names of all materials that make up the mixture

   c. the names of the three materials that are in greatest quantity in the mixture

   d. the names of the materials in the mixture that share the same class

17. If there's an incident involving hazardous materials, you or your employer must call the National Response Center if

   a. no one involved requires hospitalization.

   b. the damage to property exceeds $50,000.

   c. a small road must close for 20 minutes.

   d. there's no damage, continuing danger, or fire.

18. When is it okay to run the vehicle's engine while loading flammable liquids?

   a. when you're within 25 feet of the engine

   b. when you need the engine to run a pump

   c. when you're loading a Class 3 liquid

   d. when you're loading the liquid into an IBC

19. Which marking is necessary for a portable tank?

   a. the material's identification number

   b. the material's shipping name

   c. the lessee or owner's name

   d. all of the above

20. How far from the nearest rail should you stop when you come to a railroad crossing while driving a vehicle transporting hazardous materials?

   a. between 15 and 50 feet

   b. between 50 and 100 feet

   c. between 100 and 150 feet

   d. between 100 and 200 feet

21. If you're involved in an accident, emergency workers will look for identifiers such as proper shipping name and hazardous materials identification number on your

   a. emergency guidebook.

   b. CDL endorsement.

   c. placards.

   d. shipping papers.

22. Propane is an example of a(n)

   a. flammable gas.

   b. corrosive.

   c. flammable liquid.

   d. oxidizer.

23. What is the purpose of package orientation markings?

   a. to show where in the vehicle a package can be placed

   b. to show the maximum weight a package can bear

   c. to show the package's correct upright direction

   d. to show what date the package should be delivered by

24. How close to the traveled part of the road can you park if you're driving a placarded vehicle that doesn't contain explosives?

a. 5 feet

b. 50 feet

c. 200 feet

d. none of the above

25. If you're transporting 500 pounds of a Division 6.1 inhalation hazard (zone A & B only) material, what placard should you use?

a. poison gas

b. flammable gas

c. poison

d. flammable

26. How many feet away from an area with an open fire should you keep your placarded vehicle?

a. 50 feet

b. 100 feet

c. 150 feet

d. 300 feet

27. What is one difference between a freight container and a cargo tank?

a. A freight container is permanently attached and a cargo tank is always portable.

b. A freight container transports unit packages and a cargo tank transports liquids or gases.

c. A freight container is primarily used on ships while a cargo tank is mainly used on trucks.

d. A freight container holds under 500 pounds while a cargo tank holds 1,000 pounds or more.

28. Which hazard class uses transport indexes to determine the amount of the material that can be loaded into a single vehicle at once?

a. Class 1

b. Class 3

c. Class 4

d. Class 7

29. A rigid or flexible portable packaging, other than a cylinder or portable tank, which is designed for mechanical handling and isn't required to have the owner's name or shipping name is called

a. an intermediate bulk container.

b. a freight container.

c. a limited quality.

d. a non-bulk package.

30. Which agency conducts the background checks that must take place before a driver can receive a hazardous materials endorsement in most states?

a. Department of Environmental Protection

b. Environmental Protection Agency

c. Transportation Security Administration

d. National Response Center

▶ Answers and Explanations

1. c. Shippers must follow "containment rules" when packaging hazardous materials to protect those who will handle the package—as well as others and the environment around the materials—from injury, death, or contamination. Drivers must also follow containment rules when loading, transporting, and unloading hazardous materials.

2. b. Placards are a communication device, a sign placed on the outside of a vehicle, that lets others know that a driver is transporting hazardous materials. They serve as a warning to others that the materials a driver is transporting are dangerous, as well as what the specific dangers are (e.g., the "FLAMMABLE" placard warns others to keep burning items like cigarettes and open flame away from the vehicle).

3. c. When local authorities designate an area as a safe place to park an unattended vehicle loaded with explosives, the area is called a safe haven.

4. d. Chemicals that are toxic to marine life are called "marine pollutants." A driver who is hauling marine pollutants must have a "marine pollutant" marking on the outside of the vehicle, even though the marking isn't actually a placard.

5. d. If you're parking a vehicle transporting Division 1.1 explosives, you should park at least 300 feet away from a structure such as a bridge, tunnel, or building, a place where people are gathered, or a spot with an open fire.

6. b. The first thing you should do when loading a vehicle is set the parking brake so the vehicle can't move while you're loading it. If you started loading hazardous materials into the vehicle and the vehicle then began to move, you could find yourself in a disastrous situation!

7. a. The best way to transport cylinders is to secure them in racks inside the vehicle. Because not all vehicles have racks, the next best method for transporting cylinders is to make sure that they're upright and on a flat surface in a box or other containment device. A cylinder can be loaded on its side only when the design allows for the relief valve to be in the vapor space.

8. c. Materials in Class 1 (explosives), Class 2.1 (flammable gas), and Class 3 (flammable liquids) should never be loaded into a trailer with a cargo heating/air conditioning unit. This is because some hazardous materials become even more hazardous when exposed to heat or a possible ignition source.

9. a. If your vehicle is parked and you can't attend to it, you must have someone else attend to it. Legally, this person must be awake (not in the sleeper berth), or must stay within 100 feet of the vehicle and have it in clear view at all times, be aware of the type(s) of hazardous material being transported and the danger they present, know what to do in the event of an emergency, and be able to move the vehicle.

10. a. Corrosive liquids should never be loaded with Division 1.5 materials, or blasting agents. You can load corrosive liquids with Division 2.3, Zone B materials, and Division 4.1 materials as long as the corrosive liquid isn't next to or above these materials.

11. c. When a driver isn't in the vehicle, he or she should keep the hazardous material shipping papers on the driver's seat. When the driver is in the vehicle, the shipping papers should be kept in a pouch on the door or in clear view and within immediate reach while the driver is wearing a seat belt.

12. b. While you're smoking or carrying a lit cigarette, cigar, or pipe, you must stay at least 25 feet away from a vehicle that contains Class 1, Class 3, Class 4, or Class 5 materials.

13. d. If you're in an accident involving hazardous materials and there's a fire, breakage, spillage, or suspected contamination involving bacteria or toxins, you or your employer must contact the National Response Center as soon as possible. It maintains a 24-hour toll-free line.

14. c. If you're stopped at a rest stop and you discover that hazardous materials are slowly leaking from your vehicle, but there's no phone around, you should stay with your vehicle and send someone else for help.

15. c. If you're transporting Class 1 (Explosives) and you become involved in a collision, remove all explosives before separating the vehicles and place the explosives at least 200 feet away from the vehicles and from occupied buildings.

16. a. A mixture is a material composed of more than one chemical compound or element. On the shipping paper for a mixture of hazardous materials, the item description should contain the technical names of the two most hazardous materials in the mixture

17. b. If there's an incident involving hazardous materials, you or your employer must call the National Response Center if the damage to property exceeds $50,000.

18. b. Always turn off your engine when you're loading a flammable liquid unless you need the engine to run a pump to load the liquid.

19. d. A portable tank should be marked with the lessee or owner's name, the shipping name of the contents, and the identification number of the material contained in the portable tank.

20. a. When you come to a railroad crossing while driving a vehicle transporting hazardous materials, you should always stop between 15 and 50 feet from the nearest rail.

21. d. If you're involved in an accident, emergency workers will look for identifiers such as proper shipping name and hazardous materials identification number on your shipping papers. It's important to have your shipping papers in the proper location at all times.

22. a. Propane is a Class 2.1 material, meaning it's a flammable gas.

23. c. Packages that contain liquids have package orientation markings, which are arrows that show which is the correct upright direction. This prevents a driver from placing a package containing liquid upside down, which might cause the liquid to leak out of the package.

24. **a.** If you're driving a placarded vehicle that doesn't contain explosives, you can park within 5 feet of the traveled part of the road. You can you park there only briefly if your work requires it.

25. **c.** Division 6.1 is used to describe a poisonous material other than a gas. It becomes an inhalation hazard when it turns into a dust, mist, or vapor.

26. **d.** You should keep your placarded vehicle at least 300 feet away from an area with an open fire.

27. **b.** The main difference between a freight container and a cargo tank is that a freight container primarily transports packages in unit form, while a cargo tank mostly transports liquids or gases.

28. **d.** Class 7 materials are radioactive materials. There are rules regulating the amount of radioactive materials that can be loaded into a single vehicle because radiation surrounds each package and then passes through all of the packages around it. The transport index establishes the degree of control necessary when transporting radioactive materials.

29. **a.** A rigid or flexible portable packaging, other than a cylinder or portable tank, which is designed for mechanical handling and isn't required to have the owner's name or shipping name is called an intermediate bulk container.

30. **c.** In most states, the agency that conducts the background checks that must take place before a driver can receive a hazardous materials endorsement is the Transportation Security Administration.

CHAPTER

12 ▶ Passenger Transport

CHAPTER SUMMARY

Operating a passenger vehicle is one of the most challenging jobs a commercial driver can have. The safety of your vehicle's passengers depends on the actions you take while driving. This is why drivers are required to take and pass the Passenger Transport Test. This chapter will explain the basic concerns associated with driving a passenger vehicle and describe the necessary precautions you must take to ensure the safety of you and your passengers.

As you learned in Chapter 1, to drive a passenger vehicle, you need to take and pass the Passenger Transport Test, which includes a knowledge test and a skills test, to receive the passenger "P" endorsement on your CDL. Passenger vehicle drivers have special responsibilities in addition to the responsibilities of a driver of any other CMV. As a driver of a passenger vehicle, you're responsible not only for the condition and safe operation of your vehicle, but also for the safety of your passengers. This is a big responsibility!

You'll need a passenger "P" endorsement for a passenger transport vehicle such as a bus, farm labor vehicle, or general public passenger vehicle. Most states require you to have a passenger "P" endorsement to drive a bus designed to transport a certain number of passengers—usually 15, not including the driver.

The Passenger Transport Test has 20 questions, and you need to answer 16, or 80 percent, of them correctly to pass. On the Passenger Transport Test, you'll be asked questions about

- vehicle inspections
- loading baggage and passengers

- rules and regulations on the road
- safety precautions

In most states, if you plan to drive a school bus designed to carry 11 or more passengers including the driver, you also need a school bus "S" endorsement on your CDL. Some states have a separate knowledge test for school bus drivers. To receive a school bus "S" endorsement on your CDL, you'll have to pass a skills test required for the class of school bus you intend to drive.

▶ Vehicle Inspections

When taking the knowledge test and skills test, you must first know how to inspect your passenger vehicle. As a driver of a passenger vehicle, you're responsible for your life, the lives of other drivers on the road around you, and the lives of your passengers. For this reason, federal and state laws require the driver to inspect the vehicle before, during, and after a trip. Federal and state inspectors may also inspect your CMV. An unsafe CMV might be put out of service until it's repaired by the driver or owner.

Many drivers work for companies that have maintenance mechanics who are responsible for checking and repairing the things mentioned in this section. As the driver, however, you must know what to inspect and be able to recognize a problem. You have to be able to check for unsafe operating conditions. To pass your knowledge and skills tests, you must demonstrate to the examiner that you know what problems to check for.

What to Inspect
During your skills test, you need to show the examiner that you understand what to look for in a pre-trip inspection, an en-route inspection, and a post-trip inspection. In Chapter 4, you learned about what to

look for when inspecting your vehicle. Before moving your vehicle, always be sure that you have the emergency equipment required by federal law. This equipment generally includes spare electrical fuses (unless the vehicle has a circuit breaker), three red reflective triangles, and a properly charged and rated fire extinguisher. In many states, school buses must also be equipped with a first-aid kit containing supplies for 10 to 24 passengers. If your vehicle has this equipment, you can start inspecting your passenger vehicle for these problems:

Problems with tires. It's extremely dangerous to drive with bad tires. Your front tires can't be recapped, retreaded, or regrooved. After a tire has been changed, you should stop in a few miles to recheck the tightness of the wheel fasteners. When inspecting your tires for problems, look for

- too much or too little air pressure
- bad tire wear
  (Remember what you learned in Chapter 4. You need at least $4/32$-inch tread depth in every major groove on front tires and $2/32$-inch on other tires. Fabric shouldn't show through the tread or sidewall.)
- cuts, leaks, and other damage
- tread separation
- dual tires in contact with each other or with parts of the vehicle
- mismatched sizes
- radial and bias-ply tires used together
- cut or cracked valve stems

Problems with wheels and rims. Damaged rims can cause a tire to lose pressure or come off. When inspecting your wheels and rims, look for

- rust around wheel fasteners
- loose wheel fasteners

- missing clamps, spacers, studs, or lugs
- lock rings that are mismatched, bent, or cracked
- signs of damage or welding repairs in wheels or rims

Defects of the suspension system. The suspension system supports the vehicle and its cargo, and it keeps the axles in place. When inspecting your suspension system, look for

- cracked or broken spring hangers, if there are any
- missing or broken leaves in any spring. (During a state or federal inspection, the vehicle will be put out of service if one-quarter or more are missing or broken or if a main leaf spring is broken. Any defect, however, should be considered extremely dangerous.)
- leaking shock absorbers
- damaged or leaking air suspension systems. (Don't move with less than 80 psi.)

Defects of the exhaust system. A broken exhaust system allows poisonous fumes to enter your passenger vehicle or bus. When inspecting your exhaust system, look for

- exhaust pipes, mufflers, tailpipes, or vertical stacks that are loose, broken, or missing
- mounting brackets, clamps, or bolts that are loose, broken, or missing
- exhaust system parts that are rubbing against fuel system parts, tires, electrical wiring, combustible parts, or other moving parts
- leaking exhaust system parts
- excessive smoke

Pre-Trip Inspection

When you take your Passenger Transport Skills Test, you'll perform a pre-trip inspection for the examiner. In Chapter 4, you learned about the seven-step pre-trip inspection method. To perform your pre-trip inspection, you should follow this method. Review Chapter 4 before you take the skills test. See Figures 12.1 and 12.2 for the pre-trip inspection "cheat sheets."

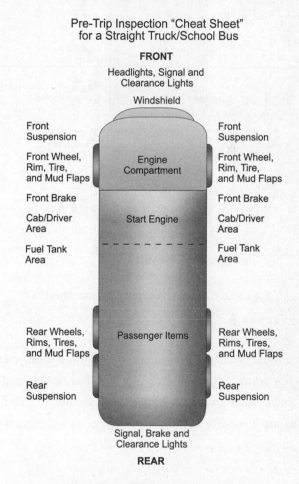

Pre-Trip Inspection "Cheat Sheet" for a Straight Truck/School Bus

Figure 12.1. Pre-Trip Inspection "Cheat Sheet" for a Straight Truck/School Bus

Before driving your passenger vehicle, you have to review the inspection report made by the previous driver. You should sign the previous driver's report only if defects reported earlier have been certified as

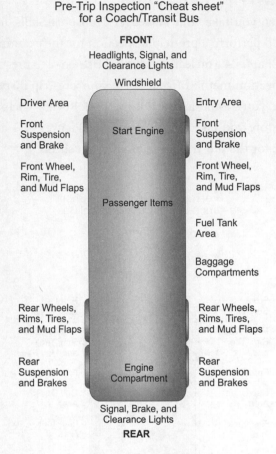

Pre-Trip Inspection "Cheat sheet"
for a Coach/Transit Bus

FRONT

Headlights, Signal, and
Clearance Lights

Windshield

Driver Area — Entry Area

Front Suspension and Brake — Start Engine — Front Suspension and Brake

Front Wheel, Rim, Tire, and Mud Flaps — Front Wheel, Rim, Tire, and Mud Flaps

Passenger Items

Fuel Tank Area

Baggage Compartments

Rear Wheels, Rims, Tires, and Mud Flaps — Rear Wheels, Rims, Tires, and Mud Flaps

Rear Suspension and Brakes — Engine Compartment — Rear Suspension and Brakes

Signal, Brake, and Clearance Lights

REAR

Figure 12.2. Pre-Trip Inspection "Cheat Sheet" for a Coach or Transit Bus

repaired or certified as not needing repairs. This is your certification that the defects reported have been fixed.

As with any CMV, make sure these things are working properly on your passenger vehicle before driving:

- service brakes, including air hose couplings if your passenger vehicle has a trailer or semitrailer
- parking brake
- steering mechanism
- lights and reflectors
- tires
- horn

- windshield wipers
- rear-vision mirrors
- coupling devices
- wheels and rims
- emergency equipment

Your passenger vehicle has some additional equipment that you must check before driving.

Emergency Exits

Before driving your passenger vehicle, you must inspect the emergency exits. Check that these exits open easily, that they're correctly marked, and that any buzzers or devices are working properly. As you check the outside of the passenger vehicle, close any open emergency exits. Close any open access panels (for baggage, restroom service, engine, etc.). You shouldn't ever drive with an open emergency exit door or window. The emergency exit signs on an emergency door or window must be clearly visible. Any red emergency door lights must work. If your passenger vehicle has a red emergency door light, turn it on at night or any other time you use your outside lights.

Passenger Vehicle Interior

People sometimes damage unattended buses or other passenger vehicles. Before driving, always check the interior to ensure the safety of your passengers. Make sure aisles and stairwells are clear of debris. Check that the following parts of your bus are in safe working order:

- **Handholds and railings.** Ensure that handholds and railings are clean and that nothing is making handholds and railings feel sharp, slippery, or hot.
- **Floor coverings.** Make sure floor coverings don't have corners folded over or sticking

up. Check that the floor coverings are clean and flat so that your passengers won't trip.

- **Signaling devices.** Make sure all buzzers and lights are working correctly. This includes the restroom emergency buzzer if your passenger vehicle has a restroom.
- **Emergency exit handles.** Your passengers will need these handles in the event of an emergency. Keep these handles clean to ensure the safety of your passengers.

The seats of your passenger vehicle have to be safe for your passengers. Always check that all seats are securely fastened to the bus. The number of passengers on your vehicle can't exceed the number of safe, adequate seating spaces, unless standing in designated areas is allowed. This excludes infants being held in arms.

In the passenger compartment of a farm labor vehicle, all cutting tools and tools with sharp edges should be placed in a covered container. All other tools, equipment, or materials carried in the passenger compartment should be secured to the vehicle. The driver and all passengers must wear their seat belts.

Roof Hatches

Some emergency roof hatches may be locked in a partially open position to allow fresh air into the passenger compartment. Don't leave them open as a regular practice, however. Keep in mind that your passenger vehicle has a higher clearance while driving with them open.

Seat Belts

Your passenger vehicle must have a seat belt in the driver's seat. Make sure you always use this seat belt for your safety. Remember, your passengers rely on you to keep them safe. Using your seat belt will keep you safe, which will help you ensure the safety of your passen-

gers. Always be sure your seat belt works properly. Wearing your seat belt is required by law!

Inspection During a Trip

You may have to show the examiner that you know what to check for during an en-route inspection. During a trip, you should

- watch gauges for signs of a problem
- use your senses to look, listen, smell, and feel for a problem
- check critical items such as tires, wheels, rims, brakes, and lights when you stop

Post-Trip Inspection

When you inspect your passenger vehicle at the end of a trip, day, or tour of duty, it may include filling out a report, sometimes called a vehicle condition report. You'll list any problems you find. The person who drives the vehicle next will have to sign your post-trip vehicle condition report. When you fill out this report, remember that you're helping to ensure the safety of the driver and passengers of the next trip.

After each shift, inspect your bus or passenger vehicle thoroughly. Passengers can sometimes damage safety-related parts such as handholds, seats, emergency exits, and windows. Report this damage at the end of every shift. This way, mechanics can make repairs before the bus departs again. Mass transit drivers should also ensure that passenger signaling devices and brake-door interlocks are working properly.

If you work for an interstate carrier and you drive buses, you have to complete a written inspection report for each bus you drive. On this report, you will note each bus and will list any defect that could affect safety or cause a breakdown. The report should also specify if there aren't any defects.

Hazardous Materials			
Hazardous Class/Division Table			
Class	Division	Name of Class or Division	Example
1	1.1 1.2 1.3 1.4 1.5 1.6	Mass Explosives Projection Hazards Mass Fire Hazards Minor Hazards Very Insensitive Extremely Insensitive	Dynamite Ammunition, Incendiaries, Flares Display Fireworks Ammunition Blasting Agents Explosive, Detonating Devices
2	2.1 2.2 2.3	Flammable Gas Nonflammable Gases Poisonous/Toxic Gases	Propane Helium Fluorine, Compressed
3	—	Flammable Liquids	Gasoline
4	4.1 4.2 4.3	Flammable Solids Spontaneously Combustible Dangerous When Wet	Ammonium Picrate, Wetted White Phosphorus Sodium
5	5.1 5.2	Oxidizers Organic Peroxides	Ammonium Nitrate Organic Peroxide Type B, Solid
6	6.1 6.2	Poison (Toxic Material) Infectious Substances	Potassium Cyanide Infectious Substances Effecting Animals, Anthrax Virus
7	—	Radioactive	Uranium
8 9 None	— — —	Corrosives Miscellaneous Hazardous Materials ORM-D (Other Regulated Material - Domestic)	Battery Fluid Polychlorinated Biphenyls (PCB) Food Flavorings, Medicines
None	—	Combustible Liquids	Fuel Oil

Figure 12.3. The Federal Hazardous Materials Table

There are special procedures for the post-trip inspection when driving a school bus. You'll learn these procedures later in this chapter.

► Loading Baggage and Passengers

You need to consider passenger safety while loading and unloading a passenger vehicle.

Baggage

Don't allow passengers to leave their carry-on baggage in a doorway or aisle. Passengers need to be able to get to emergency exits quickly in the event of an emergency. The aisle should be clear of anything that could trip you or other passengers. Make sure baggage and freight are secured in a way that avoids damage. Also make sure they're secured in a way that allows you to move freely and easily, allows passengers to exit using emergency exits, and protects passengers from injuries if carry-on baggage falls or shifts.

You must also be aware of the restrictions on certain types of baggage.

Hazardous Materials

Watch for cargo or baggage that contains hazardous materials and wastes. Most hazardous materials and wastes can't be carried on a bus.

The Federal Hazardous Materials Table (see Figure 12.3) shows what materials are hazardous. They pose a risk to health, safety, and property during transportation. The rules require shippers to mark containers of hazardous materials with the material's name, identification number, and hazard label. Watch for any of the nine different 4-inch, diamond-shaped hazard labels (for examples, see Figure 12.4). Don't transport any hazardous materials unless you're sure the rules allow it. Remember, to transport some hazardous materials, you need placards and a hazardous materials endorsement on your CDL.

Passengers sometimes board a passenger vehicle or bus with an unlabeled hazardous material. They might not know it's unsafe. Don't allow passengers to carry hazards such as car batteries and gasoline. Medically prescribed oxygen that's in a passenger's possession and in a container designed for personal use is allowed.

A wheelchair transported on a passenger vehicle or a bus (except a school bus) must have brakes or some mechanical means of holding it still while it's raised or lowered on a wheelchair platform. Batteries have to be spill-resistant and must be securely attached to the wheelchair. Wheelchairs can't contain flammable fuel.

Forbidden Hazardous Materials

Passenger vehicles and buses may carry small arms ammunition labeled ORM-D, emergency hospital supplies, and drugs. You can carry small amounts of certain other hazardous materials if the shipper can't send them any other way. Passenger vehicles and buses, however, must never carry the following:

- Division 2.3 poisons, liquid Division 6.1 poisons, tear gas, and irritating materials
- more than 100 lbs. of solid Division 6.1 poisons
- explosives in the space occupied by people, except small arms ammunition
- labeled radioactive materials in the space occupied by people
- more than 500 lbs. total of allowed hazardous materials, and more than 100 lbs. of any one class

Animals

Transporting animals is generally prohibited except for certified service, guide, and signal animals used by passengers with physical or mental challenges.

Figure 12.4. Examples of HAZMAT Labels

Passengers

Always make sure your passengers are safely on your passenger vehicle and seated, if appropriate, before closing the doors and pulling away. Allow passengers enough time to sit down or to brace themselves using handholds or railings before you depart. Starting and stopping movements should be as smooth as possible to avoid injuring any passengers.

Standee Lines

Passengers can't stand forward of the rear of the driver's seat. Passenger vehicles and buses with a designated standing area need to have a 2-inch line on the floor must be marked in (or some other way) to show passengers where they can't stand. This is called the **standee line**. All standing passengers must stay behind this line.

▶ Rules and Regulations on the Road

At Your Destination

When you arrive at your destination or at intermediate stops, you're required to announce the following information:

- the location
- the reason for stopping
- the next departure time
- the bus number

Remind passengers that if they get off the vehicle, they should take their carry-on baggage with them. Most companies don't take responsibility for lost or stolen carry-on baggage. If the aisle is on a lower level than the seats are, remind your passengers to watch their step. It's best to remind them of this before you

come to a complete stop. This way, they're reminded before they're standing. Charter bus drivers shouldn't allow passengers on the bus until the departure time. This helps prevent theft or vandalism of the passenger vehicle.

At Stops

Your passengers could stumble while getting on or off your passenger vehicle or when the passenger vehicle starts or stops. Warn your passengers to watch their step when exiting the vehicle. Wait for them to sit down or brace themselves before you depart. Allow them plenty of time to do so. As you've learned, start and stop as smoothly as you can to avoid injuring a passenger.

Passenger Supervision

Passenger management is necessary while driving. Many charter and intercity carriers have passenger comfort and safety rules. Make sure you explain the rules at the start of every trip to avoid trouble concerning these rules later. Be sure to mention rules that concern smoking, drinking, or using electronic devices including cell phones at the beginning of the trip. While driving, in addition to keeping your eye on the road ahead, to the sides, and behind you, scan the inside of your passenger vehicle. You might have to remind your passengers of some of the rules or instruct them to keep their arms, heads, and legs inside the vehicle at all times.

Disruptive Passengers

You may occasionally have to deal with a passenger who's disruptive, unruly, or under the influence of alcohol or drugs. You have to ensure the safety of such passengers and that of other passengers. Don't discharge a passenger where he or she may be unsafe. It may be safer to wait to unload a disruptive passenger at the next scheduled stop or well-lit area where there are other people. Many companies have guidelines for handling disruptive passengers. If it's unsafe to continue traveling with an unruly passenger and you must discharge the passenger before the next scheduled stop, contact local law enforcement agents before discharging the passenger. Wait for officers to arrive before making the passenger exit the passenger vehicle.

Railroad Crossings

In some states, it's required that you stop at railroad crossings, while in other states, it's required only that you slow down. To ensure the safety of your passengers, however, you should always stop your passenger vehicles at railroad crossings. Stop your passenger vehicle or bus between 15 and 50 feet before railroad crossings. Look and listen in both directions for trains. Be sure to look in all directions. Passenger vehicles and buses can be very loud, which may prevent you from hearing a train. You should open your forward door if it improves your ability to see or hear an approaching train. After a train has passed, and before crossing the tracks, be sure there's not another train coming in either direction on other tracks.

If your passenger vehicle has a manual transmission, you should never change gears while crossing the tracks.

You don't have to stop, but you must slow down and check for other vehicles, under these conditions:

- at streetcar crossings
- where a police officer or flagman is directing traffic
- at railroad tracks that run alongside and on the roadway within a business or residential district
- if the railroad track is within the intersection and the traffic control signal is showing green

- at crossings marked as "exempt" or "abandoned"

Drawbridges

Always stop at drawbridges that don't have a signal light or traffic control attendant. You must stop at least 50 feet before the draw of the bridge. Check to see if the draw is completely closed before you cross. If there's a traffic light that's showing green, or if the bridge has an attendant or traffic officer who controls traffic whenever the bridge opens, you don't need to stop, but you must slow down.

▶ Safety Precautions

Common Accidents

The most common passenger vehicle and bus accidents happen at intersections. Always use extra caution at intersections, even if a traffic signal or stop sign controls other traffic. Passenger vehicles—especially school and mass transit buses—could scrape off mirrors or hit passing vehicles when pulling out from a stop. Keep in mind the clearance of your passenger vehicle—remember, your passenger vehicle takes up a lot of space. Watch out for poles and tree limbs at stops. Know how much space your passenger vehicle needs to accelerate and merge with traffic. Wait for that gap to open before leaving a stop. Never assume other drivers will brake to give you room when you signal or start to pull out.

Destructive and fatal crashes on curves almost always result from excessive speed. This is especially true in inclement weather such as rain or snow, which can make the road very slippery. Banked curves always have a safe design speed. In good weather, the posted speed is safe for cars. This speed is usually too high for many CMVs, including passenger vehicles and buses.

With good traction, a bus may roll over; with poor traction, it might slide off the curve. If your passenger vehicle leans toward the outside on a banked curve, you're driving too fast. Always reduce your speed as you approach curves!

Prohibited Practices

Never engage in any distracting activities while driving. This includes having unnecessary conversations with passengers, talking on a cell phone, and eating and drinking.

Don't tow or push a disabled passenger vehicle that has passengers aboard the vehicle unless having the passengers get off the vehicle would be unsafe. Tow or push the passenger vehicle only to the nearest spot where it would be safe to discharge your passengers. Always follow your employer's guidelines for towing or pushing disabled vehicles or buses.

Don't ever have unnecessary conversations with passengers or talk on a cell phone while you're driving. This could distract you and cause an emergency.

Fueling Your Vehicle

Avoid fueling your passenger vehicle with passengers on board unless it's absolutely necessary. In some states, it's prohibited to fuel your vehicle while passengers are aboard unless the vehicle is fueled by diesel and in an open area or in a structure open at both ends. Never refuel in a closed building with passengers on board. The nozzle of the fuel hose must be in contact with the intake of the fuel tank when refueling. You should never allow your passenger vehicle or bus to be fueled if

- the engine is running
- a radio on the vehicle or bus is transmitting
- the vehicle is close to any open flame or ignition source (including people who are smoking)

Brake-Door Interlock

Sometimes urban mass transit coaches have a brake and accelerator interlock system. The brake-door interlock applies the service brakes and holds the throttle in an idle position when the rear door is open. The interlock releases when you close the rear door. Don't use this safety feature in place of the parking brake. Safety requires the use of the parking brake.

▶ School Buses

If you intend to drive a school bus designed to carry 11 or more passengers, including the driver, you may need a school bus "S" endorsement on your CDL. Some states have a separate knowledge test for school bus drivers. In fact, some states require special training with a specific amount of hours in order to obtain an "S" endorsement. You'll also have to pass a skills test required for the class of school bus you intend to drive. This special school bus "S" endorsement is designed to keep students safe as they travel to and from school. To drive a school bus, you must be thoroughly familiar with all the specific school bus procedures, laws, and regulations in the state and school district where you plan to drive.

Medical Examinations

Some states and school districts require school bus drivers to have a special medical examination. Some of these regulations require school bus drivers to obtain a medical examination every 2 years and to get a signed and dated medical examination form. The bus driver medical examination form can be completed and signed by only a licensed medical doctor, a licensed osteopathy, or a nurse practitioner. If the examination is conducted by a physician's assistant or an advanced practicing nurse, the examination form must also be signed by a supervising or collaborating physician.

Some states have additional requirements concerning how often school bus drivers must get medical examinations.

Danger Zones

One of the most important things to remember when driving a bus is the danger zones. A **danger zone** is any area outside the bus that extends as much as 15 feet from the front bumper, 15 feet from the left and right sides of the bus, and 15 feet behind the rear bumper. Children are in the most danger of being hit, either by another vehicle or by their own bus, in these danger zones. The area to the left of the bus should always be considered especially dangerous because of passing vehicles. Figure 12.5 shows a school bus's danger zones.

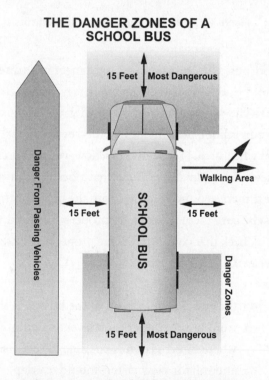

THE DANGER ZONES OF A SCHOOL BUS

Figure 12.5. The Danger Zones of a School Bus

Using Your Mirrors

Properly adjusting and using all mirrors is essential to safely operate your school bus. It's important that you observe the danger zones around your school bus.

Always look for students, traffic, and other objects. You must always check each mirror before operating the school bus to ensure a maximum viewing area consistent with the vision requirements of Federal Motor Vehicle Safety Standard No. 111, "Mirror Systems." Always check the mirrors during your pre-trip inspection. If necessary, have the mirrors adjusted to ensure you can clearly observe all areas around your school bus. It's just as important to make sure all your mirrors are clean before you start your route.

Outside Left and Right Side Flat Mirrors

Your outside left and right side flat mirrors are mounted at the left and right front corners of your school bus, at the side or front of the windshield. They're used to monitor traffic and to check clearances and students on the sides and to the rear of the bus. There's a blind spot immediately below and in front of each mirror and directly in the back of the rear bumper. The blind spot behind the bus extends 50 to 150 feet and could extend up to 400 feet, depending on the length and width of the bus.

Check that your mirrors are properly adjusted so you can see

- 200 feet, or 4 bus lengths, behind the bus
- along the sides of the bus
- the rear tires touching the ground
- 6 inches of pavement in front of the rear tires

Figure 12.6 shows how the outside left and right side flat mirrors should be adjusted.

Outside Left and Right Side Convex Mirrors

If your school bus is equipped with convex mirrors, they're located below the outside flat mirrors. They're used to monitor the left and right sides at a wide angle.

**LEFT AND RIGHT SIDE
FLAT MIRRORS**

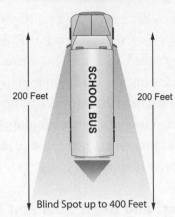

200 Feet   200 Feet

Blind Spot up to 400 Feet

Figure 12.6. Left and Right Side Flat Mirrors

**LEFT AND RIGHT SIDE
CONVEX MIRRORS**

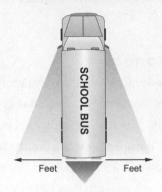

Feet   Feet

Blind Spot up to 400 Feet

Figure 12.7. Left and Right Side Convex Mirrors

These mirrors provide a view of traffic, clearances, and students at the sides of the bus. These mirrors, however, present a view of people and objects that doesn't accurately reflect their size and distance from the bus.

Check that your mirrors are properly adjusted so you can see

- the entire side of the bus up to the mirror mounts
- the front of the rear tires touching the ground
- at least one traffic lane on either side of the bus

Figure 12.7 shows how the outside left and right side convex mirrors should be adjusted.

Outside Left and Right Side Cross-View Mirrors

Your outside left and right side cross-view mirrors are mounted on the left and right front corners of your school bus. They're used to see the danger zone directly in front of the bus, which isn't visible by direct vision, and to view the danger zones to the left and right sides of your school bus, including the service door and front wheel areas. These mirrors, however, also present a view of people and objects that doesn't accurately reflect their size and distance from the bus. The driver must be sure these mirrors are properly adjusted.

Check that your mirrors are properly adjusted so you can see

- the entire area in front of the bus from the front bumper at ground level to a point where direct vision is possible; direct vision and mirror view vision should overlap
- the right and left front tires touching the ground
- the area from the front of the bus to the service door

LEFT AND RIGHT
CROSS-VIEW MIRRORS

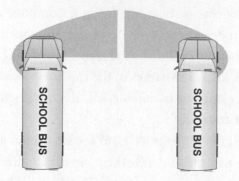

Figure 12.8. Left and Right Cross-View Mirrors

Figure 12.8 shows how the left and right side cross-view mirrors should be adjusted.

Overhead Inside Rearview Mirrors

Your school bus's overhead inside rearview mirror is mounted directly above the windshield on the driver's side area of the bus. This mirror is used to monitor passenger activity inside the bus. It provides limited visibility directly behind the bus if the bus is equipped with a glass-bottomed rear emergency door. There's a blind spot directly behind the driver's seat and a large blind spot beginning at the rear bumper, which could extend more than 400 feet behind the bus. You must use the exterior side mirrors to monitor traffic that approaches and enters this area.

Check that this mirror is properly adjusted so you can see

- the top of the rear window in the top of the mirror
- all the students including the heads of the students directly behind your driver's seat

Loading and Unloading

Unfortunately, students are killed every year while getting on and off their school buses. In fact, each year, more students are killed while getting on and off their school buses than are killed as passengers inside of their school buses. For this reason, knowing what to do before, during, and after loading and unloading students is critical. Knowing the correct loading and unloading procedures will help you avoid unsafe conditions that could result in injuries and fatalities during and after loading and unloading students.

Approaching a Stop

The school district that you work in will establish official routes and official school bus stops. All stops must be approved by the school district prior to making the stop. Never change the location of a bus stop without approval from the appropriate school district official.

Always use extreme caution when you approach a school bus stop. Remember that students might not always behave in the safest manner while you're approaching. You're in a very demanding situation when you enter these bus stop areas. It's essential that you understand and follow all state and local laws and regulations regarding approaching a school bus stop. This involves properly using your mirrors, your alternating flashing lamps, and your moveable stop signal arm and crossing control arm, if your school bus is equipped with them.

When approaching a school bus stop, follow these precautionary measures:

- Approach the bus stop cautiously at a slow rate of speed.
- Look carefully for pedestrians, traffic, and other objects before, during, and after coming to a complete stop.
- Check all your mirrors continuously to monitor your danger zones for students, traffic, and other objects.

- Activate your alternating flashing amber warning lamps at least 300 feet before the school bus stop.
- Bring the school bus to a full stop on the right side of the roadway with the front bumper at least 10 feet from students at the designated stop. This forces the students to walk to the bus, which will give you a better view of their movements.
- Place the transmission in "Park" (if there's no "Park" shift point, use "Neutral") and set the parking brake every time you stop.
- If it's possible, open the service door far enough to activate the alternating red lamps when traffic is a safe distance from the school bus.
- Check a final time to be sure that all traffic has stopped before completely opening the door, which will signal to students that it's safe to approach.

Loading Procedures

As you just learned, knowing the proper loading procedures can save the lives of your student passengers. Be sure that you perform a safe stop every time you're preparing to load students. Make sure students wait in a designated location for the school bus, facing the bus as it approaches. Remember, when you open your door, you're signaling to the students that it's all right to approach the bus. Check that it's safe for students to approach the bus before you signal them by opening the door. Students should board the bus only after they're signaled to do so. If students don't wait in the designated location, or if they don't wait for your signal to approach the bus, tell the students once they board your bus and tell the adult that supervises the school bus stop or a school administrator. Periodically remind the students of the proper loading procedures.

When students board the bus, have them fill up the middle rows first. Continue to monitor all mirrors while students are boarding the bus. Count the number of students at the bus stop before you open your door. Then, be sure that all students board the bus. If possible, know the names of the students at each bus stop. If a student is missing, ask the other students where that student is.

Tell the students to board the school bus slowly and in single file, and have them use the handrail. The dome light should always be on if students are loading in the dark.

Wait until all students are seated and facing forward before moving the bus. In some states, students may be required to wear seat belts on school buses. If this is the case, don't move the bus until all students are wearing their seat belts.

Check all your mirrors before moving. Make sure no students are running to catch the bus. If you can't account for a student who was outside, secure the bus, turn off the engine, take the key, set the brake, and check around and underneath your school bus. *Never* leave the key unattended in the ignition. Anyone, including a student, could attempt to drive your school bus, possibly resulting in multiple injuries or fatalities. If you have to leave the driver's seat, always remove the key from the ignition and take it with you.

When you've accounted for all students, prepare to leave by

- closing the door
- engaging the transmission
- releasing the parking brake
- turning off the alternating flashing red lamps
- checking all your mirrors again

When it's safe, move the bus and continue your route. This loading procedure is essentially the same wherever you load students, but sometimes slight differences are necessary. For instance, when students are loading at the school campus, you should

- turn off the ignition switch, or turn it to the "accessory" position, if required to operate the red loading lamps
- remain seated to supervise loading
  If you must leave the driver's compartment in the event of an emergency or to assist a student, remove the key from the ignition. (As you've already learned, don't leave the key unattended in the ignition.)

Unloading Procedures on the Route

Unloading students is a little different from loading students. Again, however, knowing the correct unloading procedures may save your student passengers' lives. Be sure to perform a safe stop at designated unloading areas by following the safe stopping procedures that you've already learned. Approach the bus stop as though students were there, even though you may not see anyone at the bus stop.

Tell students to remain seated until they're told they can exit the bus. Check all your mirrors continuously, looking into the danger zones. Count the number of students while unloading to confirm the location of all students before you pull away from the stop. Tell students to exit the bus and to walk at least 15 feet away from the side of the bus to a position where you can see all the students clearly.

When the students have unloaded, check all your mirrors again. Make sure no students are around or are returning to the bus. If you can't account for a student outside the bus, secure the bus, turn off the engine, take the key, set the brake, and check around and underneath your school bus.

When you've accounted for all students, prepare to leave by

- closing the door
- engaging the transmission
- releasing the parking brake
- turning off the alternating flashing red lamps
- checking all your mirrors again

When it's safe, move the bus and continue the route. If you miss a student's unloading stop, *don't back up.* There could be a pedestrian, car, or other object in your blind spot. Be sure to follow the local procedures in this case.

Procedures for students who must cross a roadway. You must understand what students should do if they must exit a school bus and cross the street. Tell students that they should always cross the roadway in front of the bus. You should understand, however, that students might not always do what they're supposed to do.

If one or more of your students must cross the roadway, they should follow these procedures. Students should

- look down the right side of the bus before exiting the bus for vehicles that are attempting to pass the bus on the right
- walk approximately 15 feet away from the school bus to a position where you can see them
- walk to a location at least 10 feet in front of the right corner of the bumper, but they should also remain away from the front of the school bus
- stop at the right edge of the roadway, so that you are able to see the student's feet
- stop and look in all directions when they reach the edge of the roadway, making sure the roadway is clear and safe

- check to see if the red flashing lamps on the bus are still flashing
- make eye contact with you
- wait for you to give the universal crossing signal before crossing the roadway
- cross, once you give the signal, at least 10 feet in front of the school bus so they remain in your view while they cross
- go back if you give the universal danger signal
- continue to cross the roadway if you give the universal crossing signal
- look for traffic in both directions, making sure the roadway is clear
- proceed across the roadway continuing to look in all directions

It's important that you use the universal crossing and danger signals with the understanding that any motorists who are stopped in the area could misinterpret a hand signal or other signal that you give to a student. Be sure to discuss these universal signals with students, and periodically remind students of these signals.

Unloading Procedures at School

State and local laws and regulations dealing with unloading students at schools are often different than unloading along the school bus route—especially in situations where unloading takes place in the school parking lot or another location that's off the traveled roadway. It's important that you understand and obey state and local laws and regulations. The procedures listed here are meant as general guidelines.

When unloading students at a school, remember to

- perform a safe stop, which you've already learned about, at designated unloading areas

- turn off the ignition switch, or turn it to the "accessory position," if required to operate the red loading lamps
- remain seated to supervise loading; if you must leave the driver's compartment in the event of an emergency or to assist a student, always remove the key from the ignition
- tell the students to remain seated until they're told to exit
- tell the students to exit in an orderly, single file manner
- observe the students as they step from the bus to see that they all move away from the unloading area promptly
- walk through the bus and check for hiding or sleeping students and items left by students
- check all mirrors to make sure no students are returning to the bus
- if you can't account for a student outside the bus, secure the bus, turn off the engine, take the key, set the brake, and check around and underneath your school bus

When you've accounted for all students, prepare to leave by

- closing the door
- starting the engine
- stepping on the service brake
- engaging the transmission
- releasing the parking brake
- turning off the alternating flashing red lamps
- checking all your mirrors again

When it's safe, pull away from the unloading area.

The Dangers of Loading and Unloading

Loading and unloading students presents unique dangers. Always focus on students as they approach the bus, and watch for any student who disappears from sight. Keep in mind that students don't always do what they're told to do. Watch for these special dangers:

Dropped or forgotten objects. Students sometimes drop something near the bus during loading and unloading. The student might then stop to pick up the object or return to pick up the object. This may cause the student to disappear from your sight at a very dangerous moment.

Tell students to leave any dropped object where it is, and move to a point of safety out of your danger zones. Tell the students to attempt to get your attention from a safe area before attempting to retrieve the object. Remember that students might not always do this. Always count the students as they approach and exit the bus, and then count the students again to make sure you can see all of them.

Handrail hang-ups. Students have been injured or killed when their clothing and accessories or even parts of their bodies get caught in the handrail or door as they exit the bus. Always closely observe all students exiting the bus to ensure they're in a safe location at least 15 feet away from the bus before moving it. Keep a close eye on the handrail and door as students are exiting. Again, always count the students as they approach or exit the bus. This way, you can count the students again to make sure they're all safe.

Post-Trip Inspection

You learned in Chapter 4 how to conduct a post-trip inspection, and you reviewed a post-trip inspection earlier in this chapter. A post-trip inspection on your school bus, however, requires a few extra steps. When your route or school activity trip is completed, you have to conduct a post-trip inspection of your bus.

Walk through your school bus, looking around thoroughly for

- articles and objects left on the bus
- hiding or sleeping students
- open windows and doors
- mechanical and operational problems with your school bus, paying special attention to items that are unique to school buses, such as mirror systems, flashing warning lamps, and stop signal arms
- damage and vandalism

Immediately report any problems or special situations to your supervisor or to school authorities.

Emergency Exit and Evacuation

Emergencies can happen at anytime. They can happen to any person in any place. You must always be prepared to handle an emergency. This could mean a crash, a stalled school bus on a railroad-highway crossing or in a high-speed intersection, an electrical fire in the engine compartment, a medical emergency with a student on your school bus, and so on. Knowing what to do in an emergency—especially before, during, and after an evacuation—can mean the difference between life and death.

Planning for Emergencies

Always be prepared and plan ahead. Study your route and the types of children you'll be transporting to determine in advance how you'll evacuate the bus, according to the types of hazards you may encounter. When it's possible, assign two responsible, older student assistants to each emergency exit. Teach them how to help the other students get off the bus. Assign another student assistant to lead the other students to safety after an evacuation.

You must realize, however, that responsible, older students may not be on your bus during an emergency. This means you must discuss emergency evacuation procedures with *all* students. Explain to students what to do in the event of an emergency, and ensure that all students know where the emergency exits are and how to work them. Explain to the students how important it is to listen to you and follow your instructions during an emergency. You should rehearse these procedures during the three annual school bus emergency drills.

Evacuation Procedures

Determine the need to evacuate. The first thing to consider is also the most important—you must first recognize that there's a hazard. If you have enough time, you should contact your dispatcher to explain the situation before deciding to evacuate the school bus. Generally, student safety and control is best maintained by keeping students on your bus during an emergency—but only if doing so doesn't expose them to unnecessary risk or injury. Remember, you have to make the decision whether to evacuate your school bus in a timely manner. To decide whether to evacuate your school bus, ask yourself these questions:

- Is there a fire or danger of a fire?
- Is there a smell of leaking fuel?
- Is there a chance the bus could be hit by another vehicle?
- Is the bus in the path of a sighted tornado, rising waters, or another natural disaster?
- Are there downed power lines?
- Would evacuating students expose them to speeding traffic, severe weather, or a dangerous environment such as downed power lines?

- Would evacuating students complicate injuries such as fractures or neck and back injuries?
- Is there a hazardous spill involved? Would it be safer to remain on the bus and not encounter this material?

Sometimes, answering these questions can help you decide if an evacuation is mandatory. You *must* evacuate the bus when

- the bus is on fire or there's a threat of fire
- a bomb is reported to be on the bus
- the bus is stalled on or adjacent to a railroad-highway crossing
- the position of the bus may change and increase the danger
- there's an imminent danger of collision
- there's a need to quickly evacuate because of a hazardous materials spill

General procedures. If you've decided that an evacuation is in the best interest of your students' safety, use these procedures. First, determine the best type of evacuation. Should you evacuate using the front, rear, or side doors, or should you use a combination of doors? Should you conduct a roof or window evacuation?

Always secure the bus before leaving to ensure that you don't accidentally add to the danger of the situation. Secure the bus by first placing the transmission in "Park," or in "Neutral" if your vehicle doesn't have a "Park" shift point. Then, set the parking brakes and shut off the engine. Remove the ignition key and take it with you. Then, activate your hazard-warning lamps.

After you've secured the bus, you should notify the dispatch office of your evacuation location, the conditions that you're evacuating under, and the kind of assistance that you require. Note that if there's a bomb or threat of a bomb present, *don't* use the bus radio or a cell phone. This could cause the bomb to detonate. Warn students not to use cell phones during bomb threats. If it's possible, dangle your radio microphone or telephone out the driver's window in case you are able to use it later—but do *not* do this during a bomb threat.

If you don't have a radio, if your radio is inoperable, or if there's a bomb or threat of a bomb, stop a passing motorist or area resident and ask the person to call for help. As a last resort, ask two responsible, older students to go for help. Tell them to stay in public and not to enter a private residence.

Tell students that you're planning an evacuation. Very quickly, if time permits, tell them the evacuation plan. Then, evacuate students from the bus. Don't move a student who you believe may have suffered a neck or spinal injury unless the student is in immediate danger on the school bus. Use special procedures to move a neck or spinal injury victim to prevent further injury.

If you have a student assistant who can lead students to safety, direct the assistant to do so. Point out a safe place for the students to go. A safe place for the students is at least 100 feet off the road in the direction of oncoming traffic. This keeps them from being hit by debris if another vehicle collides with the bus. Lead students upwind of the bus if there's a fire. Lead students as far away from railroad tracks as possible and in the direction of any oncoming train. Lead students at least 300 feet upwind of the bus if there's a risk from spilled hazardous materials.

If the bus is in the direct path of a sighted tornado and an evacuation is ordered, escort students to a nearby ditch or culvert if shelter in a building isn't readily available. Direct them to lie facedown with their hands covering their heads. They should be far enough away so the bus can't tumble onto them. Avoid areas that are subject to flash floods. Walk through the bus to make sure no students are still on the bus. Retrieve your emergency equipment, including your first-aid kit.

Join the waiting students. Account for all students and check that they're safe. Protect the scene as much as you can. Set out emergency warning devices, as necessary and appropriate. Prepare information for emergency responders.

Railroad-Highway Crossings

You already learned about railroad crossings in Chapter 3, as well as earlier in this chapter. When driving a school bus, however, crossing railroads has an additional risk. Keep in mind that the safety of your student passengers is in your hands, and remember these points when you come to railroad-highway crossings.

Types of Crossings

Passive crossings. A passive crossing doesn't have any type of traffic control device. You have to stop at these crossings and follow the proper procedures. The decision to proceed, however, rests solely with you. When crossing passive crossings, you must recognize the crossing, search for a train using the tracks, and decide if there's sufficient clear space to cross safely. Passive crossings have yellow circular advance warning signs, pavement markings, and crossbucks to assist you in recognizing the crossing.

Active crossings. An active crossing has a traffic control device installed at the crossing to regulate traffic. These active devices may include flashing red lights, flashing red lights with bells, or flashing red lights with bells and gates.

Warning Signs and Devices

Advance warning signs. These round, black-on-yellow warning signs (see Figure 12.9) are placed ahead of a public railroad-highway crossing. The advance warning sign tells you to slow down, look and listen for a train, and be prepared to stop at the track if a train is approaching.

ADVANCE WARNING SIGN

Figure 12.9. Advance Warning Sign

Pavement markings. Pavement markings (see Figure 12.10) have the same meaning as advance warning signs. They have an "X" with the letters "RR" and a no-passing marking on two-lane roads. There's also a "No Passing Zone" sign on two-lane roads. There may be a white stop line painted on the pavement before the railroad tracks. The front of your school bus must stay behind this line while you're stopped at the crossing.

PAVEMENT MARKINGS

Figure 12.10. Pavement Markings

Crossbuck signs. These signs mark passive crossings. They require you to yield the right-of-way to a train. When the road crosses more than one set of tracks, a sign below the crossbuck specifies the number of tracks. (See Figure 12.11 for an example of a crossbuck sign specifying three tracks.)

Flashing red light signals. At many active railroad-highway crossings, the crossbuck sign has flashing red lights and bells. When the lights begin to flash, a train is approaching. You're required to yield

CROSSBUCK SIGN SPECIFYING THREE TRACKS

Figure 12.11. Crossbuck Sign Specifying Three Tracks

the right-of-way to a train. If you see the flashing red lights, *stop!* Check the crossbuck sign to see if there's more than one track. Make sure all tracks are clear before you cross.

Gates. Many active railroad-highway crossings also have gates with flashing red lights and bells. Always stop when the lights begin to flash. This means you'll stop before the gates lower across traffic lanes. Remain stopped until the gates go back up and the lights have stopped flashing. Proceed only once it's safe. If the gate stays down after the train passes, don't drive around the gate. Instead, contact your dispatcher. (See Figure 12.12

A RAILROAD CROSSING WITH FLASHING RED LIGHT AND GATES

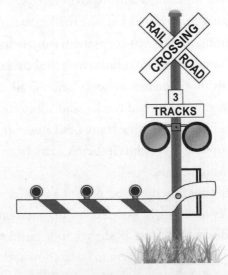

Figure 12.12. A Railroad Crossing with Flashing Red Lights and Gates

for an example of a railroad crossing with flashing red lights and gates.)

Recommended Procedures

Many state and local laws and regulations will govern how you operate your school bus at railroad-highway crossings. It's important for you to understand and obey all of these state and local laws and regulations. Check with your company to make sure you know all the company regulations, and check with your school district to learn the school district regulations. Remember, school buses must stop at *all* crossings. You have to ensure that it's safe before crossing any tracks.

Your school bus is one of the safest vehicles on the highway. A school bus doesn't have an edge, however, when it's involved in a crash with a train. A train's size and weight prevent it from stopping quickly. The train doesn't have an emergency escape route. You should always try to prevent crashes involving your school bus and a train by following all recommended procedures.

As you approach a crossing, take these precautions:

- *Slow down!* Shift to a lower gear if your bus has a manual transmission. Always test your brakes.
- Activate the hazard lamps about 200 feet before the railroad crossing. Make sure the drivers around you know what you're intending to do.
- Always scan your surroundings and check for traffic behind you.
- Stay to the right of the roadway, if it's possible.
- Choose an escape route in the event of a brake failure or if problems exist behind you.

When you're at the crossing, follow these procedures:

- Stop no closer than 15 feet and no farther than 50 feet from the nearest rail. This is where you have the best view of the tracks.
- Place the transmission in "Park," or "Neutral" if your vehicle has no "Park" shift point. Press down on the service brake or set the parking brake.
- Turn off all radios and noisy equipment. Ask your student passengers to be silent.
- Open the service door and your driver's window. Look and listen carefully for an approaching train.

If you've decided there's no train approaching, you're ready to cross the track. When crossing the track, follow these steps:

- Close the service door before you cross.
- Check the crossing signals a final time before you proceed.
- At a multiple-track crossing, stop only before the first set of tracks. When you're sure that no train is approaching on any track, proceed across all the tracks until you've completely crossed them.
- Cross the tracks in a low gear. Don't change gears while crossing.
- If the gate comes down after you've started to cross, drive through it even if it means you'll break the gate.
- After you've cleared all tracks completely, turn off the hazard lights, turn on the master switch and radio, and return all equipment that you shut off back to normal operating condition.

Special Situations

What to do if your bus stalls or gets trapped on the track. If your bus stalls or gets trapped on the tracks, get all your students off the bus and off the tracks immediately. Move everyone far from the bus at an angle away from the tracks, but moving in the direction that the train is coming from. If the train collides with the empty bus, you'll have a better chance of avoiding debris if you are behind the collision rather than in front of it. Then, contact your dispatcher and the proper authorities.

A law enforcement officer is at the crossing. If a law enforcement officer is at the crossing, obey that officer's directions. If there's not an officer and you believe the signal is malfunctioning, contact your dispatcher to report the situation and ask for instructions about what to do.

Your view of the tracks is obstructed. Plan your route so it provides maximum sight distance at railroad-highway crossings. Don't attempt to cross the tracks unless you can see far enough down the tracks to be *sure* that there's no train approaching. Be particularly careful at passive crossings. Even if active railroad signs indicate that the tracks are clear, look and listen to make sure it's safe to proceed across the tracks.

Your containment or storage areas. Know the length of your bus and the size of the containment area at railroad-highway crossings on your school bus route. Also know the size of any containment area at a railroad-highway crossing in the course of a school activity trip. Part of your responsibility is to know your route! If your bus won't fit, don't proceed! When approaching a crossing with a signal or stop sign on the opposite side, pay close attention to how much room there is. Be *sure* your bus has enough containment or storage area to completely clear the railroad tracks on the other side if there's a need to stop. Generally, you should add 15 feet to the length of your school bus to determine an acceptable containment or storage area.

Student Management

A big part of driving a school bus is managing students. To get your students to and from school safely and on time, you have to be able to concentrate on driving. Don't ever deal with on-bus problems while loading and unloading students. Loading and unloading requires *all* your concentration and attention. Don't take your eyes off what's happening outside the bus. Be sure to count the students, as you've already learned. If there's a behavior problem on the bus while students are loading, wait to deal with the problem until the students who are loading are safely on the bus and seated. If there's a behavior problem on the bus while students are unloading, wait until the students who are unloading are safely off the bus and have moved away from the bus. If it's necessary, pull the bus over to deal with the problem.

Handling a serious problem may be more difficult. Always follow the procedures and regulations of the school district you work in. Follow these procedures for discipline and refusal of rights to ride the bus. *Never* turn a student away. *Never* discharge a student from the bus except at the school or at the student's designated school bus stop. If you feel the offense is serious enough that you can't safely drive the bus, call for a school administrator or the police to come. They can remove the student, if appropriate. You can't. Always remember to follow your school district's procedure for requesting help.

If you have to deal with a serious problem, remember these tips:

- Stop the bus. Park in a safe location off the road, such as a parking lot or a driveway.
- Secure the bus. If you leave your seat, remember to take the ignition key with you.
- Stand up and speak to the offenders. Speak in a courteous manner, but use a firm voice. Remind the offenders of what behavior is

expected of them. Don't show anger. Show the students that you're serious and that you mean business.

- If the discipline problem requires a change of seating, tell the student to move to a seat near you.

Antilock Braking System (ABS)

Vehicles Required to Have ABS

Vehicles are required to have ABS if they're air brake equipped vehicles—trucks, buses, trailers, and converter dollies—that were built after March 1, 1998, or if they're hydraulically braked trucks and buses with a gross vehicle weight rating (GVWR) of 10,000 lbs. or more that were built after March 1, 1999. Most school buses built before these dates have been voluntarily equipped with ABS. Your school bus will have a yellow ABS malfunction lamp on the instrument panel if it's equipped with ABS.

How ABS Helps

When you brake hard on slippery surfaces in a vehicle without ABS, your wheels might lock up. When your steering wheels lock up, you lose control of the steering. When your other wheels lock up, you could skid or spin the vehicle.

ABS helps you to avoid these situations by ABS preventing wheel lockups. You may or may not be able to stop faster with ABS, but you should be able to steer around an obstacle while braking and avoid skids caused by overbraking.

Braking with ABS

When you drive a vehicle with ABS, you should brake as you normally would. Use only the braking force that's necessary to stop safely and to stay in control. Brake the same way, regardless of whether you have ABS on the bus. In emergency braking, however, don't pump the brakes on a bus with ABS. As you slow down, monitor your bus and back off the brakes—if it's safe to do so—to stay in control.

If Your ABS Isn't Working

You'll still have normal brake functions without your ABS. Drive and brake as you normally would. Vehicles with ABS have yellow malfunction lamps to tell you if something isn't working properly. The yellow ABS malfunction lamp is on the bus's instrument panel. As a system check on newer vehicles, the malfunction lamp comes on at start-up for a bulb check, and then it quickly goes out. On older systems, the lamp could stay on until you're driving over 5 mph. If the lamp stays on after the bulb check, or goes on once you're already driving, you may have lost ABS control on one or more of your wheels. Remember, if your ABS malfunctions, you still have regular brakes. Drive normally, but get the system serviced as soon as you can.

ABS Safety Tips

Remember these safety tips about your ABS. ABS won't

- compensate for bad driving habits such as driving too fast, tailgating, or driving less carefully
- prevent power or turning skids, but it should prevent brake-induced skids; however, it won't prevent those caused by spinning the drive wheels or going too fast in a turn
- shorten your stopping distance, but it will help maintain vehicle control
- increase or decrease your stopping power; it's an add-on to your normal brakes, not a replacement
- change the way you normally brake. Under normal brake conditions; ABS matters only

when a wheel would normally lock up due to overbraking

- compensate for bad brakes or poor brake maintenance

Remember, you're still your vehicle's best safety feature! Drive so you don't have to use your ABS. Your ABS is there for emergencies only. If you need it, your ABS could prevent a serious crash.

Special Considerations for Safety

Strobe Lights

Some school buses are equipped with roof-mounted, white strobe lights. If your school bus has these lights, the overhead strobe light should be used when your visibility is limited. If you can't easily see the area around you, including in front, behind, or beside the school bus, use the overhead strobe light to help. Your visibility could be only slightly limited, or it could be so bad that you can't see anything at all. In any of these instances, you must understand and obey the state and local laws and regulations concerning the use of these overhead strobe lights.

Driving in High Winds

Strong winds affect the handling of your school bus. The side of a school bus is like the sail on a sailboat. Strong winds can push the school bus sideways. They can even move the school bus off the road and, in extreme conditions, cause it to tip over.

If you're caught in strong winds, keep a strong grip on the steering wheel with both of your hands. Try to anticipate strong gusts of wind. Slow down! This will lessen the effect of the wind. If it's too strong to continue, pull off the roadway and wait. Contact your dispatcher to get more information about what to do.

Backing

Backing your school bus is extremely dangerous. It's dangerous to your students, and it increases your risk of a collision. For this reason, it's strongly discouraged. You should try to drive in such a manner that prevents you from having to back your school bus. If you find that there's no other safe way to move your bus, you'll have to back your bus. This is the only circumstance that you should back. *Never* back a school bus when students are outside of the bus.

If you have no choice but to back your school bus, follow these procedures:

- Post a lookout, preferably inside the school bus looking out the rear window. The lookout can warn you about obstacles, people approaching, and other vehicles. The lookout shouldn't give you directions about how to back the bus.
- Ask everyone on the bus to be extremely quiet.
- Constantly check all your mirrors and the rear windows.
- Back slowly and smoothly.

If no lookout is available, secure your vehicle by setting the parking brake, turning off the motor, and removing the keys from the ignition. Walk to the rear of the bus to determine if the way is clear.

If you have to back at a student pick-up point, load students before backing. Watch for latecomers at all times. Be sure that all students are in the bus before backing. If you have to back at a student drop-off point, back before unloading your students. Never back after you've unloaded students.

Tail Swing

Your school bus can have a tail swing of up to 3 feet. Tail swing is the distance between your drive tires and the rear of the bus. What is important to remember is that the bus pivots on the drive tires, not at the rear of the bus. Think about your bus having a building close to the right side and you need to make a left turn. If you turn the wheel too sharply to make the left turn,

the right rear corner of the bus will impact the building. So always check your mirrors before and during any turning movements to monitor the tail swing. This is especially important when pulling away after loading or unloading students.

Chapter 12 Review Quiz

1–5: Circle the correct answer.

1. Which mirror is mounted directly above the windshield on the driver's side of the school bus?
   a. outside right side cross-view mirror
   b. overhead inside rearview mirror
   c. outside left side convex mirror
   d. outside right side flat mirror

2. Most states require you to have a passenger "P" endorsement to drive a bus designed to transport _____ passengers, not including the driver.
   a. 5
   b. 11
   c. 15
   d. 25

3. Your school bus can have a tail swing of up to
   a. 3 feet.
   b. 7 feet.
   c. 15 feet.
   d. 17 feet.

4. On your school bus, the outside left and right side convex mirrors can be used to monitor
   a. the danger zone directly in front of the bus.
   b. clearances and students on the sides and to the rear.
   c. the left and right sides at a wide angle.
   d. passenger activity inside the bus.

5. Passenger vehicles and buses must never carry more than _____ of solid Division 6.1 poisons.
   a. 15 lbs.
   b. 100 lbs.
   c. 500 lbs.
   d. 1,000 lbs.

6–10: Indicate whether each statement is true or false.

____ 6. If you must refuel your passenger vehicle while passengers are on board, you should refuel in a closed building.

____ 7. You must evacuate your school bus when the bus is on fire or if there's a threat of fire.

____ 8. Transporting animals—including certified service, guide, and signal animals used by passengers with physical and mental challenges—is always prohibited.

____ 9. If your ABS isn't working correctly, you should immediately pull over and contact your dispatcher.

____ 10. You should never drive with an open emergency exit door or window.

Check your answers on page 296.

Passenger Transport Endorsement Practice Test

1.	ⓐ	ⓑ	ⓒ	ⓓ
2.	ⓐ	ⓑ	ⓒ	ⓓ
3.	ⓐ	ⓑ	ⓒ	ⓓ
4.	ⓐ	ⓑ	ⓒ	ⓓ
5.	ⓐ	ⓑ	ⓒ	ⓓ
6.	ⓐ	ⓑ	ⓒ	ⓓ
7.	ⓐ	ⓑ	ⓒ	ⓓ
8.	ⓐ	ⓑ	ⓒ	ⓓ
9.	ⓐ	ⓑ	ⓒ	ⓓ
10.	ⓐ	ⓑ	ⓒ	ⓓ

11.	ⓐ	ⓑ	ⓒ	ⓓ
12.	ⓐ	ⓑ	ⓒ	ⓓ
13.	ⓐ	ⓑ	ⓒ	ⓓ
14.	ⓐ	ⓑ	ⓒ	ⓓ
15.	ⓐ	ⓑ	ⓒ	ⓓ
16.	ⓐ	ⓑ	ⓒ	ⓓ
17.	ⓐ	ⓑ	ⓒ	ⓓ
18.	ⓐ	ⓑ	ⓒ	ⓓ
19.	ⓐ	ⓑ	ⓒ	ⓓ
20.	ⓐ	ⓑ	ⓒ	ⓓ

21.	ⓐ	ⓑ	ⓒ	ⓓ
22.	ⓐ	ⓑ	ⓒ	ⓓ
23.	ⓐ	ⓑ	ⓒ	ⓓ
24.	ⓐ	ⓑ	ⓒ	ⓓ
25.	ⓐ	ⓑ	ⓒ	ⓓ
26.	ⓐ	ⓑ	ⓒ	ⓓ
27.	ⓐ	ⓑ	ⓒ	ⓓ
28.	ⓐ	ⓑ	ⓒ	ⓓ
29.	ⓐ	ⓑ	ⓒ	ⓓ
30.	ⓐ	ⓑ	ⓒ	ⓓ

▶ Passenger Transport Endorsement Practice Test

Choose the correct answer. Mark the letter on the answer sheet on page 283.

1. While driving a school bus, how many feet from the nearest rail should you stop when you're at a railroad-highway crossing?
   a. no closer than 2 feet and no farther than 15 feet
   b. no closer than 15 feet and no farther than 50 feet
   c. no closer than 50 feet and no farther than 200 feet
   d. no closer than 200 feet and no farther than 400 feet

2. On passenger vehicles and buses with designated standing areas, a 2-inch line on the floor or some other marking that shows passengers where they can't stand is called
   a. a containment area.
   b. a brake-door interlock.
   c. a standee line.
   d. none of the above.

3. Which of the following hazardous materials can you transport on a passenger vehicle in the space occupied by people?
   a. emergency hospital supplies
   b. explosive ammunition
   c. labeled radioactive materials
   d. irritating tear gas

4. As with any CMV, before driving your passenger vehicle, you should perform a pre-trip inspection. During your pre-trip inspection, which of the following should you make sure is in proper working order?
   a. the steering mechanism
   b. the windshield wipers
   c. the service and parking brakes
   d. all of the above

5. If you must get a disruptive student off your school bus, what should you do?
   a. Discharge the student at the next scheduled school bus stop.
   b. Pull over immediately, discharge the student, and call the school.
   c. Discharge the student within a mile of his or her designated school bus stop.
   d. Pull over and call a school official or the police to come and remove the student.

6. Which of the following are you required to announce at your destination or intermediate stops?
   a. your first name
   b. your next stop location
   c. the reason for stopping
   d. the bus route

7. How far does the danger zone extend around all sides of a school bus?
   a. 15 feet
   b. 50 feet
   c. 100 feet
   d. 400 feet

8. At a drawbridge, you should always stop if the bridge has
   a. a bridge attendant and light.
   b. no signal light or officer.
   c. an officer controlling traffic.
   d. a light that's showing green.

9. Which of the following is a practice prohibited while driving a passenger vehicle or bus?
   a. talking on your cell phone
   b. answering passenger questions
   c. pulling over to use the restroom
   d. using your radio to contact police

10. If your school bus is equipped with convex mirrors, they're used to monitor
   a. the danger zone in front of the bus.
   b. passenger activity inside the bus.
   c. clearances to the sides and rear of the bus.
   d. the left and right sides at a wide angle.

11. How many feet before you arrive at a bus stop should you activate your alternating flash amber warning lamps?
   a. 10 feet
   b. 50 feet
   c. 300 feet
   d. 400 feet

12. During which of these emergencies must you evacuate your school bus?
   a. There's a hazardous spill outside the bus.
   b. A bomb is reported to be on the bus.
   c. Power lines are downed outside the bus.
   d. The bus is near the path of a sighted tornado.

13. If your bus comes equipped with a brake-door interlock, before you can go forward, you must
   a. turn on the parking brake.
   b. close the rear door.
   c. shift the manual transmission.
   d. use the service brake.

14. When you drive with ABS, you should brake
   a. the same as you normally would.
   b. harder than you normally would.
   c. softer than you normally would.
   d. none of the above.

15. You should be especially careful at a passive railroad-highway crossing because there's
   a. pavement markings and bells.
   b. a flashing red light and gate.
   c. no traffic control device.
   d. an officer controlling traffic.

16. When you unload your school bus at the school, you should walk through the bus while you're still at the school to look for
   a. sleeping students.
   b. damaged seats.
   c. unbuckled seat belts.
   d. dirty handrails.

17. Which of the following emergency equipment are you required to have on your passenger vehicle?
   a. spare electrical fuses
   b. three red reflective triangles
   c. a rated fire extinguisher
   d. all of the above

18. Which of these mirrors on your school bus should you properly adjust to monitor traffic and to check clearances and students on the sides and to the rear of the bus?
a. outside left and right side convex mirrors
b. outside left and right side flat mirrors
c. outside left and right side cross-view mirrors
d. overhead inside rearview mirrors

19. When you unload students at a scheduled bus stop, how far away should you tell students to walk from the side of the bus?
a. 15 feet
b. 50 feet
c. 100 feet
d. 300 feet

20. If your passenger vehicle has a red emergency door light, turn it on when you
a. begin to drive 25 mph.
b. start your vehicle's engine.
c. use your outside lights.
d. open the emergency door.

21. Which of the following should you do before closing the doors of your passenger vehicle and pulling away?
a. Tell passengers to take carry-on baggage with them if they leave the bus.
b. Contact your dispatcher to tell him or her of any problems you foresee.
c. Announce your location, the next departure time, and the bus number.
d. Allow your passengers enough time to sit down or to brace themselves.

22. One of your passengers would like to bring aboard your bus a bag that contains a car battery. What should you do?
a. Allow the passenger to come aboard, but make her sit in the back of the bus.
b. Tell her that car batteries are forbidden cargo, and don't allow it on the bus.
c. Allow the bag aboard your bus, but collect an extra fare from the passenger.
d. Take the bag containing a car battery, and put it in the baggage compartment.

23. While conducting your pre-trip inspection, you should sign the inspection report made by the previous driver
a. when you receive the report from the driver.
b. after you return from your next scheduled trip.
c. as soon as defects are scheduled for repair.
d. after defects have been certified as repaired.

24. If you're driving a passenger vehicle, when must you wear your seat belt?
a. anytime that your vehicle is moving
b. if your passengers wear seat belts
c. when you're driving faster than 15 mph
d. only on any curved, wet, or icy roads

25. You should never refuel your passenger vehicle if
a. the fuel hose nozzle is contacting the intake of the fuel tank.
b. you've already unloaded all your passengers.
c. a radio on your passenger vehicle is transmitting.
d. your passenger vehicle's engine has been shut off.

26. When loading baggage and freight onto a passenger vehicle, it should be secured to
   a. allow the driver to move freely and easily on the bus.
   b. protect passengers from falling and shifting baggage.
   c. enable passengers to access emergency exits.
   d. all of the above.

27. If you're driving a passenger vehicle on a banked curve in good weather, you should
   a. reduce your driving speed.
   b. drive the speed that's posted.
   c. hit your accelerator before the curve.
   d. hit your brake after entering the curve.

28. How many pounds of solid Division 6.1 poisons can you load onto passenger vehicles and buses?
   a. fewer than 10 lbs.
   b. up to 100 lbs.
   c. up to 500 lbs.
   d. more than 500 lbs.

29. After unloading your school bus at the school, you've accounted for all the students and you're preparing to leave. What is the last thing you should do?
   a. Check underneath the bus.
   b. Release the parking brake.
   c. Check all your mirrors again.
   d. None of the above.

30. If you drive a school bus and one of your student passengers must cross a roadway after unloading, to what location should they walk to wait for your signal to cross the street?
   a. to a place at least 10 feet in front of the right corner of the bumper
   b. to a place at least 10 feet in the back left corner of the bumper
   c. to a place at least 15 feet away from the back left corner of the school bus
   d. to a place at least 100 feet from the back bumper of your school bus

► Answers and Explanations

1. **b.** While driving a school bus, if you're approaching a railroad-highway crossing, you should stop no closer than 15 feet and no farther than 50 feet from the nearest rail. This is where you have the best view of the tracks.

2. **c.** On passenger vehicles and buses with designated standing areas, a 2-inch line on the floor or some other marking that shows passengers where they can't stand is called a standee line.

3. **a.** Passenger vehicles and buses may carry small arms ammunition labeled ORM-D, emergency hospital supplies, and drugs. Passenger vehicles may never carry explosives, labeled radioactive materials, and irritating materials such as tear gas, especially in the space occupied by people.

4. **d.** As with any CMV, before driving your passenger vehicle, you should perform a pre-trip inspection. During your pre-trip inspection, you should make sure the steering mechanism, windshield wipers, service brakes, and parking brakes are in proper working order. You should also check the lights and reflectors, tires, horn, rear-vision mirrors, coupling devices (if equipped), wheels and rims, and emergency equipment.

5. **d.** If you must get a disruptive student off your school bus, pull over and call a school official or the police to come and remove the student. Never discharge the student anywhere except at the school or at the student's designated bus stop.

6. **c.** At your destination or intermediate stops, you're required to announce the location, the next departure time, the bus number, and the reason for stopping.

7. **a.** The danger zones are any areas outside the bus that extend as much as 15 feet from the front bumper, 15 feet from the left and right sides of the bus, and 15 feet behind the rear bumper.

8. **b.** At a drawbridge, you should always stop if the bridge has no signal light or officer controlling traffic. You don't need to stop, but you must slow down, if the drawbridge has a bridge attendant and light, an officer controlling traffic, or a light that's showing green.

9. **a.** Talking on your cell phone, or any other activity that can distract you while you're driving, is a prohibited practice while driving a passenger vehicle or bus. You may answer passenger questions, pull over to use the restroom, or use your radio to contact police.

10. **d.** If your school bus is equipped with convex mirrors, they're used to monitor the left and right sides of the bus at a wide angle. Use the outside left and right side cross-view mirrors to view the danger zone in front of the bus. Use your inside rearview mirror to monitor passenger activity inside the bus. Use your outside left and right side flat mirrors to check clearances to the sides and rear of the bus.

11. c. You should activate your alternating flash amber warning lamps at least 300 feet before you arrive at a bus stop.

12. b. You must evacuate your school bus if there's a bomb reported to be on the bus.

13. b. If your bus comes equipped with a brake-door interlock, the interlock applies the service brakes and holds the throttle in an idle position when the rear door is open. Before you can go forward, you must close the rear door.

14. a. When you drive with ABS, you should brake the same as you normally would.

15. c. You should be especially careful at a passive railroad-highway crossing because there's no traffic control device. Passive crossings have yellow circular advance warning signs, pavement markings, and crossbucks, but they don't have traffic control devices such as flashing red lights, bells, gates, or officers to control traffic.

16. a. When you unload your school bus at the school, you should walk through the bus while you're still at the school to look for sleeping and hiding students.

17. d. In a passenger vehicle, the emergency equipment that you're required to have includes spare electrical fuses (unless your vehicle has circuit breakers), three red reflective triangles, and a properly charged and rated fire extinguisher.

18. b. To monitor traffic and to check clearances and students on the sides and to the rear of your school bus, be sure that you properly adjust the outside left and right side flat mirrors on your school bus.

19. a. When you unload students at a scheduled bus stop, you should tell students to walk at least 15 feet away from the side of the bus. Since the danger zone extends 15 feet from the bus in all directions, you can see all of the students clearly if they walk 15 feet away from the bus.

20. c. If your passenger vehicle has a red emergency door light, you should turn it on at night or any other time you use your outside lights.

21. d. Before closing the doors of your passenger vehicle and pulling away, you should always allow your passengers enough time to sit down or brace themselves by grabbing handholds and rails.

22. b. Car batteries and gasoline are cargo that's forbidden on a passenger vehicle. If one of your passengers would like to bring aboard your bus a bag that contains a car battery, you should tell her that car batteries are forbidden cargo, and don't allow the bag with the car battery on the bus.

23. d. While conducting your pre-trip inspection, you should sign the inspection report made by the previous driver only after any defects have been certified as repaired or certified as not needing repairs.

24. a. If you're driving a passenger vehicle, you must wear your seat belt anytime that your vehicle is moving.

25. c. You should never refuel your passenger vehicle if a radio on your passenger vehicle is transmitting. You should only refuel if the fuel hose nozzle is contacting the intake of the fuel tank, you've already unloaded your passengers, and your vehicle's engine has been shut off.

26. d. When loading baggage and freight onto a passenger vehicle, it should be secured to allow the driver to move freely and easily on the bus, protect passengers from falling and shifting baggage, and enable passengers to access emergency exits.

27. a. If you're driving a passenger vehicle on a banked curve in good weather, you should reduce your driving speed. The speed that's posted is safe only for cars driving in good weather.

28. b. A passenger vehicle or bus must never carry more than 100 lbs. of solid Division 6.1 poisons.

29. c. After unloading your school bus at the school, you've accounted for all the students and you're preparing to leave. The last thing you should do is check all your mirrors again. Always give your mirrors one final check before deciding it's safe to pull away from the unloading area at a school.

30. a. If you drive a school bus and one of your student passengers must cross a roadway after unloading, tell the student to walk to a place at least 10 feet in front of the right corner of the bumper and wait for your signal to cross the street.

Appendix ▶

▶ Chapter 1 Review Quiz Answers

1. b.
2. d.
3. b.
4. a.
5. b.
6. a.
7. a.
8. c.
9. b.
10. d.
11. False. You can take all the knowledge tests over and over again until you pass. Note that some states require you to renew your permit if you fail a written test three times. However, they do not limit the number of times you can renew a permit.
12. True
13. True
14. False. When you stop and reverse the direction of your vehicle to better position it, it's called a pull-up.
15. True

▶ Chapter 2 Review Quiz Answers

1. a. lane changes; b. merges; c. turns; d. tight spaces and congested roads
2. a. exhaust; b. engine; c. hydraulic; d. electric
3. c.
4. b.
5. b.
6. a.
7. c.
8. a.
9. d.
10. d.
11. b.
12. d.
13. b.

▶ Chapter 3 Review Quiz Answers

1. (a) obey all fog-related warning signs; (b) drive at a slower rate of speed; (c) leave your low beams on; (d) always be prepared to stop for an emergency.

2. b.
3. d.
4. c.
5. a.
6. b.
7. b.
8. d.
9. b.
10. b.
11. c.
12. a.
13. d.

▶ Chapter 4 Review Quiz Answers

1. b.
2. c.
3. b.
4. a.
5. c.
6. c.
7. b.
8. c.
9. False. Aside from the driver, a number of people may inspect a CMV, including the motor carrier, state or federal inspectors, state police officers, and Motor Carrier Investigators.
10. True
11. True
12. False. Left rear turn signals can be red, yellow, or amber.

▶ Chapter 5 Review Quiz Answers

1. d.
2. b.
3. a.
4. b.
5. d.
6. a.
7. c.

8. a.
9. False. When securing a load on a flatbed, you should use one tie down per every 10 feet of cargo, with at least two tie downs.
10. True
11. True
12. False. To balance the cargo in a trailer, you should load the lightest cargo on top of the heaviest cargo in a tiered effect.

▶ Chapter 6 Review Quiz Answers

1. b.
2. d.
3. a.
4. d.
5. b.
6. c.
7. a.
8. True
9. False. In a dual air brake system, the primary air brake system controls the regular brakes on the rear axle or axles. The secondary air brake system controls the brakes on the front axle and sometimes also on one rear axle.
10. True
11. False. If your service brakes are working correctly, they won't pull your CMV to one side when you test them.
12. False. An ABS on only the trailer makes the trailer less likely to swing out. An ABS on only the tractor makes it easier to maintain control with less chance of jackknifing.

▶ Chapter 7 Review Quiz Answers

1. c.
2. b.
3. a.
4. b.
5. b.

6. a.
7. b.
8. a.
9. False. All trailers and converter dollies made after 1975 are equipped with spring brakes. Most trailers and dollies made before this time have only air operated emergency brakes.
10. True
11. True
12. False. You should never back under the trailer at an angle. You could push the trailer sideways and break the landing gear.
13. True

► Chapter 8 Review Quiz Answers

1. a.
2. c.
3. b.
4. a.
5. False. You should use your mirrors to see the position of your vehicle during the offset back/left exercise. Never lean out of your window or open your door.
6. True
7. False. Don't change gears when making a turn during the Road Test.
8. True

► Chapter 9 Review Quiz Answers

1. c.
2. b.
3. a.
4. a.
5. You release a converter dolly's brakes by opening the air tank petcock. If the dolly has spring brakes use the dolly parking brake control.
6. It should be slightly lower than the center of the fifth wheel and raised slightly when the converter dolly is pushed underneath it.

7. False. If you use the speed retarder on slippery roads, you may lose traction and skid.
8. True
9. True
10. True
11. False. The kingpin is located on the upper fifth wheel.
12. False. The "crack-the-whip" effect affects the last trailer in a double or a triple.

► Chapter 10 Review Quiz Answers

1. b.
2. a.
3. c.
4. b.
5. c.
6. b.
7. True
8. False. The amount of liquid a driver puts in a tank depends on three factors: the amount the liquid will expand, the weight of the liquid, and the legal weight limits.
9. False. Wet roads usually double the normal stopping distance.
10. True
11. True

► Chapter 11 Review Quiz Answers

1. b.
2. a.
3. b.
4. a.
5. b.
6. a.
7. c.
8. a.
9. False. The consignee is the person to whom a shipment is delivered.

10. False. An IBC is a rigid or flexible portable packaging, other than a cylinder or portable tank, that's designed for mechanical handling.
11. True
12. False. The abbreviation "UN" stands for "United Nations."
13. True
14. True
15. False. A driver must always know the reportable quantity of the material being transported, in case the material spills while in transit. The abbreviation "RQ" on a package or shipping paper is also an indicator that the package contains a hazardous material.

▶ **Chapter 12 Review Quiz Answers**

1. b.
2. c.
3. a.
4. c.
5. b.
6. False. You should never refuel your passenger vehicle while passengers are onboard unless it's absolutely necessary. Never refuel in a closed building with passengers onboard.
7. True
8. False. Transporting animals is generally prohibited except for certified service, guide, and signal animals used by passengers with physical and mental challenges.
9. False. If your ABS isn't working correctly, you can drive as you normally would, but get the system serviced as soon as possible.
10. True

▶ Key Contacts for Commercial Drivers by State

ALABAMA

Alabama Department of Public Safety
Driver License Division

Mailing Address:
P.O. Box 1471
Montgomery, AL 36102
Walk-In:
301 South Ripley St.
Montgomery, AL 36104
Phone: 344-242-4400
Email: info@dps.state.al.us
Website: www.dps.state.al.us

Alabama Department of Revenue
Motor Vehicle Division, Motor Carrier Services

Mailing Address:
P.O. Box 327620
Montgomery, AL 36132-7620
Walk-In:
50 North Ripley Street, Room 1239
Montgomery, AL 36104
Phone: 334-242-1170
Email: Use online form
Website:
www.ador.state.al.us/motorvehicle/index.html

Alabama Department of Transportation
Public Affairs Bureau

Mailing Address:
1409 Coliseum Boulevard
Montgomery, AL 36110
Walk-In:
P.O. Box 303050
Montgomery, AL 36130-3050
Phone: 334-242-6358
Website: www.dot.state.al.us/docs/Information

ALASKA

Alaska Department of Transportation
Division of Motor Vehicles

Mailing/Walk-In Address:
1300 West Benson Boulevard
Suite 200
Anchorage, AK 99503
Phone: 907-269-5551
Email: dmv_webmaster@admin.state.ak.us
Website: www.state.ak.us/dmv

ARIZONA

Arizona Department of Transportation
Motor Vehicle Division

Mailing Address:
P.O. Box 2100
Phoenix, AZ 85001-2100
Walk-In:
2739 East Washington Street
Phoenix, AZ 85034
Phone: 602-255-0072
Email: mvdinfo@azdot.gov
Website: www.azdot.gov/mvd

ARKANSAS

Arkansas Department of Finance and Administration
Office of Motor Vehicle

Mailing/Walk-In Address:
1900 West Seventh Street
Suite 2042
Ragland Building
Little Rock, AR 72201
Phone: 501-682-4692
Fax: 501-682-4756
Website: www.arkansas.gov/dfa/motor_vehicle/

Arkansas Department of Finance and Administration
Office of Driver Services

Mailing Address:
P.O. Box 1272
Little Rock, AR 72201
Walk-In:
1900 West Seventh Street
Room 2067
Ragland Building
Little Rock, AR 72201
Phone: 501-682-7060
Fax: 501-682-7688
Website: www.arkansas.gov/dfa/driver_services/

Arkansas State Highway and Transportation Department

Mailing Address:
P.O. Box 2261
Little Rock, AR 72203

Walk-In:
10324 Interstate 30
Little Rock, AR 72209
Phone: 501-569-2000
Email: Info@ArkansasHighways.com
Website: www.arkansashighways.com

CALIFORNIA

California Department of Motor Vehicles

Mailing/Walk-In Address:
4700 Broadway
Sacramento, CA 95820
Phone: 800-777-0133
Email: Use the automated email system available on the DMV website.
Website: www.dmv.ca.gov

COLORADO

Colorado Department of Revenue
Division of Motor Vehicles

Mailing/Walk-In Address:
1881 Pierce St.
Lakewood, CO
Phone: 303-205-5600
Email: mvadmin@spike.dor.state.co.us
Website: www.revenue.state.co.us/mv_dir/home.asp

CONNECTICUT

Connecticut Department of Motor Vehicles

Mailing Address:
60 State Street, Room 239
Wethersfield, CT 06161

Walk-In:

60 State Street, Room 239

Wethersfield, CT 06161

Phone: 860-263-5700

Email: dmv.phonecenter@ct.gov.

Website: www.ct.gov/dmv

DELAWARE

Delaware Division of Motor Vehicles

Mailing Address:

P.O. Box 698

Dover, DE 19903

Walk-In:

303 Transportation Circle

Dover, DE 19903

Phone: 302-744-2500

Email: dot-public-relations@state.de.us

Website: www.dmv.de.gov

DISTRICT OF COLUMBIA

DC Department of Motor Vehicles

Mailing Address:

301 C Street NW

Washington, DC 20001

Walk-In:

301 C Street NW

Washington, DC 20001

Phone: 202-727-5000

Email: Use online form

Website: dmv.dc.gov

FLORIDA

Florida Department of Highway Safety and Motor Vehicles
Division of Driver Licenses

Mailing Address:

504-A Capital Circle S.E

Tallahassee, FL 32301-3817

Walk-In:

504-A Capital Circle S.E

Tallahassee, FL 32301-3817

Phone: 850-617-2000

Email: HSMV-info@flhsmv.gov

Website: www.flhsmv.gov

GEORGIA

Georgia Department of Motor Vehicles
Department of Driver Services

Mailing Address:

P.O. Box 80447

Conyers, GA 30013

Walk-In:

2206 Eastview Parkway

Conyers, GA 30013

Phone: 678-413-8400

Email: Use online form

Website: www.dds.ga.gov

HAWAII

Hawaii Department of Transportation
Public Affairs Office

Mailing/Walk-In Address:
Aliiaimoku Building
869 Punchbowl Street
Honolulu, HI 96813
Phone: 808-587-2160
Fax: 808-587-2313
Email: dotpoa@hawaii.gov
Website: www.state.hi.us

City of Honolulu Department of Customer Services
Motor Vehicle, Licensing, and Permits Division

530 South King Street
Room 302A
Honolulu, HI 96813
Phone: 768-4385
Email: csd@honolulu.gov
Website: www.honolulu.gov

IDAHO

Idaho Transportation Department
Division of Motor Vehicles/Driver Services Section

Mailing Address:
P.O. Box 7129
Boise, ID 83707-1129
Walk-In:
3311 West State Street
Boise, ID 83707-1129
Phone: -208-334-8735
Email: Use online form
Website: www.itd.idaho.gov/dmv

ILLINOIS

Illinois Office of the Secretary of the State
Driver Services Department

Mailing/Walk-In Address:
2701 S. Dirksen Parkway
Springfield, IL 62723
Phone: 217-782-6212
Email: Use online form
Website:
www.cyberdriveillinois.com/departments/drivers/

Illinois Department of Transportation

Mailing/Walk-In Address:
2300 S. Dirksen Parkway
Springfield, IL 62764
Phone: 217-782-7820
Email: Use online form
Website: www.dot.state.il.us

INDIANA

Indiana Bureau of Motor Vehicles

Mailing Address:
100 N. Senate Ave
Indianapolis, IN 46204
Walk-In:
100 N. Senate Ave.
Room N402
Indianapolis, IN 46204
Phone: 317-233-6000
CDL Help Desk: 317-615-7335
Email: Use online form
Website: www.in.gov/bmv

Indiana Department of Revenue
Motor Carrier Services Division

Mailing/Walk-In Address:
5252 Decatur Boulevard
Suite R
Indianapolis, IN 46241
Phone: 317-615-7200
Email: IndianaCDL@dor.in.gov
Website: www.in.gov/dor.3408.htm

IOWA

Iowa Department of Transportation
Motor Vehicle Division

Mailing Address:
P.O. Box 9204
Des Moines, IA 50306-9204
Walk-In:
6310 SE Convenience Boulevard
Ankeny, IA 50021
Phone: 800-532-1121
Fax: 515-237-3152
Website: www.dot.state.ia.us/mvd

Iowa Department of Transportation
Office of Motor Carrier Services

Mailing Address:
P.O. Box 10382
Des Moines, IA 50306-9204
Walk-In:
6310 SE Convenience Boulevard
Ankeny, IA 50021
Phone: 515-237-3264
Fax: 515-237-3257
Email: omcs@dot.iowa.gov
Website: www.dot.state.ia.us/omcs

KANSAS

Kansas Department of Revenue
Division of Motor Vehicles
Motor Carrier Services

Mailing Address:
P.O. Box 12003
Topeka, KS 66612-2003
Walk-In:
Kansas Corporation Commission (KCC) Building
1500 SW Arrowhead Road
Topeka, KS 66614
Phone: 785-271-3145
Fax: 785-271-3283
Email: mc@kdor.state.ks.us
Website: www.ksrevenue.org/vehicle

Kansas Department of Revenue
Division of Motor Vehicles
Driver's Licensing

Mailing Address:
Docking State Office Building
P.O. Box 2188
Topeka, KS 66601-2128
Walk-In:
Docking State Office Building
915 SW Harrison Street
First Floor
Topeka, KS 66612-2021
Phone: 785-296-3963
Email: driver_license@kdor.state.ks.us
Website: www.ksrevenue.org/vehicle

KENTUCKY

Kentucky Transportation Cabinet
Division of Motor Vehicle Licensing

Mailing Address:
P.O. Box 2014
Frankfort, KY 40602-2014
Walk-In:
200 Mero Street
Frankfort, KY 40622
Phone: 502-564-6800
Email: KYTCMVLHelpDesk@ky.gov
Website: www.kytc.state.ky.us/mvl

Kentucky Transportation Cabinet
Division of Motor Carriers

Mailing/Walk-In Address:
200 Mero Street
Frankfort, KY 40622
Phone: 502-564-4540
Email: dmc@ky.gov
Website: www.kytc.state.ky.us/dmc/

LOUISIANA

Louisiana Department of Public Safety
Office of Motor Vehicles

Mailing Address:
P.O. Box 64886
Baton Rouge, LA 70896
Walk-In:
7979 Independence Boulevard
Baton Rouge, LA 70806
Phone: 877-368-5463
Email: Use online form
Website: www.omv.dps.state.la.us

Louisiana Department of Transportation

Mailing/Walk-In Address:
1201 Capitol Access Road
Baton Rouge, LA 70804-9245
Phone: 225-379-1232
Email: Use online form
Website: www.dotd.louisiana.gov

MAINE

Department of the Secretary of State, State of Maine
Bureau of Motor Vehicles

Mailing/Walk-In Address:
19 Anthony Ave
Augusta, ME 04333
Phone: 207-287-3330
Website: www.state.me.us/sos/bmv

MARYLAND

Maryland Department of Transportation

Mailing/Walk-In Address:
7201 Corporate Center Drive
Hanover, MD 21076
Phone: 410-865-1097
Email: mdta@mdot.state.md.us
Website: www.mdot.state.md.us

Maryland Motor Vehicle Administration

Mailing/Walk-In Address:
6602 Ritchie Highway NE
Glen Burnie, MD 21062
Phone: 800-950-1682
Email: MVACS@mdot.state.md.us
Website: mva.state.md.us

MASSACHUSETTS

Massachusetts Registry of Motor Vehicles

Mailing Address:
P.O. Box 55889
Boston, MA 02205-5889
Walk-In:
630 Washington Street
Boston, MA 02114
Phone: 617-351-4500
Email: Use online form
Website: www.mass.gov/rmv

MICHIGAN

Michigan Department of State

Mailing/Walk-In Address:
Michigan Department of State
Lansing, MI 48918-0001

Phone: 888-767-6424
Email: Use online form
Website: www.michigan.gov/sos

Michigan Department of Transportation

Mailing Address:
P.O. Box 30050
Lansing, MI 48909
Walk-In:
State Transportation Building
425 West Ottawa St.
Lansing, MI 48909
Phone: 517-373-2090
Email: Use online form
Website: www.michigan.gov/mdot/

Michigan Public Safety Commission

Mailing Address:
P.O. Box 30221
Lansing, MI 48909
Walk-In:
6545 Mercantile Way
Suite 7
Lansing, MI 48911
Phone: 517-241-6180
Email: Use online form
Website: www.michigan.gov/mpsc/

MINNESOTA

Minnesota Department of Public Safety
Driver and Vehicle Services

Mailing/Walk-In Address:
Driver and Vehicle Services
445 Minnesota St. Ste 168
St. Paul, MN 55101-5175
Phone: 651-297-5029
Email: motor.vehicles@state.mn.us
Website: www.dps.state.mn.us/dvs/

Minnesota Department of Transportation
Office of Freight and Commercial Vehicle Operations

Mailing/Walk-In Address:
Transportation Building
395 John Ireland Boulevard
Saint Paul, MN 55155-1899
Phone: 651-215-6330
Fax: 651-366-3718
Email: info@dot.state.mn.us
Website: www.dot.state.mn.us

MISSISSIPPI

Mississippi Department of Public Safety
Motor Carrier Safety Division

Mailing/Walk-In Address:
1900 Woodrow Wilson Drive
Jackson, MS 39216
Phone: 601-987-1212
Website: www.dps.state.ms.us/mcsd

MISSOURI

Missouri Department of Revenue
Division of Motor Vehicle & Driver Licensing

Mailing/Walk-In Address:
301 West High Street
Harry S. Truman State Office Building, Room 470
Jefferson City, MO 65101
Phone: 573-526-2407
Email: dlbmail@dor.mo.gov
Website: www.dor.moi.giv/mvdl

Missouri Department of Transportation
Division of Motor Carrier Services

Mailing/Walk-In Address:
105 E. Capitol Avenue
Jefferson City, MO 65102
Phone: 888-275-6636
Website: www.modot.mo.gov/mcs/

MONTANA

Montana Department of Justice
Motor Vehicle Division

Mailing Address:
P.O. Box 201430
Helena, MT 59620-1430
Walk-In:
303 North Roberts
Scott Hart Building, Second Floor
Helena, MT 59620-1430
Phone: 406-444-1772
Email: mvd@mt.gov
Website: www.doj.mt.gov/driving/

Montana Department of Transportation
Motor Carrier Services Division

Mailing Address:
P.O. Box 201001
Helena, MT 59620-1001
Walk-In:
2701 Prospect Avenue
Helena, MT 59620-1001
Phone: 406-444-7638
Website:
www.mdt.mt.gov/mdt/organization/mcs.shtml

NEBRASKA

Nebraska Office of Highway Safety

Mailing Address:
P.O. Box 94612
Lincoln, NE 68509-4789
Walk-In:
301 Centennial Mall South
Lincoln, NE 68508
Phone: 402-471-2515
Website: www.dmv.ne.gov

NEVADA

Nevada Department of Motor Vehicles

Mailing/Walk-In Address:
555 Wright Way
Carson City, NV 89711
Phone: 702-486-4368
Email: info@dmv.state.nv.us
Website: www.dmvnv.com

NEW HAMPSHIRE

New Hampshire Department of Safety
Division of Motor Vehicles

Mailing/Walk-In Address:
23 Hazen Drive
Concord, NH 03305
Phone: 603-271-2371
Email: webcoordinator@safety.state.nh.us
Website: www.nh.gov/safety/dmv

NEW JERSEY

New Jersey Motor Vehicle Commission

Mailing Address:
P.O. Box 160
Trenton, NJ 08666-0403
Walk-In:
120 S. Stockton & Front Street
Trenton, NJ 08611
Phone: 888-486-3339
Website: www.state.nj.us/mvc

NEW MEXICO

New Mexico Taxation & Revenue
Motor Vehicle Division

Mailing Address:
Joseph Montoya Building
P.O. Box 1028
Santa Fe, NM 87504-1028
Walk-In:
Joseph Montoya Building
1100 S. St. Francis Drive
Santa Fe, NM 87504-0630
Phone: 888-683-4636
Website: www.tax.state.nm.us

NEW YORK

New York Department of Motor Vehicles

Mailing Address:
Swan Street Building, Room 136
Empire State Plaza
Albany, NY 12228

Walk-In:
6 Empire State Plaza
Albany, NY 12228
Phone: 800-342-5368
Email: Use online form
Website: www.nydmv.state.ny.us

NORTH CAROLINA

North Carolina Division of Motor Vehicles

Mailing Address:
3148 Mail Service Center
Raleigh, NC 27699-3101
Walk-In:
1100 New Bern Avenue
Raleigh, NC 27697-3148
Phone: 919-715-7000
Email: Use online form
Website: www.ncdot.org/dmv/

NORTH DAKOTA

North Dakota Department of Transportation
Drivers License and Traffic Safety

Mailing Address/ Walk-In:
608 East Boulevard, Department 801
Bismarck, ND 58505-0700
Phone: 701-328-3225
Email: cpadilla@nd.gov
Website: pmu.dot.state.nc.us/dmv

OHIO

Ohio Department of Public Safety
Bureau of Motor Vehicles

Mailing Address:
P.O. Box 16520
Columbus, OH 43216-6520
Walk-In:
1970 West Broad Street
Columbus, OH 43223-1101
Phone: 614-752-7500
Email: Use online form
Website: www.bmv.ohio.gov

OKLAHOMA

Oklahoma Department of Public Safety

Mailing Address:
P.O. Box 11451
Oklahoma City, OK 73136-0415
Walk-In:
3600 N. ML King Avenue
Oklahoma City, OK 73111
Phone: 405-521-3101
Email: comment@dps.state.ok.us
Website: www.dps.state.ok.us

OREGON

Oregon Department of Transportation
Department of Motor Vehicles Headquarters

Mailing Address:
355 Capitol St. N.E.
Salem, OR 97301-3871

Walk-In:

1905 Lana Ave NE

Salem, OR 97314

Phone: 888-275-6368

Email: Use online form

Website: www.oregon.gov/ODOT/

PENNSYLVANIA

Department of Transportation
Driver and Vehicle Services

Mailing Address/Walk In:

1101 South Front Street

Harrisburg, PA 17104

Phone: 800-932-4600

Email: Use online form

Website: www.dmv.state.pa.us

RHODE ISLAND

Division of Motor Vehicles

Mailing Address/Walk In:

100 Main Street

Pawtucket, RI 02860

Phone: 401-462-4368

Email: Use online form

Website: www.dmv.ri.gov

SOUTH CAROLINA

Department of Motor Vehicles

Mailing Address:

P.O. Box 1498

Blythewood, SC 29016

Walk In:

10311 Wilson Boulevard - Building C

Blythewood, SC 29016

Phone: 803-896-5000

Email: help@scdmvonline.com

Website: www.scdmvonline.com

SOUTH DAKOTA

South Dakota Motor Vehicles Division

Mailing Address/Walk In:

445 East Capitol Avenue

Pierre, SD 57501

Phone: 605-773-3541

Email: motorv@state.sd.us

Website: www.state.sd.us/drr2/motorvehicle

TENNESSEE

Tennessee Department of Safety
Drivers License Issuance

Mailing/Walk-In Address:

1150 Foster Avenue

Nashville, TN 37243

Phone: 615-253-5221

Website: state.tn.us/safety/index.htm

TEXAS

Texas Department of Public Safety
Driver License Division

Mailing Address:

5805 North Lamar Boulevard

Austin, TX 78752-4422

Walk-In:
P.O. Box 4087
Austin, TX 78773-0001
Phone: 512-424-2000
Email: Use online form
Website: www.txdps.state.tx.us

UTAH

Utah Department of Public Safety
Driver License Division

Mailing/Walk-In Address:
210 North 1950 West
Salt Lake City UT 84134
Phone: 801-279-7780
Email: dmv@utah.gov
Website: www.dmv.utah.gov

VERMONT

Vermont Department of Motor Vehicles

Mailing/Walk-In Address:
120 State Street
Montpelier, VT 05603-0001
Phone: 802-828-2000
Email: CommissionersOffice@state.vt.us
Website: www.aot.state.vt.us/

VIRGINIA

Virginia Department of Motor Vehicles

Mailing Address:
P.O. Box 27412
Richmond, VA 23269

Walk-In:
2300 West Broad Street
Richmond, VA 23269
Phone: 866-368-5463
Email: Use online form
Website: www.dmv.virginia.gov

WASHINGTON

Washington Department of Licensing

Mailing Address:
P.O. Box 9030
Olympia, WA 98507-9030
Walk-In:
1125 Washington Street SE
Olympia, WA 98504-2283
Phone: 360-902-3900
Email: drivers@dol.wa.gov
Website: www.dol.wa.gov/

WEST VIRGINIA

West Virginia Department of Transportation
Division of Motor Vehicles

Mailing/Walk-In Address:
Building 3, Capitol Complex
1800 Kanawha Boulevard East
Charleston, WV 25305
Phone: (800) 642-9066
Email: dot.info@wv.gov
Website: www.wvdot.com

WISCONSIN

Wisconsin Department of Transportation
Drivers and Vehicles

Mailing Address:
P.O. Box 7979
Madison, WI 53704
Walk-In:
2001 Bartillon Drive
Madison, WI 53704
Phone: 608-266-2353
Email: driverrecords.dmv@dot.state.wisconsin.us
Website: www.dot.wisconsin.gov.

WYOMING

Wyoming Department of Transportation
Driver Services

Mailing/Walk-In Address:
5300 Bishop Boulevard
Cheyenne, WY 82009-3340
Phone: 307-777-4800
Email: Use online form
Website: www.dot.state.wy.us

CANADA

Ontario Ministry of Transportation
Drivers and Vehicles

Mailing Address:
1800 Bank Street, Suite 5
Ottawa, ON K1C 1G7
Walk-In:
1570 Walkley Rd.
Ottawa, ON KIV 5P6
Canada
Phone: 613-523-1048
Email: Use online form
Website: www.mto.gov.on.ca

▶ Transportation Agencies

Federal Motor Carrier Safety Administration

Office of Motor Carrier Standards

Mailing/Walk-In Address:
1200 New Jersey Avenue, SE
Washington, D.C. 20590

Phone: 800-832-5660
Website: www.fmcsa.dot.gov

Federal Highway Administration

Mailing/Walk-In Address:
1200 New Jersey Avenue, SE
Washington, DC 20590

Phone: 202-366-0660
Website: www.fhwa.dot.gov/

Federal Transit Administration

Mailing/Walk-In Address:
East Building
1200 New Jersey Avenue, SE
Washington, DC 20590

Phone: 202-366-4043
Email: Use online form
Website: www.fta.dot.gov/

Motor Carrier Safety Service Centers

Eastern Service Center

Mailing/Walk-In Address:
802 Cromwell Park Drive, Suite N
Glen Burnie, MD 21061

Phone: 443-703-2240
Website: www.fmcsa.dot.gov

Territory: Connecticut, District of Columbia, Delaware, Maine, Massachusetts, Maryland, New Hampshire, New Jersey, Pennsylvania, Rhode Island, Puerto Rico, Vermont, West Virginia

Midwestern Service Center

Mailing/Walk-In Address:
19900 Governors Drive, Suite 210
Olympia Fields, IL 60461

Phone: 708-283-3577
Website: www.fmcsa.dot.gov

Territory: Iowa, Illinois, Indiana, Kansas, Michigan, Missouri, Minnesota, Nebraska, Ohio, Wisconsin

Southern Service Center

Mailing/Walk-In Address:
1800 Century Boulevard, NE
Suite 1700
Atlanta, GA 30345-3220

Phone: 404-327-7400
Website: www.fmcsa.dot.gov

Territory: Alabama, Arkansas, Florida, Georgia, Kentucky, Louisiana, Mississippi, North Carolina, Oklahoma, South Carolina, Tennessee, Texas

Western Service Center

Mailing/Walk-In Address:
Golden Hills Office Centre
12600 West Colfax Avenue
Suite B-300
Lakewood, CO 80215

Phone: 303-407-2350
Website: www.fmcsa.dot.gov

Territory: American Samoa, Alaska, Arizona, California, Colorado, Guam, Hawaii, Idaho, Mariana Islands, Montana, North Dakota, Nevada, Oregon, South Dakota, Utah, Washington, Wyoming

National Highway Traffic Safety Administration

Mailing/Walk-In Address:
1200 New Jersey Avenue, SE
West Building
Washington, DC 20590

Phone: 1-888-327-4236
Email: Use online form
Website: www.nhtsa.dot.gov

Transportation Security Administration

Mailing/Walk-In Address:
601 South 12th Street
Arlington, VA 22202-4220

Phone: 866-289-9673
Email: TSA-ContactCenter@dhs.gov
Website: www.tsa.gov

▶ Online Resources

American Trucking Associations
www.truckline.com
The American Trucking Associations, Inc. represents the interests of the trucking industry. Their Website provides information on federal regulations, safety issues, and other concerns relevant to commercial truck drivers.

Canadian Trucking Alliance
www.cantruck.com
A federation of provincial trucking associations with more than 4,500 carriers.

eTrucker.com
www.etrucker.com
A community of truckers and trucking companies throughout the United States that provides drivers with information about the issues that affect their business. The Website includes polls, surveys, forums, and up-to-the-minute coverage of transportation news.

I10 Trucking.com
www.i10trucking.com
Designed by truckers for truckers, this site provides CMV drivers with information and resources, including tips for driving in certain states, the updated trucking news, safety advice designed for female CMV drivers, and resources to help CMV drivers stay healthy on the road.

Newbiedriver

www.newbiedriver.com

Dedicated to those new to CMV driving, this site provides novice drivers with inside views on the trucking world and with many helpful tips, including how to set up a CB radio, which travel-related purchases might be tax deducible, tips on how to increase the amount of money you earn as a CMV driver, and much more.

Thetrucker.com—America's Trucking Newspaper

www.thetrucker.com

An online newspaper with up-to-date information on the trucking business, highways, and legislation that affects the industry.

The Trucker's Report

www.thetruckersreport.com

This Website offers news and announcements of interest to CMV drivers across the country. Includes driving tips, truck facts, and a trucker forum where CMV drivers can share information.

Truck News

www.trucknews.com

Truck News provides Canadian trucking news, a directory of trucking companies and suppliers, truck driving jobs and used trucks listings.

Glossary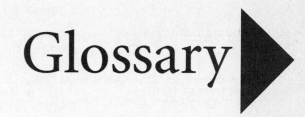

Definitions and explanations of terms used in your text and the industry.

► A

Adverse conditions	Unfavorable driving conditions including driving in snow, rain, or ice as well as driving at night or in the mountains.
After-trip inspection report	A list of any problems found with the vehicle after the trip has been completed that allows the carrier to know if there is anything that should be repaired before the vehicle goes back out on the road; also called post-trip inspection or vehicle condition report.
Age requirement	A driver must be 21 years old in order to obtain a Class A CDL. Some states allow drivers to get Class A, Class B, and Class C CDLs at age 18 as long as drivers don't cross state lines, transport passengers, or carry hazardous materials.
Air governor	A device that "governs," or controls, the amount of air pressure in the compressor.
Air service line	A device that carries air from the tractor to the trailer(s) and is controlled by the amount of pressure applied to the foot brake or the trailer hand valve; also called the control line or signal line.
Air storage tanks	Storage tanks that hold enough air to stop a vehicle a few times even if the air compressor stops working; also called air tanks or air reservoirs.
Air tank drains	Drains located on the bottom of the tanks where oil and water accumulate. Air tanks should be drained daily to keep a CMV working properly.
Air tank petcock	A valve on an air tank that releases air when turned.

Ammeter	A device that measures electric current and voltage from the battery; also called voltmeter.
Antilock brake system (ABS)	A computerized system that keeps a vehicle's wheels from locking up when the driver brakes hard.
Application pressure gauge	A device that shows how much air pressure a driver is applying to the brakes.
Apron	A surface for resting the trailer on the fifth wheel.
Automated transmission	A type of transmission in which the driver must depress the clutch only to start and stop the vehicle; shifting is automatic when the CMV is in motion.
Automatic transmission	A type of transmission that automatically changes gear ratios when the CMV is in motion.
Axle weight	The weight transmitted to the ground by an axle or a set of axles.

▶ B

Baffled tank	A tank with compartment walls with holes so that the liquid in the tank can flow through the compartment. This slows the liquid's movement, reducing the impact of the forward-and-backward surge.
Big-rig (slang)	A combination vehicle.
Black ice	A layer of ice so thin and clear that the road appears wet rather than icy.
Blind spots	Places the driver can't see in the mirrors that make changing lanes challenging.
Blocking	A securing element that fits snugly against cargo and may be used in the front, back, or sides of cargo.
Bobtail tractor (slang)	A tractor without trailers attached to it.
Bracing	A securing element used to keep cargo from moving within a trailer or cargo compartment.
Brake drums	The wheels on the axles are bolted to the brake drums, which are located at each end of the CMV's axles. A braking mechanism is inside the drum.
Brake lag	The extra time needed to stop when driving a vehicle with air brakes because the air must travel through the brake lines.
Brake linings	Along with the brake shoes, these devices press against the brake drum creating friction to slow or stop the vehicle. This also creates heat.
Brake pedal	The pedal the driver pushes down to apply the brakes. The harder the driver pushes the pedal, the harder the brakes are applied; also called the foot pedal, the foot brake, or the treadle valve.
Brake shoes	Along with the brake lining, these devices press against the brake drum creating friction to slow or stop the vehicle. This also creates heat.

Braking distance	The distance it takes for a vehicle to stop once the driver's foot has pushed the brake.
Bulkheads	Wall-like structures that can be used to divide large liquid tanks into several smaller tanks.
Bundled	Logs and other cargo that are tied together in groups.
Button-hook turn	A turn in which a vehicle swings wide into another lane.

▶ C

Caliper	A device similar to a large c-clamp that squeezes the brake lining pads against a rotating disc.
Cargo	Freight.
Chemical Transportation Emergency Center (CHEMTREC)	Agency that provides technical information to emergency personnel about specific hazardous materials.
Chock	A wedge used to secure the trailer wheels.
Combination vehicles	Vehicles with five or six axles that also consist of a tractor or a truck and a trailer that's used to haul cargo over long distances across one or more states.
Compression braking	A braking method in which the driver of an automatic transmission selects a low range to improve engine braking when driving down grades.
Consignee	The person or company to whom goods are being shipped.
Controlled braking	A braking method in which brakes are applied as hard as possible without locking the wheels.
Convex mirrors	Curved mirrors that allow the driver to see more than flat mirrors, but make objects seem smaller and farther away; also called fisheye, bug-eye, or spot mirrors.
Converter dolly	An assembly, or group of parts, with one or more axles and a fifth wheel, that is used to convert a semitrailer to a full trailer or create doubles and triples; also called converter gear.
Countersteering	Technique used to get the vehicle back on course after a skid by turning the wheel back in the other direction.
Coupling	The act of attaching tractors and trailers or trailers and other trailers.
Coupling device capacity	Rating for coupling devices that refers to the maximum weight they can pull or carry.
Cut-in level	The level at which air pressure falls to about 100 psi, and the governor allows the compressor to pump air.
Cut-out level	The level at which the air pressure rises and reaches between 120 and 130 psi, and the governor stops the compressor from pumping additional air.

▶ D

Danger zones	Any area outside a bus or passenger vehicle that extends 15 feet from the front and rear bumpers and 15 feet from either side of the vehicle. It's especially difficult to see people within these danger zones.
Dead axles	Axles not connected to the drivetrain.
Deadhead miles	Miles driven without cargo.
Disc brakes	A type of foundation brake where air pressure acts on a brake chamber and a slack adjuster.
Disqualifications	Instances that disqualify a driver from operating a CMV for a period of time or life due to events such as driving under the influence of alcohol.
Double (slang)	A tractor with two trailers attached to it; also called a double-trailer rig.
Drawbar	A bar, usually made of metal, that connects a truck and a trailer; also referred to as the "tongue" of the trailer.
Drive tires	Powered tires that provide traction to push the vehicle through snow and water.
Driver requirements	A list of requirements established by the Commercial Motor Vehicle Safety Act of 1986 and the Motor Carrier Safety Improvement Act (MCSIA) of 1999 that drivers must meet in order to obtain a CDL.
Driving axle	Part of the drivetrain.
Dual air brake system	Contains two separate air brake systems—the primary air brake system and the secondary air brake system—with one set of controls. This protects heavy-duty CMVs from complete brake failure.
Dual parking control valve	A valve system found on CMVs with a separate air tank that allows the driver to release the spring brakes. One of the valves is used to put on the spring brakes and another is used to release them, so the driver can safely move the vehicle out of harm's way in an emergency.

▶ E

Emergency brake system	A braking system used during an emergency such as brake failure.
Emergency line	Supplies air to the trailer air tanks, controls the combination vehicle's emergency brakes, and allows the emergency brakes to come on if the air pressure in the emergency line drops; also called the supply line.
Encroachment	Occurs when any part of a driver's vehicle crosses over boundaries; results in a loss of points during an examination.
Endorsement	A special permission to operate some vehicles not granted by a regular CDL. It is usually indicated by a letter or number code. Some endorsements require passing a knowledge test while others require passing both a knowledge test and a skills test.

Escape ramp	A long upgrade or a long bed of loose material such as gravel designed to stop runaway vehicles without injuring drivers or passengers.

 F

Federal Motor Carrier Safety Regulations (FMCSR)	A large body of regulations for CDLs created by the U.S. Department of Transportation Federal Motor Carrier Safety Administration (FMCSA).
Fifth wheel	A locking device used to connect a semitrailer to a tractor.
Forward-and-backward surge	Occurs when the driver brings the CMV to a stop and the liquid in the tank surges back and forth. A sudden stop can cause liquid to surge so violently against the front of the tank that it can move the stopped vehicle forward.
Foundation brake	Located at the end of each brake.
Front-brake limiting valve	A valve found on CMVs made before 1975 that was supposed to reduce the chances of skidding on slippery surfaces if the control was switched from "normal" to "slippery." This device was found to be inefficient.
Front-wheel skids	Skids that occur because a driver is driving too fast for weather conditions, the CMV's tires lack tread depth, or a CMV's cargo is loaded so that there is not enough weight on the front axle.
Full trailer	A trailer with both the front and rear axles that can stand on its own without support. A full trailer can be attached to a semitrailer, a single-unit truck, or another full trailer.

▶ **G**

Glad hands	Coupling devices used to connect the service and emergency air lines from the tractor or truck to the trailer.
Gross combination weight (GCW)	The total weight of a powered unit plus the trailer or trailers and cargo.
Gross combination weight rating (GCWR)	The maximum GCW specified by the manufacturer for a particular combination of vehicles plus the load.
Gross vehicle weight (GVW)	The total weight of a single vehicle and its load.
Gross vehicle weight rating (GVWR)	The maximum GVW, as specified by the manufacturer, for a single vehicle and its load.

▶ H

Hazard	Any condition or person on or near a road (driver, pedestrian, cyclist, etc.) that poses a risk to the driver or other persons.
Hazard classes	Nine categories and subdivisions in which hazardous materials are divided by type of material and the risks associated with that material.
Hazardous material	Any material that poses a risk to people, property, and the environment.
HAZMAT	Abbreviation for hazardous material; also abbreviated HM.
Hydroplane	Driving hazard in which water or slush collects on the roadway and a vehicle's tires can't make contact with the road, resulting in a loss of traction.

▶ I

Identification number	A number used to identify the material's proper shipping name; also called UN/NA identification number.
Intrastate	Traveling within the state.

▶ J

Jug-handle turn	An improper turn where the driver starts the turn by swinging to the left. This could result in drivers trying to pass the CMV on the right and increase the possibility of a collision.

▶ K

Kingpin	A device that attaches the semitrailer to the tractor. It's always located in the center of the front of the semitrailer.
Knowledge test	A written exam that tests knowledge by asking the driver to answer multiple-choice questions.

▶ L

Language requirement	Drivers must be able to speak and read English well enough to communicate with officials and other drivers, make entries in records and reports, and understand road signs.

Liquid surge	Occurs when driving a CMV with a tank only partially filled with liquid, allowing the substance to move around in the tank. This can cause handling problems for the driver.
Load	The amount of cargo a CMV can safely haul.
Load locks	Long poles that extend from wall to wall within a trailer to prevent cargo from falling.
Loading pallets	Devices used to ensure that pallets don't lean and fall.
Long combination vehicles (LCVs)	Double-trailer combinations or triple-trailer combinations where at least one trailer is longer than 28 feet.
Low air-pressure warning signal	A red warning light and buzzer that indicate the air pressure has fallen below 60.

▶ M

Marking	The descriptive name, identification number, instructions, cautions, weights, specification, or UN marks or combinations thereof, required on outer packaging of hazardous materials.
Medical requirement	Requirement by the federal government requiring drivers to undergo a physical and mental examination before applying for a commercial driver learner's permit to ensure that they don't have any conditions that could interfere with their ability to operate CMVs.
Modulating-control valve	A control handle on the dashboard that allows the driver to gradually apply the spring brakes to avoid coming to a screeching halt.

▶ N

NA	Abbreviation for North America.
National Response Center	An agency that helps coordinate emergency response efforts and acts as a resource for police and firefighters. Certain incidents involving CMVs hauling hazardous materials must be reported to this agency.

▶ O

Offset back/left	An exercise in which the driver is asked to back into a space that's to the left rear of the vehicle.
Offset back/right	An exercise in which the driver is asked to back into a space that's to the right rear of the vehicle.

Offtracking	Driving hazard in which a vehicle goes around a corner and its rear wheels follow a different path than its front wheels.
Outage	Liquid expanding as it warms inside the tanker. It's the main reason drivers can't load full cargo tanks.
Overload	A CMV that's carrying too much cargo.
Oversized vehicles	Vehicles that exceed the maximum vehicle length and width set by state law.
Oversteering	Turning the wheel more sharply than the vehicle can stand, which can cause skidding.

▶ P

Parallel park (conventional)	Exercise in which the driver is asked to parallel park in a space to the right of the vehicle.
Parallel park (driver side)	Exercise in which the driver is asked to parallel park in a space to the left of the vehicle.
Parking brake system	Used when the driver applies the parking brake.
Perception distance	The distance a vehicle moves from the time that the driver's eyes spot a hazard until the driver's brain recognizes it.
Pintle hook	A hook on the rear of a truck used to tow trailers.
Placard	Diamond-shaped sign placed on the outside of the vehicle warning others that the driver is transporting certain hazardous materials.
Primary air brake system	In a dual-air brake system, the system that controls the regular brakes on the rear axle or axles. Both the primary and secondary air brake systems supply air to the trailer, if one is attached.
Pull-up	Stopping and reversing the direction of the vehicle to better position it.
Pup trailer (slang)	A short semitrailer with a single axle.
Pushrod	A rod pushed out by air pressure that moves the slack adjuster.

▶ R

Reaction distance	The distance the vehicle moves from the time the driver's brain recognizes the hazard until the driver's foot moves off the accelerator and pushes the brake pedal.
Rearward amplification	An event that often occurs when a driver changes lanes too quickly. The force used to steer the vehicle amplifies as it travels through the trailer, resulting in an increase in the likelihood that the trailer will tip over.
Rear-wheel braking skid	Occurs when the rear drive wheels lock. Most commonly caused by excessive braking or acceleration.

Reefer (slang)	A refrigerated trailer.
Relay valves	The service line is connected to these valves, which connect the trailer air tanks to the trailer air brakes allowing the trailer brakes to be applied very quickly in an emergency.
Restriction	A limitation on a CDL that restricts the type of vehicle a driver is allowed to operate. Given when a driver fails to pass or take required examinations.
Retarders	Adjustable devices that help slow down the vehicle without causing major brake wear. The four main types of retarders are (1) exhaust, (2) engine, (3) hydraulic, and (4) electric.
Rims	The outer part of the wheels to which the tires are attached.
Rocky Mountain Double (RMD)	A type of LCV where a tractor pulls a 45- to 48-foot trailer and a 20- to 28-foot trailer.

▶ S

S-cam drum brake	The most common type of foundation brake.
Safety release valve	A device that protects the tank and the entire air brake system from too much pressure.
Secondary air brake system	In a dual air brake system, the secondary air brake system controls the brakes on the front axle and sometimes also on one rear axle. Both the primary and secondary air brake systems supply air to the trailer, if one is attached.
Semi (slang)	A semitrailer.
Semitrailer	A trailer with only rear axles that can't stand on its own without being attached to a tractor. A tractor-trailer combination consisting of a tractor and a semitrailer is the most common type of combination vehicle.
Service brake system	The brake system used most often during normal driving.
Shipping paper	A shipping order, bill of lading, manifest, or other shipping document serving a similar purpose and containing the information required by Sec. 172.202, 172.203, and 172.204.
Side-to-side surge	Occurs when the driver brings the CMV to a stop and the liquid in the tank surges side to side, which can cause the CMV to roll over.
Single (slang)	A tractor pulling a semitrailer.
Single-unit truck	A vehicle with three or four axles where the cargo-carrying unit is mounted on the same chassis as the engine, the cab, and the drive train; also called a straight truck.
Skidding	When a vehicle's tires lose their grip on the road.
Skills test	A performance test on an approved course with an examiner. The test requires drivers to demonstrate their abilities on the vehicles for which applying for licenses.

Slack adjuster	A device that twists the brake camshaft, which turns the s-cam. One end of the slack adjuster is attached to the pushrod and the other end is attached to the brake camshaft.
Snub braking	Braking technique used for long steep downgrades that involves using the brakes to gradually slow down.
Specialized hauling vehicles (SHVs)	Common single-unit trucks designed to haul very heavy cargo that can't be divided into parts (milk, gravel, construction materials) over short distances within one state.
Spring brakes	Powerful brakes used as a backup in case all the air in the air tanks is released. When the air releases, the springs put on the brakes; also called fail-safe brakes.
Surface Transportation Assistance Act (STAA) double-trailer combination	Vehicle consisting of a tractor pulling two 28-foot trailers permitted to travel on a certain network of federal highways referred to as the "National Network" (the NN).
Stab braking	Applying the brakes all the way and releasing them when they lock up.
Stale green light	A light that's already green when the driver sees it and has probably been green for a while. Drivers should assume that this light will soon change and are encouraged to slow down.
Standee line	A 2-inch line on the floor of passenger vehicles or buses that shows passengers where they can't stand. All passengers must stand behind this line for their safety.
Steering axle	The front axle on most CMVs.
Steering tires	Tires that provide traction to help steer the vehicle.
Stop-light switch	A light that turns on when the brake pedal is depressed, warning people behind the vehicle that the driver is coming to a stop.
Straight line backing	An exercise in which the vehicle is backed up in a straight line between lines or cones without touching or crossing over the boundaries.
Supply pressure gauge	Device located on the air tank that tells drivers how much pressure is in the air tank.
Suspension system	Supports the vehicle and its load while keeping the axles in place.

▶ **T**

Tandum	Two trailers together; also called twin trailers.
Tensile strength	A material's resistance against tearing.
Tie downs	Securement devices used to tie down cargo to keep it from falling off.
Tire billy	A device used to check the air pressure of tires.
Tire load	The maximum safe weight a tire can carry at a specified pressure.
Total stopping distance	The sum of the perception distance, reaction distance, and braking distance. The driver's speed greatly affects the total stopping distance.

Traction | The friction between the tires and the road.

Tractor protection valve | A device that keeps air in the brake system of the tractor or truck so the driver can still control the vehicle's brakes if the trailer breaks away or develops a bad air leak. The valve will automatically close if the air pressure drops too low, keeping air in the brakes of the tractor.

Traffic emergency | Serious situation in which two or more vehicles are about to collide.

Trailer air supply control valve | A knob or lever that's pushed in to supply the trailer with air and pulled out to shut off the air and engage the emergency brakes. This valve will automatically close if the air pressure drops too low.

Trailer hand valve | Controls the operation of the trailer brakes, but should only be used to test the brakes. If used while driving, it could cause the trailer to skid or jackknife. Also called the "trolley valve" or "Johnson bar."

Trailer Skid | Also called trailer jackknife; occurs when the trailer's wheels lock up and the trailer swings around.

Triple (slang) | A tractor with three trailers attached to it; also called a triple-trailer rig.

Triple-trailer combinations | A long combination vehicle (LVC) consisting of two trailers, each of which are 28 feet long.

Truck-trailer combination | A single-unit truck pulling a full trailer.

Turnpike double (TPD) | A long combination vehicle (LCV) in which the tractor pulls two trailers, each of which are 45 to 53 feet long.

▶ U

Unbaffled tank | Long cylindrical tanks with no divisions inside, allowing the liquid to move freely inside without any obstructions to slow it down. This can cause a strong forward-and-backward surge; also called smooth bore tanks.

Uncoupling | The act of separating tractors and trailers or trailers and other trailers.

Underloading | Occurs when the driver loads too little weight on the driving axle.

▶ V

V-belt | V-shaped fan belt.

Vehicle emergency | When tires, brakes, or other important parts of a vehicle fail.

▶ **W**

Wedge brakes   A type of foundation brake in which the chamber pushrod pushes a
                         wedge between the ends of the brake shoes.

Wigwag   A mechanical arm that drops into the driver's field of vision when the air
                         pressure in the air brake system drops below 60 psi.